Humanism Challenges Materialism in Economics and Economic History

Humanism Challenges Materialism in Economics and Economic History

EDITED BY RODERICK FLOUD,
SANTHI HEJEEBU,
AND DAVID MITCH

The University of Chicago Press
Chicago and London

The University of Chicago Press, Chicago 60637
The University of Chicago Press, Ltd., London

Published 2017.
Printed in the United States of America

26 25 24 23 22 21 20 19 18 17   1 2 3 4 5

ISBN-13: 978-0-226-42958-8 (cloth)
ISBN-13: 978-0-226-42961-8 (e-book)
DOI: 10.7208/chicago/9780226429618.001.0001

Library of Congress Cataloging-in-Publication Data

Names: Floud, Roderick, editor. | Hejeebu, Santhi, editor. | Mitch, David Franklin, 1951– editor.
Title: Humanism challenges materialism in economics and economic history / edited by Roderick Floud, Santhi Hejeebu, and David Mitch.
Description: Chicago ; London : The University of Chicago Press, 2017. | Includes bibliographical references and index.
Identifiers: LCCN 2016028692 | ISBN 9780226429588 (cloth : alk. paper) | ISBN 9780226429618 (e-book)
Subjects: LCSH: Economics—Philosophy. | Economic history—Philosophy. | Humanism. | Values. | Social values. | McCloskey, Deirdre N.
Classification: LCC HB72 .H826 2017 | DDC 330.01—dc23 LC record available at https://lccn.loc.gov/2016028692

♾ This paper meets the requirements of ANSI/NISO Z39.48-1992 (Permanence of Paper).

Contents

INTRODUCTION

RODERICK FLOUD, SANTHI HEJEEBU, AND DAVID MITCH

Economics and economic history have been dominated in recent decades by a peculiar orthodoxy. It stresses materialistic motives to human action and a singular representation of choice as optimization with constraints. The doctrine enlightens new entrants to the discipline with such powerful notions as the role of incentives and the principle that there is no such thing as a free lunch. Foundational economic ideas can illuminate the enigmas experienced in "the business of everyday life," delivering the tale of allocative efficiency in a world of scarcity and diminishing returns. Beyond the basics, deeper engagement with the discipline requires mastering increasingly rigorous mathematics and statistics. For all their definitiveness and elegance, however, formal economic models still equip analysts to make only the thinnest of observations about the lived experience of economic change. As Robert Solow long ago observed, "The practical utility of economics comes not primarily from its high-powered frontier, but from fairly low-powered reasoning. But the moral is not that we can dispense with high-powered economics, if only because high-powered economics seems to be such an excellent school for the dispensing of low-powered economics."[1] The recent financial crisis has made painfully clear the limits of such schooling.

The Great Recession has unsettled economists and their discipline. The queen of England is reputed to have asked, on a visit to the London School of Economics, "Did no one see this coming?" Economics students around the world have been vociferous in their demands for changes in the syllabus and the inclusion of alternative approaches to the dominant neoclassical paradigm. Faith in markets has been replaced in many countries by demands for regulation and even for criminal sanctions against those who took advantage of previous laxity in rules and standards. Meanwhile, politicians and markets agonize about the possibility of further crises; the age, only ten years ago, when a leading British politician could proclaim "the end of boom and bust" has long gone.

None of this greatly surprised those economists and economic historians, small in number though they were, who had for some time challenged interpretations of both past and present in the work of the dominant schools of modern economics. They pointed to the incapacity of traditional models to explain invention and understand altruism. They argued that a simple faith in the ability of markets to clear and to achieve the optimum allocation of resources was insufficient both to explain major events in economic history and to act as a guide to contemporary political and economic decisions. Explaining even the most salient facts of modern economic life—the long duration of growth and the remarkable technological advances—requires pushing the boundaries of orthodox methods.

Not surprisingly, the chorus of dissent *within* economics continues to accelerate. At the research level, complexity models compete alongside traditional efficiency models for the imagination of graduate students. The result is that economics has taken on a much more behavioral turn, in which specifying the social context of economic decision making proves paramount to the outcome. In the newer areas of the discipline, neither the uniqueness nor the stability of economic outcomes is guaranteed. Empirical techniques in economics are also churning. The old confidence in significance tests, for example, has been shaken by mounting evidence of its limitations. Recently, the US Supreme Court weighed in. In the case of *Matrixx vs. Siracusano*, the high court ruled against statistical significance, long a favorite tool in the economist's arsenal, as sufficient evidentiary grounds to insulate a party from liability (Ziliak 2011). Once-common concepts have become indefensible both in court and at the research frontier. While these shifts may be seen as overdue corrections, part of the healthy evolution of any field, we believe something deeper is stirring.

A broad array of scholars insists that economists articulate the values, beliefs, and norms embedded in their practice. The resistance to do so reflects our training. Conventionally, economists are trained to distinguish between normative and positive views of well-being and to remain focused on the latter. For economists, well-being or welfare is typically defined as the fulfilment of preferences. Since preference orderings must be consistent and formally defined, and the decision maker must be informed and self-interested, the economist's boundary line between normative and positive perspectives proves more porous than it might appear. As Hausman (2013) explains, "Taking welfare to match the satisfaction of preference specifies how to find out what is good for a person rather than committing itself to any substantive view of a person's good." As the breach in the normative-positive distinction widens, the desire for more substantive discussions of what is "good" and "right" in economics grows more intense.

Some scholars, most notably Amartya Sen, have called for the reengagement of economics with ethics. Martha Nussbaum and Sen (1993) have emphasized the development of human capabilities as pivotal to economics. Hilary Putnam and Vivian Walsh (2011) advocate an end to value-free economics by demonstrating the inseparability of facts, theories, and values. These philosophers urge applied economists and economic historians to deepen their awareness of their practice. Does economics contain a moral and ethical code that enhances narratives of the past and also warrants its seemingly universal acceptance? Can economics as a method of inquiry share the concerns of the humanities and other social sciences without reducing the complexity of human decision making to material calculation?

The chapters in this volume address these questions in contemporary and historical contexts. They seek to employ insights from the humanities to provide perspectives that go beyond self-interested behavior and that enrich understanding of human responses even in materialistic situations. The approach is decidedly cross-disciplinary, for while some quarters of economics treat a discussion of values and norms as a tinkering of the utility function or a change in the structure of the model, we believe that less formalism can yield more insight. The contributors to the volume are scholars of history, politics, rhetoric, theology, epistemology, gender studies, and of course economics. They reject a blind faith in materialism, even while acknowledging its indispensability and the importance of "low-powered" economic reasoning. They embrace the central role of values and beliefs in explaining economic decisions and major discontinuities in economic history. They understand economics as a language of political and social discourse, as one of many ways of knowing the world. Put succinctly, they emphasize humanistic over materialistic perspectives.

The challenge of humanism to materialism, in economics and economic history, can be seen as proceeding on three levels of analysis. The first is that of *individual* values and beliefs, informing actions that determine material outcomes. Economists are comfortable with the notion of autonomous individuals making reasonable choices governing their own well-being. Indeed, sometimes the conventional logic can lead to unconventional wisdom. When individuals act on nonmaterial impulses, however, economists face a wider, less predictable range of behaviors. When nonmaterial values drive the everyday heroism of firefighters or the devotion of scholars, clergy, and social workers, for example, such values precipitate long-term material benefits or costs. Similarly, when an employee's individual identity leads an employer to emphasize qualities other than productivity, the returns to labor will not follow the prediction of standard theory. Such situations are in fact commonplace. A more humanistic economics should begin where the model of individual utility maximization most surprises—that is, in situations where either its compelling logic upends conventional wisdom or its explanatory power appears spent.

A second front on which humanism challenges materialism is at the level of *collective* beliefs and values. In the neoclassical orthodoxy, the individual remains the unit of analysis, abridging the reality of social groups and categories. In reality, shared values and beliefs—the traditionally sanctioned desirability of male offspring, for example—have enormous implications for overall economies and societies. Economists are increasingly returning to the role of values and institutions in influencing economic performance, even when narrowly defined in terms of income per capita. And they are increasingly recognizing the importance of equity and inequality in evaluating economic systems, as evidenced by the recent attention garnered by Thomas Piketty's work (2014) on inequality trends in capitalist systems.

A third front in the humanistic challenge to economic materialism is *methodological.* Thinking of formal economic logic as a type of language recasts economics as only one of many possible methods for studying materialism. Economics as a specialized language welcomes specialists in rhetoric, philosophy, and history into the center of debates over the allocation of real goods and services. Economics as a language engenders pluralistic ways of knowing, transcending the narrow scientific positivism famously asserted by Milton Friedman (1953). It also makes possible a more robust, more historically informed elucidation of the values and beliefs normalized within the profession as well as those associated with the phenomenon of long-run economic growth in the West.

The chapters in this volume reflect the desire for deeper meaning in economics, a desire that has gained new urgency in recent decades. It has led to new interdisciplinary subfields such as social network analysis, epitomized by the work of David Easley and Jon Kleinberger (2010). We have also seen the development of fields such as economic psychology and "identity economics," as represented by George Akerlof and Rachel Kranton (2010). The experimental methods used by a new generation of economists such as Roland Fryer, winner of the 2015 Clark Medal (for the most significant contribution to economic knowledge by a researcher under age forty), are indicative of the new openness. The Institute for New Economic Thinking and the Mercatus Center at George Mason University both reflect disaffection with economic positivism, even while taking broadly opposing policy positions. The techniques and methods for gaining insights in these new fields are far more diverse than those available just a few decades ago.

Diverse and robust methods aid the important task of developing the story of long-run capitalist growth. In economic history, a subfield as old as the economics profession, evidentiary voids can be treacherously large and experiments obviously impossible. Economic historians vigorously deploy rhetorical techniques to ensure that highly rarefied knowledge becomes accessible and relatable. Among the wide-ranging subfields of the discipline, economic history may be especially amenable to a methodology infused with humanism.

The humanistic challenge to materialism in economics and economic history has been particularly associated with the career of Deirdre McCloskey. A scholar of exceptional breadth and depth, McCloskey has returned time and again to her first love, the economic history of Great Britain. Her impact on that topic has been long-lasting and pervasive. She was, in the 1960s and 1970s, one of the leaders of the "new" economic history, the application of economic theory and quantitative methods to topics that were often well-worn but that were newly illuminated. McCloskey's work was characterized by clear prose and fierce logic, as in one of her most significant contributions, the article "Did Victorian Britain Fail?" (1970). In this and in "From Damnation to Redemption: Judgments on the Late Victorian Entrepreneur" (1971), written with L. G. Sandberg, she adopted a neoclassical framework to argue that the British economy at the end of the nineteenth century performed well under constraints and that the choices of techniques used in British industry were consistent with factor prices and, in particular, the relative costs of labor and capital. She drew on her own important work on the British iron and steel industry. Demonstrating the economist's unique capacity to tackle historical enigmas, these articles were influential for a whole generation of scholars of the late nineteenth-century economy.

Perhaps in the long run, even more influential was McCloskey's editorial work, beginning with *Essays on a Mature Economy: Britain after 1840* (1971), which brought together the first set of papers on the new economic history of Britain, and then in the two volumes of *The Economic History of Britain since 1700* (1981), edited together with Roderick Floud. These volumes, and subsequent editions (with various editors) of what became *The Cambridge Economic History of Modern Britain* (1994, 2004, and 2014), demonstrated McCloskey's skill as a rhetorician. Each edition brought together the leading economic historians working on modern British economic history; McCloskey demanded that they should write lucidly and without jargon, showing off the achievements of the new economic history in analysis and the marshalling of theory. The result was a series that has become the leading textbook of its subject, a godsend—as many have said—to generations of students and their teachers, summing up in an accessible manner the major findings of detailed research. As an editor, she ruffled a few feathers—academics are often protective of their prose—but naturally persisted and, with her coeditors, achieved a transformation of the way in which British economic history is done. Her own contributions, notably "The Industrial Revolution 1780–1860: A Survey" (1981), are still much quoted, in part because of their lucid exposition of techniques such as total factor productivity analysis.

McCloskey also contributed significantly to economists' understanding of the role of foreign trade in Britain's growth, before turning to consider the economic rationale and ultimate disappearance during the "enclosure movement" of the open field system that characterized much of British agriculture from the Middle Ages to the nineteenth century. She has returned, most recently and with a very much wider perspective, to the origins of the British Industrial Revolution and to the concept of Bourgeois Virtues that she sees as crucial to the transformation of a small, offshore island into the workshop of the world.

From her landmark contributions in economic history, McCloskey remained intensely optimistic about markets while simultaneously developing insights into the nature of economic argumentation. It was the disjuncture between the conclusions of price theory and the common knowledge gleaned from the humanities and personal experience that ultimately led her to champion a humanistic challenge to materialism. As in her editorial achievements, she aims for a more articulate economics. First, she insists that the discipline explain the values, norms, and beliefs embedded in its practice. Moreover, in her recent work (McCloskey 2006, 2010), she finds changes in values and norms to be central to understanding the historical development of capitalism and its twenty-first-century sustainability.

Unlike the Schumacher-inspired humanistic economics of the 1970s, McCloskey does not make the sharp distinction between needs versus wants. Nor does she reject the psychology of utilitarianism wholesale. Instead, she describes prudential behavior as virtuous, complementing other virtues that sustain polite and commercial society. Her approach appears akin to the New Institutional Economics associated with Douglass North and Elinor Ostrom. While the New Institutionalists regard group norms or "rules of the game" as pivotal to economic outcomes, McCloskey's approach is more expansive. It too uncovers implicit and explicit norms in historical and contemporary behavior. The McCloskey tradition, by contrast, does not take values as exogenous and unidimensional. Values, she argues, are multidimensional and endogenous to the way actors conceive and speak about the world. Thus a serious engagement with values requires a more far agile discourse than is possible with the optimization models of economics.

Second, McCloskey urges economists to articulate *how they know* and *how they persuade*. In her seminal work on the rhetoric of economics, McCloskey recast the discipline as a discourse. As a language or disciplined way of communicating, economics relies on literary devices such as metaphor to persuade. The orthodox language of economics, she shows, limits what economists can ask, how they observe facts, and how they generate insights. In her 1983 article in the *Journal of Economic Literature*, "The Rhetoric of Economics," McCloskey held a mirror to the profession that it had never seen before. The new reflection offered economists the potential to align their methods more closely with those of both humanists and scientists. A more self-knowing economics is necessarily more humanistic, but not less material. Stated differently, the McCloskey tradition does not disdain materialism per se, but rather the narrowness and rigidity with which material gain is valorized and promoted. In so doing, the McCloskey tradition aims for scholarship that is more inclusive, more interdisciplinary. "It is the pluralistic idea," writes Stephen Ziliak of McCloskey, "that if you are going to claim to know something you are obliged to examine all the ways of knowing it—in theory, mathematics, sciences, criticism, literature, art, poetry, statistics, history, language, philosophy, rhetoric and, no less importantly, through personal experience" (Ziliak 2010, 302). The McCloskey critique pivots not on market-based growth itself but on the course tools—narrative, mathematical, and epistemological—that conventional economics relies on to make sense of it.

This volume displays humanistic challenges to materialism in the McCloskey tradition. We begin with a set of chapters that illustrate *individual* values, beliefs, and norms shaping material outcomes. The first two essays consider whether the humanistic approaches that McCloskey advocates require a modification in the application of Chicago price theory. In chapter 1, Richard Sutch explores the growing belief in the value of savings in nineteenth-century America. A wealthy Philadelphia merchant, Condy Raguet, promoted a modern notion of savings through the establishment in 1816 of the Philadelphia Saving Fund Society. Raguet envisioned savings as private virtue, a way of self-healing from the pain of a low-growth economy. Raguet aimed not to maximize return on investment but to mitigate depositors' material insecurity, to promote happiness through consumption smoothing, then a rare opportunity for the working classes. The historical case illustrates "a respectable bourgeois blend of materialism and humanism."

The next study directly challenges conventional portrayals of economic behavior at the individual level. In chapter 2, Robin Bartlett explores the performance of gender identity in economic life. She explains how notions of maleness and femaleness constrain individual action to a heteronormative script. Rejecting such binaries can be personally costly, even while complying with them limits the functioning of free markets and the insights of the economics profession. The career of Deirdre McCloskey offers a focal point within which Bartlett locates the complex interplay of individual identity and the ideals of free markets, democracy, and personal freedom.

A second set of essays illustrates *collective* values, beliefs, and norms shaping material outcomes. In chapter 3, Stanley Engerman delivers a historical macroeconomic perspective. He examines the growth of ideological commitment to, and also hostility against, the rise of capitalism as a dominant economic system. He elucidates the roles of government in setting the preconditions and altering the rate of capitalist growth. He questions the links between capitalist growth and a range of social evils, noting that poverty, inequality, war, imperialism, famine, and slavery all predate modern capitalism. Does capitalism tend to accentuate these evils in the long run? Does it corrode culture as detractors, such as Karl Polanyi, argued? Engerman shows that capitalistic growth generally correlates with increased freedoms in political and economic choices.

Engerman's contrasting of societies, in terms of their commitments to capitalist growth, underscores the humanistic point that economies are socially embedded. The varied ways in which economic growth flourishes or withers reflect more than factor endowments and aggregate production functions. Economic growth reflects a society's common values and shared beliefs, an argument McCloskey masterfully develops in her treatise on bourgeois virtues. Alterations of religious belief have long played a role in understanding the Industrial Revolution, and in chapter 4, Robert Nelson considers the impact of McCloskey's work in this field. Nelson intertwines a Lutheran ethical system with the development of the welfare state in Nordic countries. For Nelson, the success of the Nordic welfare state in the twentieth century is built squarely upon "a critical value foundation and other cultural supports" provided by Lutheranism. Economists and theologians have complementary concerns, he concludes.

Compared to their neoclassical descendants, classical political economists were far more lucid about the moral and ethical dimensions of their craft. In chapter 5, Jack Goldstone, a student of revolutions in preindustrial societies, concurs with McCloskey's notion that broad changes in ethical judgments invigorated modern rates of economic growth. For Goldstone, shared values—notions of justice and appropriate social hierarchy, for example—constrain the powers of government and elites. As values change, as the constraints on action are eased, societies rapidly reorder the world along new priorities.

He argues that in expounding a view of human nature that includes a wider range of virtues than the prudence and self-interest featured in mainstream economics, McCloskey is actually returning to the rich economic and moral philosophy originally expounded by Adam Smith.

A third set of chapters engages the methodology of economics, especially as it bears upon public policy. Echoing Goldstone, in chapter 6 Stephen Engelmann also envisages an economy as an ethical reckoning among its participants. As a political theorist, Engelmann finds a contradiction between McCloskey's rhetoric of virtues, her classical liberalism, and her libertarianism, which Engelmann describes as an elevation of the market as a principle of governance. He distils McCloskey's ethics into a form of suppressed politics, an insistence on virtues other than self-interest but never amounting to collective action that could ultimately impact market outcomes. By suppressing politics in economic discourse, Engelmann argues, McCloskey fuels a growing disenchantment with public policy and reduces political questions to matters of private virtue.

The authors of chapter 7, Peter Boettke and Virgil Storr, do not share Engelmann's concern. Both prominent "Austrian" economists, they embrace McCloskey's *Homo loquens*, the speaking human, as one of their own. The authors consider the extent to which an emphasis on economic reasoning as a form of rhetoric parallels systems of economics such as the Austrian school. Seminal contributors to this school, such as Ludwig von Mises, F. A. Hayek, and Israel Kirzner, all discussed the vital role of persuasion in markets. Like McCloskey, the authors view economics as a mode of discourse in which the beliefs and values of actors determine how, what, and how much gets traded. For Boettke and Storr, "the market" is not orchestrated by an esoteric auctioneer but is rather a cacophonic social focal point needing thick description. Their approach to public policy therefore emphasizes restraint and humility.

In chapter 8, by Paul Turpin, the confrontation of beliefs and values against material calculation is made tangible in recent policy debates over health care in the United States. Turpin shows how economic considerations can be effectively neutralized when their moral content is underarticulated or marginalized. He demonstrates how the *pathos* or emotional framework from which economic arguments are viewed bears on consideration of the argument itself. Thus the rhetoric of economic disputation takes center stage in explaining the twists and turns of economic policy.

In chapter 9, John Nelson casts economics as a paradigm of knowledge whose rhetorical style is materialistic even as its substantive inquiries are expansive and deeply humane. Like Turpin, Nelson views economic inquiry as inseparable from the moral commitments it encompasses, and those moral commitments inevitably appear in an aesthetic dimension. The aesthetics of economic inquiry, in other words, expresses a moral texture. Recognizing the rhetoric of economics as a style of inquiry holds the potential for a more meaningful, more pluralistic politics. Nelson suggests that the "rhetoric of economics can lead from a practical take on disciplinary epistemology into a novel political economy of the bourgeoisie."

In chapter 10, Steven Landsburg brings us full circle, back to individual decision making and the value of low-powered reasoning focused exclusively on selfish material ends. To a young Professor McCloskey and the young student Landsburg, the Chicago approach to price theory produced astonishing results—powerful conclusions—that upturned common sense. Landsburg vividly describes the sense of triumph that iconoclastic results produced. Like McCloskey in her Chicago school days, Landsburg uses a deductive and empirical approach to real problems, such as the crime rate in contemporary Hyde Park. The capacity to illuminate everyday experiences through a small set of intuitive principles remains the central attraction of economics. Such principles can highlight unintended consequences and locate hidden beneficiaries and overlooked victims of public and private action. Built upon an intense emphasis on the value of prudent choices, Landsburg argues, economics makes a singular contribution to the human sciences.

Although this volume's title features economics and economic history, a number of the essays in this volume would not normally be classified in either category as conventionally defined. This would include the essays by John Nelson and Paul Turpin on rhetoric, the essay by Stephen Engelmann on political theory, and arguably that of Robin Bartlett on gender identity and that of Robert Nelson on Lutheran theology and the Nordic welfare state. Nevertheless, in their engagement with core principles and methodologies, each of these chapters centrally features economics and economic history.

Together, the essays demonstrate the multisided challenge of humanism to materialism. The three fronts—individual, collective, and methodological—create new seams for cross-disciplinary learning. The essays respect the analytic power of microeconomic principles while simultaneously acknowledging the limits of that training and suggesting alternative approaches for locating meaning. Each essay engages its substantive concerns—personal identity, capitalist growth, and republican virtues, for example—while also leaning on the fulcrum of humanistic challenges to materialism. While the ideas have coherence and merit on their own, it is certainly the case that Deirdre McCloskey has had a salient influence on their emergence. Indeed, McCloskey's own career might be summarized succinctly by the volume title.

Unfolding over four decades, McCloskey's exploration of humanistic challenges to materialism has led her to advocate virtue ethics as a central intellectual and personal paradigm. Virtue ethics does not reduce human values to universal prudential behavior in response to variations in prices and incomes, as in Stigler and Becker's "De Gustibus Non Est Disputandum"(1977), by their own acknowledgement an adventure in Max U wonderland. Virtue ethics emphasizes individual moral character in contrast to ethical approaches that emphasize either (1) duties and adherence to rules or (2) allowances for the consequences of actions. To possess a virtue is not just to have a tendency to act in a certain way or to avoid certain actions, nor is it just the possession of a one-dimensional character trait. Virtue ethics depends on selecting actions on the basis of judging situations so that the question of the appropriateness of the action to the needs of the situation is the central concern.

In *The Bourgeois Virtues: Ethics for an Age of Commerce* (2006), McCloskey introduces the four cardinal or what are alternatively called pagan virtues and the three Christian or theological virtues. The four cardinal virtues of justice, courage, temperance, and prudence feature prominently in Plato's *Republic*. The cardinal virtues are embodied in the different segments of Plato's well-ordered ideal society, as well as in the works of Cicero, and were acknowledged by such early Christian fathers as St. Ambrose and St. Augustine. The three theological virtues of faith, hope, and love (or alternatively charity) were stated especially prominently by the apostle Paul in 1 Corinthians 13:13: "And now abideth faith, hope, charity, these three; but the greatest of these is charity" (KJV).

For McCloskey, virtue ethics features prominently as an explanation of history. As in Smith's *Theory of Moral Sentiments* (1790 [1759]: part VI), McCloskey describes economic actions as imbibing the virtue of prudence. She maintains, however, that prudential behavior alone cannot account for large moments in history. Ethical systems embedded in the culture of society play a major role. McCloskey argues that adherence to the seven virtues can actually explain the onset of modern economic growth and, more specifically, why the Industrial Revolution occurred first in Britain. The position is not without controversy. Some economic historians insist on stronger empirical evidence for the argument either that a change in values was the central factor behind modern economic growth or that material factors were not major contributing factors. Specialists also argue that McCloskey provides inadequate evidence or explanation for the fundamental change in values she claims has occurred. Critics charge that she makes no allowance for reverse causation from material and institutional changes to changes in values. Yet even her critics concede the importance, originality, and erudition of her ideas.

The virtues that McCloskey sees as enabling long-run growth are mirrored in her own life. They figure prominently in her intellectual practice and in her relationships with colleagues and students. McCloskey's career has wonderfully embodied all seven of the virtues, providing a worthwhile guide to her character and contributions.

We start with the pagan or cardinal virtues and with the most prosaic of all—prudence or, alternatively, practical wisdom. One constant throughout McCloskey's career has been her insistence on the importance in magnitude. Her recurrent query in evaluating arguments is "How much oomph does it have?" The factor of twelve attributable to modern economic growth has oomph. Statistical significance does not. McCloskey's touchstone question in evaluating how to allocate scarce intellectual resources is whether the issue in question matters, and ultimately matters to humanity.

However neither man nor McCloskey has lived by bread alone. The undeniable power of Chicago price theory made McCloskey's change of approach so difficult for many others and so remarkably brave for her. As she ventured to new interdisciplinary boundaries, she demonstrated the virtue of courage, a willingness—indeed eagerness—to explore new and unknown connections. Courage is essential to all intellectual life, but especially at the forefront of new fields, such as the rhetoric of economics, the rhetoric of inquiry, and intellectual and spiritual approaches to the Industrial Revolution. Her public and deeply personal *Crossing* (2000) likewise testifies to an extraordinary capacity to travel where there are few precedents.

Justice is often described as the primary pagan virtue. Justice entails balance and respect where such is called for but also calling out when respect is not warranted. McCloskey has been a staunch iconoclast in calling out what she regards as false gods and idols—excessive formalism in economics, irrelevant positivism, meaningless statistical testing.

The virtue of temperance—the controlling of desire—is a virtue one might not associate with McCloskey, given her bold and unconventional choices both intellectually and in her life in general. Yet temperance is the virtue most cultivated by and most implicit in McCloskey's insistence on multiple ways of knowing. Her methodology calls for comparative epistemology, in which detailed inquiries must improve on learning in diverse fields. Intellectual temperance involves controlling the desire to privilege one's native discipline, a quality McCloskey has shown in abundance.

We next turn to the more transcendent Christian or theological virtues. Faith in McCloskey's explication is a sense of identity and origins (2006: chapter 10). Faith in action, this sense of identity, facilitates persistence in the midst of doubt and uncertainty. Numerous contributors and participants in the conference that first discussed these chapters spoke of how it was McCloskey's advocacy and persistence with hostile and hidebound editors that ultimately turned their manuscripts into published books. These include Steven

Landsburg, with his *Armchair Economist* (1993); Robert Nelson's *Economics as Religion* (2001); and George de Martino, with his *Economist's Oath* (2011), a project McCloskey supported in discussion with publishers. Faith is closely associated with conviction. McCloskey's conviction that a more expansive and inclusive economics will enrich economic inquiry made possible a staggering number of books, articles, journals, and dissertations.

Hope is the forward-looking virtue: having an eye on the destination. For McCloskey, the text provides the arena for hope, the promise of clearer expression and thus clearer thinking. In McCloskey's case, this has shown up tangibly in the indispensable task of lucid written communication. Even those who would otherwise be unsympathetic to McCloskey's views on methodology have openly embraced her advocacy of clear writing and have required their own students to read and master McCloskey's treatises on the writing of economics. Hope expresses the possibility of a good beyond one's immediate circumstances and control. McCloskey's guidelines offer hope that as arguments are clarified and more fully cohere, a destination will emerge. Many contributors spoke of McCloskey's insistence on written clarity and walking the walk with detailed comments on draft after draft of their manuscripts as critical in their own endeavors.

The greatest of the virtues according to the apostle Paul is love. McCloskey agrees. It is certainly the case that whatever task McCloskey undertakes, or whomever she undertakes to motivate, she does so with the greatest of enthusiasm—in other words, love. She is the one who jumps up ramrod straight to make her point and to raise her hand high to underscore it. This infectious enthusiasm has inspired generations of graduate students in such far-flung fields as price theory and rhetorical criticism. Colleagues, supporters and detractors alike, have all benefited from her unconstrained love of inquiry.

We hope that the following essays illuminate the virtues Deirdre McCloskey has displayed throughout her scholarly career. We are confident that they will advance emerging literatures in which humanism challenges materialism.

Notes

1. Cited in Colander (2006, 31). Solow's 1964 observation rings more true a half century later, when the mathematical barriers to entry in economics are formidable.

References

Akerlof, George A., and Kranton, Rachel E. 2010. *Identity Economics: How Our Identities Shape Our Work, Wages, and Well-Being*. Princeton, NJ: Princeton University Press.

Colander, David. 2006. *The Stories Economists Tell*. Columbus: McGraw-Hill Education.

De Martino, George. 2011. *The Economist's Oath: On the Need for and Content of Professional Economic Ethics*. New York: Oxford University Press.

Easley, David, and Kleinberger, Jon. 2010. *Networks, Crowds, and Markets: Reasoning about a Highly Connected World*. New York: Cambridge University Press.

Emmett, Ross, ed. 2012. *Elgar Companion to the Chicago School of Economics*. Chicago: University of Chicago Press.

Floud, Roderick, and McCloskey, D. N., eds. 1981. *The Economic History of Britain since 1700*. Cambridge: Cambridge University Press.

Friedman, Milton. 1953. *Essays in Positive Economics*. Chicago: University of Chicago Press.

Hausman, Daniel M. 2013. "Philosophy of Economics." In *The Stanford Encyclopedia of Philosophy*, edited by Edward N. Zalta. Winter 2013 edition. http://plato.stanford.edu/archives/win2013/entries/economics/.

Landsburg, Steven E. 1993. *The Armchair Economist*. New York: Free Press.

McCloskey, D. N. 1981. "The Industrial Revolution 1780–1860: A Survey." In *The Economic History of Britain since 1700*, edited by Roderick Floud, and D. N. McCloskey. Cambridge: Cambridge University Press.

McCloskey, D. N. 1985. *The Rhetoric of Economics*. Madison: University of Wisconsin Press.

McCloskey, D. N. 2000. *Crossing: A Memoir*. Chicago: University of Chicago Press.

McCloskey, D. N. 2006. *The Bourgeois Virtues: Ethics for an Age of Commerce*. Chicago: University of Chicago Press.

McCloskey, D. N. 2010. *Bourgeois Dignity: Why Economics Can't Explain the Modern World*. Chicago: University of Chicago Press.

McCloskey, D. N. 1970. "Did Victorian Britain Fail?" *Economic History Review* 23: 446–59.

McCloskey, D. N., and L. G. Sandberg. 1971. "From Damnation to Redemption: Judgments on the Late Victorian Entrepreneur." *Explorations in Economic History* 9: 89–108.

McCloskey, D. N., ed. 1971. *Essays on a Mature Economy: Britain after 1840*. London: Methuen.

McCloskey, D. N. 1983. "The Rhetoric of Economics." *Journal of Economic Literature* 21 (2): 481–517.

Nelson, Robert. 2001. *Economics as Religion: From Samuelson to Chicago and Beyond*. University Park: Pennsylvania State University Press.

Nussbaum, Martha, and Amartya Sen, eds. 1993. *The Quality of Life*. Oxford: Clarendon.

Piketty, Thomas. 2014. *Capitalism in the Twenty-First Century*. Translated by Arthur Goldhammer. Cambridge, MA: Belknap Press.

Putnam, Hilary, and Walsh, Vivian. 2011. *The End of Value-Free Economics*. New York: Routledge.

Smith, Adam. 1790 (1759). *The Theory of Moral Sentiments*. London: A. Millar. Library of Economics and Liberty Online. Retrieved January 5, 2016, from http://www.econlib.org/library/Smith/smMS6.html.

Stigler, George J., and Becker, Gary S. 1977. "De Gustibus Non Est Disputandum." *American Economic Review* 67 (2): 76–90.

Ziliak, Stephen. 2010. "Deirdre N. McCloskey." In *The Elgar Companion to the Chicago School of Economics*, edited by Ross Emmett, 301–5. Cheltenham: Edward Elgar.

Ziliak, Stephen. 2011. "Matrixx v. Siracusano and Student v. Fisher, Statistical Significance on Trial." *Significance* 8 (3): 131–34.

1

Philanthropic Endeavors, Saving Behavior, and Bourgeois Virtues

RICHARD SUTCH

> Economic change in all periods depends, more than most economists think, on what people believe.
>
> JOEL MOKYR[1]

In 1816, near the end of November, Condy Raguet, the president of a fledgling insurance company and a newly elected Pennsylvania state representative, encountered his friend Richard Peters at the southeast corner of Fourth and Chestnut near Philadelphia's Carpenters' Hall. Raguet had recently received reports from England on the operation of several savings banks. These newly created Scottish and English banks provided a philanthropic service to the laboring class.[2] With the subject fresh on his mind, he "immediately," by his own account, asked his friend to join with him to establish a similar institution in Philadelphia.

It was probably unseasonably cold. Philadelphia is always cold in late November. But that particular November was "indeed a cold blustering month, and there [were] rain storms and snow storms; cold north-west and north-east winds, . . . froze very hard several nights, and some days were cold enough to sit by a good fire" (Peirce 1847, 220–21).[3] In person, Raguet was tall, slender, and according to an acquaintance, "remarkably straight, with much of a military air . . . and was always dignified in his deportment" (quoted in Camurça 1988, 181).

Peters and Raguet walked together eagerly discussing the idea when they met Clement Biddle and Thomas Hale in the financial district. They too joined in support of the proposal. Mr. Raguet was a man of local repute, and it was not difficult for him to recruit eight additional men of prominence as trustees. He was also a man of resolve. Only a few days later, an organizational meeting was held, and soon after, on December 2—less than two weeks since his chance encounter with Peters—the Philadelphia Savings Fund Society opened its doors for business. It was the first savings bank established in the United States.

FIGURE 1.1 Condy Raguet, founder of the Philadelphia Savings Fund Society. It is likely that Raguet pronounced his name: rah-gay, as the French would say it. However, his cousin, Henry Raguet, a friend of Sam Houston, moved to Texas, and the Raguet Elementary School in Nacogdoches, Texas, which is named for Henry, has adopted: ray-GAY (voice on the school's answering machine, accessed February 15, 2015). Source: Willcox (1916: facing page 16).

A local newspaper published the society's objectives:

> To promote economy and the practice of saving amongst the poor and laboring classes of the community—to assist them in the accumulation of property that they may possess the means of support during sickness or old age—and to render them in a great degree independent of the bounty of others—is a duty incumbent upon all, who by their services or advice have it in their power to effect so desirable an end. . . . [Our] design is to afford a secure and profitable mode of investment *for small sums* (returnable at the will of the depositor on a short notice) to mechanics, tradesmen, laborers, servants *and others* who have no friends competent or sufficiently interested in their welfare, to advise and assist them, in the care and employment of their earnings.[4]

The reason for saving presumed by Raguet and his compatriots was to provide "support during sickness or old age." That same motive has remained the primary objective for saving and wealth accumulation for at least the next two hundred years. From today's perspective, we might add a few other provisions for the future—saving for children's education, saving for a down payment on a home, saving to leave an inheritance—but why we save is straightforward. We save today, consuming less than we might, so that we can consume more than we earn at some point in the future.

It might seem, then, that there is nothing very remarkable about the aims of the Philadelphia Saving Fund Society. Yet what is curious about this story of America's first savings bank might not be obvious to modern readers. Saving—putting aside some portion of current income for protection against whatever the future might bring—was a novel concept at the time. Saving was not commonly mentioned in letters and diaries originating from the newly independent states of America—that is, "saving" in the sense of saving money. There were plenty of references to saving lives, saving souls, and saving seed.[5]

"Thrift" would be a word more frequently encountered, but its sense at that time did not suggest the act of saving money. Thrift was a moral virtue: the virtue of frugality. Frugality, moreover, was part of an ethical package, bundled with other bourgeois virtues: honesty, hard work, charity, sobriety, stewardship, and the like (McCloskey 2006). Saving money was not the object of frugality. The frugal person would avoid extravagance, minimize waste, and improve efficiency. The fruit of this parsimony need not be the accumulation of wealth; the practice of thrift was advocated to increase the individual's capacity for charitable deeds. The English cleric John Wesley, whose ministry was the founding inspiration for the Methodist movement, gave a sermon in 1744 on stewardship titled "On the Use of Money," which contained the catchphrase "Gain all you can, save all you can, give all you can." With "save all you can," Wesley challenged his listeners to live frugally. Avoid "elegant epicurism. . . . Despise delicacy and variety." Do not waste money on "superfluous or expensive apparel, or by needless ornaments. Waste no part of it in curiously adorning your houses; in superfluous or expensive furniture; in costly pictures, painting, gilding, books; in elegant rather than useful gardens." Do not "throw away money upon your children. . . . Do not leave it to them to throw away." If there is a surplus, "give to the poor." Do "good to them that are of the household of faith" (Wesley 1872). The goal of frugality was to demonstrate the ability to discipline oneself by the use of reason.

When he set out to promote "the practice of saving," Condy Raguet used the word "saving" in a different, modern sense: setting aside some portion of earnings for future use. In 1816, that was a rather novel definition. Noah Webster's *Compendious Dictionary* of 1806, with "the definitions of many words amended and improved," recorded these definitions:

> **Saving**, a[djective]. frugal, careful, near, excepting.
>
> **Save**, v[erb]. to preserve from danger or ruin, rescue, lay up, keep frugally, spare, except.
>
> and
>
> **Frugal**, a[djective]. thrifty, sparing careful, saving of expense without meanness.

Webster's 1828 edition was more expansive and explicitly a compendium of *American* English. It recorded five definitions, but not Mr. Raguet's:

1. Preserving from evil or destruction; hindering from waste or loss; sparing; taking or using in time.
2. Excepting.
3. Frugal; not lavish; avoiding unnecessary expenses; economical; parsimonious. But it implies less rigorous economy than parsimonious; as a saving husbandman or housekeeper.
4. That saves in returns or receipts the principal or sum employed or expended; that incurs no loss, though not gainful; as a saving bargain. The ship has made a saving voyage.
5. That secures everlasting salvation; as saving grace.

Saving was not often mentioned outside of the few cities of the time because it was not a primary concern for early American farmers. Most Americans were not "mechanics, tradesmen, laborers, or servants"—the clients the Philadelphia Saving Fund Society reached out to assist. Around that time, approximately 82 percent of the white (nonslave) population lived in rural areas and were directly engaged in agriculture. More to the point, the great bulk of the farms they resided on were self-sufficient, owner-occupied, family enterprises. Aside from the tobacco plantations operated with slave labor in Virginia and further south, most agricultural production was still small-scale and intended to meet the needs of local consumers and not for export to distant markets. The farmer's income consisted of the physical product of the family's labor, and very little if any was sold for coin. Barter was the usual means of exchange, and the goods received in return were more often than not intended for immediate consumption. Apart from saving seed and storing grain, saving for the future was not common among American farmers. Their future was taken care of in another way. Family members, particularly grown children, were obligated by custom and law to provide support in sickness and also to give relief from the infirmities of old age. If that protection failed, neighbors might step forward to help. "Give to the poor," John Wesley advised the community.

Saving seed and storing grain are examples of prudence that require careful frugality. Such activities sustained the agricultural enterprise and preserved the farm from danger or ruin in the following year. Deirdre McCloskey properly describes this behavior as "necessary thrift" (McCloskey and Nash 1984; McCloskey 2011, 64–65). But this "desperate saving," as she describes it, is not saving as an economist would have it. Saving is technically defined as *disposable* income minus consumption (Sutch 2006, 287). But if saving and storing seed is compelled by the command of nature, the value of the grain saved must be subtracted from gross income (just like taxes paid are subtracted) to arrive at disposable income. Disposable income is what the income earner has left over (after taxes, fines, and other obligatory dues—including saved seed) to consume or accumulate as he or she wishes.

But the fact of the matter is that most Americans did not accumulate. Most didn't need to save. The few who did save might have had no easy means beyond hoarding to do so. And hoarding cash—say, in a sock or a hole in the ground—was considered sinful.[6] In the Gospel of Matthew, Jesus relates the *Parable of the Talents* (Matthew 25:14–30). A master berates his servant who had hidden his master's talent (a unit of money), which was given to him for safekeeping, in a hole: "You wicked and slothful servant. . . . You ought . . . to have deposited my money with the bankers, and at my coming I should have received back my own *with interest*. . . . Throw out the *unprofitable* servant into the outer darkness, where there will be weeping and gnashing of teeth" (Matthew 25:24–30, emphasis supplied).

Those of European descent in America before the nineteenth century invested in their economy but rarely invested at a distance or earned interest. Land was cleared, homes and outbuildings were erected, walls and fences and wagon roads were engineered and built with the exercise of a great amount of hard labor. As a consequence, the land was made more productive. To gain that advantage, some consumption was sacrificed as the labor devoted to farm building was diverted from the production of crops, hunting and fishing, and other activities required to provision the farm family. Yet the growth in output that can be attributed to these kinds of intimate investments would be approximately matched by the growth in the population. Virgin land would not need to be cleared; new farms would not need to be built, except to provide for a growing population. If output grows only as fast as population, per capita output remains unchanged.

Just because saving money was rare in this world does not mean that there was no wealth. In agrarian America, most wealth was land and the permanent improvements on the land. And some landowners were wealthier than others. Indeed, if you owned enough land, you could join the landed gentry, rent to others, and live off the rents without the trouble of engaging in hard labor yourself, like the eighteenth-century English aristocrats portrayed in BBC costume dramas. But whether you were a small farmer or an aristocrat, your objective would be to preserve what wealth you owned and ultimately to pass it on to your heirs. In this world, most wealth was inherited (or appropriated from the aboriginal population with or without the color of law). If asked to explain your wealth, your probable answer would be that you were born into a wealthy family.

Raguet was wealthy by the standards of both his time and ours.[7] He had inherited from his French-born father, Claudius, who had amassed a fortune first as a privateer during the Revolution and then as a ship owner involved in the lucrative carrying trade across the Atlantic. Condy Raguet established himself as an independent merchant at age twenty-two. Six years later, he built a "mansion" on Chestnut Street. He owned land in rural Pennsylvania and Virginia. He was a successful merchant and private banker (Camurça 1998, 47–56, 308–13).

Even before his inspiration to establish a savings bank, Raguet had become interested in the problem of the insecurity of old age and the power of compound interest. With some experience in underwriting marine insurance, he interested himself in working out the principles of life annuities. It is probable that he was one of the private underwriters who organized the Pennsylvania Company for the Insurances on Lives and Granting Annuities, the first life insurance company in North America (Murphy 2010, 1–2). In any case, he was an early director. The company was granted a charter in March of 1812 just as the tensions that preceded the declaration of war against the United Kingdom made ocean travelers and wealthy Americans reluctant to purchase insurance from English underwriters.

The insurance business got under way in 1814 after a public address was published (Yorke et al. 1814). As a director of the company, Raguet was a signer of the advertisement. He became the company's president in May of 1816 (Morris 1896, 24–27). During his tenure, the primary business was in insuring lives at sea (typically for a single voyage) and selling life annuities, a novel concept at the time (Buley 1953, I:33). According to an advertisement in *Paxton's Philadelphia Directory* signed by Raguet and the company's actuary, Jacob Shoemaker, "a person aged 60 years would receive 11 3/4 per cent. per annum" for the rest of his or her life (Paxton 1818: n.p. at xxviii). If the Pennsylvania Company invested the monies received at 7 percent (the current rate on US Treasury bonds), this advertised annuity implies an expected thirteen years and one month of life remaining at age sixty. Shoemaker had calculated a life table based on the records of the Philadelphia Episcopal Church and the Philadelphia Board of Health and concluded that a sixty-year-old would have between 13.71 and 13.75 years of additional life (Morris 1896: table 1, 117–21).

According to the *Address*, "The object for which annuities were instituted was to enable persons not having a sufficient income to maintain themselves, or not being able to pursue their usual occupations for support, to provide against the infirmities of old age, inability to labor, or some other mischance which might reduce them to want" (Yorke et al. 1814, 102–3). Raguet's advertisement went on to point out that by saving $2.98 per year from age eighteen to age sixty, enough would be accumulated to produce an annuity of $100 per year for life (about $40,000 in today's living standards; Williamson 2015). Clearly, Raguet had thought deeply about the advantages of saving before he learned of the Scottish savings banks.

The economist who studies economic development is interested in the provision of funding for investment—funding *at a distance*. There would be macroeconomic consequences for economic growth quite apart from the advantages to the individual saver. Economists have known ever since they were shocked by the magnitude of "Solow's residual" that the most important ingredients in the formula for per capita growth are the optimistic ideas, the novel innovations, and the dreams that are the stuff of technological advancement.[8] The phenomenal rise in per capita income that occurred in the United States between 1816 and 2008 was generated by adopting new technologies (steam and steel and hybrid corn) and creating new institutions (banks, corporations, and public high schools). Contrary to some thinking, the expanding abundance was not (primarily) the consequence of providing each worker with more capital. It was advancing technology—not accumulating wealth—that mattered most. For reviews of the evidence, see Oded Galor (2005) and Joel Mokyr (2005, 2010a). For a passionate defense of the role of new ideas and some straight thinking that puts the role of capital accumulation in its place, see Deirdre McCloskey (2010a and 2011).

But an absence of new ideas proved to be a problem before the nineteenth century. To be an innovator, you have to believe that progress is possible—that there is a potentially better way to power a river boat, or to remove the seeds from the cotton boll, or to manufacture a comb from a tortoise shell.[9] To be a financial innovator, you need to believe in the creative power of a bank. Americans before Condy Raguet's time had little reason to believe in progress. Sustained economic growth was beyond their experience (Clark 2010). To be sure, they thought the standard of living they enjoyed was higher than in Europe but that good fortune could be explained by the abundance of land, the absence of landlords, and—they dared to think—the favor of Providence.

But even this privileged standard seemed fixed and frozen. Americans at the start of the nineteenth century lived no better than the previous generation.[10] The long view of European history seemed to indicate there would be good years and bad years, few would be rich and many poor, but the *average* welfare of the population would remain constant over the generations (Persons 1954). Measured by the standards of today, it was low.

Thomas Malthus had a simple explanation for this stagnation, which he articulated in his influential book *Essay on the Principle of Population as It Affects the Future Improvement of Society*. Published anonymously at the close of the eighteenth century (1798), the book interpreted abundance as pernicious. When the standard of living rose (because, perhaps, of an advance in technology), men and women would marry early and have many children. The population would grow more rapidly than output expanded, and this pace would soon push output per capita back down. Any economic gains would be temporary. It retrospect, Malthus had the facts on his side. The provocative economic historian Gregory Clark, in his brief summary of the economic history of the world, could assert with the confidence that comes with hard evidence "the average person in the world of 1800 was no better off than . . . his or her ancestors of the Paleolithic or Neolithic" (2007, 1 and 5).

If growth is not to be, then one individual can improve his or her lot only at the expense of others. An economy without progress is like a zero-sum game, like a round of poker where the winnings of the winners exactly equal the losses of the losers. The chief economic preoccupation in such a world is not improving one's position but rather defending what one has from the encroachment of others. The rules that maintain the distribution of wealth are thus of uppermost importance. If this situation is not to generate class war and become unstable, society must settle into an uneasy stasis. In that context, new ideas are threatening. The status quo is maintained by an allegiance to tradition. A new design for a plow, or a new scheme for fertilizing the soil, or a proposal to experiment with planting rutabagas, not only would fly in the face of the traditional ways of doing things but would seem morally suspect. To gain from such activities would, it was feared, be at the expense of one's neighbors. Better to fall into line.

The Philadelphia Savings Fund Society was a new—even threatening—idea. The founders anticipated opposition and sought to justify their intent "to promote the happiness of a large portion of the community." The depositors would be winners. There would be no losers. This bank would be a positive-sum venture. The opening paragraph of the pamphlet announcing their plan directly addressed the obstacle:

> With many, the novelty of any scheme is a sufficient objection to it; and with more, jealousy of the interference of others in concerns not their own, and of efforts to interpose between them and established habits, furnish strong grounds for objection to purposes such as the Society is desirous to achieve. But while it is admitted that opposition to new projects is often well founded, and that the distrust which is felt towards those, who unsought offer counsel, is frequently justifiable, the motives which have dictated the following [plan for a savings bank] . . . have their origin in sincere wishes to promote the happiness of a large portion of the community. (Quoted in Willcox 1916, 31–32)

The economic paralysis of Raguet's day was the consequence of a self-fulfilling prophesy. The long history without growth had produced a culture of tradition and a near-universal fear of change. Innovation was stifled and growth refused to happen. The economy wasn't growing because it hadn't been growing. What would be needed to break out of this trap of circular thinking, as Joel Mokyr has argued (echoing McCloskey), is the popular inculcation of a "culture of growth" (Mokyr 2014). A culture of growth: hold that thought, because it will be useful in what follows.

If an ideology based on the zero-sum logic of economic stasis was an obstacle to technical change, so too was the lack of saving. Both saving *and* investment are needed to bring new ideas to fruition. Savings were required to fund the innovation. As Robert Solow observed, "Much, perhaps nearly all, innovation must be embodied in new plant and equipment to be realized at all" (1957, 316). So the lack of voluntary saving in 1816 and, indeed, its absence in British North America before the Revolution and during the early years of the new nation help explain the absence of economic growth in the decades before 1820.

The presence of saving to fund investment, however, is not enough to guarantee rapid economic growth. It must be investment at arm's length—investment at a distance. The thinker or inventor who has a new and potentially productive idea is someone who, generally speaking, has insufficient savings stored up to turn his or her plans into machines, factories, and going concerns. And most savers are not themselves inventors, engineers, or entrepreneurs. So to connect saving to technological progress, an intermediary is required to collect the savings from the savers and put the capital in the hands of the builders. Intermediaries of this sort were absent or rare before 1816. Without them, little progress would be made. That observation gives significance to Raguet and Peters's impulse to create a financial intermediary to collect the savings of the poor. The funds accepted would be comingled and invested on behalf of the savers. At first, the Philadelphia Savings Fund Society invested only in "safe" assets: "All sums received, are by the immutable rules of the Institution, to be invested in the public funds of the nation, and of the safety of such investments none can doubt" (quoting a pamphlet advertising the Savings Fund Society published in 1817; Willcox 1916, 32). The savings of the poor were channeled into the infrastructures of government. As the savings bank movement took on momentum, their investments funded canals, water works, and private entrepreneurs (Olmstead 1976, chapter 4; Payne and Davis 1956, chapter 6; Welfling 1968, 27–29).

Fifteen days after the Society opened for business, it made its first investment, purchasing $450 of US government bonds yielding 7 percent per annum.[11] When the yields on the US bonds retreated somewhat, the Society invested in Philadelphia City bonds at "approximately" 7 percent (Willcox 1916, 157; Carter et al. 2006, series Cj1192). Soon mutual savings banks were making personal loans. The Philadelphia Society guaranteed its depositors a return "fixed at *near five per cent*," and in case profits exceeded expenditures, the surplus would be divided among the depositors proportionately (Willcox 1916, 27). Such returns were unavailable to the workingmen, domestic servants, and others. As the Society put it,

> The usual situations in which many individuals are placed do not furnish the opportunities to preserve . . . [their] frugal savings. The continual occupations of the industrious mechanic frequently exclude him from a knowledge of the methods by which his earnings, beyond what is required for his support, can be protected and advantageously invested. A profitable employment of these fruits of his labour and economy is generally beyond his attainment; and all persons who like him could gather the means of future fortune from small earnings carefully managed suffer the same inconveniences. The honest and faithful domestic, whose weekly or monthly wages exceed by a few shillings or dollars the sums required by his necessities—the apprentice, whose early skill in his business enables him to gain by "over work," in each month a few dollars—the day labourer, who in the busy and profitable months of spring, summer and autumn, finds himself possessed of more than his support and that of his family demands; all of these it is presumed would most willingly deposit these gains in some place of profit and safety, and they have heretofore sought in vain for such advantages. (Quoted in Willcox 1916, 33)

Raguet's zeal to enable the poor to accumulate "ample resources for the evening of existence"—as the Society quaintly phrased it—might seem today to be a benevolent eccentricity (Willcox 1916, 37, quoting an 1817 pamphlet published by the Society). But he was not alone in this humanitarian impulse. By the end of 1816, the Society's board had swollen to twenty-one members; all were drawn from the elite of Philadelphia's bourgeois society.[12] And the bank they organized was not for profit; it was a philanthropic endeavor. Raguet and the managers of the Society served without pay and covered the expenses of the bank out of their own pockets. They claimed their only object was "not their own but the benefit of others" (Willcox 1916, 32). Their professed disinterest in financial gain, they hoped, would inspire confidence in the novel institution. But we should look for a deeper motive.

The first depositor was Curtis Roberts, a black domestic servant in Raguet's own household (Willcox 1916, 141–42). Perhaps Raguet reasoned that if his manservant—a freeman, not a slave—could become financially independent, then he would not regard Raguet as his patron and look to him for maintenance in old age. Of course, the founders had issued an invitation to a much wider segment of Philadelphia's population than the servants of the trustees. The call was directed at laborers, mechanics, apprentices, and all who were "industrious and frugal" (advertisement in *Paxton's Philadelphia Directory* for 1818, np at xii). Applicants were screened and the well-to-do were refused.

The Society was designed not just to serve the poor but to improve them morally. An 1817 pamphlet published by the bank and aimed at the elite of Philadelphia society explained that its intention was "to promote industry, temperance and morality" (Willcox 1916, 32). The bourgeoisie patronized the poor to improve them, to wean them from aversion to hard work and from imprudence. The well-to-do of Philadelphia supported a long list of civic and charitable institutions designed to bourgeoisify the lower classes. These included the Philadelphia Hospital for the Poor, the Philadelphia Orphan Society, Charles Willson Peale's famous museum, the American Philosophical Society, the Philadelphia Asylum for the Mentally Ill, the Washington Benevolent Society of Pennsylvania, the Female Hospitable Society for the Relief and Employment of the Poor, and the Philadelphia Association for the Instruction of Poor Children (Kashatus 1994). The historian Thomas Haskell attributes this patronizing impulse, this "humanitarian sensibility," not to a "random outburst of altruism" or a heightened sense of morality but to new ways of thinking associated with the recent ascendency of an entrepreneurial class located in a handful of late colonial cities (Haskell 1985, I:339 and 341). The important point for the present argument is that the new thinking included an emphasis on habits of economy, self-reliance, and "utilitarian individualism" (Bellah et al. 1985, 27). These attitudes were nascent in 1816 and largely confined to the city merchants, but they would soon spread and prove essential preconditions for mass saving.

Raguet was an affluent member of the gentlemen elite: a merchant, an entrepreneur, and what was then regarded as a "practical man of affairs." In a portrait painted when Condy Raguet was fifty-two (that would be 1836), he wore a dark coat and a broad high collar that clasped under a silk neckerchief that marked him as a man of wealth and distinction.[13] He was a founding member of the Swedenborgian New Jerusalem Church in Philadelphia, whose doctrine stressed free will and espoused a simple theology of love and beneficence (Gouge 1842; Hunt 1842, 543; Scharf and Westcott 1884, 1432–33). He was also a political economist, an admirer of Adam Smith, a correspondent of David Ricardo, and an ardent proponent of free trade (Raguet 1839; Dorfman 1946, 602–3 et passim; Martin 1987).[14]

What is significant about Raguet's story is not that he was somehow unique or essential. I feature him simply as an exemplar of McCloskey's bourgeois merchant, an autodidact: genteel, alert, entrepreneurial, and philanthropic. As McCloskey herself might say, Raguet's story is an example of creative arbitrage, buying an idea low (from the Scottish) and selling it high (to his Philadelphia peers; McCloskey 2010, 23). But Raguet's kind was ubiquitous in the port cities of the Northeast in 1816. If Raguet hadn't proposed the idea, others would have surely done so. In Philadelphia, one of his friends, perhaps Peters or Biddle, might have taken on his role. After all, the idea of a savings bank philanthropy was up for grabs. Just a few days after the Philadelphia Fund for Savings opened its doors on December 2, 1816, the "Provident Institution for Savings in the Town of Boston" set up a nearly identical business on December 13. Baltimore, Maryland, and Salem, Massachusetts, were not far behind, accepting deposits beginning in March and April of 1818 (Payne and Davis 1956; Keyes 1876, I:43, 91, and II:377). The "Bank for Savings in the City of New York," planned in 1816, was delayed for three years while the state legislature debated a law to govern mutual savings banks, but it opened in 1819 (Olmstead 1976, 16; Keyes 1876 I, chapter 28). By 1820, there were ten such banks in the United States, fifteen in 1825, and fifty-two in 1835 (Payne and Davis 1956, 18).

In 1840, there were sixty-one savings banks in the United States. At that point, the idea of saving as a precaution against times of want and for securing one's comfort in old age was no longer novel. It had gone viral. And this virtue no longer required the prompting and assistance of do-gooders like Raguet. It had become—almost overnight—the identifying characteristic of the American individualist. The responsible man conducted his affairs so as not to become a burden on his children or a mendicant for public support. Writing in 1840, Richard Henry Dana, in his great narrative *Two Years before the Mast*, could claim that Americans were distinguished as a "money saving people" (Dana 1840, 155).

While the early savings banks pioneered and popularized the industry, they were not the only institutions to arise that accepted deposits of savings.

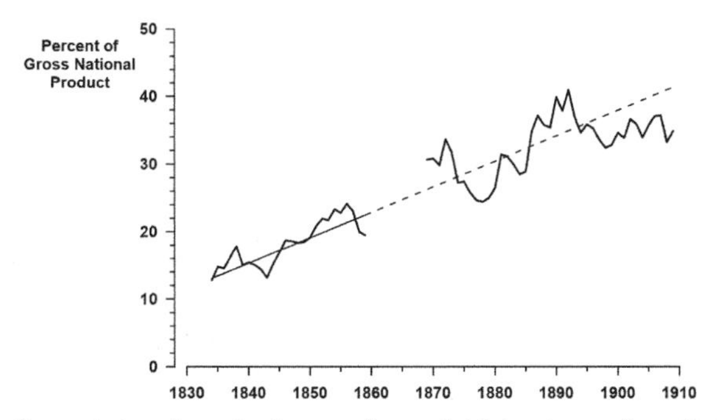

FIGURE 1.2 Gross private savings rate, 1830–1910. Source: Sutch (2006, 3:292, figure Ce-E).

It was not long before commercial banks, insurance companies, and building and loan societies eagerly competed to collect the savings of the working class. Commercial banks, which first appeared in 1782 and were organized to facilitate large mercantile transactions, particularly transatlantic deals, did not accept small deposits at the outset (Wright 2001 and 2011). However, they began to broaden their business after 1819. They soon introduced personal banking accounts that paid interest and took small deposits from individuals. The spread of these commercial banks was phenomenal. By 1840, there were 735 in the United States located in 414 distinct towns and cities (online database to accompany Warren Weber's 2006 study updated on July 27, 2011).

Saving rates rose over the course of the nineteenth century until they stood at over 25 percent of gross product at the century's end (see figure 1.2; Sutch 2006 volume 3: figure Ce-E, p. 292). And saving was widespread even among the working class (Sutch 2011 and 2015). What had happened? What had happened "almost overnight"? Three things.

First, before American industrialization began, there was a stable, family-based set of institutions that governed economic transfers from producers to dependents. These included patriarchy, dynastic inheritance, high fertility, and grown children's responsibility for the support of their aging parents. Beginning in the early nineteenth century, the old-age support mechanisms began to break down, and when they did, it prompted a realignment of all the elements of that institutional cluster. One response was a shift away from the extended family to the nuclear family as the economic unit. Subsequent generations had fewer children, saved to accumulate assets, and then drew upon that wealth to finance their consumption in old age (Sutch 1991). Thus "life-cycle saving" replaced the premodern system. Saving money was an invention of early modernity and, I argue, was a critical component in the emergence of a market economy (Hunter and Yates 2011, 9). The "life-cycle transition" picked up steam in the mid-1840s. It was well under way by 1870 and was nearly complete by 1920. Planned self-financed retirement came to be a common phenomenon (Carter and Sutch 1996). These transformations in family strategies mattered: "Where children directly provide for their parents' old age, fertility will be high—perhaps too high to allow for economic development. Where physical and financial assets—perhaps together with credible government pledges—secure parents' old age, fertility will be low and parents will invest in their children's education and other nurturing that enhances their adult productivity" (Carter, Ransom, and Sutch 2004, 274).

The savings bank movement may have hastened the life-cycle transition. The pioneer students of the mutual savings bank movement, Lance Davis and Peter Payne, concluded as much: "The semi-benevolent philosophy that gave rise to the mutuals did much to remove the small savers' fear of banks and bankers, and, by providing a safe and profitable depository for savings, the mutuals probably increased the propensity to save among the working classes" (Davis and Payne 1958, 405–6).[15]

Second, life-cycle savers found a rewarding place in the banks—both commercial banks and savings banks—to deposit their savings. And the banks proved to be transforming. Davis and Payne continue: "Moreover, the mutuals certainly made small savings available for productive investment, especially after the founders had given way to a business-oriented management in the conduct of the operations of the banks. Although it appears that almost all of the banks' direct investment in industry and trade took the form of private loans, their willingness to absorb public issues must also have freed funds for investment in manufacturing concerns" (Davis and Payne 1958, 406).

The savings banks invested the savings of the working class, and many of those investments financed new innovations that were the motive force behind the economic growth, which began sometime between 1816 and 1830 (Rhode and Sutch 2006, 16–19). James S. Gibbons, writing in 1858, described the transforming role of banking:

> Any one who has travelled among our country villages, out of the immediate influence of cities, has occasionally been struck by the neglect of natural advantages, the lack of energy, the rudeness of life and character, and the almost savage features of the common people. But on visiting the same place after an interval of a few years, he has seen a total change: a larger population, a better class of buildings, an air of thrifty growth, and a manifest increase of comfort. The old lethargy has disappeared; a new life has been infused into everything; even the countenances of the people are softened; a less brutal and more

> intelligent spirit beams from their eyes. A *bank* has been the starting point of this new career; the mill-dam has been built across the little streams of capital, and the social machinery is brought into play. (Gibbons 1858, 12–13)[16]

To modern ears, this passage sounds like it might have been seasoned with a touch of hyperbole. Gibbons was apparently aware of this problematic reading. He writes in the preface, "Some of the scenes . . . would perhaps be accepted as caricature, if not vouched for as literally true" (v). And other observers have made much the same observation. Howard Bodenhorn reviewed the evidence and concluded Gibbons's view of the impact of banks "was largely correct" (2000, 213).

Third, once economic growth became visible, widespread, and widely shared, Mokyr's promised "culture of growth" began to replace the self-defeating, self-fulfilling prophesies of the zero-sum world. Growth was not only possible but socially desirable as well. New ideas came to be seen as a positive-sum proposition. The system of financial intermediaries (which in time included building and loan associations, insurance companies, and pension plans) developed rapidly and proved eager to invest in innovation (Ransom and Sutch 1987; Ransom, Sutch, and Williamson 1993). Technical change was then propelled along by the regular appearance of new ideas offered up by hopeful and optimistic would-be entrepreneurs who could (at least in normal times) find investors to bet on their success.

Raguet did not start this process. I have made him stand in for all those in 1816 who were beginning to see the economic potential of their new country and were bold enough to become part of the creative process (Skeen 2003). Yet we still might ask, what was it about that cold day in November of 1816 that prompted him to a simultaneous act of benevolence and innovation? It is pure speculation on my part, but perhaps it was the cold weather. The year 1816 is still remembered as the "year without a summer." Throughout the Middle Atlantic states, New England, the Maritime Provinces of Canada, and most of western Europe, temperatures, particularly in the summer months, were historically low, abysmally cold. The abnormal weather that year was almost certainly the consequence of the cataclysmic eruption of Mt. Tambora in the Dutch East Indies (at the time under British occupation and now Indonesia) in April 1815. This explosion was the largest known historic volcanic eruption, ejecting approximately 140 billion metric tons of magma (equivalent to fifty cubic *kilometers* of dense rock). An estimated 60 billion metric tons of sulfur entered the stratosphere, forming a sulfate aerosol veil that circled the earth and filtered out sunlight for months (Oppenheimer 2003).[17]

The result was abnormally low temperatures in North America throughout 1816 (Skeen 2003, chapter 1; Munger 2012).

Philadelphia was not spared. Charles Peirce religiously chronicled the weather in Philadelphia for thirty-four years from 1813 to January 1847.[18] Here is what he reported and thought about the summer of 1816:

> April— . . . Jack Frost came along mounted upon a cold, boisterous north-wester, and made every thing tremble and shiver before him. . . . ice formed on several nights, half an inch thick, which destroyed all the buds, and almost every green thing. (Peirce 1847, 75)
>
> May— . . . this month . . . was really a frosty jade. Her frowns were many, and her smiles few. . . . Every green thing was either killed or withered. A melancholy hue appeared to seal the fate of all vegetable life. . . . Corn was re-planted two or three times, and very little ever came to perfection. . . . (94–95)
>
> June—The medium temperature of this month was only 64,[19] and it was the coldest month of June we ever remember; there were not only severe frosts on several mornings, but on one morning there was said to be ice. Every green herb was killed, and vegetables of every description very much injured. (116)[20]
>
> July—The medium or average temperature of this month was only 68,[21] and it was a month of melancholy foreboding, as during every previous month since the year commenced, there were not only heavy frosts, but ice, so that very few vegetables came to perfection. It seemed as if the sun had lost its warm and cheering influences. One frosty night was succeeded by another, and thin ice formed in many exposed situations in the country. . . . Indian corn was chilled and withered, and the grass was so much killed by repeated frosts, that the grazing cattle would scarcely eat it. . . . Very little rain fell during the month. (134–35)
>
> August— . . . such a cheerless, desponding, melancholy summer month . . . This poor month entered upon its duties so perfectly chilled, as to be unable to raise one warm, foggy morning, or cheerful sunny day. . . . ice in many places half an inch thick. It froze Indian corn, which was in the milk, so hard, that it rotted up on the stock, and farmers mowed it down and dried it for cattle-fodder. . . . Indian corn, raised in Pennsylvania in 1815, sold (for seed to plant in the spring of 1817,) for four dollars per bushel. (157)

For Peirce, and probably for Raguet, the year was "melancholy," "foreboding," and "cheerless." Vegetables and crops were ruined. Prices of food rose as the year progressed. In Philadelphia, the wholesale prices of Indian corn (maize) around this time typically varied between fifty-eight and eighty-two cents per bushel. But in 1816 and 1817, prices skyrocketed. In July 1816, when Peirce reported that the corn was "chilled and withered," corn grown in the county was selling for $1.22 (exceeding even the wartime high in recorded in 1815).

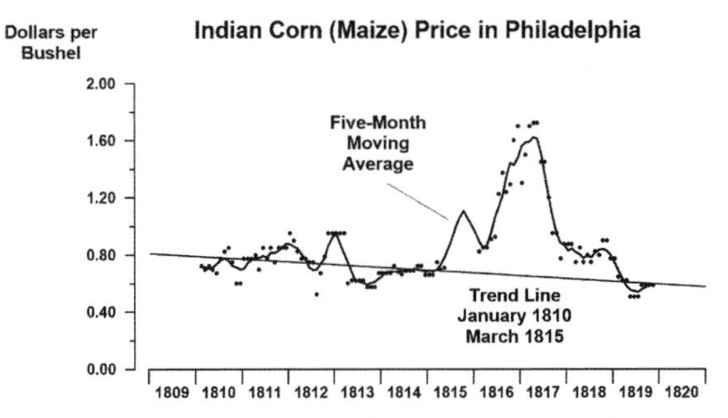

FIGURE 1.3 Indian corn (maize) price in Philadelphia, 1809–20. Source: Cole (1938, 151–91).

By December, when Raguet opened the doors of the Savings Fund Society, it had reached $1.70. The high prices naturally lingered through the winter and reached a peak of $1.73 in May of 1817.[22]

We can only guess at Raguet's specific concerns about the weather's impact on the laboring class as he braced for winter. A New Jersey newspaper expressed serious concern in November—a concern that was probably shared by many: "From every appearance, at present, we have reason to believe the poor will have a distressing winter; that there will be many thousands in every part of our country, who must, before the spring, feel the finger of poverty forcibly pressing upon them; that there will be many actual sufferers among those who now live tolerably comfortable. The prospect is dreary, it is disheartening. . . . What many of the poor are to do God only knows! . . . The times certainly call for the indulgence of creditors, and the liberality of the rich" (*New-Jersey Journal*, November 26, 1816, 4). It would not be surprising if Raguet was both distressed and moved to action.[23]

At the time, no one had a scientific explanation for the surpassingly abnormal weather. Various bizarre theories were floated. Some thought that sunspots were blotting out the sun's rays (Munger 2012, 28–35). Yet 1816 was on the declining phase of one of the normal eleven-year sunspot cycles and fell into a longer period of decreased sunspot activity, called the Dalton minimum (Wagner and Zorita 2005). Some thought the bad weather was related to earthquakes. The New Madrid (Missouri) earthquakes of 1811 and 1812 were another scientific mystery still fresh in memory in 1816 (Valencius 2013). To those with strong religious convictions, the weather might be seen as a divine message. Some saw it as a sign of the apocalypse, others as a call to more virtuous habits (Munger 2012, 64–68). As a Swedenborgian, Raguet might have been particularly inclined to benevolence. He knew that the severe weather, the failed crops, the high price of food would be particularly hard on the urban working class who had made no "provision for the casualties of life." Yet as an exemplar of the bourgeoisie, Raguet would be disinclined to gratuitous charity. He believed that alms would encourage idleness: "He is the most effective benefactor to the poor, who encourages them in habits of industry, sobriety and *frugality*."[24]

The Philadelphia Savings Fund Society was, as its centennial historian, James Willcox, put it "the child of benevolence and political economy" (1916, 11). If that marriage was not a respectable bourgeois blend of materialism and humanism, what is?

Notes

My thanks to Susan B. Carter, Farley Grubb, Joel Mokyr, and Alan Olmstead for their valuable comments on an earlier draft. Joshua Herbstman helped me understand the Treasury notes and bonds of 1815. The conference participants proved to be a helpful audience, curious about Raguet's story and eager to explore its ramifications. We had a remarkably stimulating discussion.

1. *The Enlightened Economy* (2010, 1), quoted with approval by Deirdre McCloskey (2010a: xiii; 2010b, 56).

2. Savings banks as a vehicle for the provident poor to protect themselves against age and want were advocated by Jeremy Bentham (1797) and Thomas Malthus (1803). The Edinburgh Saving Bank was instituted in 1814 (Keyes 1876, 18). Raguet undoubtedly knew of the Scottish and English banks, because Philadelphia's leading newspaper, *Paulson's Advertiser*, had recently published an extensive seven-part article on the subject drawing extracts from the *Edinburg Review* (*Paulson's Advertiser*, November 8–16, 1816). The year 1816 saw an outpouring of publications and pamphlets in Great Britain advocating savings banks; see the review of this literature in Griffiths (1816). According to James Willcox (1916, 28), Raguet probably also had access to George Rose's *Observations on Banks for Savings* (1816). Another prominent treatment was the book by John Beaumont (1816). It is also possible that Raguet read of the schemes in his own copy of the *Edinburgh Review* (letter from Clement Biddle to Condy Raguet [1829], reproduced in Willcox 1916, 19), and he may even have had a hand in placing the article in *Paulson's Advertiser*. The crescendo of interest in England culminated the following year when Parliament created (and subsidized) a national system of Trustee Savings Banks (Fishlow 1961).

3. The date was "on or about" Wednesday, November 20, 1816. Letter from Clement Biddle to Condy Raguet [1829], reproduced in Willcox (1916, 19).

4. The story of Raguet's founding of the Savings Fund Society is related by James Willcox (1916, 17–27). The newspaper "address" to the public is reproduced in Roy Foulke (1941, facing page 140, italics in the original). A detailed biography by Zelia SáViana Camurça covers Raguet's political, diplomatic, and editorial careers (1988). In the diplomatic service, he first held the position of US Consul in Rio de Janeiro (1822–25) and then represented the US government as the first *Chargé d'Affaires* to the newly independent government of Brazil (1825–27).

5. A search of references in American books published before 1816 and digitized by Google and the Archive of Early American Newspapers confirms the very infrequent use of the word "saving" in its modern sense.

6. Of course, we will never know how many saved and buried gold and silver coins nor how much. One of the virtues of coin is its durability in such environments. However, the residents

of the British colonies complained constantly about the shortage of specie. They had yet to mine gold or silver, and the British Crown did not allow them to mint coins (Grubb 2012). During the War of 1812, circulating specie disappeared and was replaced by paper money issued by the Treasury (Raguet 1815).

7. Apparently, a few years later, he encountered a serious setback during the economic downturn of 1819 with a "wave of monetary disasters" and unfortunate speculations in coal lands (Camurça 1998, 131). But in 1816, he was rich.

8. Robert Solow, employing a "crude application of American data" for 1909–49, calculated that the fraction of the change in productivity *unexplained* by capital deepening was 87.5 percent—this fraction is Solow's residual: "About one-eighth of the total increase (in productivity per worker) is traceable to increased capital per man hour, and the remaining seven-eighths to technical change" (Solow 1957, 316). Solow later suggested that even he was "startled" by the small size of the contribution by capital (Solow 1987: xx). Also see Solow (1956); Edward Denison (1962); and Solow (1987: xx–xxii).

9. The stories of Robert Fulton's steamboat (1807) and Eli Whitney's cotton gin (1794 patent validated in 1807) are well known and well documented. The story of comb making and the invention of a machine to saw the comb's teeth (1817) by David E. Noyes is less so. It is told by Bernard Doyle (1925, 52).

10. The best conjecture of economic historians is that there was little difference between the American per capita income of 1774 and that of 1816. If anything, this index may have fallen (Lindert and Williamson 2014: figure 4.2), although in retrospect the wars in Europe (Napoleon and the consequent disruption of trade) and North America (the American Revolution and the War of 1812) had a lot of influence on the economic trends experienced by Condy Raguet's generation.

11. Willcox describes the purchase as "$450 United States 6% loan at a premium of 1%" (1916, 157). This bond was undoubtedly an issue of the 6 percent "stock of 1813" (Hessler 1988, catalog number X71). During the just-concluded war with Great Britain, Congress, desperate to raise money to conduct military operations, authorized the president to sell $16 million worth of "stock certificates" (i.e., Treasury bonds) bearing an interest of 6 percent at a price "not limited to par" (Act of February 8, 1813; US Statutes at Large, 798). However, by selling below par, the government would not raise the full $16 million that Congress deemed was necessary. So an attractive alternative was offered: the investor would pay the full-face value and receive an additional premium as an "annuity" (Bayley 1882, 50). In December of 1816, the going rate on Treasury securities remained at 7 percent, thus the Philadelphia Society received a thirteen-year 1 percent annuity as the premium for paying par for the 6 percent bond. Images of the bond and the certificate of annuity are provided by Gene Hessler (1988, 89–90). Treasury notes were also issued under the 1815 act in denominations ranging from $3 to $50, which the government used to pay for supplies, to pay soldier's salaries, and to pay interest (dividends) on the public debt. These notes would be received by the Treasury at any time at face value for payment of taxes, duties, and public lands. But they could also be exchanged (with a minimum of $100) for the 7 percent bonds. The privilege of paying duties and taxes with the low-denomination notes meant that those instruments circulated as currency (Kagin 1984, 82–86). It is probable that some of the deposits into the Savings Fund were made with these notes, since gold and silver specie was scarce and state bank notes were still heavily discounted (Raguet 1815). For a discussion of Treasury obligations during this period, see Rafael Bayley (1882, 48–60); for images of the notes, see Hessler (1988, catalog number X83 and pp. 102–6).

12. Twelve of twenty-one were identified as "merchants" in Philadelphia's city directories, including Raguet (Robinson 1816, 1817; Paxton 1818). Three were "gentlemen"; the others included an attorney at law, a broker, the director of an insurance company, a shipbuilder, a sugar refiner, and Philadelphia's postmaster. They were all young, in their thirties or early forties. Raguet and Biddle were thirty-two; Peters, thirty-six; and Hale, forty-three (Ancestry.com). They were joined by one older man, Andrew Bayard, fifty-five, whom they invited to serve as the society's president (Willcox 1916, 24). Bayard was president of the Commercial Bank of Pennsylvania, prominent in the social and business life of the community, distinguished, and respected. He still wore a white wig, a fashion that by then was rapidly dying out (Willcox 1916, 103, and portrait following 100). I suspect he was selected to give standing to the society at the outset. He served until his death in 1832 but acted more as a figurehead than a supervisor or executive officer (Willcox 1916, 101).

13. The oil painting is reproduced in Willcox (1916: facing page 16), and an engraving based on the painting appears in the book by Harrison Morris (1896, following page 26).

14. At the time of the founding of the Philadelphia Savings Fund Society, he had already taken up the role of a political economist, having published *An Inquiry into the Causes of the Present State of the Circulating Medium of the United States* the year before (Camurça 1998, 308–13).

15. George Alter, Claudia Goldin, and Elyce Rotella have a similar conclusion: "Savings banks, by making it easier and safer for individuals to save, encouraged the increase of savings that generated growth at the macrolevel" (1994, 736).

16. Also quoted by John James (1978, 3). I have restored Gibbons's original spelling and punctuation.

17. The magnitude of the sulfur ejection has been estimated from Antarctic ice core samples (Cole-Dai, Mosley-Thompson, and Thompson 1997).

18. This diarist was not the famous American philosopher Charles Sanders Peirce (1839–1914) but an earlier Peirce who was a vernacular scientist and bookseller in Philadelphia.

19. Peirce calculated the "medium" (mean) as the average of three readings taken at sunrise, at 2 p.m. and at 10 p.m. (Peirce 1847: vi). For comparison, in 1815 the mean June temperature was seventy-three; in 1817 it was seventy-four.

20. June 6 through 10 saw five consecutive nights with "*severe frosts*" (Hazard 1828, 385, emphasis in original).

21. The mean July temperature for 1814 was seventy-three; for 1815 and again in 1817 it was seventy-four; for 1818 it was seventy-five.

22. Monthly wholesale prices were collected from local newspapers by Anne Bezanson and are reported in Arthur Cole (1934, 151–91). The "typical" prices I have reported are based on the data for 1809–14 and 1818–20.

23. On November 15, less than a week before Raguet and Peters met in the street, a meeting of Philadelphia Quakers received an appeal to aid Native Americans in western New York who were said to be starving because their crops had been wiped out by the frosts (Munger 2012, 26). Since many of his friends were Quakers, it is quite possible that this sad news reached Raguet (Baltzell 1958, 238–39).

24. This quotation is from a communication of the Philadelphia Society reported to the periodical *The Christian Disciple* (Boston) and printed in the December 1816 issue (quoted by Emmerson Keyes 1876: I, 38–39; emphasis in the original). The historian of Philadelphia's aristocracy, Nathaniel Burt, gave this bourgeois view a slightly disdainful reading: "At once to do good and to condescend—what sweeter avocation for an Old Philadelphian?" (1963, 167).

References

Aghion, Philippe, and Durlauf, Steven N., eds. 2005. *Handbook of Economic Growth*. Vol. 1, Parts A and B, Atlanta, GA: Elsevier.

Alter, George, Goldin, Claudia, and Rotella, Elyce. 1994. "The Savings of Ordinary Americans: The Philadelphia Saving Fund Society in the Mid-Nineteenth Century." *Journal of Economic History* 54 (4): 735–67.

Baltzell, E. Digby. 1958. *Philadelphia Gentlemen: The Making of a National Upper Class*, Free Press. Reprinted with a "New Introduction by the Author." Piscataway, NJ: Transaction, 1989.

Bayley, Rafael A. 1882. *The National Loans of the United States, from July 4, 1776, to June 30, 1880*. 2nd ed. Prepared for the *Tenth Census of the United States*. Washington, DC: Government Printing Office.

Beaumont, John Thomas Barber. 1816. *An Essay on Provident Banks, for Savings, &c*. London: Cadell and Davies.

Bellah, Robert N., Madsen, Richard, Sullivan, William M., Swidler, Ann, and Tipton, Steven M. 1985. *Habits of the Heart: Individualism and Commitment in American Life*. Berkeley, CA: University of California Press.

Bodenhorn, Howard. 2000. *A History of Banking in Antebellum America: Financial Markets and Economic Development in an Era of Nation-Building*. New York: Cambridge University Press.

Buley, R. Carlyle. 1953. *The American Life Convention: 1906–1952*. 2 vols. New York: Appleton-Century-Crofts.

Burt, Nathaniel. 1963. *The Perennial Philadelphians: The Anatomy of an American Aristocracy*. Little, Brown. Republished with new material. Philadelphia: University of Pennsylvania Press, 1999.

Camurça, Zelia SáViana. 1988. *Condy Raguet: His Life, Work, and Education*. PhD diss. in education, University of Pennsylvania. http://repository.upenn.edu/dissertations/AAI8908315.

Carter, Susan B., and Sutch, Richard. 1996. "Myth of the Industrial Scrap Heap: A Revisionist View of Turn-of-the-Century American Retirement." *Journal of Economic History* 56 (1): 5–38.

Carter, Susan B., Gartner, Scott Sigmund, Haines, Michael R., Olmstead, Alan L., Sutch, Richard, and Wright, Gavin. 2006. *Historical Statistics of the United States*. Millennial ed. 5 vols. New York: Cambridge University Press.

Carter, Susan B., Ransom, Roger L., and Sutch, Richard. 2004. "Family Matters: The Life-Cycle Transition and the Antebellum American Fertility Decline." In Guinnane, Sundstrom, and Whatley 2004, 271–327.

Clark, Gregory. 2007. *A Farewell to Alms: A Brief Economic History of the World*. Princeton, NJ: Princeton University Press.

Clark, Gregory. 2010. "The Macroeconomic Aggregates for England, 1209–2008." *Research in Economic History* 27: 51–140.

Cole-Dai, Jihong, Mosley-Thompson, Ellen, and Thompson, Lonnie G. 1997. "Annually-Resolved Southern Hemisphere Volcanic History from Two Antarctic Ice Cores." *Journal of Geophysical Research: Atmospheres* 102 (D14): 16761–71.

Cole, Arthur Harrison. 1938. *Wholesale Commodity Prices in the United States, 1700–1861: Statistical Supplement, Actual Wholesale Prices of Various Commodities*. Cambridge, MA: Harvard University Press.

Dana, Richard Henry, Jr. 1840. *Two Years before the Mast: A Personal Narrative of Life at Sea*. Originally published 1840. New York: Harper. New edition of 1869, Boston: Fields, Osgood, and Co.

Davis, Lance Edwin, and Payne, Peter Lester. 1958. "From Benevolence to Business: The Story of Two Savings Banks." *Business History Review* 32 (4): 386–406.

Denison, Edward F. 1962. *The Sources of Economic Growth in the United States and the Alternatives before Us*. Committee for Economic Development, Supplementary Paper No. 13, January.

Dorfman, Joseph. 1946. *The Economic Mind in American Civilization: 1606–1865*. 2 vols. New York: Viking.

Doyle, Bernard W. 1925. *Comb Making in America: An Account of the Origin and Development of the Industry for Which Leominster Has Become Famous . . .* Privately printed for the Viscoloid Company.

Fishlow, Albert. 1961. "The Trustee Savings Banks, 1817–1861." *Journal of Economic History* 21 (1): 26–40.

Foulke, Roy A. 1941. *The Sinews of American Commerce*. New York: Dun & Bradstreet.

Galiani, Sebastian, and Sened, Itai, eds. 2014. *Institutions, Property Rights, and Economic Growth: The Legacy of Douglass North*. New York: Cambridge University Press.

Galor, Oded. 2005. "From Stagnation to Growth: Unified Growth Theory." In Aghion and Durlauf 2005, 171–293.

Gibbons, James S. 1858. *The Banks of New-York, Their Dealers, the Clearing House, and the Panic of 1857*. Printing of 1864, copyright 1858, first printing 1859. New York: D. Appleton.

Gouge, William M. 1842. "Obituary [of Condy Raguet]." *Journal of Banking*, July 1841/July 1842, 309–10.

Griffiths, Ralph. 1816. "Tracts on Savings-Banks." *Monthly Review, or Literary Journal Enlarged* 81: 85–94.

Grubb, Farley. 2012. "Chronic Specie Scarcity and Efficient Barter: The Problem of Maintaining an Outside Money Supply in British Colonial America." *NBER Working Paper*, no. 18099.

Guinnane, Timothy W., Sundstrom, William A., and Whatley, Warren, eds. 2004. *History Matters: Essays on Economic Growth, Technology, and Demographic Change*. Stanford, CA: Stanford University Press.

Hall, Bronwyn H., and Rosenberg, Nathan, eds. 2010. *Handbook of the Economics of Innovation*. Atlanta, GA: Elsevier.

Haskell, Thomas L. 1985. "Capitalism and the Origins of the Humanitarian Sensibility." *American Historical Review* 90 (2): 339–61; and 90 (3): 547–66.

Hazard, Samuel, ed. 1828. "The Effects of Climate on Navigation, &c." *The Register of Pennsylvania: Devoted to the Preservation of Facts and Documents, and Every Other Kind of Useful Information Respecting the State of Pennsylvania* 2 (1): 23–26; 2 (6): 379–86.

Hessler, Gene. 1988. *An Illustrated History of U.S. Loans: 1775–1898*. Dover, DE: Dover Litho Printing.

Hunt, Freemont, ed. 1842. "Sketch of the Life and Character of Condy Raguet." *Merchants' Magazine and Commercial Review* 7 (5): 542–43.

Hunter, James Davidson, and Yates, Joshua J. 2011. "The Question of Thrift." In Yates and Hunter 2011, 3–33.

James, John A. 1978. *Money and Capital Markets in Postbellum America*. Princeton, NJ: Princeton University Press.

Kagin, Donald H. 1984. "Aspects of the Treasury Notes of the War of 1812." *Journal of Economic History* 44 (1): 69–88. Reprinted with editorial adjustments and illustrations as Kagin, Donald H. 2013. "Treasury Notes of the War of 1812." *The Numismatist* 126 (2): 35–49.

Kashatus, William C., III. 1994. "The Inner Light and Popular Enlightenment: Philadelphia Quakers and Charity Schoolings, 1790–1820." *Pennsylvania Magazine of History and Biography* 118 (1/2): 87–116.

Keyes, Emerson W. 1876. *A History of Savings Banks in the United States from Their Inception in 1816 down to 1877.* 2 vols. New York: Bradford Rhodes.

Lindert, Peter H., and Williamson, Jeffrey G. 2014. "American Incomes 1650–1870: New Evidence, Controlled Conjectures." Paper presented at meetings of the Development of the American Economy Program of the National Bureau of Economic Research, March 1. Preliminary version dated January 27. Quoted with permission.

Malthus, Thomas Robert. 1798. *An Essay on the Principle of Population, as It Affects the Future Improvement of Society with Remarks on the Speculations of Mr. Godwin, M. Condorcet, and Other Writers.* Published anonymously. London: J. Johnson.

Martin, Thomas L. 1987. "Neglected Aspects of the Economic Thought of Condy Raguet." *History of Political Economy* 19 (3): 401–13.

McCloskey, Deirdre N. [Donald], and Nash, John. 1984. "Corn at Interest: The Extent and Cost of Grain Storage in Medieval England." *American Economic Review* 74 (1): 174–87.

McCloskey, Deirdre N. 2006. *Bourgeois Virtues: Ethics for an Age of Commerce.* Chicago: University of Chicago Press.

McCloskey, Deirdre N. 2010a. *Bourgeois Dignity: Why Economics Can't Explain the Modern World.* Chicago: University of Chicago Press.

McCloskey, Deirdre N. 2010b. "Review of *The Enlightened Economy: An Economic History of Britain 1700–1859* by Joel Mokyr." *History Today* 60 (5): 56.

McCloskey, Deirdre N. 2011. "The Prehistory of American Thrift." In Yates and Hunter 2011, 61–87.

Mokyr, Joel. 2005. "Long-Term Economic Growth and the History of Technology." In Aghion and Durlauf 2005, 1113–80.

Mokyr, Joel. 2010a. "The Contribution of Economic History to the Study of Innovation and Technical Change: 1750–1914." In Hall and Rosenberg 2010, 11–50.

Mokyr, Joel. 2010b. *The Enlightened Economy: An Economic History of Britain 1700–1859.* New Haven: Yale University Press.

Mokyr, Joel. 2014. "Culture, Institutions, and Modern Growth." In Galiani and Sened 2014, 151–90.

Morris, Harrison Smith. 1896. *Sketch of the Pennsylvania Company for Insurances on Lives and Granting Annuities; Founded MDCCCIX* [1809]. Philadelphia: J. B. Lippincott.

Munger, Michael Sean. 2012. "1816: 'The Mighty Operations of Nature': An Environmental History of the Year without a Summer." MA thesis, Department of History, University of Oregon.

Murphy, Sharon Ann. 2010. *Investing in Life: Insurance in Antebellum America.* Baltimore, MD: Johns Hopkins University Press.

New Jersey Journal. 1816. "Communication." *New-Jersey Journal* [Elizabethtown], November 26, 4.

Olmstead, Alan L. 1976. *New York City Mutual Savings Banks, 1819–861.* Chapel Hill: University of North Carolina Press.

Oppenheimer, Clive. 2003. "Climatic, Environmental and Human Consequences of the Largest Known Historic Eruption: Tambora Volcano (Indonesia) 1815." *Progress in Physical Geography* 27 (2): 230–59.

Paulson's Advertiser. 1816. "On Savings Banks." Seven Parts, and "An Encouragement for Persons. . . ." *Paulson's American Daily Advertiser* [Philadelphia], November 8, 9, 11, 12, 13, 15, and 16, 1816: pp. 3, 3, 3, 2, 2, 2, 3, and 3.

Paxton, John Adems. 1818. *The Philadelphia Directory and Register for 1818: Containing the Names, Professions, and Residence of All the Heads of Families and Persons in Business.* Philadelphia: E. & R. Parker.

Payne, Peter Lester, and Davis, Lance Edwin. 1956. *The Savings Bank of Baltimore, 1818–1866: A Historical and Analytical Study.* Baltimore, MD: Johns Hopkins University Press.

Peirce, Charles. 1847. *A Meteorological Account of the Weather in Philadelphia from January 1, 1790, to January 1, 1847.* Philadelphia: Lindsay & Blakiston.

Persons, Stow. 1954. "The Cyclical Theory of History in Eighteenth Century America." *American Quarterly* 6 (2): 147–63.

Raguet, Condy. 1815. *An Inquiry into the Causes of the Present State of the Circulating Medium of the United States.* Philadelphia: Moses Thomas.

Raguet, Condy. 1839. *A Treatise on Currency and Banking.* 1st ed. London: Ridgway, Piccadilly, and J. Miller; 2nd ed. Philadelphia: Grigg and Elliot.

Ransom, Roger L., and Sutch, Richard. 1987. "Tontine Insurance and the Armstrong Investigation: A Case of Stifled Innovation, 1868–1905." *Journal of Economic History* 47 (2): 379–90.

Ransom, Roger L., Sutch, Richard, and Williamson, Samuel H. 1993. "Inventing Pensions: The Origins of the Company-Provided Pension in the United States, 1900–1940." In Schaie and Achenbaum 1993, 1–44.

Rhode, Paul W., and Sutch, Richard. 2006. "Estimates of National Product before 1929." In Carter et al. 2006, 3:12–20, 57–70.

Robinson, James. 1816. *The Philadelphia Directory for 1816: Containing the Names, Trades, and Residence of the Inhabitants.* Printed for the publisher, 1816.

Robinson, James. 1817. *Robinson's Original Annual Directory for 1817: Being an Alphabetical List of More than 22,000 Merchants, Mechanicks, Traders, &c. of Philadelphia.* Whitehall, 1817.

Rose, George. 1816. *Observations on Banks for Savings.* 3rd ed. London: Cadell and Davies.

Schaie, K. Warner, and Achenbaum, W. Andrew, eds. 1993. *Societal Impact on Aging: Historical Perspectives.* New York: Springer.

Scharf, John Thomas, and Westcott, Thompson. 1884. *History of Philadelphia, 1609–1884.* 3 vols. Philadelphia: L. H. Everts.

Skeen, C. Edward. 2003. *1816: America Rising.* Lexington: University Press of Kentucky.

Solow, Robert M. 1956. "A Contribution to the Theory of Economic Growth." *Quarterly Journal of Economics* 70 (1): 65–95.

Solow, Robert M. 1957. "Technical Change and the Aggregate Production Function." *Review of Economics and Statistics* 39 (3): 312–20.

Solow, Robert M. 1987. "Growth Theory and After." Nobel lecture, December 8, 1987. Reprinted in Robert M. Solow, *Growth Theory: An Exposition.* 2nd ed. New York: Oxford University Press, 2000, ix–xxvi.

Sutch, Richard. 1991. "All Things Reconsidered: The Life-Cycle Perspective and the Third Task of Economic History." *Journal of Economic History* 51 (2): 271–88.

Sutch, Richard. 2006. "Saving, Capital, and Wealth." In Carter et al., 3:287–332.

Sutch, Richard. 2011. "Hard Work, Non-employment, and the Wealth-Age Profile: Evidence of a Life-Cycle Strategy in the United States during the Nineteenth Century." Paper presented at the National Bureau of Economic Research, Development of the American Economy, program meeting, Cambridge, MA, March 5. Draft of February 17.

Sutch, Richard. 2015. "Capital [i.e. Wealth] in the Nineteenth Century: Definition, Distribution and Disposition." Paper presented at the All-UC Economic History Group/Caltech Conference, "Unequal Chances and Unequal Outcomes in Economic History," Pasadena, CA, February 6.

US Statutes at Large, 13th Congress, 3rd Session. 1815. "An Act to Authorize the Issuing of Treasury Notes for the Service of the Year One Thousand Eight Hundred and Fifteen." Originally published 1815. Reproduced in US Library of Congress, *A Century of Lawmaking for a New Nation: U.S. Congressional Documents and Debates, 1774–1875*, [online database] *US Library of Congress*, 213–16.

Valencius, Conevery Bolton. 2013. *The Lost History of the New Madrid Earthquakes*. Chicago: University of Chicago Press.

Wagner, Sebastian, and Zorita, Eduardo. 2005. "The Influence of Volcanic, Solar and CO2 Forcing on Temperatures in the Dalton Minimum (1790–1830): A Model Study." *Climate Dynamics* 25 (2/3): 205–18.

Weber, Warren E. 2006. "Early State Banks in the United States: How Many Were There and When Did They Exist?" *Journal of Economic History* 66 (2): 433–55.

Webster, Noah. 1806. *A Compendious Dictionary of the English Language; in Which, Five Thousand Words Are Added to the Number Found in the Best English Compends; the Orthography Is, in Some Instances, Corrected; the Pronunciation Marked by an Accent or Other Suitable Direction; and the Definitions of Many Words Amended and Improved; to Which Are Added for the Benefit of the Merchant, the Student, and the Traveller, I. Tables of the Moneys, II. Tables of Weights and Measures, III. Divisons of Time, IV. An Official List of the Post-Offices in the United States, V. The Number of Inhabitants in the United States, with the Amount of Exports, IV* [sic, should be VI]. *New and Interesting Chronological Tables of Remarkable Events and Discoveries*. Hartford, CT: Hudson and Goodwin. Database online, Ancestry.com, 1997.

Webster, Noah. 1828. *American Dictionary of the English Language, intended to exhibit, I. The origin, affinities and primary signification of English words, as far as they have been ascertained. II. The genuine orthography and pronunciation of words, according to general usage, or to just principles of analogy. III. Accurate and discriminating definitions, with numerous authorities and illustrations. To which are prefixed, an introductory dissertation on the origin, history and connection of the languages of Western Asia and of Europe, and a concise grammar of the English language*. Facsimile of 1st ed. of 1828. Chesapeake, VA: Foundation for American Christian Education.

Welfling, Weldon,. 1968. *Mutual Savings Banks: The Evolution of a Financial Intermediary*. Cleveland, OH: Press of Case Western Reserve University.

Wesley, John. 1872. "Sermon 50: The Use of Money" *The Sermons of John Wesley*. Wesley Center Online. http://wesley.nnu.edu/john-wesley/the-sermons-of-john-wesley-1872-edition/sermon-50-the-use-of-money/.

Willcox, James M. 1916. *A History of the Philadelphia Savings Fund Society*. Philadelphia: Lippincott.

Williamson, Samuel. 2015. "Seven Ways to Compute the Relative Value of a U.S. Dollar Amount, 1774 to present." *Measuring Worth*. http://www.measuringworth.com/uscompare/.

Wright, Robert E. 2001. *Origins of Commercial Banking in America, 1750–1800*. Lanham, MD: Rowman & Littlefield.

Wright, Robert E. 2011. "Governance and the Success of U.S. Community Banks, 1790–2010: Mutual Savings Banks, Local Commercial Banks, and the Merchants (National) Bank of New Bedford, Massachusetts." Paper presented at the Business History Conference. *Business and Economic History On-Line* 9: 2.

Yates, Joshua J., and Hunter, James Davidson, eds. 2011. *Thrift and Thriving in America: Capitalism and Moral Order from the Puritans to the Present*. New York: Oxford University Press.

Yorke, Samuel, Bohlen, John, Raguet, Condy, Shoemaker, Jacob, et al. 1814. *An Address from the President and Directors of the Pennsylvania Company for Insurances on Lives and Granting Annuities, to the Individuals of the United States upon the Beneficial Objects of That Institution*. J. Maxwell for the Company. Reprinted in Morris 1896, 91–116.

2

Queering McCloskey's Feminism in Location and History

ROBIN L. BARTLETT

Introduction

Ideas develop in conversations. In open and inclusive conversations, new possibilities emerge and the seeds of innovation are sown. Innovation leads to economic, social, and political progress. McCloskey believes that government rules and regulations squelch open conversations and thus thwart innovation and growth (2015). A more insidious set of rules and regulations, however, may hamper open conversations even more. The unexamined assumption of heteronormativity can keep a virtuous society, producing in unfettered free markets, from reaching its full potential.

Heteronormativity is the assumption that all males and females are and should be attracted to members of the supposed opposite sex for reproductive purposes. Reproduction takes place in the nuclear family. As a result, there is a cultural bias, a heteronormative bias, built into every economic conversation, institution, and system. Many feminist scholars focus on the male/female or man/woman component of heteronormative conversation. They examine the causes and consequences of the almost universally observed differential growth in the economic, social, and political fortunes of men as opposed to women. They also examine the growth and development of families and family structures.

Queer scholars focus on the heterosexual/other sexualities component of the heteronormativity conversation. *Queer* can be used as a derogatory term for human beings who exhibit nonconforming gender expressions and sexual behaviors. Used as such, it is a way of policing and enforcing gender expressions and sexual norms. *Queer* can be used as an adjective, but context is everything. Queer scholars, however, use the word as a verb. To queer is to study, to question, those who transgress the cultural norms. Some believe that straying from the traditional gender and sexual norms will destroy the family. It may. Whether or not it does depends on the connections between and among biological sex, gender identity, gender expression, gender roles, and sexual identities and the purposes to which they are put.

While academics study the causes and consequences of nonconforming gender expressions and sexual behaviors from a privileged perspective, there are those who actually transgress the gender and social norms in everyday life. Their voices are not to be ignored. They may be able to provide insight into what it means to be a man or a woman, to be heterosexual or other, and to go through life alone or in a family unit. McCloskey is one of those rare human beings who contributes to the intellectual discussion of these issues with a personal narrative of her gender-crossing journey. A review of her life and feminist work reveals her many transgressions. She transgressed the masculine norms of the economics profession by transitioning from a biological male to a woman. She transgressed cultural gender expectations when she demonstrated how a human being born, raised, and socialized as a male/man could adapt to and acquire the traditional physical, psychological, and emotional characteristics of a female/woman. One of her most important intellectual contributions is that her work transgresses the content and methodology of economics, giving scholars a glimpse of how to transcend disciplinary boundaries. One of her most important queer contributions is her blending of privileged and marginalized voices to provide a fuller understanding of economic life.

Conversations

Academic life is conversation. Economists tend to converse about the material aspects of life. They portray human beings as robotic calculators: rational human beings scurrying around maximizing their satisfaction within the constraints of time and resources, given their "tastes and preferences." McCloskey argues that economists' conversations, though instructive, are limited in scope and depth by their dependence on mathematical models and statistical significance. In contrast, humanists rarely stray from their stories and metaphors. In general, scholars across the academy engage in very scripted, methodologically skewed conversations to describe and understand the human condition.

"Real life" is conversation too. Human beings observe and try to understand what they see. Unlike economic "man," as envisioned by economists, human beings observe with lenses filtered or tinted by an array of cultural beliefs and norms. For example, casual observation would suggest that the real world is made up of two kinds of human beings: males/men and females/

women. Further observation might suggest that males and females may be two different species of human beings, given their visible differences in physical appearances, activities, mannerisms, and speech patterns. Moreover, it may appear that males and females are attracted to each other and that the primary purpose of that attraction is to engage in sexual intercourse to reproduce. Often, males and females live together in one household and share childrearing and household responsibilities. Couples tend to have one person specialize in market or nonmarket work. However, this is just one possible interpretation of these observations of male and female interactions. The assumption that all human beings behave in these ways is the assumption of heteronormativity. Furthermore, since it is believed that most human beings engage in this behavior, it is considered the norm. Heteronormativity is so normalized that few question it.

Human beings often rely on other human beings for interpretation of what they observe. These other human beings may be parents, teachers, government officials, or religious leaders. Human beings may also rely on their own inner voices and personal experiences. When interpretations seem reasonable and fit with everyday lived experiences, they become traditions, accepted beliefs, and norms. It is generally accepted that "This is the way we do things." Once interpretations have reached this status, they typically go unspoken and exist in the background of everyday decision making.

As time passes, these beliefs and norms may be questioned. When these beliefs and norms no longer correspond to everyday experiences, human beings begin to engage in conversations about them both in the academy and at the kitchen table. For example, for decades in the United States, the Barbie doll was considered to have the ideal female body type. Her boyfriend, Ken, a well-chiseled white male, possessed the ideal male body type. Generations of female tweens starved themselves to have a twenty-five-inch waist, while male tweens drank protein shakes to bulk up to attain a forty-two-inch chest. Eventually, professionals, parents, and tweens observed that the human body does not even closely resemble that of Barbie or Ken. Efforts to achieve these body types were counterproductive and harmful.

Economists leave it to psychologists, sociologists, or political scientists to grapple with beliefs and norms. They set them aside and assume they are captured in the phrase "tastes and preferences." Thus economic "man" maximizes "his" utility under the constraints of time and resources, given "his" tastes and preferences. But the reality is that "tastes and preferences" have not remained constant since Paul Samuelson wrote his dissertation *Foundations of Economic Analysis: The Observational Significance of Economic Theory* (1941). Just as the norms related to physical appearance embodied for girls and boys in Barbie and Ken have changed, so too have those for women and men and their interactions. Yet, in the West, many human beings hold on to the ideal that a man should marry a woman, have children, and live happily ever after. The unspoken assumption of heteronormativity is buried deep in the "tastes and preference" clause.

What follows in this chapter is a reflection on the ways that McCloskey's work and life evolved and how they challenge the norms of the economics profession, gender norms, the discipline of economics, and in particular, heteronormativity. The challenges are profound, particularly when they are observed and interpreted within a historical context. The context is the academy and the intellectual conversations that brewed with successive waves of activism: feminists in the 1980s; gays, lesbians, and bisexuals in the 1990s; and queers in the 2000s. As academic conversations expanded to investigate commonly held beliefs and norms through the lenses of these marginalized groups, their findings allowed human beings to be freer, to "be," to reach their human potential.

Time has given scholars across the academy the opportunity to engage in conversations that are deconstructing the impact of the heteronormative script on the construction of gender, sexuality, and the basic institution of the nuclear family. Moreover, scholars are examining the impact of heteronormativity on the larger systems within which human beings live. The impact of the unspoken assumption of heteronormativity cannot be overstated or overlooked. The creative and productive potential that is trapped inside of each human being, confined by societal norms, legal restrictions, and economic inequities institutionalized by these norms, is lost to society, to its economic growth, and to its accumulated wealth. Even a virtuous society, a society filled with virtuous men and women exchanging in unencumbered free markets, will not reach its full economic potential until men, women, and families are freed from the norms of heteronormativity.

McCloskey's feminist work illustrates the workings of the heteronormative script. McCloskey's transition from a biological male to a woman is accompanied not only by changes in her writing style and in her physical appearance but also by changes in her scholarly productivity. After her transition, she took on the persona of Aunt Deirdre. She produced three major books in ten years. One might ask, were her female content interests and more inclusive methodologies always there? Were they repressed by the acceptable male interests of the profession? Did transitioning or crossing allow her to free up energy previously used to keep her cross-dressing and eventually her gender identity secret? Or did transitioning to a woman allow her to reenvision and to reinterpret her previous economic beliefs about men and women?

Whatever the cause or connection, her current work is shaking the economic profession's understanding of the roles that human beings play through their conversations in developing not only human and physical capital but wealth.

The 1980s: A Feminist, Biological Male, Free-Market Economist

The 1980s were a time of intellectual ferment and growth as scholars rediscovered the ignored or devalued works of women and began incorporating them into their fields. Much of the early work focused on documenting the marginalized place of women in the economy, society, and politics. Patriarchy seemed to be omnipresent, and more concerning, it did not seem to be a recent phenomenon. An obvious question, of course, was why. It was a question that was rarely raised before women entered the academy in reasonable numbers. Women in the academy changed the conversations. The work that grew out of these conversations became known as the New Scholarship on Women (Brown 1984).

While few mainstream economists were taking part in these conversations, several trailblazing works from scholars in other disciplines appeared: Gilligan (1982) and Hyde (1981) in psychology; Keller (1983) in science; and Rich (1980) and Lorde (1978) in poetry and literature. In addition, Hyde (1985) illustrated schematically, in the first chapter of *Half the Human Experience: The Psychology of Women*, all the ways bias, or beliefs and norms, can filter into and distort the objective scientific method. These are only a few of the classic works of the 1980s.

Peggy McIntosh's (1983) five-phase model was used in the 1980s to measure the progress different disciplines were making in integrating women into their scholarly literature. Each phase focused on not only content but also methodology. McIntosh's five phases are (1) womanless; (2) women as notables; (3) adding women and stirring; (4) women as deviants, anomalies, and problems; and (5) women re-visioning.

In the "womanless" phase, the discipline's canon and its methods are seen as universal. In the " women as notables" phase, the works of exceptional women economists from the past are dusted off and reexamined. The canon and its methods are not questioned. The point of this phase is that women can become economists if they have the talent and are willing to make the sacrifices to do so. The "adding women and stirring" phase includes women and their issues in traditional economic analyses. Interestingly, traditional economic models did not do a good job of describing the economic behaviors of women. More questions were raised than answered. The "women as deviants, anomalies, and problems" phase must be entered to make progress.

In this phase, scholars look outside of their disciplines for content and new methodologies to capture the nuances of women's economic behaviors. Changing content and methods, however, changes disciplinary boundaries. So McIntosh's "women re-visioning" phase suggests that new disciplines will be created and have multidisciplinary content and multimethodological ways of knowing. It is important to note that no discipline has made it to this phase. McIntosh's model can be used to show the progress that economists have made in creating and integrating the New Scholarship on Women into economics. It can also help locate McCloskey's feminist work in the academic conversations that were taking place when she wrote them.

Phase 1: The "Womanless" Phase. In the 1980s, economics was a discipline in which the laws and principles were well established and generally accepted. Neoclassical economics was the core. The methodology consisted of abstract mathematical models of economic activity and the use of regression and statistical analysis for empirical work. Rational economic man maximized his utility within the constraints of time and resources, given his "tastes and preferences." Firms maximized their profits in competitive markets. Macroeconomics was built upon microeconomics. Aggregate economic output was just the sum of all the individual and firm outputs. McCloskey (2002) would call this phase "Samuelsonian economics." In phase 1, practitioners consider their work universal, gender-blind, objective, and ahistorical. There is no reason to believe that women would behave any differently than men in making economic decisions, and there is no reason to believe that economics would be any different as a discipline with women in the conversation. Heteronormativity is an unspoken norm.

Phase 2: The "Women as Notables" Phase. Also in the early 1980s, economists began to discover and introduce the work of women economists missing in action. The works of "woman notables" such as Coman (1857–1915), who wrote the first article in the first issue of the *American Economic Review*, were rediscovered. Coman focused on development economics and particularly on the Far West (Ohio). Similarly, the prophetic work in Gilman's book *Women and Economics* (1966 edition), written in 1898, was also recovered. Gilman believed that men and women were becoming physically and mentally weaker as they distorted their bodies and minds to find a socially acceptable mate. In phase 2, the content and methodology of the disciplines are not questioned. Any human being can become an economist. It is an economic choice. Heteronormativity is still hidden in "tastes and preferences."

Phase 3: The "Adding Women and Stirring" Phase. In addition to rediscovering lost female economists, Kreps (1971), Blaxall and Reagan (1976), and Lloyd and Niemi (1979) were adding and stirring women into the content of economics. Conventional economic models and statistical methods were used to document and explain the observed differentials in wages and occupational distributions between men and women.

Bartlett (1985) disaggregated the Phillips curve by gender to demonstrate the differential impacts of monetary and fiscal policy actions on male and female workers. Bergmann (1986) developed an occupational crowding model to explain the wage differential by demonstrating how women are disproportionately tracked into a few occupations (teaching, nursing, and secretarial occupations), thereby lowering their wages as compared to men, who were afforded more occupational choices. Goldin (1990) demonstrated that the observed wage gap between men and women had improved over the previous century but economists' ability to explain the remaining differential was becoming more difficult. The New Scholarship on Women made its way into the economics classroom with Blau and Ferber's (1986) classic text *Men, Women and Work.*

In economics, "adding women and stirring" focused on content and not methodology. Beliefs about biological sex and gender expression or what it means to be a man or woman were not questioned. For example, labor force participation studies offered participants only two categories from which to choose—"male" or "female"—to denote their sex or gender. Moreover, gender and biological sex were considered the same. The number of respondents who did not fit neatly into one of those categories is unknown. Moreover, the heteronormative script can be found in other survey questions. Respondents are provided four options to check to indicate their family status: "single," "married," "divorced," or "widowed." If at least 10 percent of the population is gay, lesbian, or bisexual (GLB) and the majority of the GLB population, like the different-sex couples population, live in households with partners, then how are the regression coefficients for the "Single" variable to be interpreted? Boulding (1990) pointed out the potential problems with inappropriate categories.

Phase 4: The "Women as Anomalies, Problems, and Deviants" Phase. Standard economic models were not able to adequately describe the economic behavior of all human beings. The tendency to add another theoretical twist or add another control variable to a regression became counterproductive. Some female economists explored alternative economic paradigms.

Heidi Hartmann (1976) used a Marxist model to tease out the connections among capitalism, patriarchy, and the observed sex segregation in the market and at home. Hartmann concluded that the system of patriarchy (the control of women's production by men) existed long before the Industrial Revolution in most societies. The factory system made it worse by pulling men away from their farms and into the cities. Their wives followed. Since married men found more gainful employment in the cities than did their wives, they became relatively wealthier. The relative economic power base of women shrank, and they became dependent on men. Even if the observed division of labor between the sexes before the Industrial Revolution was not hierarchical, the Industrial Revolution made it so.

Amott and Matthaei (1991) used a socialist feminist model to explain these observed differences. In their model, biology is destiny. Biological sex determined whether a human being would be designated as a boy or girl. Boys were socialized to be men and could enter one of many primary occupations: doctors, lawyers, college professors, mechanics, airline pilots, and plumbers. Girls were socialized to be women and could enter one of the few secondary occupations: teachers, secretaries, nurses, and homemakers. Men went into primary occupations with opportunities for advancement and thus increased pay. Women went into secondary occupations with few, if any, opportunities for career advancement and thus stagnant pay.

It was within these intellectual conversations that McCloskey (1983) published her classic article "The Rhetoric of Economics" in the *Journal of Economic Literature*. Both mainstream and feminist economists took note, but for very different methodological reasons. At first glance, this article does not seem to be feminist in either its content or its methodology. McCloskey examined the types of rhetoric that scholars use in different disciplines to make their arguments. She noted that economists tend to use facts and logic to make their arguments. Those in the humanities used stories and metaphors. Having pointed out the differences between economics and other disciplines, McCloskey concluded that mainstream economists could develop more inclusive economic theories and a richer understanding of economic behavior if they mindfully wove narratives and metaphors into their explanations. Nonetheless, economists continued to boast that no other social science had the rigorous mathematical models, extensive data sets, and statistical techniques that economics did. McCloskey cautioned them that this arrogance could be to their peril. Such a narrow theoretical and methodological tool kit limited their ability to completely describe and thus understand economic reality.

In her article, McCloskey made a list of attributes used to describe the sciences and nonsciences. The following is figure 2.1, taken from her 1983 article.

On the left side of figure 2.1 are the words McCloskey used to describe the assumed attributes of science. These attributes are ones that most individuals would agree have masculine connotations and are generally attributed

Scientific*	Humanistic*
Fact*	Opinion*
Objective*	Subjective*
Positive*	Normative*
Vigorous**	Sloppy**
Precise*	Vague*
Things*	Words*
Cognition*	Intuition**
Hard*	Soft*

FIGURE 2.1 "The task of science is to move the line" (McCloskey 1983, 510).
* Words that were in the 1983 version and remained in the 1985 version
** Words that were removed ("vigorous" and "sloppy") or moved ("intuition") in the 1985 version

to men: words like *fact*, *objective*, and *hard*. On the right side of figure 2.1 are the attributes she assigned to nonscience. These attributes are ones that most individuals would agree have feminine connotations and are generally attributed to women: words like *opinion*, *subjective*, and *soft*. *Fact*, *objective*, and *hard* are the preferred intellectual attributes and are seen as the best way to go about knowing. *Opinion*, *subjective*, and *soft* are intellectual qualities that are not to be trusted to reveal the truth. Conversations in the academy clearly favor the scientific approach over the nonscientific approach because it is more masculine.

Moreover, if male attributes correspond to the superior intellectual attributes needed for of science, and if female attributes correspond to the inferior intellectual attributes of nonscience, then it follows that men are better thinkers than women and, by default, should be the decision makers in and out of the workplace. This illustrates how easily a misguided interpretation based on a spurious correlation can become a widely held belief and thus an unquestioned norm. Over half of the world's population would be excluded from leadership and policy-making positions because of the inferior attributes they are presumed to possess. Moreover, what this half of the world's population knows because of its presumed inferior attributes is ignored or dismissed in conversions.

McCloskey takes the list of implicit masculine/feminine attributes for the science/nonscience binary from her article and makes them the explicit masculine/feminine attributes of the science/nonscience binary in her book *The Rhetoric of Economics* (1985a) two years later. Her new science/nonscience list, interestingly, has some new attributes. Other attributes have been removed from her original list. The words with three asterisks in figure 2.2 were added to her list. The change in her list of attributes of the science/nonscience binary made feminist economists take note, particularly with regard to her adding the words "male" to the left side and "female" to the right side.

Scientific*	Humanistic*
Fact*	Value***
Truth***	Opinion*
Objective*	Subjective*
Positive*	Normative*
Rigorous***	Intuitive***/ Intuition**
Vigorous**	Sloppy**
Precise*	Vague*
Things*	Words*
Cognition*	Feeling***
Hard*	Soft*
Yang***	Yin***
Male***	Female***

FIGURE 2.2 "The task of science is to move the line" (McCloskey 1985b, 43).
* Words that remained in the 1985 version
** Words that were removed or moved in the 1985 version
*** Words that were added

McCloskey adds three words in addition to "male" (truth, rigorous, yang) to the left side of figure 2.2 and drops one word, "vigorous." McCloskey's choice of words is never accidental. On the right side of the figure, she adds three additional attributes to "female" on the nonscience side (value, feeling, and yin) and she subtracts "sloppy" and moves "intuition" up the list to correspond with the science attribute of "rigorous." Her new list makes the attributes found in the science/nonscience binary correspond remarkably well with the socially constructed attributes of the male/female, man/woman binary. Thus male scientific voices are privileged. This juxtaposition gives males an inherent monopoly on truth and on decision making. The attributes on the "other" side of the figure, the nonscience side, are often used to dismiss women's ways of knowing (see Belenky et al. 1986). Feminist economists realized that McCloskey, who was still biologically a male, was writing as a feminist. She was validating women's ways of knowing and doing economics. McCloskey was suggesting that our economic understanding of the origins and impacts of segmented markets on women and the economy could be more complete and richer if narratives, art, or even music were added to the traditional economic explanations. The disappointments that women feel and the barriers they face are hidden in the numbers found in statistical tables and behind the lines on charts.

Such a shift or expansion in methodology has not happened. Even McCloskey's privileged white male voice has gone unheeded with regard to methodology. While female and male economists are continuing to add to the New Scholarship on Women, they are running up against disciplinary boundaries, restrictive ways of knowing, and unexamined vestiges of heteronormativity.

Phase 5: Women Re-visioning. Another way to locate McCloskey's contribution to feminism and economics is to situate it in a three-dimensional truth space. The three dimensions are "content," "methodology," and "voice." Figure 2.3 contains a three-dimensional figure with these dimensions appropriately labeled.

Axis A represents the degree to which the content of academic inquiry is abstract/ahistorical or grounded/historical. For example, theoretical physicists observe, hypothesize, and test their hypotheses. They work out the mathematical possibility of the big bang theory with little to no physical evidence. On the other extreme are scholars grounded in physicality. Artists in particular would be on this extreme, together with trend watchers in the social sciences, anthropologists in the field, and scanners of archival and other historical documents and data. Axis B represents a continuum of methodological approaches from the scientific method to critical theory. Chemists would be found at the scientific extreme of Axis B and English, other languages, classics, history, philosophy, and religion scholars would be found at the opposite extreme. Finally,

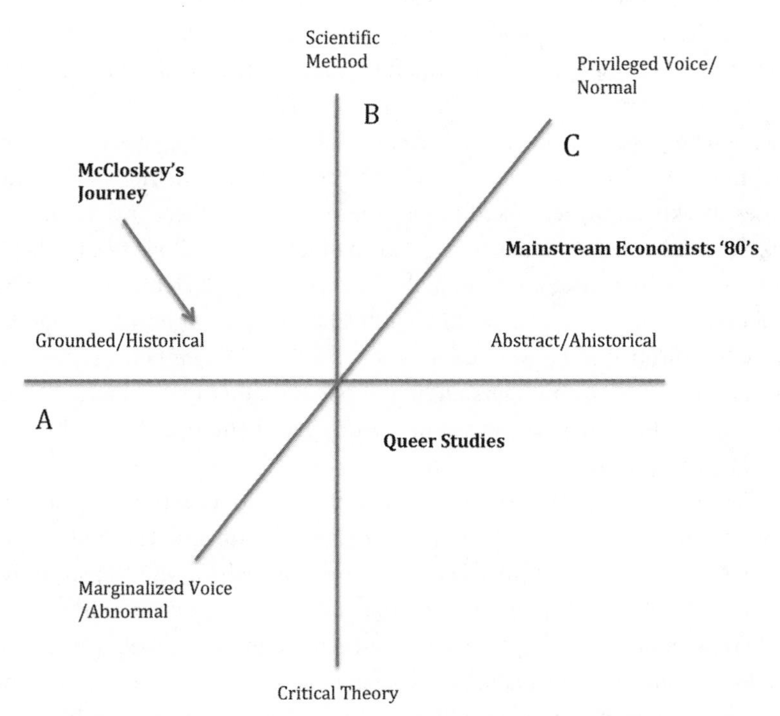

FIGURE 2.3 The truth space: Science/nonscience, abstract/grounded, and privilege/marginalized voice.

Axis C represents the strength of the scholar's voice. Privilege and power allow individuals or groups to have a louder voice or influence with which to establish societal norms. The more a scholar aligns with accepted individual and professional norms, the more power the scholar's work has to influence other scholars. As a white, male, heterosexual, Harvard-educated, neoclassical economist, McCloskey's ideas were well respected, but as a woman, her ideas were sometimes ignored. As she recalls in a London *Times* (1996a) interview and in video found on her website of an Oxford talk in 2010, only when a man repeated the point she had just made, the assembled group of men heard her idea. So who is able to speak and whose voice is heard in the conversation on beliefs and norms are important.

McCloskey is calling for a more balanced approach to understanding human economic behavior and the systems within which human beings live. The center of figure 2.3 is a multidisciplinary, multimethodological space where inclusive, open conversations take place. There is no hierarchy between disciplinary contents. There is no hierarchy between methodologies. And finally, the idea and conclusions agreed upon by the privileged and marginalized after an open conversation are as close to the truth that human beings can get. Talking and listening to marginalized voices are now legitimate ways to go about knowing. McIntosh's fifth stage would be multidimensional, as represented in figure 2.3.

Figure 2.3 is a compilation of several ideas. First, it represents aspects of McIntosh's model. Expanded disciplinary content and methods can come closer to explaining real life. Second, the notion that there is a conjective truth (a truth that lies somewhere between objective and subjective truths) is McCloskey's. McCloskey gave a Phi Beta Kappa lecture at Denison University in 1985 on the meaning of conjective truth. She spoke about how it is impossible to be objective and how one should not be dismissed for being subjective. Both claims assume an understanding of self and other that is humanly impossible. Adding the perspectives of the privileged and marginalized voices builds on McIntosh's and McCloskey's work.

The economics profession as a whole is at the abstract extreme of the content axis in figure 2.3. The canon remains that of mathematical modeling of the free market system. Its methods are regression analysis with statistical significance on Axis B. While some feminist and heterodox economists developed different methodologies, mainstream economists are still wearing methodological blinders. The inability to take in concrete information may be why the economics profession was blindsided by the recent housing bubble and its aftermath. McCloskey (1998b) feels the work of Bergmann, who simulated economic activity, was a small step in the right direction. McCloskey's feminist methodological critique of economics and other disciplines was ahead of her time.

The 1990s: A Feminist, Biological Male/Woman, Free-Market Economist

In terms of McIntosh's model, economists were catching up with their colleagues in the other disciplines. Jacobsen (1994), Feiner (1994), Bartlett (1996, 1997) and Bartlett and Haas (1997) published works that demonstrated the impact of more inclusive content on economic theory. The International Association for Feminist Economics (IAFFE) was founded in 1992. Feminist economists from around the world gathered annually to present their work and engage in conversations with feminists from other cultural backgrounds. IAFFE soon began publishing *Feminist Economics*, the only outlet for feminist economists' work other than more politically heterodox publications. Ferber and Nelson (1993) published the first compilation of theoretical pieces by feminist economists in *Beyond Economic Man*. McCloskey's (1993) work on "conjectivity" was published in this issue. In it, she aligns masculinity with objectivity and femininity with subjectivity from her previous American Economic Association (AEA) presentation on the consequences of the feminine (1985b, 1989). She notes that while most women economists are not willing to throw out neoclassical economics, they are willing to explore what are considered to be more female interests, such as children and family. McCloskey (1989) also hopes that women could humanize Gary Becker's modeling of the family as a "business enterprise" to one with shared goals, responsibilities, and connections among its members. In terms of macroeconomic policy, McCloskey (1993) claims that with women in economics, there would be no need for a paternalistic government. Society would need less intervention from government sources because women would intervene. Women would be more human (motherly). It seems as if McCloskey (1989) is now leaning toward a nature (essentialist) as opposed to nurture (constructionist) explanation for male/female differences. Yet McCloskey's reasons for these differences are in the opening sentences of her 1989 (earlier version 1985) AEA presentation: "The main point is that because men and women live somewhat differently they differ on average in their ways of approaching economics. The secondary point is that the way certain women actually or might or should approach economics is good" (McCloskey 1989, 1).

Note that she does not say that men and women are inherently different; they are just socialized differently. Differences in upbringing manifest themselves in the different topics women choose to investigate and the ways that they choose to investigate them. Butler (1990), a queer theorist, would agree with her. She claims that gender would not exist. It is socially constructed.

Disciplines acquire the trappings of those within it. McCloskey notes that economics is a very masculine discipline, and the topics tend to be of more interest to men than to women. The rules of economic conversation are ones that allow participants to score points. The economist with the most points wins the Nobel Prize. Engaging in intellectual discourse for the purpose of ultimately coming to a joint understanding, a conjective truth, of an issue is viewed as a waste of time and energy. Thus conversations in economics are typically combative. There is little listening. McCloskey concludes that "putting the allegedly feminine and the allegedly masculine into conversation with each other, will, I say, enrich neoclassical Economics" (1993, 76).

McCloskey's Feminist Perspective. In an interview after her transition, when asked what feminism means to her, McCloskey responded, "Feminism is the radical notion that women are people" (2000b, 363). Although she uses the word "radical," she would not fall into the category of radical feminist. Feminist economists have developed many theories about the origins of the observed differences between men and women in the market and at home. These theories are based on the unquestioned heteronormative script.

Conservative feminist economists claim that the observed male/female differences in income and occupational segregation are the result of choices that women freely make. For example, the gender wage gap exists because women make different choices about their labor force participation than men do. Women maximize their utility within the constraints of time and resources given their culturally defined heteronormative tastes and preferences just as men do. Rational economic women decide to go into jobs that complement their childbearing and child rearing needs. The jobs require less specific and more general education and training. In addition, these jobs have more flexible hours and do not demand the long hours of career-track occupations. And even if women are not in baby production mode, they may still decide to do other things with their time because of their caring and supportive tendencies: volunteering for their church, assisting teachers in their local school, or engaging in civic activities. The impact of these free choices is that women earn less than men do because they have less human capital and crowd into occupations that can use their caring and cooperative tendencies.

Conservative feminist economists focus on the individual and believe that women can do whatever they want, but they have to make tough choices. Yet those choices have very different opportunity costs. Veering from the heteronormative script can be personally, socially, economically, and politically costly. The societal norm, the heteronormative script embedded in those tastes and preferences, is that women will be mothers and men will be fathers living together in traditional marriages. Women (and in particular men) who decide not to marry, not to marry men (or women, in the case of men), or not to have children are often suspect and marginalized.

Liberal feminist economists argue, by contrast, that the observed wage and occupational differences between males and females are the result of institutional barriers: family expectations, school curriculums, religious beliefs, and governmental prohibitions deter girls and women from developing their full human potential and deter them from pursuing their interests. Families socialize "baby girls" differently than they do "baby boys" because of assumed biological differences and reproductive imperatives. "Baby girls" need to be treated more gently because they are assumed to be physically more fragile. "Baby boys" are handled with rougher physical interactions because they are assumed to be sturdier. Girls are socialized differently than boys are by their families to prepare them for the demands of parenthood. Girls are taught to be feminine: dependent, weak, emotional, and cooperative. Boys are taught to be masculine: independent, strong, rational, and competitive. In schools, girls acquire the skills to further carry out their biological imperative and are directed to more "feminine" subjects and occupations. Boys are directed into the more "masculine" subjects and endeavors. By the time most girls mature into women, their heteronormative gender role has been internalized. Motherhood, with temporary attachments to the labor force in traditionally female jobs, is their future. Unfortunately, that leaves a woman economically, politically, and socially dependent on a man for her and her children's economic well-being, social status, and political influence.

Similarly, in school, boys are prepared to become providers and protectors for the women who bear and rear their children. Boys are directed toward masculine subjects and occupations, propelling them into a world of competitively incentivized, hierarchical organizations to make a living. Men also internalize the heteronormative script and pass it along to their offspring.

To begin to break down the institutional walls of this bifurcated world of boys and girls, men and women, liberal feminists suggest that families and schools encourage girls to be educated to the same extent possible and in the same ways that boys are educated. Liberal feminists accept the obvious biological differences between girl babies and boy babies, but they also expect that girl babies and women are perfectly capable of competing on par with men in the workforce and in government. With more balanced socialization and education, women are qualified for a wider range of family and work options. The impact will be that women will be less dependent on men and can support themselves. The current reality is that few professional women can be found at the top of the income distribution. Women still assume the majority of the housework and childcare, no doubt affecting their productivity at both tasks. The underlying heteronormative script is still operative at home.

Radical feminist economists, thirdly, believe that institutions define individuals and individuals define institutions. Radical feminists can be separated into two groups. One group believes that the institution of marriage, as defined by patriarchy, defines women. This model suggests that men need women to serve as the mothers of their children and to support their household needs. Men want children so that they can pass along their biological lineage (bloodline) and wealth. Men marry women to control their bloodline. Maternal claims are rarely disputed. It is obvious who gave birth. Until very recently, paternity could be disputed or denied. Thus the assumption is that there is no need to educate women and there is no reason for women to be in the public spheres of commerce and government. The value-added of women, the contribution of women, to economic wealth is the genetic material passed along through birth and the care they provide to offspring. This is an extreme form of the heteronormative script. Yet it may arguably be the most pervasive script internationally.

A second subset of radical feminists believes that men are violent human beings. Whether they are innately violent or taught to be violent through institutions has not been unraveled. Bergmann (1981) concludes that being a housewife is one of the most dangerous occupations that a woman can enter because of the likelihood of physical and mental abuse from her husband. In addition, when measured by the divorce rate, housewives have the highest unemployment rate among all workers. However, there are other explanations for male violence toward women. The hierarchical institutions of family and work as they have evolved since the Industrial Revolution may have put unrealistic role expectations and demands on husbands and wives as they live in isolated, monogamous relationships. In *Yellow Wallpaper*, Gilman (1973 reprint) illustrates how a nineteenth-century housewife goes mad given the limited gender roles imposed on her by society's heteronormative script. Or the economic emergence of women into traditionally male fields may anger some men who think it is their birthright to have the best jobs, that they are entitled to the best jobs. In either event, the benefits of marriage to men and women are changing. Despite the growing turmoil within families, the nuclear family is still seen as the ideal, the norm.

Two policy recommendations come from radical feminists: (1) separatism and (2) challenge/change the existing institution of marriage. The first recommendation means that women and men should live in separate spaces. In *Herland*, a science fiction utopian novel, Gilman (1970 reprint) writes about a tribe of women who live high up in the jungle at the beginning of the Amazon River. They reproduce and raise children without men. "Herland" residents' goal for the reproductive process is not quantity but quality. Each member of the tribe contributes to the most important task of educating the children. They teach them everything they collectively know. Their goal is to make Herland's children the smartest and most creative human beings possible in order to sustain life and to make their lives better. The current reality is that many women and men already live in separate spaces. Some women leave their marriages because of abusive husbands. Husbands leave their marriages for a whole array of reasons: pressures to provide, irresponsibility, immaturity, and/or other women or men.

These models assume that the heteronormative script is how it should be. Female tastes and preferences are different from male tastes and preferences because it is generally accepted that women are the human beings who give birth and raise children and men are the human beings who provide and protect the women having their offspring. The heteronormative script outlines how men and women will talk, dress, and walk to attract a mate. This script outlines how boys and girls will be educated to prepare them for their roles as mothers and fathers. The underlying assumption of the heteronormative script is that the purpose of life for all human beings is to reproduce. Given the goal of reproduction, the heteronormative script requires nuclear families.

Women who choose to live with other women or alone may just not want to be around men. Some women are not interested in discussing the topics most men like to talk about or engaging in activities men like. Sports and war talk can grow tiresome. Conquering and destroying seems counterproductive. Instead, some women like to talk about relationships, hopes, dreams, and challenges. Thus these women may prefer to live or socialize with women in sexual or nonsexual relationships. Some people may just be loners. But withdrawal from the company of men is not without its price of ridicule. Males who choose to live in different household arrangements also challenge the heteronormative script.

McCloskey's Queer Perspective. McCloskey would find herself in good company with conservative feminists. She believes that women would act like men in terms of maximizing utility under constraints, given the prevailing norms underwriting the "tastes and preferences" assumption. McCloskey believes that men and women should be treated equally. She does seem to think that there are some essential differences, whether they are innate or learned. *Crossing: A Memoir* (1999a) provides a unique personal lens, that of a male-to-female transgendered woman, with which to explore the concepts of what it means to be a woman and what it means to be a man in today's US society. In

Crossing, we learn that Deirdre McCloskey had been born a biological male. She had been married, had two children, and had a successful career as Donald N. McCloskey, the Harvard-educated, Chicago-tenured, microeconomist and economic historian. For the first fifty-three years of his life, he followed the heteronormative script for men (more or less).

But Donald had a secret. Since the age of eleven, he liked dressing in women's clothes. Why? Who knows? But his inner gender identity was telling him to do it, and he seemed to get a great deal of pleasure from it. He knew better than to let anyone in on his secret. A man wearing women's clothes was a serious transgression of society's gender expression norms. It was considered abnormal. Males do not wear women's clothing. The heteronormative script has males wearing pants. Pants signaled that he was a strong, rational, and competitive man. Dresses signaled that he was a gentle, emotional, and cooperative woman. Men cannot be women. Men have to act like men.

Shortly after he married his wife, he told her about his secret. He and his wife considered his cross-dressing a hobby and negotiated his supposed hobby into their marriage. Donald's life with his family went on—he was happy. As he grew older and the children left home, his desires to cross-dress and to be read as a woman grew stronger. Whenever possible, Donald, a.k.a. Jane, took advantage of every opportunity to dress like a woman and to be with other heterosexual cross-dressers. He wanted to be free and in a nonjudgmental environment with others who he thought were like him: a biological male, heterosexual cross-dresser.

The *desire* to be a woman, however, became overwhelming when he learned of the possibility that he could *actually* be a woman. The Internet put people and resources that he never knew existed at his fingertips. One day, on a trip back from Chicago to Des Moines, he realized not only that he could be a woman but also that in fact he was a woman.

The decision to physically change his biological sex and gender expression was not that of a rational economic man maximizing his utility with the constraints of time and money, given his tastes and preferences. It made no rational sense. Donald had made a list of all the anticipated cost and benefits (McCloskey 1999a, 51–52). The anticipated costs far outweighed the benefits. But it was not a matter of costs and benefits; his inner identity of a woman had to "be." In the introduction to *Crossing*, McCloskey writes, "My gender crossing was motivated by identity, not by a balance sheet" (McCloskey 1999a, xiii). When questioned by a reporter about when she first knew she was a woman from the inside, she responded that the question did not make sense, "because it takes a prudential answer when the matter is identity. . . . Asking why a person changes gender is like asking why a person is a Midwesterner or thoughtful or great souled: she just is" (McCloskey 1999a, 177).

Dee, a.k.a. Jane, had to spend two years living as a woman before she could have the operation. This is a very dangerous time for transgender human beings because they stick out like a sore thumb. She quickly began observing and learning the mannerisms and conversational styles of women. She said it was like learning the culture of another country. Perfecting her gender presentation and expression took time, effort, and money. As she describes it, "Passing as a woman is not a problem that natural-born women have. They get no practice thinking about it. . . . It therefore takes an actress to see what makes a born man into an acceptable woman" (McCloskey 1999a, 158). Moreover, in public, "a figure is assumed male until enough gender clues contradict the hypothesis" (McCloskey 1999a, 159). If miscues are given, confusing the onlooker, the figure can be seen as a threat. Getting gender expression right was critical to her living as a female. She notes, "Gender is something done, a performance, not an essence springing from genitals or chromosomes" (McCloskey 1999a, 164).

Jane also found herself doing those things that women do: cooking for events, cleaning up after gatherings, and developing friendships. There was much to learn about gender roles, the things that women typically do, although they seemed to come naturally to her. At the conclusion of one of her gender-crossing gatherings, Jane realized it was time to clean up: "Jane started going around the room with a big trash bag. In a roomful of born women, half would have risen to help, and the other half would have at least made a cooperative gesture. None of the cross dressers moved" (McCloskey 1999a, 33). Jane was not just a biological male, heterosexual cross-dresser. Jane was a woman. She began to realize that "being a woman is what you do, she thought, not what you wear. Caring, watching, noticing. It might be difficult for gender crossers to make this transition with their wives. The male habit of being served persists. 'Act like a man'" (McCloskey 1999a, 34).

She was fearful of being "read" and the violence that could follow. As she noted, "You can't change your gender in private, so I can't stay discreetly in the closet" (McCloskey 1999a, 89). Jane's ability to pass as a woman in a heteronormative environment was critical for her safety and survival. Transgendered violators of the heteronormative script are particularly vulnerable. The extent of Jane's worries is revealed in her recollection of a potty stop on an interstate highway and her encounter with a janitor. She had to use the facilities. There was no going on down the road. She would run the risk of getting beaten up if "read" as a man dressed as a woman in the men's restroom. Yet she would cause a fuss if read as a man in the women's restroom. A janitor was walking in and out of the building attending to his chores. So she waited until she thought the women's restroom was completely empty and the janitor was out of sight. Upon exiting the building, the janitor yelled, "Hey fella." She and the male janitor had a male, eye-to-eye standoff: "Violence is dangerous to both sides in the game of men" (McCloskey 1999a, 39). You do not want to start something you cannot finish. Fortunately, she was tall.

Deirdre was fearful about losing her job. She was surprised by the support she received from the dean when she made an appointment to tell him. He was happy she had not become a socialist and that his affirmative action numbers were now better. He even joked about the female salary discount. Deirdre advised gender crossers to get support from the top: "The lower people will discriminate in fear of imagined gender anxieties at the top and will indulge their own. But the top people have fewer anxieties, not more. Later, when a male-to-female professor of chemistry came out at the University of Tennessee, the president was impatient with the anxieties of his subordinates: 'Grow up,' he said" (McCloskey 1999a, 94). And if the person at the top is not supportive, Deirdre recommended finding a job elsewhere. Better to start over in a new state where you can write the story.

Deirdre ran into other some unexpected costs with the legal and psychiatric professions. On two occasions, a family member had Deirdre committed to hospitals against her will. She was arrested twice and taken to the psychiatric floors of nearby hospitals for evaluation. When Dee questioned her family member's motives, the family member said that it was done out of love and to protect "Donald" from doing something that "he" would later regret. Deirdre's encounters with the legal and psychiatric professions were bad enough, but adding insult to injury for an economist, it cost her thousands of dollars in unnecessary hospital bills and lawyers' fees. There was no way Donald could have anticipated the real cost of becoming Deirdre. But she drew a lesson from her experiences: "Certainly the psychiatrists know very little about gender crossing. Even the experts. The conclusion to be drawn from the fact of ignorance reminded Deirdre of her economic views about government policies: Since we know so little about the economy, or about gender crossing, better laissez-faire" (McCloskey 1999a, 148).

If Deirdre adhered to the heteronormative script, she would now be attracted to men rather than women. In her usual analytical way, however, she reports, "The conventional statistic for male-to-female crossers formerly heterosexual is that a third go on loving women, a third come to love men, and a third are asexual. Sexual preference and gender preference are not connected, contrary to the simplicities of the 1930s psychoanalysis and the 1990s homophobia. Who you love is not the same as who you are" (McCloskey 1999a, 10). However, on several occasions, she has noticed men coming out of church or in other social gatherings. She has even gone so far as to daydream about a tall man sweeping her off her feet. Love can come in a variety of bodies.

Her description of the male-gendered world of Donald and the female-gendered world of Deirdre is a story that can only be told from the inside out. At one point she muses, "She had started to forget what the actual experience, how it felt. . . . She forgot what it felt like to not understand relationships because you find them boring. Or to feel that you are by rights the local hero. Or, to feel that people are to serve you. Or more superficially and most fundamentally to think of men as 'we' and women as 'they.'" (McCloskey 1999a, 209). Deirdre's gender identity was that of a woman.

McCloskey was and is a conservative, feminist, biological male/woman, free market economist. She feels that men and women, consistent with the current cultural gender norms, perform complementary roles—that is, men are more rational and competitive and women are more caring and cooperative. Together, they can create a whole human being. However, she is not ignoring the possibility that human beings have and can develop all of these attributes. But given her time and location in the conversation, she wants to go through the world expressing her gender identity as a traditional woman, doing those things that women have traditionally done, and being treated as a woman. She misses her traditional heteronormative family and wishes that her wife and children could have understood that she had to "be." Unfortunately, given the heteronormative script, they have to "be" who they are. As McCloskey reminisces, she had the perfect family: a wife, two children, and a good job. She was happy in her former life as a biological male heterosexual firmly committed to traditional family values. But the heteronormative script left her and her family few options. If human beings could redefine the family and its purpose, the changes that could follow are unimaginable. Given the failure of marriage as it is currently configured, the gender roles and sexual behaviors it demands, change would be a good thing if it allows human beings to at least be who they are.

There is a spark, a voice, a spirit, something inside of every human being that tells them who they are: man, woman, neither, both, or some combination. Living life is the process of becoming that individual. Unfortunately, some human beings' inner gender identity is blocked, ignored, or repressed out of fear of transgressing social norms and being left alone and unprotected. How that inner gender identity is expressed and lived should be up to the individual, but the heteronormative script circumvents most individual efforts.

If biological female and male babies do not necessarily have corresponding inner girl and boy identities and are forced by the heteronormative script to grow up as the other, then their human potential is misdirected, and society as a whole loses their full contributions.

The pervasive male/female and heterosexual/other binaries support the heteronormative script. Binaries usually give rise to hierarchies. One component of the binary is considered to be superior to, more valued than, the other. Superiority gives rise to power and privilege. For example, men are assumed to have the attributes necessary for making tough business decisions. They are seen as aggressive, competitive, and rational: just what is needed to win in a competitive market. Men's way of interacting and conducting business becomes the norm for all business dealings. Hierarchies are hard to change once they are established because they become embedded in every economic exchange, institution, and system. Those in superior or privileged positions can keep it that way.

The 2000s: A Conservative, Feminist, Woman Free-Market Economist

From the gay movement of the 1980s and the emergence of gay and lesbian studies of the 1990s, came queer studies in the 2000s. *Feminist Economics* (1998) published a special issue on GLB issues. Jacobsen and Zeller (2008) produced the first queer economics reader. GLB issues made their way into economics, if only at the margins.

During this decade, McCloskey became a strong advocate for transgender men and women with her public writings about her transition (1999b, 2006b, 2007a). She also had a very public debate with Bailey that started with her review (2007b) of his pseudoscientific book *Queer Science* (2007b). Bailey interviewed transgender men and women without their informed consent or knowledge of the real purpose to which the information from these interviews would be put. From his reckless research, Bailey concluded that transgender human beings are indeed mentally ill as described in the DSM-IV. And even without having met McCloskey, he publicly provided her his diagnosis of her condition as "autogynephilia." The exchange between McCloskey and the other parties involved illustrates how unfounded scientific findings or claims make their way into the news and destroy innocent lives.

Transgressing the Economics Profession. McCloskey's work on the rhetoric of economics and her feminist work on economics are transgressive or queer in many ways. Suggesting that economists should expand their methodological repertoire to become better economists went against the norms of the economics profession. Yet their models and empirical studies failed to predict the housing bubble, the fall of Wall Street, and the resultant Great Recession. Could their myopic methodologies be the source of their failure? Did their models miss the human vices of greed, laziness, and envy?

When she began conversing with feminist economists, her male colleagues wondered what was to be gained. What could these women know or have to offer her that they did not already know and have to offer? What was to be gained? When McCloskey (1995) let it be known that she was transitioning from a biological male to a woman, she transgressed the very notions of what it means to be a male, a man, a female, and a woman. Whether intentional or not, McCloskey was challenging the heteronormative script.

McCloskey writes about how economics is a male game in *Crossing* (1999a). A recent study of the American Economic Association by Fourcade, Ollion, and Algan (2015) confirms McCloskey's claim. Harragan (1977) was one of the first women to spell out the rules of the game for other women. Private and public enterprises are organized as military units. Each unit has a chain of command that is never to be circumvented. Strategies are conveyed through sports metaphors, mostly from American football. For example, knowing the difference between "going up the middle" and "an end run" is very important. Women economists who do not learn the rules of the game, or choose not to play by those rules, will not last long in the economics profession.

Boys learn the ethics of the game very early. Girls are not taught them because they are not expected to be in the game. Kimmel (2008) and Katz (2006) refer to it as the "Bro Code." Men have a sense of entitlement with respect to their positions in life. They have a code of silence about each other's behaviors. Stay out of other men's business. Nonetheless, if their status is challenged by outsiders, they will "circle the wagons" for protection. McCloskey pulls back the curtain on the economics profession's limited ability to provide answers. In doing so, she transgresses the "Bro Code." As she writes, "They are not listening, she thought, as boys often don't in the excitement of the sandbox. I have come upon a criticism of modern Economics that makes the field seem boyishly silly, but the boys can't see the silliness and draw proud attention to their new sand castles. Look, Aunt Deirdre, look at what I have done" (McCloskey 1999a, 179).

Transgressing Gender. When *Crossing* (1999a) came out, economists across the country were talking. "Did you read *her* book?" "Unbelievable." She was in all the newspapers and magazines (Bullard 1997; Kumin 1999; Morgenthaler 1998; Wilson 1996). What some economists said made those of us who are queer feel uneasy and threatened. If the sanity of Deirdre N. McCloskey, the former Donald N. McCloskey, could be questioned, it was fair warning of the potential consequences to all who would challenge the norm. The heteronormative male privileges to gawk, to wander, to rule were no longer hers: "They came down to viewing the male-to-female gender crosser as a weird man rather than as another woman, or for that matter as another human being. They are like other misunderstandings, the knowledge we confidently believe we have of the other. If you have been scorned or misunderstood as a Black or a Jew or a short person or a fat person—or as a woman—you've felt it" (McCloskey 1999a, 352).

She was a biological male who transitioned to a woman. Members of the profession met her with suspicion. Some male economists did not want to claim her as one of them. Her previous male privilege, however, kept them relatively silent and protective in public. Both conservative and liberal female economists also had trouble accepting her as one of them. When being nominated for a seat on the Committee on the Status of Women in the Economics Profession (CSWEP), some female free market economists argued that she had not been brought up as a woman, so how could she know the challenges that women face in the profession? The president of the AEA denied her nomination for the seat on CSWEP. Some feminist female economists worried that her previous feminist writings would be discredited and by association so would their writings. Some felt that they were losing a trusted male ally. After all, his voice was louder and more privileged than theirs were.

Beginning with an analysis of biological sex, the academic conversation has gotten much richer. A strict male/female dichotomy does not exist. Instead, the labels male and female represent the opposite ends of a chromosomal, hormonal, and reproductive organs matrix continuum. Human beings are born with some combination of male and female chromosomes, hormones, and/or one or more sets of reproductive organs that places them somewhere on the male/female continuum. Most of this goes unnoticed and/or unspoken.

Gender identity is a deeply innate psychological feeling of who a human being is: a man, a woman, both a man and a woman, or neither a man nor a woman. A biological male (female) with a gender identity of woman (man) is called transgendered. Some transgendered human beings are more to one end of the spectrum than the other. Gender identity can be expressed by performing masculine or feminine personas. Gender expression refers to all of an individual's visible characteristics and behaviors, including clothing, mannerisms, and speech patterns. Those who express their gender identity in masculine ways are called men, and those who express their gender identity in feminine ways are called women. However, human beings in the middle portions of this masculine/feminine continuum can present as androgynous or gender queer. Some transgender human beings are found here.

Similarly, with respect to sexual identity, there is a heterosexual/homosexual (same sex/different sex) continuum representing the degree to which individuals experience sexual attraction toward the same sex or a different sex. Kinsey's famous survey found that only 10 percent of the population is exclusively heterosexual or homosexual. Since then, several studies confirm his findings. The most recent one is *Sex by the Numbers* by Spiegelhalter (2015). As with biological sex, gender identity, and gender expression, there is tremendous variation in sexual behavior. Sexual and gender identity are independent aspects of an individual's identity. So the presumed linear connection from being born biologically female, to feeling like a woman on the inside, to acquiring feminine attributes, to being attracted to biological males is tenuous at best. The fragility of the gendered assumptions of human beings in the heteronormative script may be the nuclear family's eventual demise.

Yet the heteronormative script is so pervasive that the economic world we live in is designed around it. The ads we read, the movies we watch, the dances we dance, and the Hallmark greeting cards we send for those special occasions in life are designed almost exclusively for gender-conforming, different-sex couples. Homosexual, bisexual, asexual, or pansexual individuals living in this heteronormative environment find it hard to even send a birthday or anniversary card. Individuals whose gender expressions or sexual practices do not coincide with the heteronormative script are often made to feel like the "other." The conveniences and feeling of belonging afforded to those who live the heteronormative script are denied to those who choose not to, or otherwise cannot, live it. Offenders often are severely punished by being ostracized or by physical and emotional abuse.

To demonstrate how pervasive, yet unnoticed, and how dehumanizing, yet ignored, the heteronormative script can be, a simple example will suffice. For example, it is a right-hander's world. Right-handed individuals make, enforce, and gain from the rules of right-handedness. Left-handed individuals do not immediately stand out. Handedness is not typically given away by just looking at an individual. Right-handed students can always find a chair that supports and fosters their natural right-handed proclivities. Left-handed students, however, know that the minute they enter the classroom, they must start looking for those "special" chairs with left-side writing arms. If left-handers cannot find a special chair, they try to make do with a right-handed chair. Left-handers are often forced to adapt to an awkward physical situation.

Right-handers' privilege is built into every facet of human life. Most writing instruments, cooking utensils, and sporting equipment are designed for right-handers. When dining out with friends or family, right-handers think nothing about where they will sit. They can be in the middle of the conversation or, if they like, off to the side. They have free choice. Left-handers, in comparison, tend to sit at the left end of the table so as not to interfere with the eating motions of right-handers. The sense of privilege registered on right-handers' faces when left-handers inadvertently bump their elbows cannot go unnoticed. Lefties are made to feel abnormal. Individuals cannot do their best work when they feel there is something wrong with them.

The example of right-handers and left-handers may seem silly, but the question must be asked: Are left-handers innately different from right-handers beyond handedness? Are left-handers inferior or defective in some way? Could they switch if they really wanted to do so? Lots of left-handers write right-handedly. Some individuals are even ambidextrous. No one has estimated the cost of being left-handed in a right-handed society. But it is probably not trivial.

The impact of the pervasive heteronormative script on the development of human potential is enormous and often goes unnoticed: it arrests the growth and development of all human beings. Queer human beings live in a world made for heteronormative human beings. They are often seen as a threat to the social order. Youths who do not fit the norms spend a great deal of time, physical and emotional energy, and money trying to fit in and survive yet be true to themselves. These are resources that could no doubt be put to more creative use. Yet the heteronormative script not only affects marginalized groups. Those in the privileged groups (males, whites, and other dominant identities) are arrested. They too spend time, physical and emotional energy, and money to keep their place of privilege: living in the right neighborhoods, socializing with the right people, and creating the ideal family. The impact is probably magnified or exaggerated, as members of the dominant groups do not want to even remotely resemble those in the marginalized groups.

The question is, how did human beings get themselves into this heteronormative predicament? How did the heteronormative script get written? How did biological sex, gender identity, gender expression, and sexual identity become linearly connected? Religious and scientific conversations played lead roles. In a film titled *A Fish Out of Water* (Dickens 2009), practitioners and theologians are interviewed about biblical support for heterosexuality. Both groups refer to Genesis (chapters 2–3 of the Bible), the Christian creation story. The story is about how God created Adam and Eve. Interpretations of those chapters by lay and fundamentalist Christians claim that God created Adam in his own image (a superior being) and that he later created Eve (a subservient being) to birth Adam's offspring and to cater to Adam's wants and needs. Since Adam was made in God's image, he was to be the head of the human household, the way God was the head of the universe. Since Eve was made from Adam, she was his to control, just like an arm or leg.

Biblical scholars, however, going back to some of the earliest Hebrew versions of the Bible, found that two words, "Ezer Kenegdo," were mistranslated from the ancient texts. The words mean "corresponding strength," not the "subservient to" translation that has been passed down. Eve was supposed to be Adam's partner, not his subordinate in life. Together they would produce children and raise them. Together they would feed them. Different-sex couples are still assumed, but not necessarily in strict heteronormative gender roles.

When asked why heterosexual behavior is the social norm, some people say it is just natural. Biologists have countered the notion that heterosexual reproduction is nature's way. First, Anne Fausto-Sterling (1993, 2000) has identified at least five sexes. In addition to males and females, there are "herms" (true hermaphrodites), "merms" (male pseudohermaphrodites) and ferms (female pseudohermaphrodites). Herms, merms, and ferms are known as intersexed individuals. Scientists have no estimate of how prevalent these individuals are because many of them were surgically altered upon birth or soon after.

Second, not all animals engage in heterosexual sex and reproduction. The long-held assumption that heterosexual reproduction is the norm has blinded some scientists to the truth sitting right before their eyes. For example, the Laysan albatross has been studied for decades. They are large birds with a life expectancy of sixty to seventy years. They migrate every November to a spot called Kana Point in the Pacific. There they find and rejoin their lifelong reproductive mates. Scientists have observed that these birds engage in behaviors that are consistent heterosexual pairs. All the pairs preened each other's feathers, made out with their mate, and engaged in mating behaviors. The pair would sit on the nest and wait for their eggs to hatch. The Laysan albatross was the poster child for the heteronormative script: one male and one female, mating for life. Lindsay Young (Mooallen 2010), who had been studying these birds since 2003, decided to take a closer look at the albatross pairs. Despite almost identical body markings, she found that one-third of the pairs were same-sex female pairs. The implications of this observation for science and scientific studies of reproduction are far reaching. Animals can change their biological sex (Crews 1994) and engage in what appears to be sexual activities with animals of the same sex (Bagemihl 1999).

Psychologists and sociologists have also weighed in on the necessity for heteronormative coupling. Some emphasize the importance of children being raised by different-sex couples. They argue that for children to be properly socialized, they need same-sex role models to learn how to behave like men and women. They need role models to teach them "appropriate" gender expression: how to present themselves as masculine and feminine. Parents know as well as anyone the price that children pay if they do not conform to established gender norms. Human beings who transgress the societal norms of gender expression and sexual behaviors are considered abnormal or queer.

Biology may not determine destiny. When the identities of human beings, which McCloskey and most economists reference as "people," are properly articulated and uncoupled, the traditional nuclear family will have to change or dissolve. If the socially constructed notions of gender disintegrate, then the heteronormative script falls apart too. Opportunities for constructing new scripts emerge. The individuals walking along Main Street and Wall Street in the future might look very different from those we see today. When the heteronormative script is deconstructed, then previously established reasons for the locations and roles of particular individuals within groups and in society will change.

Transgressing Free Markets. During this decade, McCloskey begins her trilogy: *Bourgeois Virtues: Ethics for An Age of Commerce* (2006a), *Bourgeois Dignity: Why Economics Can't Explain the Modern World* (2010), *Bourgeois Equality: How Ideas, Not Capital, Enriched the World* (2016). These books are her interpretation of how the Industrial Revolution came about and the economic impact it had on human beings. She has come full circle in her intellectual interests, but with a deeper understanding of how cultural norms affect change. In her trilogy, she demonstrates how a free market system without government interventions has enriched human existence to a level never seen before the Industrial Revolution because cultural norms changed. The reasons for the Industrial Revolution are complex and play out in conversations.

McCloskey is in the middle of the current debate over the creation of growth, wealth, and growing income disparities around the world. In response to Thomas Piketty's claim in *Capital in the Twenty-First Century* (2014) that since the return on capital tends to be greater than the return on labor, the distribution of income is skewed, McCloskey (2014) suggests that he may be making the same mistake that Introductory Economics students make by confusing a change in demand with a change in the quantity demanded to come to his conclusion. McCloskey's other work on the determinants of growth (2006a, 2010) precedes that of Piketty.

McCloskey is a strong advocate of capitalism and free markets. However, McCloskey transgresses one more time. Markets are not enough unless there is a virtuous society to regulate human vices. She also argues that the world's wealth grew not because of the usual suspects of increased labor and capital productivity but because the conversations about the bourgeoisie, capitalism, and international trade changed positively over time, inspiring innovation. Changing ideas about the role of the bourgeoisie were the impetus for the Industrial Revolution. When conversations occur and persuasive arguments are made, ideas change. Then beliefs change and then cultural norms change.

McCloskey is not worried about the immense income inequality that is created in this process. She would say, "Let the rich get richer; they deserve it." The promise of astronomical rewards to encourage entrepreneurs to take extraordinary risks of time, money, and energy is necessary for them to provide the market with new products. The Henry Fords, Mark Zuckermans, Steve Jobses, Oprah Winfreys, and Bill Gateses of the world have earned their rewards. Moreover, the world is a better place because of their inventions even if monopolies evolve. No worry—other monopolies seeing the excess profits will evolve and destroy them. The market system can work out errant competition.

With regard to the other end of the income distribution, McCloskey says the poor are much better off now than they were before the Industrial Revolution. McCloskey falls back on a saying first made popular by John F. Kennedy in a speech referring to his macroeconomic policies: "A rising tide lifts all ships." Some improvement is better than no improvement. It is the inventors and entrepreneurs who catapulted the human population to a new standard of material wealth. She suggests that government regulation is to blame for the paucity of innovative people and their creations.

So in true libertarian fashion, she recommends the elimination of government rules and regulations hampering the free market system. She argues that market signals adequately inform consumers and business enterprises. Governments do not need to sculpt economic outcomes. The market outcome is the right outcome. The role of government is only to provide for the common defense, to protect individual property rights, and to enforce the laws.

But what about the market's excesses, imperfections, and externalities? McCloskey's response is that a virtuous society ensures that the free market system delivers on its promise. People will not just rely on prudence and maximize profits. In their daily interactions with other human beings, because they will be virtuous in those interactions, they will be generous, fair, and honest. Reflecting on the impact her transition to a woman had on her thought processes, she says, "It changes one's attitude toward Economics, which is a boys' game and is single minded. The single-minded game among economists is to find the prudence in everything, even though it's obvious to women that love without prudence is there too. Look you have forgotten the love" (McCloskey 1999a, 257).

Tough Love. Yet we do need government for more than the common defense, protecting property rights, and enforcing laws. Price-gouging drug monopolies, savings-squandering Wall Street investors, and employment-reducing relocations of assembly plants happen all the time and cause economic hardships for the most vulnerable. Those on the left have proposed democratic socialist alternatives. They too are dependent on a virtuous society. In some ways, if they follow a heteronormative script, their policies can be even more paternalistic than those of free market economists.

But there is a middle ground that McCloskey never explores because she is waiting for the Schumpeterian "gales of creative destruction" to get rid of the current monopolies. The problem with waiting for the "gales of creative destruction" is that in the meantime, many human beings and their families could be irreparably harmed. It is not unlike waiting for the massive unemployment of the Great Depression to end by letting crippled market forces clear markets. McCloskey inadvertently has suggested a gendered solution. Not all things male are bad. If human beings are going to play the free market game, then they need some rules to play by. And more important, they need a referee. Relying on self-regulation is not enough. A virtuous society is not enough.

The more competitive free markets are, the better they can provide for society's economic needs. The more monopolistic free markets are, the more consumers lose out even with a virtuous society. Players of the free market game need a set of common rules. The Antitrust Act gave us two very simple rules that seem to have been forgotten and need to be dusted off. First, human beings who engage in the exchange of goods and services in for-profit and not-for-profit enterprises both in and out of the market place can do anything they want as long as they do not monopolize, conspire with competitors to monopolize, or naturally evolve into a monopoly. Second, human beings in these enterprises cannot collude with other human beings to fix prices. If they do, the government steps in to remedy the situation. Not-for-profit and non-market exchanges have been added. Just as big corporations cannot monopolize a market without government intervention, men cannot monopolize marriage, churches, and academia without government remedies. Heteronormative couples cannot monopolize marriage.

With these two rules in place and the government acting as the referee, human beings can play the free market game. They get to keep the profits they rightfully earned by being creative, taking risks, and providing something that other human beings want. However, they also get to incur the losses they earned when being creative, taking risks, and providing something other human beings did not want. The government does not bail them out.

Why is it that human families, a locus of nonmarket production, are not seen in this way? If families serve an economic purpose, then men cannot be granted monopoly rights over the production of the other human beings in families. While this may not be as much of an issue here in the United States, it is in other corners of the world.

McCloskey's discussion about the importance of rules for males in their games is instructive. Right now, the only rule is "If it is legal, it is OK to do." A lot is being left to virtuous behavior and self-regulation. Males would never play American football without rules. Think of all the possibilities for injuries and mishaps on a field without rules and officials enforcing them. Even with the current rules of football, there are significant injuries.

Rules help us get from here to there in a mannerly and safe way. For example, traveling on Interstate 70, or any other major highway, without lane markings, speed limits, and state troopers to enforce the rules would be hazardous. The game of driving is to get where you want to go in the least amount of time with the least amount of expense. Drivers go to drivers' training schools to get a license. In the schools, novice drivers learn to pass on the left and to signal their intentions. The state troopers are like referees in a sporting event. Tickets are agreed-upon penalties. Troopers keep the game fair and safe, at least safer than it would be without lane markers, speed limits, and no state troopers.

The truth is that societies need governments to keep other human beings from monopolizing and causing harm. Free markets without rules may be as bad as government-controlled markets. Every game (on the playground, at work, and at home) needs an uninterested referee because human beings are not without their vices. But there is the rub. McCloskey's fears of government and the psychiatric profession are well founded. Religious teachings and scientific diagnoses codified in laws have done great harm to GLBT human beings. They can still be fired from their places of work for their gender expression or sexual behaviors in the United States. Transgendered men and women are still considered mentally ill. The heteronormative script lurks unexamined in cultural norms.

McCloskey

While the feminist works of McCloskey mentioned were not necessarily intended for the purposes to which this author has employed them, they illustrate her journey from the country of men to a country of women. Her journey occurred during the intellectual ferment of the women's movement, the political awakening of the gay movement, and finally the culture-bending queer movement. She was definitely in on the conversations in ways that she may not have even known. Her work transgressed the norms of the economics profession, gender norms, and the discipline of economics.

Back in the middle of the academic and social conversations of the 1980s, 1990s, and 2000s, no one could have predicted the changes in gender and sexual norms that have occurred since then. The conversations changed on many levels, and so did the cultural norms. The conversations go on. The academic and real-life conversations underpinning the transgender movement, of which McCloskey is now a part, will help unravel the impact of the heteronormative script on individuals' and society's collective lives.

McCloskey's personal history includes a history of being a feminist, a conservative one at that. She has a history of living as a successful man. She also has a history of living in a nuclear family. She has a history of living now for more than twenty years as a woman without a traditional family. She probably has a more complete understanding of what it means to be a man and what it means to be a woman than most human beings. She probably has the most visceral understanding of the impact of the heteronormative script on human beings.

The reality is that human beings are biologically, socially, and culturally complex. One aspect of identity does not necessarily follow from the other. The traditional nuclear family may become a smaller percentage of all households. Human beings who live alone, in same-sex and different-sex pairs, and in some combination of same-sex and different-sex groupings may increase. Gay and lesbian couples have been redefining families for as long as they have existed. Members of these newly organized and freely chosen families could decide when and how to raise children differently. For example, an intergenerational model could exist. Younger different-sex couples could produce children and older related or unrelated adults could rear them in the same household. Or several adults could decide to parent in the same household. The animal world may provide suggestions, no matter how outlandish that may seem. The wolf pack model is one such suggestion. They take turns being the alpha male and female for mating purposes, and then the other members of the pack share in the rearing of the offspring. The elephants have a modified separatist model. Their family structure is matriarchal. Eliminating the heteronormative script would free human beings to be who they are and to go about organizing families or other living arrangements as places to grow and realize their human potential.

The pool of human talent is much wider and deeper than current human social, economic, and political structures have allowed it to be. The heteronormative script could also be a reason for the paucity of innovative human beings. Whether the misdirection of human resources by the heteronormative script is greater or less than the misdirection of physical or human resources by government regulation and intervention into the market is yet to be determined.

McCloskey's work provides the tools to re-vision the content and methodology of economics and to move into McIntosh's fifth phase, "women re-visioning." But re-visioning of economics necessitates a better understanding of "people" and their biological, social, and cultural natures. The profession and society would be better off if human beings were allowed to tap into the potential of all of their identities without the accompanying fears that waste so many human resources. A "re-visioned" economics profession would probably look and act very differently from the men and women seen at annual conventions, in graduate schools, and in front of classrooms.

References

Aboleve, Henry, Barale, Michele, and Halperin, David, eds. 1993. *The Lesbian and Gay Studies Reader*. New York: Routledge.

Amott, Teresa L., and Matthaei, Julie A. 1991. *Race, Gender, and Work: A Multicultural History of Women in the United States*. Boston: South End Press.

Badgett, M. V. Lee, and Prue Hyman. 1998. "Explorations—Introduction: Towards Lesbian, Gay, and Bisexual Perspectives in Economics: Why and How They May Make a Difference." *Feminist Economics* 4 (2): 49–54.

Bagemihl, Bruce. 1999. *Biological Exuberance: Animal Homosexuality and Natural Diversity*. New York: St. Martin's Press.

Bailey, J. Michael. 2003. *The Man Who Would Be Queen: The Science of Gender-Bending and Transexualism*. Washington, DC: Joseph Henry Press.

Barnhurst, Kevin G., ed. 2006. *Media/Queered: Visibility and Its Discontents*. Retrieved September 3, 2015, from http://www.deirdremccloskey.com/gender/queer.php.

Bartlett, Robin L. 1985. "Integrating the New Scholarship on Women into an Introductory Economics Course." Paper presented at the Gender and Race in the Economics Curriculum session at the meeting of the American Economic Association, New York, NY, December.

Bartlett, Robin L. 1996. "Discovering Diversity in Introductory Economics." *Journal of Economic Perspectives* 10 (3): 141–53.

Bartlett, Robin L., ed. 1997. *Introducing Race and Gender into Economics*. London: Routledge.

Bartlett, Robin L., and Haas, Paul. 1997. "Race, Gender, Class and the Natural Rate of Unemployment." *Challenge: The Magazine of Economic Affairs* 40 (6): 85–96.

Belenky, Mary Field, Clinchy, Blythe McVicker, Goldberger, Nancy Rule, and Tarule, Jill Mattuck. 1986. *Women's Ways of Knowing: The Development of Self, Voice, and Mind*. New York: Basic Books.

Bergmann, Barbara R. 1981. "The Economic Risks of Being a Housewife." *American Economic Review* 71 (20): 81–86.

Bergmann, Barbara R. 1986. *The Economic Emergence of Women*. New York: Basic Books.

Blau, Francine, and Ferber, Marianne. 1986. *The Economics of Men, Women and Work*. Englewood Cliffs, NJ: Prentice Hall.

Blaxall, Martha, and Reagan, Barbara, eds. 1976. *Women and the Workplace: The Implications of Occupational Segregation*. Chicago: University of Chicago Press.

Boulding, Kenneth E. 1990. "Taxonomy as a Source of Error." *Methodus* 2 (1): 17–21.

Brown, Peggy A., ed. 1984. "The New Scholarship on Women." *Forum for Liberal Arts Education* 6(5).

Bullard, Charles. 1997. "Iowans Accepted Sex Change, Professor Tells ISU Audience." *Des Moines Register*, October 11: 2.

Butler, Judith. 1990. *Gender Trouble*. London: Routledge.

Coman, Katherine. 1911. "Some Unsettled Problems of Irrigation." *American Economic Review* 1 (1): 1–19.

Crews, David. 1994. "Animal Sexuality." *Scientific American*, January.

Dickens, Ky. 2009. *A Fish Out of Water*. Chicago: Yellow Wing Productions.

Fausto-Sterling, Anne. 2000. "The Five Sexes, Revised." *The Sciences*, July/August.

Fausto-Sterling, Anne. 1993. "The Five Sexes." *The Sciences*, March/April.

Feiner, Susan F. 1994. *Race and Gender in the American Economy: Views from across the Spectrum*. Englewood Cliffs, NJ: Prentice Hall.

Ferber, Marianne A., and Nelson, Julie A., eds. 1993. *Beyond Economic Man: Feminist Theory and Economics*. Chicago: University of Chicago Press.

Fourcade, Marion, Ollion, Etienne, and Algan, Yann. 2015. "The Superiority of Economists." *Journal of Economic Perspectives* 29 (1): 89–114.

Gilligan, Carol. 1982. *In a Different Voice: Psychological Theory and Women's Development*. Cambridge, MA: Harvard University Press.

Gilman, Charlotte Perkins. 1966. *Women and Economics*. New York: Harper and Row.

Gilman, Charlotte Perkins. 1973. *Yellow Wallpaper*. New York: Feminist Press.

Gilman, Charlotte Perkins. 1970. *Herland*. New York: Pantheon.

Goldin, Claudia. 1990. *Understanding the Gender Gap: An Economic History of American Women*. New York: Oxford University Press.

Harragan, Betty Lehan. 1977. *Games Mother Never Taught You to Play: Corporate Gamesmanship for Women*. New York: Warner Books.

Hartmann, Heidi. 1976. "Capitalism, Patriarchy, and Job Segregation by Sex." *Signs* 1 (3): 137–69.

Hyde, Janet Shibley. 1985. *Half the Human Experience: The Psychology of Women*. 3rd ed. Lexington, MA: D. C. Heath.

Hyde, Janet Shibley. 1981. "How Large Are Cognitive Gender Differences? A Meta-analysis Using w2 and d." *American Psychologist* 36 (8): 892–901.

Jacobsen, Joyce, and Zeller, Adam, eds. 2008. *Queer Economics: A Reader*. London: Routledge.

Jacobsen, Joyce P. 1994. *The Economics of Gender*. Malden, MA: Blackwell.

Katz, Jackson. 2006. *The Macho Paradox: Why Some Men Hurt Women and How All Men Can Help*. Naperville, IL: Sourcebooks.

Keller, Evelyn Fox. 1983. *A Feeling for the Organism: The Life and Work of Barbara McClintock*. New York: Freeman.

Kimmel, Michael. 2008. *Guyland: The Perilous World Where Boys Become Men*. New York: HarperCollins.

Kreps, Juanita. 1971. *Sex in the Marketplace: American Women at Work*. Baltimore, MD: Johns Hopkins University Press.

Kumin, Maxine. 1999. "The Metamorphosis." *New York Times*. Retrieved September 11, 2002, from http://pfc.org.uk/reviews/mcc-nyt.htm.

Lloyd, Cynthia B., and Niemi, Beth T. 1979. *The Economics of Sex Differentials*. New York: Columbia University Press.

Lorde, Audre. 1978. *Uses of the Erotic: The Erotic as Power*. Trumanburg, NY: Out and Out Books, distributed by The Crossing Press.

McCloskey, Donald N. 1983. "The Rhetoric of Economics." *Journal of Economic Literature* 21: 481–517.

McCloskey, Donald N. 1985a. *The Rhetoric of Economics*. Madison: University of Wisconsin Press.

McCloskey, Donald N. 1985b. "Some Consequences of a Feminine Economics." Paper presented at the Gender and Race in the Economics Curriculum session at the meeting of the American Economic Association, New York, NY, December.

McCloskey, Donald N. 1989. "Some Consequences of a Feminine Economics." Paper presented at the meeting of the American Economic Association, December.

McCloskey, Donald N. 1993. "Some Consequences of a Conjective Economics." In Ferber and Nelson 1993, 67–93.

McCloskey, Deirdre N. 1995. "Other Things Equal: Some News That at Least You Will Not Find Boring." *Eastern Economic Journal* 21 (4): 551–53.

McCloskey, Deirdre N. 1996a. "It's Good to Be a Don If You're Going to Be a Deirdre." *Times (London) Higher Education Supplement*, August 23: 1. Video retrieved April 13, 2016, from http://www.deirdremccloskey.com/gender/index.php.

McCloskey, Deirdre N. 1998a. "Happy Endings: Law, Gender and the University." *Journal of Gender, Race and Justice* 21: 77–85.

McCloskey, Deirdre N. 1998b. "Simulating Barbara." *Feminist Economics* 4 (3): 181–86.

McCloskey, Deirdre N. 1999a. *Crossing: A Memoir*. Chicago: University of Chicago Press.

McCloskey, Deirdre N. 1999b. *Slate Diary (On Line Magazine)*, entries for November 29, 1999, November 30, 1999, December 1, 1999, December 2, 1999, and December 3, 1999. Retrieved January 12, 2016, from http://www.deirdremccloskey.com/docs/pdf/Article_243.pdf and can also be found at Slate.com.

McCloskey, Deirdre N. 2000a. "Crossing Economics." Special issue on "What Is Transgender?" *International Journal of Transgenderism* 4 (3): July–Sept. Retrieved September 3, 2015, from http://www.deirdremccloskey.com/gender/queer.php.

McCloskey, Deirdre N. 2000b. "Other Things Equal: Free-Market Feminism 101." *Eastern Economic Journal* 26 (3): 363–65.

McCloskey, Deirdre N. 2002. "Other Things Equal: Samuelsonian Economics." *Eastern Economic Journal* 283: 425–30.

McCloskey, Deirdre N. 2006a. *The Bourgeois Virtues: Ethics for an Age of Commerce*. Chicago: University of Chicago Press.

McCloskey, Deirdre N. 2006b. "Queer Markets." In *Media/Queered: Visibility and Its Discontents*, edited by Kevin Barnhurst. Retrieved June 2, 2015, from http://deirdremccloskey.com/gender/queer.php.

McCloskey, Deirdre N. 2007a. "Free to Be She—or He." *Toronto Globe and Mail*, October 20.

McCloskey, Deirdre N. 2007b. "Queer Science." Review of *The Man Who Would Be Queen*, by J. Michael Bailey. *Reason*, November. Retrieved June 2, 2015, from http://deirdremccloskey.com /gender/bailey.php#review.

McCloskey, Deirdre N. 2008. "Mr. Max and the Substantial Errors of Manly Economics." Symposium: Gender and Economics. *Econ Journal Watch* 5 (2): 199–203.

McCloskey, Deirdre N. 2010. *Bourgeois Dignity: Why Economics Can't Explain the Modern World*. Chicago: University of Chicago Press.

McCloskey, Deirdre N. 2014. “Measured, Unmeasured, Mismeasured, and Unadjusted Pessimism: A Review Essay of Thomas Piketty’s *Capital in the Twenty-First Century*.” *Erasmus Journal for Philosophy and Economics* 7 (2): 73–115.

McCloskey, Deirdre N. 2015. “It Was Ideas and Ideologies, Not Interests or Institutions which Changed in Northwestern Europe, 1600–1848.” *Journal of Evolutionary Economics* 25: 57–68.

McCloskey, Deirdre N. 2016. *Bourgeois Equality: How Ideas, Not Capital, Enriched the World*. Chicago: University of Chicago Press.

McIntosh, Peggy. 1983. “Interactive Phases of the Curricular Re-vision: A Feminist Perspective.” Working Paper No. 124, Center for Research on Women, Wellesley College, Wellesley, MA.

Mooallen, J. 2010. “Can Animals Be Gay?” *New York Times*, March 29.

Morgenthaler, Eric. 1998. “Just One of the Girls.” *Worth*, March: 98–104, 50.

Piketty, Thomas. 2014. *Capital in the Twenty-First Century*. Cambridge, MA: Harvard University Press.

Rich, Adrienne. 1980. “Compulsory Heterosexuality and Lesbian Existence.” In Aboleve, Barale, and Halperin 1993, 227–54.

Samuelson, Paul A. 1941. *Foundations of Economic Analysis*. Cambridge, MA: Harvard University Press.

Spiegelhalter, Bruce. 2015. *Sex by Numbers: What Statistics Can Tell Us about Sexual Behavior*. London: Profile Books.

Wilson, Robin. 1996. “Leading Economist Stuns Field by Deciding to Become a Woman.” *Chronicle of Higher Education*, February 16, A17.

3

The Spread of Pro- and Anticapitalist Beliefs

STANLEY L. ENGERMAN[1]

Introduction

In the preface and acknowledgments to *Bourgeois Dignity: Why Economics Can't Explain the Modern World* (2010: xi–xiv), Deirdre N. McCloskey makes (at least) two major arguments about the study of capitalism after the Industrial Revolution. One is the importance of ideas and ideology, not only economic and material forces, in generating modern economic development. While the causes of modern economic growth have continued to be widely debated, with numerous hypotheses still under consideration, my primary attention is on the second of her arguments—on the question of whether capitalism has been a "good thing" for the population, including the "poor people." McCloskey concludes that it is "something that's pretty good, not perfect, not a utopia, but probably worth keeping in view of the worse alternatives so easily fallen into." Not blind to problems, McCloskey concludes, "I reckon we should keep it—though tending to its ethics." I will describe the long history of arguments made for and against aspects of capitalism and place them in some historical perspective.[2]

In this essay, I wish to describe the reactions of those people who experienced the changes brought about by the onset and development of capitalism—why some thought it was "a good thing" but others believed equally strongly that it was "a bad thing" and what advocates of either position felt should be done to either further improve or correct the problems that were created and what desired alternatives were to be considered. It is thus intended to be more a history of ideas than a history of the economic changes.

What Was (and Is) Capitalism?

The term *capitalism* is quite widely used, but as with such broad and key terms, definitions vary quite widely and have been applied to many different things. We will see that capitalism has been used to describe many quite different economic societies and institutions without agreement on its precise definition. According to the *Oxford English Dictionary*, the term was first used in 1854, although some variations had been introduced earlier.

Perhaps the best way to start is to describe what appear to be some central characteristics of most uses of the term. In the introduction to volume 1 of *The Cambridge History of Capitalism*, Larry Neal lists "four elements . . . common in each variant of capitalism." These are (Neal 2014, 2):

1. private property rights;
2. contracts enforceable by third parties;
3. markets with responsive prices; and
4. supportive governments.

The degree to which any of these elements exist will vary historically, as will be the nature of the constraints that affect their implementation.

It is widely accepted that the rise of capitalism began in the eighteenth century first in the Netherlands, then in Britain, and after that elsewhere in Western Europe and in the European offshoots in the Americas. There were earlier aspects of economic life that had some features of capitalism, but those did not shape other aspects of society as was to happen later. Capitalism brought about economic, political, and moral changes and had impacts not only on those directly affected but also on many not directly affected by these changes. Because of its broad scope and widespread effects, it has become a widely discussed and debated movement generating an extensive amount of controversy.

The Debates about Capitalism

This essay will discuss several different aspects of this controversy, since there are many different questions and different types of approaches and evidence that have been central to the debate. Some of the concerns relate to empirically based arguments about the actual changes brought about by capitalism and about the actual impacts of the economic and policy changes introduced in its aftermath. There are debates about the theoretical underpinnings of different economic systems, if they were to operate in terms of their underlying logic, based on some theoretical models. Linking the empirical and theoretical discussions is the ideology that emerges in describing and evaluating the different economic systems and understanding the relation among their many overall changes. The belief in a particular ideology can, at times, lead to incorrect or clouded ideas, either because people actually believe these ideological arguments or, rather, because the propositions reflect mainly the requirements of debate and are used mainly in an attempt to convince others. In general, ideologies can influence belief and behavior if they lead to firm beliefs as to what happened, whether or not they are correct. Because of the broad range of attitudes and criticisms possible, there are a number of quite different issues involved in the evaluation of changes due to capitalism.

Capitalism is a term that is often intended to describe a large number of somewhat different social, political, and economic changes. Any evaluation of capitalism is inevitably controversial given its major, far-reaching influences on all aspects of the human condition. Some aspects of the changes capitalism has generated have been considered to have led to unique and large benefits to society, while others have been seen as imposing large costs—some expected, some unanticipated. To reach one answer, plus or minus, is seemingly impossible. Some costs may seem to be avoidable with appropriate economic or political actions, while others appear to be inherent in the nature of the capitalist system and thus are not avoidable without a different economic and political system. The comparison of capitalism with other economic systems—such as feudalism, mercantilism, fascism, socialism, and communism—is complex given the many aspects that are to be considered. It also depends on whether the comparisons of alternatives are based on theoretical considerations or on a study of the actual behavior in such systems. Thus some comparisons cannot be made, since the alternatives have not yet been tried.

Issues about Capitalism

These changes in the major ways of life and belief systems that influenced human well-being raise questions that most people do care about and thus have led to frequent heated attacks on, and defenses of, capitalism. Changes in the belief system accompanying economic changes, as well as changes in the preferred role of the government, provide some explanation for the ensuing controversies. It is of interest that anticapitalism has been an argument made not only by those apparently hurt by the effects of capitalism but frequently by those who apparently have benefited from capitalistic growth but are concerned with its issues of altruism, cultural life, morality, and equity and with its impact on others. Those who attack capitalism on moral grounds are often of the belief that people's desire for money making is not always a good thing. Many major advocates of capitalism, such as Mises (1972, 15–21) and

Schumpeter (1950, 143–55), regard intellectuals as major proponents of an "anti-capitalist bias," whose hostility increases, instead of diminishing, with every achievement of capitalist evolution. These very heated debates began with the initial development of capitalism and have continued into the present day, often with similar arguments presented over time even though the nature of capitalism has changed. There are, however, some newer arguments that have emerged as capitalism has evolved. Some attacks are concerned only with some specific aspects of the developmental outcome of the system, while others are related to the overall nature of the system. Defenders sometimes deal with only part of the outcome of the system, while others concern themselves mainly with the broad system in all its aspects.

Capitalism versus Other Economic Systems

Several different comparisons of capitalism with other economic systems have figured in recent debates. Within Europe, the attack on capitalism has come from the right as well as the left, from religious-based beliefs as well as from secular ideologies. Anticapitalist ideology developed among Catholics in the late nineteenth century as well as among twentieth-century fascists. The success of fascist ideology probably peaked in the 1930s with the then apparently greater economic success of fascist Germany and Italy compared to the West in recovering from the Depression (Weber 1964; Cohen 1988). Central to the belief of most variants of fascism were the advantages of a form of corporatism and centralized political and economic control that differentiated those systems from capitalism. There was also a broad attack on individualism and liberalism, based on a strong belief in the nation-state and the value of a collectivist society. Private property was accepted, but it was required to conform to the goals of the state or the church. The Catholic Church, after the *Rerum Novarum* of Pope Leo XIII in 1891, was concerned with the conditions of labor. It still believed in private property but argued that relations in the economy should be set by the moral concerns of Christian charity, not by those of an unfettered free market. The post–World War II Christian Democrats in Europe carried forward similar beliefs. Another important argument by conservatives was an attack on capitalism's negative impacts in debasing society's culture and in its deleterious effects on individual belief and behavior.

The more frequent critique of capitalism has come from the left. The rise of communism led to extended debates in the twentieth century about the role of planning and central control of the economy as a way to increase and stabilize growth. This argument was often based on theoretical arguments but at times drew upon empirical arguments with compilations of statistical data. In many cases, however, these data were themselves controversial and their usefulness dismissed. A noncommunist liberalism attacked capitalism based on its presumed negative effect on economic growth and also frequently on the creation of a large number of people living in poverty (however defined). Another critique, not as obviously political, was a religious-based bias against the seeking of wealth by individuals rather than their pursuit of a "good life," by which is meant acceptance of a more communal and religious way of life.[3] This religious critique of the effect of capitalism in generating immorality was frequent in the early days of the rise of capitalism, and this view, with a more secular component, still has adherents today. Recently, religious movements have prompted a widespread discussion of social reform, which has influenced the nature of the capitalist economy.[4]

Changes via Capitalism

In describing pro- and anticapitalist beliefs, it is useful to understand exactly the nature of the comparisons of capitalism and noncapitalist society that are being made. The specifics of the criticisms will influence the judgments made regarding the benefits and costs of capitalism. There are three basic comparisons that have been made, which are based on quite different counterfactuals, and different arguments are presented for different time periods:

1. Did capitalism create new negative features in society that did not exist before?
2. Did capitalism mainly continue, or perhaps even exaggerate, some earlier evils from precapitalist societies?
3. Was capitalism considered evil because even though it generated higher incomes and other benefits, these did not mitigate or eliminate early evils, and its economic success, moreover, brought more attention to existing evils?

Capitalism is consistent with, if not necessarily the cause of, the occurrence of dramatic changes in occupations, incomes, and locations, as well as changes in the relative importance of different economic and political sectors.[5] These inevitably led to changes in relative and absolute political and economic status, upsetting elites from the previous society, and as Engels claimed, could also lead to a deterioration in living and working conditions for laborers. The development of machine production and the rise of factories led to a shift in the nature of employment of labor and in the structure of asset ownership away from the earlier importance of land ownership toward financial assets, together with a shift from rural to urban locations, and possibly changes in the degree of inequality in society.[6] The extent of inequality has changed over time, as suggested by the so-called Kuznets curve or by other descriptions of the time pattern of inequality. The Kuznets curve posits rising inequality in the early stages of economic growth, followed by a reversal of the trend with the continuation of economic growth. Recent works by Piketty and others have argued, by contrast, that inequality may increase as economic growth continues.[7] Whether a shift in political and economic power is to be seen as a social benefit, and to whom, may be unclear, since it could lead either to greater control by the wealthy elite or else to a shift that ultimately increases the power of previously lower classes. Over the long term, in most capitalist societies, the benefits of political actions have generally become more favorable to those previously excluded. This did not necessarily mean, however, a shift in the power of decision making. The initial, and perhaps later, changes with the rise of capitalism may, however, have strengthened the ruling elite.[8]

There are some historical aspects of material changes due to capitalism that are accepted by many, though not all, scholars. It is often argued that capitalism has been economically productive in that it has led to substantially, and persistently, higher rates of growth of income, capital, and consumption than had been the case in early centuries, as well as to greater growth than in most noncapitalist nations. The early, and leading, critics of capitalism, Marx and Engels, commented in 1848 that the growth in capitalistic economies exceeded that of earlier generations, despite its increased variability and the immiseration of factory workers (and, more generally, the working class).[9] Rapid growth and structural changes have been major features of capitalist economies. This came with some related economic and demographic benefits—higher incomes, enhanced life expectation, lower infant mortality, increased stature, and a larger population and labor force—although the greater population may itself have created some negative effects in reduced per capita income. Higher average per capita income obviously did not necessarily mean increases for all in the population; it could have left, or created, some impoverishment. It is possible, however, that all members of society may have a higher absolute standard of living even when the relative distribution of income worsens and disparities among individuals increase.[10]

At issue, also, is the question of how long the increased economic growth of capitalist economies can be sustained. Many economists, including Malthus (1993), Marx (1936), Mill (1895, 1:334–40), Marshall (1949, 144–45), Max Weber, Hansen, Schumpeter, and Olson, have argued that capitalist growth would, at some time, come to a halt, whether due to a limited potential for further technological change, increased bureaucracy, overpopulation, decay of the entrepreneurial spirit, class warfare, or disappearance of needed natural resources.[11] Some believed that the cessation of growth would lead to social collapse and chaos, with class warfare and social upheaval, and ultimately to socialism or communism, but Mill, for example, thought that although growth rates would ultimately decline, the resulting stationary state would have major human advantages.[12]

There has also appeared some correlation of capitalism with a generally more democratic society and with increased freedom of political and economic choice by individuals. This is not an inevitable correlation, and clearly democracy does not mean "full freedom." There are limitations due to the nature of labor contracts and societal rules reflecting communal decisions. There are constraints imposed by natural conditions, issues related to various forms of competition between individuals (including envy), and limitations on income due to differences in talent and productivity that can generate unhappiness and make individuals consider themselves unfree, at least relative to others and to their aspirations. The relation of expanded voting and education to capitalism has a long history. The increased role of individuals as consumers, able to make their own purchasing decisions, has often been seen as a central result of capitalistic development, which some regard favorably, while others stress its negative aspects in the presumed degrading of individuals and society.[13]

Capitalism is based on there being a greater proportion of free, neither slave nor serf, labor than in other systems, with each individual free to make geographic and occupational decisions regarding mobility and work choices, and the freedom to respond to changing wage rates and working conditions. There are also, traditionally, in capitalist societies, relatively freer markets, freer trading in goods and services, and freer capital flows, internally as well as internationally. While the markets for goods, services, and factors of production are seldom completely free under capitalism, they are generally freer than they are in other types of economic systems, particularly those with centralized planning and powerful controls over individuals.

The shifts in political power stemming from the development of capitalism can take quite different forms. These differences reflect the nature of resource and factor endowments and economic institutions, as well as the nature of the production process. These changes will be influenced by population density and by whether the area has been long settled or has been relatively newly colonized by foreign powers. Engerman and Sokoloff (2012) argue, for example, that political power in the American colonies was influenced by climate, resources, and the size of the population, which determined which crops would profitably be grown. (See also Acemoglu, Johnson, and Robinson 2002.) Since the scale of production varied by crops, the ratio of landowners to agriculture workers varied in different parts of the Americas. Those areas, such as Latin America and the Caribbean, which produced and exported sugar and mining products, tended to have large-scale producing units and highly concentrated political and economic power. Those regions producing grains, such as those on the North American mainland, tended to have small landholdings and a high ratio of landholders to agricultural laborers. These latter regions tended to have a broader dispersion of political power and more equality of economic conditions.

Other possible causes of changes in political and economic power can be related (or unrelated) to market conditions. Although serfdom on the European continent formally ended in the mid-nineteenth century at a time of expanding capitalism, serfdom ended earlier in England, in the fourteenth century, probably as a result of the population decline caused by the Black Death. With the ensuing labor scarcity and the competitive bidding by landowners for the reduced number of agricultural laborers, those formerly enserfed were able to gain their freedom. Yet an increased land-labor ratio did not always lead to enhanced freedom as it had in England, as seen by the role of labor scarcity in leading to the "second serfdom" in Eastern Europe, also after the Black Death. Labor scarcity was also a major factor in the economically successful (for the Europeans) enslavement of Africans in the Americas.

There was a major shift of political power in nineteenth-century England, with the increased political power of the merchant middle class and manufacturers in contrast to the landed gentry. This was argued, at the time, by Marx and Engels (2002, 221): "The bourgeoisie has at last, since the establishment of Modern Industry and of the world market, conquered for itself, in the modern representative State, exclusive political sway." This reflected changes in the structure of demand and supply for output, with the declining importance of agriculture and the shifting locational and industrial composition of the labor force. The outcome of the change was seen most clearly in the parliamentary debates on the Corn Laws in the 1840s, with the shift to freer trade championed by the middle classes in opposition to the "landed interests." Similar types of changes occurred elsewhere within Europe, leading to shifts in political power and in the distribution of income and wealth. This political shift became a source of an anticapitalist attack—an attack based more on the changing rank-ordering and levels of income and political power than on the evil aspects of commercial behavior or the lifestyles of the wealthy.

Capitalism and the Role of Government

One of the problems in agreeing on any definition of capitalism concerns the nature and magnitude of the role assigned to the government. For some, laissez-faire capitalism means a complete absence, or a very limited role, of government. Others will consider capitalism to be consistent even with a relatively large government as long as there are basically unfettered markets for labor, for goods, and for capital. Today's capitalism differs in many ways from what many economists, following their interpretation of Adam Smith, have conceived of as capitalism.

An important characteristic of late nineteenth- and twentieth-century capitalism, for example, was its association with expanded suffrage, higher government expenditures on public goods and infrastructure, higher taxation, and increased government regulation of the economy—changes that provided for further shifts in economic and political power.

The issue of the government's role in the economy is significant in defining the importance of what some might call laissez-faire capitalism at any time. Some governmental role can be seen as important and necessary for a capitalist economy to emerge, persist, and spread. The basic question is not whether a large government exists and plays a role in the economy but what precisely the government does and who benefits from government activity. Do government measures help spur economic development and/or equity, or are they just reflections of rent-seeking activities, benefiting only the ruling class?

Two examples will indicate that some government role is consistent with what its advocates definitely still regarded as capitalism. This can be seen by examining the beliefs of two mid-nineteenth-century advocates of capitalist economic growth: Henry Carey (1852) in the United States and Friedrich List (1956), in Germany.[14] Both were strong believers in the importance of tariffs, among other interventions. List also argued that the state should build an extensive railroad network, while Carey argued for the benefits of a restrictive land policy to take advantage of the benefits of scale economies and urbanization in the earlier-settled areas of the United States.

The classic work on public finance by Musgrave (1959) divides the role of the government into three parts: stabilization (over the course of the business cycle), redistribution, and allocation. Redistribution can be done via a direct transfer of private or government collected funds, or else as part of the tax-expenditure pattern providing goods and services in a manner different from the burden of taxation.[15] Allocation refers to the government provision of goods and services desired by the public. These can include a broad variety of goods and services: defense, education, infrastructure, and so on. Stabilization reflects the role of the government in avoiding business cycles, reducing unemployment, and holding down the rate of inflation, all by means of monetary and fiscal policies. Stabilization policies will also have important implications for allocation and redistribution, which, however, may politically serve to constrain stabilization.

It is no doubt a frequent desire of those with low (or high) incomes to have more, whether absolutely or relative to the shares of the wealthier. More income is desired to achieve higher levels of consumption of necessities, as well as to obtain higher levels of consumption of luxuries. Redistribution of incomes could be accomplished by differential tax and expenditure policies, as voted on by the national legislature or imposed by the executive. Presumably the relative numbers of below- (and above-) average incomes will influence the voting on the amount of redistribution attempted. And in general, the higher the rate of overall taxation, the greater the possibilities for redistribution via progression in the tax schedule.

The debate regarding the allocation function of government concerns the type of goods that are considered to be better provided by the government than by the private sector—so-called public goods. The most important of these public goods have traditionally been defense, transportation, and education. The first two of these are generally (at least in the United States) provided at the national level, while education is provided on the state and local levels. At times, the government may also provide economic goods and services that could otherwise be considered private goods, such as banks and internal improvements, or even some manufactured goods.

Other functions of governments involve relatively small expenditures but can have significant effects on the economy, such as the role played by government regulation of labor and product markets in the interests of business, workers, and/or consumers. This is usually done by specific agencies of the government with the granted power to interfere with private businesses. Another important government function is the development of the legal system, which sets the range of permissible behavior.

The role of the government in the economy can vary over time based on the nature of political circumstances and perceived economic needs. Some of the early theoretical debates on the role of the government in the economy appeared to advocate an almost completely laissez-faire economy, with a very limited government role, compared with an economy with heavy government involvement. This was basically an inappropriate comparison. Rarely is it argued that the government should play absolutely no role in the economy, since, at the very least, someone has to set and enforce the overall "rules of the game." Rather, as Robbins (1952) pointed out in his discussion of the economic policy concerns of the English classical economists, the disagreement was about what precisely should be the role of the government and what should be its limits vis-à-vis the private sector. He pointed out that "what distinguishes the Classical outlook from the authoritarian system is not a denial of the necessity for state action on the one side and an affirmation on the other, but rather a different view on what kind of action is desirable" (192). Thus an extended role of regulation and control by the government can be consistent with most definitions of the essential characteristics of a capitalist system. Thus tariffs on imported goods and restrictions on immigration may exist, yet there may be relatively free internal labor and product markets. To many, this could still be regarded as basically capitalism. Indeed, flexibility and adaptability of the government's role may be essential for the survival of any form of capitalism.

The early stages of capitalism may have meant limited government activities, particularly in the cases of England and France. In some measure, the decline in the government role reflected the transition from mercantilism to freer trade. Nevertheless, by the 1840s, in England, there was still a large range of government involvement with economic policies, and this was also the case at this time in the United States and other European nations. Tariffs had long been considered a policy consistent with so-called laissez-faire capitalist societies, which also had laws dealing with property rights, patents, labor standards, immigration, and related items. Hacker (1954, 71), primarily describing England in the 1840s, stated that "the idea of laissez-faire is a fiction. For the state, by negative action—that is, by refusing to adopt certain policies can affect economic events just as significantly as when its interaction occurs."[16] England, in the eighteenth century, saw the expansion of tariff protection for certain key industries, which continued through the middle of the nineteenth century. There was an expansion of government spending by the British during the Napoleonic Wars, leading to a rise in the government share of GNP to over 20 percent, mostly for military purposes. Despite his arguments, which aimed to limit the number of government regulations, Adam Smith supported the Navigation Acts (which regulated and constrained foreign trade) and government provisions of infrastructure, and he also argued that "defense is more important than opulence" (Smith 1937, 431).[17] The main issue was not whether the government should play any economic role but, more precisely, what exactly the role of government should be. Today, there has been a widespread acceptance of a larger share of government taxes and expenditures in most professed capitalist economies, although the magnitude and the precise nature of the desired governmental role do vary with particular nations and advocates.[18]

Precapitalist Evils

Certain negative social and economic aspects that exist within capitalism did not, however, originate with capitalism but often go back a long time, much before the emergence of capitalism; they are present in contemporary societies that are not considered to be capitalist. Discussions of capitalism often point to its presumed role in generating poverty, income inequality, wars, imperialism, famines, and slavery, but those making these claims often do so without studying whether these conditions may have existed earlier, or whether they exist, at present, under alternative systems.

Alfred Marshall (1949, 600–601) pointed out: "There is then need to guard against the temptation to overstate the economic evils of our own age, and to ignore the existence of similar and worse evils in earlier ages; even though some exaggeration may for the time stimulate others, as well as ourselves, to a more intense resolve that the present evils still no longer be allowed to exist."

Even before the advent of capitalism, characteristics such as markets for trade among different individuals and groups over short or long distances, and responses to changing relative prices, affected individual production decisions. The hiring and control of labor, legally free or coerced, have long existed in many societies, as has an interest in obtaining wealth and/or power. Weber (1961, 207–70) pointed to aspects of capitalism that long preceded its contemporary variant and argued that it was the increased rationality that came with capital accounting, formal rules of trade, free labor, and the development of trust that came to be considered the basis of emerging capitalism.

There were earlier stages of so-called commercial or financial capitalism, but as noted above, the customary dating of the rise of modern capitalism is the emergence, in the late eighteenth century, of capitalism in the Netherlands and in England. Capitalism came with the development, particularly in England, of early industrialization and capitalist agriculture in the period generally referred to as the Industrial Revolution. Over the next half to three-quarters of a century, the system of industrial and agricultural capitalism spread to the United States, particularly to the northern states, and then to the nations of Northwestern Europe—particularly Belgium, France, and Germany. Ultimately, it spread to other parts of the world, with the geographic extension of industry based on what some might call the modernization of the means of production and, more recently, globalization in the world economy.

The spread of capitalism, especially after the European revolutions of 1848, brought new perspectives to bear concerning the characteristics of markets, property rights, and controls over labor, and it also established a basis for the legitimacy of the ruling class. In some arguments (e.g., by Marx and Engels), this period saw a seeming worsening of laboring conditions, but others (e.g., Ashton) argue that it was more of a heightened awareness of past and present problems than the generation of new difficulties.

Engels, in *The Condition of the Working Class in England* (1968), argued that capitalism created new social evils resulting from the problems caused by urbanization and industrial changes. T. S. Ashton's response in Hayek (1954) to this claim was to argue that inferior housing had long been a problem in England. Ashton did not deny that urban housing conditions in the 1800s were wretched, but he claimed that they were then not deteriorating, a point earlier made, in 1830, by T. B. Macaulay (1965, 146).[19]

There are some broader indictments of capitalism based on various negative developments. Many of those, however, had a long history and did not emerge only with the rise of capitalism (Weber 1961, 207–9, 261). Empires and wars have long been part of human history, and some of the more brutal wars clearly preceded the development of capitalism. These wars include the several Crusades and the military adventures of the Mongols under Genghis Khan and Tamurlane, all of which involved quite high mortality. Genghis Khan, for example, killed an estimated 5 percent of the world's population in the early thirteenth century, while Tamurlane's subsequent geographic expansion in the late fourteenth century led to possibly the largest landed empire in history (Burbank and Cooper 2010, 4, 93–115, 446). Among the many empires before capitalism, pointed to by Burbank and Cooper in their book *Empires*, were the Egyptian, Roman, Chinese, Greek, Byzantine, Islamic, Carolingian, Mongol, Persian, Ottoman, Spanish, Hapsburg, Aztec, and Inca, as well as those of the British, French, and Russians. Schumpeter's chapter "Imperialism in Practice" begins with the histories of the Egyptian, Assyrian, and Persian Empires. Some of these empires lasted a long time—Burbank and Cooper (2010, 4, 18, 21, 42, 444) state that the Ottoman Empire lasted six hundred years, a succession of Chinese dynasties lasted for more than two thousand years, the Roman Empire in the West lasted some six hundred years, and the Byzantine Empire in the East lasted for about another millennium. Schumpeter (1951) denies a link between capitalism and imperialism, describing imperialism as "atavistic in character," a point repeated by Hirschman (1977). Davis and Huttenback (1986) argue that imperialism was not financially a profit-making proposition for the British colonizers, being mainly a form of internal redistribution from the British lower and middle classes to their upper classes, a point earlier made by Marx (Marx and Engels 1968, 165–72): "It may well be doubted whether, on the whole, this dominion does not threaten to cost quite as much as it can ever be expected to come to," and "it is evident that the advantage to Great Britain from her Indian empire must be limited to the profits and benefits which accrue to individual British subjects, [which] are very considerable."[20]

A similar point was made by Karl Marx in his discussion of British imperialism in India:

> Now, sickening as it must be to human feeling to witness those myriads of industrious patriarchal and inoffensive social organizations disorganized and dissolved into their units, thrown into a sea of woes, and their individual members losing at the same time their ancient form of civilization and their hereditary means of subsistence, we must not forget that these idyllic village communities, inoffensive though they may appear, had always been the solid foundation of Oriental despotism, that they restrained the human mind within the smallest possible compass, making it the unresisting tool of superstition, enslaving it beneath traditional rules, depriving it of all grandeur and historical energies. We must not forget the barbarian egotism which, concentrating on some miserable patch of land, had quietly witnessed the ruin of empires, the perpetration of unspeakable cruelties, the massacre of the population of large towns, with no other consideration bestowed upon them than on natural events, itself the helpless prey of any aggressor who deigned to notice it at all. We must not forget that this undignified, stagnatory, and vegetative life, that this passive sort of existence evoked on the other part, in contradistinction, wild, aimless, unbounded forces of destruction, and rendered murder itself a religious rite in Hindustan. We must not forget that these little communities were contaminated by distinctions of caste and by slavery, that they subjugated man to external circumstances instead of elevating man to be the sovereign of circumstances, that they transformed a self-developing social state into never changing natural destiny, and thus brought about a brutalizing worship of nature, exhibiting its degradation in the fact that man, the sovereign of nature, fell down on his knees in adoration of Hanuman, the monkey, and Sabbala, the cow.
>
> England, it is true, in causing a social revolution in Hindustan, was actuated only by the vilest interests, and was stupid in her manner of enforcing them. But that is not the question. The question is, can mankind fulfill its destiny without a fundamental revolution in the social state of Asia? If not, whatever may have been the crimes of England she was the unconscious tool of history in bringing about that revolution. (Marx and Engels 1968, 40–41)

Wars, too, have a long precapitalist history, although it appears that, as described by Pinker (2011), there have been declines in the overall extent of violence over time despite the great changes in the technology of warfare that came with and after the Industrial Revolution. Keeley (1996) argues that early North American Indian societies were frequently at war with each other, as were those in Africa and Asia. Only 4 percent of the 157 tribes in the United States he studied were considered to be truly peaceful, and their wars often had mortality rates higher than those experienced in capitalist warfare. In the three centuries between 1500 and 1815, ending with the Pax Britannica, the major northwestern European powers were at war about three-quarters of the time, and this led to about ten million deaths, five million of them French—a figure comparable to the numbers of Africans brought to the Americas in the transatlantic slave trade.[21] It may seem strange that it was about 1400 that the Europeans ended the enslavement of other Europeans, due perhaps to developments in European religions. This ending of the enslavement of Europeans and the emergence of the enslavement of Africans might be explained by the racism that came to characterize the period. What, however, is difficult to understand is the acceptance of wartime murder, rape, pillage, and related war crimes made acceptable by the new "just war" arguments at a time when the enslavement of Europeans (but not their killing) was forbidden. Even in the Pax Britannica, the British and other European nations were at war with indigenous peoples in tropical Africa and Asia.[22]

Twentieth-century warfare among states in Africa and in Asia has occurred in societies not generally considered capitalist. The sixteenth-century Aztecs were noted for their warlike behavior, slavery, imperial conquest, and as in some other early societies, human sacrifice. With technological changes, wars may have seemed to become more deadly, but warfare with high death rates clearly antedates the onset of capitalism (Hoffman 2015).

Similarly, slavery has also been one of the longest-lasting and most ubiquitous of all human institutions (Engerman 2007a). Even in the years when capitalist societies had slavery, the numbers of their slaves were sometimes smaller than the numbers in noncapitalist slave societies at the same time. Slavery of whites did occur, particularly among Mediterranean Muslim societies, with estimates of more than one million slaves in the years between 1500 and 1800. This slavery did differ from most cases, since white slaves were more frequently ransomed to European powers than were African and Asian slaves (Davis 2003). Ancient societies, such as Greece and Rome, as well as numerous others, had large numbers of slaves, and slavery had long existed in Africa and Asia both before and after legal slavery was ended by the

European capitalistic nations. Indeed, one of the reasons that the transatlantic slave trade had expanded so rapidly after European contract with Africa was that the Europeans tapped into ongoing African trading relations, with their extensive internal as well as external slave trades with North Africa and the Middle East.

It has been argued that the New World slavery of the European powers, based on capitalist agriculture, was harsher than slavery elsewhere, but it remains the case that European capitalist societies were the first major areas to end the slave trade and slavery. This was done by political action taken in the colonizing nations, except for the case of French Haiti. Even before that, however, the economic success of capitalism had, in places, led to an end to internal slavery in Europe by reducing the number of instances of famine and threatened starvation, which had led to the practice of voluntary slavery as a means of survival.[23] Blackstone (1979: I:410–54) suggests that wealthy nations were the first to end voluntary slavery, as they provided poor relief through the government and by wealthy individuals. Another factor reducing voluntary slavery was the reduction in violence, reducing the number of captives who became slaves, as well as making less important the need for slavery for protection and safety.

Similarly, the practice of serfdom characterized much of Europe outside England until the nineteenth century, when it was abolished by law at about the same time as the European nations ended their slavery in the Americas and elsewhere, also with compensation provided to landowners, not the former serfs (Blum 1978).

A decline in the number and extent of famines occurred after the onset of capitalism; subsequently, the most deadly famines have occurred in noncapitalist societies, as has been detailed by Ó Gráda. Ó Gráda dates the last famine in England to the mid-eighteenth century. Perhaps the greatest historical population decline was the estimated 80 percent decline in the Americas, due mainly to diseases brought over by Europeans. This decline has, by some, been attributed to imperialism, but whether this geographic imperialism can be attributed to the presence of capitalism at that time is less clear.[24]

Other problems that exist under capitalism but had existed prior to the emergence of capitalism and persisted in noncapitalistic societies include forms of coerced labor such as unregulated indentured labor, contract labor, debt bondage, sharecropping, and today's sex slavery. Serfdom throughout Europe was finally ended by 1864 as a result of European state actions. Environmental destruction due to economic and political expansion was a marked characteristic of Soviet Russia's drive for economic betterment, leading to several major disasters that, it is argued, are not too dissimilar from those in the capitalist

United States. As described above, while modern capitalism led to the expansion of colonization, the geographic movement by more powerful states to capture weaker areas has similarly had a rather long history and characterizes noncapitalist societies even at the present day. There have also been changes in attitudes toward women and children and their roles in society that came with the emergence of capitalism, disrupting the patterns found in earlier and noncapitalist societies.

Similarly, earlier societies had their share of immiseration and absolute and relative poverty. Agricultural work has always been difficult, time-consuming, and physically exhausting, and in the past there were frequent cyclical fluctuations due to harvest failures and famines, as well as major uncontrolled outbursts of diseases and epidemics. The Black Death of the fourteenth century reduced European population, by some estimates, by between 25 and 50 percent. The decline of Native Americans after 1500 was even larger. The premodern world was characterized by numerous epidemics due to various diseases, a number of which have now disappeared. These major epidemics, famines, and wars with large-scale losses of life had major effects on social and political structures, with significant impacts on the nature of the cultures and communities in which they occurred, in addition to their human and economic costs. This was true even when their occurrence could not be attributed, directly or indirectly, to the existence of capitalism. Indeed, medical and pharmaceutical gains provided by capitalist innovation have resulted in significant declines in death rates and greatly increased life expectancies throughout the world.

It could be argued that the greater wealth of capitalist societies and a greater centralization of political power may have raised the expectations of the population about the ability of capitalist societies to solve various problems by expanding such policy measures as poor relief, highly progressive taxation, and other means of income redistribution. Also to be considered is whether the belief that these problems could now be solved by heightened attention to these difficulties led to disappointment with the consequences resulting from the interventions. People had hoped to see a more successful resolution of these problems, since there was now a possibility that they could be handled by human intervention, an outcome that people could not have hoped for in the past.

Globalization and Capitalism

The expansion of world economic relations to a greater extent than had occurred in earlier centuries has been accompanied by what some call the New Globalization. This has been influenced by the important role played by the

International Monetary Fund and the World Bank, controlled by the Western powers. Some have argued that capitalism has led to greater inequality among nations. It has long been claimed that the imperialism of the richer, more powerful economic powers at the expense of poorer colonies had served to restrict the economic gains to the populations of the poor nations. The argument that imperialism led to increased inequality among nations has gone through two stages, and these have been applied to Africa, Asia, and Latin America. Initially, it was argued that exploitation was the result of Europeans charging high prices for their exports while paying low prices for their imports from Africa. This argument was questioned after the calculation of the British terms of trade by Imlah (1958), which demonstrated that the terms of trade had turned against Britain and in favor of those African nations that it traded with.[25] A different mechanism was then introduced to explain the exploitation of colonies and other low-income nations, a mechanism that has been described as dependency theory: the Europeans were now seen as charging low prices for their exports to discourage colonial production of manufactured commodities such as textiles and iron, and in addition, higher prices were paid for slaves exported from Africa to provide incentives to Africans to devote resources to capturing and exporting slaves rather than to industrial production.

There is, however, a counterargument that has recently been made about the possible drawbacks of globalization—difficulties created not for the developing nations but rather for the developed nations. It has been argued that the outsourcing of manufacturing output to less developed nations has reduced employment and income in the developed nations and reduced their share of industrial production.

The presumed deleterious aspect of world trade patterns has been developed into a critique of capitalism's worldwide impact as part of a continuing long debate over the effects of trade policies among nations. It is claimed that the possibilities for economic growth in the less-developed world would be greater if poorer nations could regulate their own trade by imposing restrictions on foreign trade and permitting themselves greater self-sufficiency rather than having free trade agreements with the developed nations. In the post–World War II era, this led to arguments about the role of the so-called import-substitution industrialization (ISI) policy of import substitution in less-developed nations. Earlier in the twentieth century, after the Russian Revolution, there was a worldwide contest between capitalism, with its relatively free markets, and communism, based on central planning (among its other characteristics), which was centered on the question of the relative ability to generate prolonged economic growth as well as to provide political freedom. In retrospect, the answer to the economic (and political) contest may now, at least to some, seem clear to the advantage of capitalism, but the long debate and the heat generated on both sides did occupy more than half of the twentieth century. The debate has recently reappeared with the discussion of whether the Chinese economic system is to be considered a variant of capitalism or rather a new and unique economic system and also whether China's economic expansion can continue at the same rapid rate.

Procapitalist Ideology

Several early economic writers in Britain and in northwestern Europe presented ideas that can be regarded as precursors of the procapitalist argument, although, as noted, the term *capitalism* was not introduced until 1854 (and then not by an economist).[26] One conventional starting point for capitalism has been the 1776 publication of Adam Smith's *Wealth of Nations*. Smith advocated free trade, free markets, and limited government, mainly because he believed these to be an advance over the policies of mercantilism with its control over international trade. Smith pointed to the role of individual choice in decisions regarding working and consumption and attacked the belief in the superior productivity of slavery and serfdom. Economic freedom, it was argued, would lead to higher rates of economic growth as well as greater individual utility. Smith's belief in laissez-faire did have some limits when compared to some other writers, since he accepted a government role in providing public goods such as infrastructure and defense, but relative to earlier writers, he clearly advocated a more limited role for government control, particularly with regard to the use of tariffs to regulate international trade.

Smith's beliefs were echoed, with some modifications, by most of the leading figures of the English classical school, generally with the belief in low or no tariffs and in allowing individual consumption decisions.[27] Not all believed, however, that capitalism could last indefinitely, but this was attributed to a number of quite different reasons. Malthus argued, from one perspective, that population growth would mean diminishing returns in agriculture, the dominant economic sector at the time, and that this would ultimately bring an end to economic and population growth due to problems of insufficiency in providing subsistence income. From another perspective, Marx and Engels believed that the end of capitalism was "inevitable," with the actions of the newly formed modern revolutionary working class leading to political change and upheaval and the onset of socialism. At the end of the nineteenth century, Weber believed that decline would set in because of the development of bureaucracy and rigid institutions, a point later made by Schumpeter and by Olson. Schumpeter presented an alternative scenario for the decline of capitalism based on its success and the loss of a strong belief in capitalism's values by its advocates. In the 1930s, Hansen believed that a decline in the rate of innovation, the slowing of population increase, and the closing of the US frontier meant that US economic growth would slow down or stop.[28]

Arguments about diminishing returns were quite frequent in the nineteenth century, with many economists (and others) combining a procapitalist sentiment with a belief in some ultimate time limit to capitalism (and also to other economic systems), but generally with no definite forecast of the time horizon or statements of what the nature of the successor system might be. An exception was W. Stanley Jevons, who in 1865 argued that British growth and economic success would end with the exhaustion of the coal fields, but he did not expect that to happen for another one hundred years.[29]

Given the existence of New World slavery in the US South and the various colonies of the European powers into the nineteenth century, there was a long debate on the relative productivity of capitalist free labor and of slave labor in producing output. The basic argument in England and in the Northern US states pointed to the benefits of free labor and the economic weaknesses of slavery and serfdom.[30] These procapitalist arguments posited the importance of incentives for free labor workers in generating greater output and promoting a greater opportunity for entrepreneurship and innovation among businessmen. Hume, however, claimed that it could be the incentives provided by necessity and hunger that provided for the exceptional benefits of free labor.[31] The argument about the effect of incentives on relative productivity is now regarded as more ideological than empirical. Nevertheless, the claims about the relative productivity of slave and free labor were important in the debates that influenced the ending of slavery and serfdom in the Western world (Drescher 2002).

The twentieth century saw several important advocates of capitalism among economists. Schumpeter pointed to the dynamic economic role of capitalism and believed that "creative destruction" would lead to continued growth. To Schumpeter, capitalism meant dramatic changes in the sectoral composition of output and in economic leadership. Schumpeter was a firm advocate of the role of capitalism and of monopolies and big businesses in spurring growth and providing for dynamic efficiency. Thus he did not believe in antitrust laws. Nor did he believe that it was capitalism that generated imperialism, given that imperialism had always existed and that it was a relic from the past. A major proponent of the virtues of capitalism, Schumpeter did, however, believe that the very success of capitalism would lead to a decline in the belief in the intellectual arguments made by its advocates, leading to a weakening of the defense of the system and ultimately "The March into Socialism" in some future year, aided by the persistence of inflation.[32]

The Austrian economist Friedrich Hayek, following the ideas of his teacher, Ludwig von Mises, similarly advocated capitalism's economic and other advantages. He believed that increased control by government would be "the road to serfdom" (also the title of his 1944 book) and expressed strong doubts about the ability of a noncapitalist system to solve the major economic problems of resource allocation. Hayek was a key figure after the Second World War in establishing and expanding the Mont Pèlerin Society, a European and American organization with political concerns and ideological views that had been influential in offsetting the arguments for state control, particularly in Europe (Hayek 1944 and Hartwell 1995).

Several decades later, University of Chicago economist Milton Friedman published a procapitalist polemic, *Capitalism and Freedom*, that emphasized both the economic and political benefits of capitalism and the political and economic drawbacks of noncapitalist systems. This quickly became the major basis for contemporary procapitalist arguments, along with *Free to Choose*, a book that Friedman coauthored with his wife, Rose.[33]

Another influential twentieth-century economist who discussed the benefits and drawbacks of capitalism was the distinguished British economist John Maynard Keynes. Keynes supported capitalism as necessary and desirable for freedom and progress, but he did point to many problems, including economic crises, that the system created. There was a need for government policies to offset those tendencies, which generated economic instability. It was also important to overcome the moral problems arising from "the principle of valuing all things in terms of money," and he provided a "condemnation of moneymaking as an end in itself." He felt, nevertheless, that capitalism was the "best alternative available" and that its continuous evolution made for continued benefits (Backhouse and Bateman 2011, 66–67, 74).

The basic procapitalist arguments were somewhat similar over time. Capitalism was seen as a productive system that led to higher per capita incomes for most of the population. This followed from the incentives given to laborers as well as those provided to businessmen to invest and innovate. The incentives to labor, based on higher wages and freedom of choice in economic decisions, included the laborer's choice between consumption and leisure.[34] This has also permitted individuals to benefit from diversity in working and consuming decisions.[35] The link of liberty and capitalism, while it may not be inevitable, appears to have been widespread—another of the benefits of capitalism and, some would argue, a positive factor independent of its economic benefits. Other noneconomic benefits of capitalism were claimed by the German sociologist Georg Simmel (1990), who contended that the money economy "is able to increase individual liberty" and would also provide for other favorable conditions of life, including "provid[ing] a civilizing influence to society," although these remain controversial points.[36]

Anticapitalist Ideology

Given that capitalism meant not only economic changes but also changes in many other aspects of social and political life, a broad range of issues are covered by the anticapitalist argument, not all of which are consistent in their implications. There are broad economic claims at issue and also questions of the political and psychological impact of the market, such as the presumed degrading cultural aspects resulting from the importance of money as a measure of value and the role of capitalism in negatively influencing individual psychology, communal relations, and the culture of society. These are presumably the result of market interactions and the evil role of the "cash nexus"—the fact that tastes and transactions were influenced by the money values of things and not their inherent value in contributing to human welfare (however defined). This, it was argued, led to a deterioration in the quality of life and to increased discontent in the population; some thought this could be changed by limiting the role of capitalism and the importance of the individual drive for economic progress.[37] Many of the arguments that point to the desire to limit capitalism, however, do not describe the mechanisms by which this desired end can be achieved, whether by coercion or by moral suasion, nor do they estimate the costs (if any) to individuals and to society of limiting the operation of the market system. Thus do we wish progress in medical care to have ended in 1850 with a life expectation of 38.3 or in 1992 with a life expectation of 72.8, with large gains at all levels of income? How do we define necessities (which presumably cannot be reduced) as opposed to luxuries (which might be considered expendable)?

The most famous of the early critiques of capitalism were in the writings of Marx and Engels, who argued that capitalism led to the immiseration of workers and forced them into unhealthy living and working conditions, even while it was contended that capitalism had generated high rates of economic growth. Thus while capitalism would lead to higher rates of economic growth than did slavery or feudalism, it generated instability and class conflict, and this would (hopefully for Marx and Engels) lead to a movement to socialism in the future. Engels's *Condition of the Working Class* raised several points regarding the standard of living of the workers, going beyond the measurement of real wages. These complaints included the adulteration of food, the deterioration of housing, increases in the number of hours worked as well as in the intensity of work, a shifting pattern of family structure, and a general deterioration in the quality of life. Boyer (1998) argues, however, that Engels's claims were based on a narrow geographic and industrial basis, primarily the cotton textile industry in South Lancashire in the 1830s (see also Engerman 1984, Boyer 2010, and Hollander 2011). The arguments of Engels have been the basis of several heated debates on the standard of living during the Industrial Revolution, with notable contrasting contributions by Hobsbawm (1958) and Hartwell (1961, 1970) and, more recently, Williamson (1985) and Feinstein (1990). Attention was also given to the periodic declines in income that occurred during economic cycles, which were often linked to difficulties that resulted from the impact of foreign trade, the involvement with other nations, and difficulties in financing business activity. The basic response to these charges by the procapitalist advocates was to argue that capitalism may have reduced the costs of such fluctuations given that they had also occurred frequently in the precapitalist era and that the gains made in the upswings outweigh the losses in recession and depression.

There were numerous other criticisms of capitalism, some based on the contention that the procapitalist belief in "laissez-faire" meant a limited government role, leading to high costs paid by individuals and society. Writing in the late nineteenth century, members of the German historical school emphasized the importance of the government's role in overcoming poverty by providing public aid and welfare, thus limiting the costs of individualism.[38] At roughly the same time, a similar critique was made by the members of the English historical school, particularly by Arnold Toynbee, whose 1884 book *The Industrial Revolution* was as much the work of a social reformer as of a historian (Toynbee 1956; see also Gide and Rist 1947). Nineteenth-century economists, such as Sismondi and Saint-Simon, had also criticized capitalism's effect on income distribution and economic stability. More recent have been the extended critiques by Karl Polanyi in his *The Great Transformation* (2001), which begins with an attack on what he regards as market-created individualism. This he sees as the cause of the possible destruction of society, since a self-adjusting market could not exist for long "without annihilating the human and natural substance of society." Polanyi argued for a much greater role of government in undertaking economic actions and attacked the policy tools of the pre-1920 economy, such as the international gold standard, which he saw as an attempt at a worldwide self-regulating market and the basic cause of the economic collapse of the 1930s. This failure was caused, he argued, by a broad attempt to avoid any economic role for governments.[39] Polanyi further argued, based on his perception of African trading patterns, that societies could develop without a market system, which meant fluctuating prices, and he argued that such a system be adopted by all societies.[40]

Capitalism and Culture

An important critique of capitalism, going beyond its economic aspects, has been the impact of capitalism on communal life and the nature of society's culture. These have recently been developed by Bell (1976) and emphasized by Appleby (2010), who describes the "vulgarity and ugliness of the pursuit of property."[41] These arguments have implications that need more exploration. In part, the outcomes of urbanization and of increased population density, with their presumed negative effects, have been caused by the growth in population that came with the onset of capitalism, generating a problem that had not previously existed on such a frequent and prolonged basis. The negative effects on culture and on individual psychology are often attributed to the "cash nexus" and the desire of individuals to achieve more consumption, presumably due to the pressures of the market system (and different from that in other economic systems). Many of these antigrowth and antimaterialism arguments, which claim that people should not be interested in obtaining more goods, have, however, generally come from individuals near the top of the income and wealth distributions. They are seldom heard from those at lower, poverty-level, incomes. While this attempt to limit growth has been advanced as a measure to limit inequality, it might have a greater effect in serving to maintain the status quo and the current level of inequality.

The impact of capitalism on the cultural achievements of society has been attributed to the larger size of the population, which resulted in relatively fewer talented people and a presumed need to lower the average quality of artistry to appeal to a larger market; this leads to declines in levels of artistic accomplishment. It also, it is argued, limits the number of those capable of superior achievements. It is not clear, however, that the growth of mass markets has in fact limited cultural achievements of symphony orchestras, opera, ballet, and live theater. In the past, cultural achievements had generally been financed and viewed only by wealthy and politically important patrons. With the advent of movies, radio, TV, records, the Internet, and related forms of media that make cultural activities more accessible to the people, it is probable that more individuals and a greater proportion of the population now have been exposed to cultural endeavors than had been the case in the past, thus having a greater influence.

Other Problems with Capitalism

Financial market failures and collapses have been given much attention, particularly in recent years, as have the roles of inflation and cyclical downturns.[42] The decentralized market has been considered inefficient relative to a centrally imposed decision-making economy; this proposition seems somewhat overstated, given the difficulties experienced by recent centrally organized economies. And while attention has been given to instability in the market system, studies of centrally planned economies have revealed similar types of cyclical difficulties in economic performance. Large economies, whatever the basic economic system, appear to have similar varieties of difficulties in coordination. These difficulties are often found in the organization and operation of large factories and other business establishments, even with public ownership. The past difficulties of noncapitalist societies, such as the USSR and the nations of Eastern Europe, indicate that some similar economic problems exist in other types of economies, whose records of growth and distribution have not been superior to those of capitalist nations.

Another critique of modern capitalism is that the nature of the political power shift that comes with the development of a wealthy elite under capitalism effectively reduces the political influence of the lower classes. The force of this argument is unclear, since the rise of capitalism was generally associated with an increase in the shares of the population able to vote and a marked increase in the level of governmental benefits received by the lower classes. Some of these improvements have no doubt been initiated by the elites for their own political reasons, but these have continued for long periods. While wealth may give disproportionate political influence, the ability of a larger proportion of the population to vote could have had some offsetting impact in equalizing political decision-making power. Most noncapitalist political systems have had a much more restricted ruling elite, with limited provision for the turnover of leadership.

Concluding Remarks

Dissatisfaction with capitalism and its outcomes has had a long and vigorous history, as has its advocacy. In some measure, this has to do with the very broad nature of the issues that are considered and the many different aspects of economic, social, and political concern that are being evaluated. Thus these long-standing debates will no doubt continue into the future, as seen in the 2011 emergence of the "Occupy Movement," a movement whose concerns ranged from the forgiveness of student loans to the size of CEO salaries. As has often been the case, there seemed to be no systematic policy advocated to replace capitalism by any alternative system. Rather, the movement was seemingly concerned with handling specific complaints raised, many of which have been dealt with within the basic framework of capitalism. What often seemed at issue were somewhat relatively marginal changes within the basic structure of what would still be considered a capitalist society. Similarly, the expanding role of the state in capitalism argues for the continued development of state-owned and -operated industries, but within a basically free enterprise society.

The current discussions of the role of capitalism have become rather murky. With the demise of communism, there seems to be no basic alternative to the basically free consumer choice society, a system consistent with quite different degrees of state control, religious restrictions, and levels of the distribution of income and wealth. While there are obviously no completely laissez-faire economies, the role of freer markets and consumer choice has spread to many nations, and the role of the broader political freedom that seems to come with economic freedom has become somewhat of a worldwide phenomenon. A wide range of policies and beliefs are now considered to be consistent with some form of capitalism, generally with the presence of some qualifying adjective before capitalism. The system, as well as the term, has shown remarkable adaptability. No doubt not quite the form of capitalism that some believe was advocated by Adam Smith, the major features of modern capitalism resemble neither nineteenth-century capitalism nor today's noncapitalist systems.

Notes

1. A shorter version of this essay was presented at the Deirdre McCloskey Festschrift Conference and the Conference for Bob Allen in Honor of His Retirement (May 2014). In addition to the honorees and attendees at these conferences, I would like to thank David Eltis, Roderick Floud, Carl Mosk, Larry Neal, and Jeffrey Williamson for helpful comments and criticisms.

2. The phrase "pretty good" was used by the entertainer Garrison Keillor and applied to the examination of capitalism by the political scientist John Mueller (1999, 2–7).

3. The recent attack on capitalism by Pope Francis, *Laudato Si*, goes much further in its critique than earlier papal encyclicals. Several of his arguments are discussed below.

4. See the recent discussion of the role of religion by Fogel (2000). There are important arguments about the role of religion in the onset of capitalism, be it Protestantism (Weber 1952) or Judaism (Sombart 1913). For a discussion of the debates on the role of religion in the emergence and development of capitalism by Simmel, Weber, and Sombart, see Muller (2010, 45–61). See Weber (1968: ch. 15) on the role of Judaism and Christianity. Weber also pointed to the institutions of Asian religions in promoting (or rather not promoting) growth. After centuries of arguments that Confucian belief was inconsistent with Chinese economic growth, in recent years that argument has been reversed. For an argument that, contrary to earlier opinions, Islam is

consistent with capitalism, see Rodinson (1973), who argues that Islam does not have the effect of retarding capitalism and that both Islam and Western religions have been consistent with capitalism.

5. This is a point stressed, strongly and influentially, by Marx and Engels (2002 [1848], 219–22) among others.

6. Nevertheless, according to Crouzet (1985), the major wealthholders in nineteenth-century England were still the landed classes. See also Rubinstein (1993).

7. Kuznets (1955). Some have questioned whether this curve would apply to other periods of economic growth. See Piketty (2014). Plato (1970, 214–15) argued that "extreme poverty and wealth must not be allowed to arise in any section of the citizen-body, because both lead to disaster." Anticipating some recent discussions, Plato prescribed an acceptable ratio of the lower limit of poverty to a maximum holding and argued that if anyone exceeded this amount, "he should hand over the surplus to the state and its patron deities, thereby escaping punishment and getting a good name for himself." Polybius (2009, 235–38), writing in the second century, argued that too great inequality would lead to "mob rule" and the destruction of society. John Stuart Mill and Alfred Marshall were particularly concerned with the effects of inheritance. Mill's proposal was to let the deceased pass on their wealth as a whole but to limit the size of any individual inheritance to only enough to provide a comfortable independence, with the rest to go to objects of public usefulness or to be spent among a larger number of individuals.

8. See Engerman and Sokoloff (2012) for a comparison of Latin America, where the initial elites were able to maintain power for several centuries, with Canada and the United States, where conditions favored the nonelite and there was a rather early shift to politically benefit the nonelite. This meant long-term differences in income levels and the provision of public goods, such as education and internal improvements. For a related argument, see Acemoglu, Johnson, and Robinson (2002).

9. Marx and Engels (2003, 224). See also Marx (1936, 405–556). See, however, Weber (1961, 134) on the "democratization of luxury." McCulloch (1830, 519) noted that "there is hardly an improvement of any sort, which has not been denounced as a useless superfluity, or as being some way injurious."

10. Several of the presumed difficulties of capitalism result from its ability to generate increased population due to increases in fertility and decreases in mortality. This leads to problems of overpopulation and declining per capita income, with a self-generated limitation to economic growth. Presumably, early societies had similar problems of overpopulation, though at a lower level and for more limited periods of time, given the limited amount of economic resources. The major difference, which can be regarded as either good or bad, is that the level of population will be higher under capitalism and that it will take a longer time for society to reach the point of population decline.

While in the Malthusian world, the presence of positive shocks to increase population will lead to a return to the equilibrium subsistence of income, there is a period during which the per capita income will be above subsistence for some indeterminate time. This is the argument underlying the claims in Meadows et al. (1974), in which the present generation benefits from conditions leading the economy back to an equilibrium level, and ultimately to economic decline, due to overpopulation, pollution, or reduced labor scarcity. A recent defender of the *Limits* points out that the time horizon for the collapse was estimated by its authors to come "sometime during the second decade of the twenty-first century, or, perhaps, not even in the twenty-first century" (Bardi 2011, 1–3, 12).

There are two ways to look at the changes in the standard of living. One is to examine the changing ownership of various consumer goods and other assets over time. See, for example, Lebergott's (1993) study of the United States in the twentieth century. The number of households owning TVs rose from 9 percent in 1950 to 93 percent in 1987 and to more than 96 percent in 2000. In 2000, more than 90 percent of the households owned at least one automobile compared with 2 percent in 1910 and 87 percent in 1989. The spread of education and suffrage in capitalist societies in the nineteenth and twentieth centuries is documented in Engerman and Sokoloff (2012). The improvements in life expectancy and the decline in infant mortality have affected most levels of income. The other is to discuss relative income shares at any moment of time.

11. See also Marx and Engels (2002) on the shift from capitalism to socialism.

12. Mill (1895: II, 336–40) comments that the stationary state "would be, on the whole a very considerable improvement on our present condition." There would be room "for all kinds of mental culture, and moral and social progress; as much room for improving the Art of Living." Mill believed that "the northern and middle states of America are a specimen of this stage of civilization in very favorable circumstances," no doubt still a contentious claim.

13. Weber (1961, 134) relates the increase in consumer choice to the needs of the military state to obtain cooperation from the general members of the population—the "democratization of luxury." Others relate the development of mass markets to declining costs of consumer goods due to improved productivity and lower raw material costs, making them more accessible to the lower-income population.

14. These arguments were made by economists in two of the relative latecomers to industrial growth, the United States and Germany, both of which were basically high-tariff countries. See Chang (2002) for an argument that early developed nations had utilized economic policies when growing that they would deny to later developers.

15. While many focus on the distribution of the tax burden, differential patterns of expenditure will also have a great influence on the nature of redistribution.

16. Hacker (1954, 73–74) also points out "that in the 1830s and 1840s so many of the remnants of the old system were swept out, as the industrialists increasingly made their power felt."

17. Smith does not quantify the nature of the trade-off.

18. For a summary of data on the range of government expenditures and revenues for today's major countries, many considered capitalist, in the late nineteenth and the twentieth centuries, see Tanzi (2011, 9–10).

19. See, in particular, Engels (1968, 9–26, 30–87, 108–49, 150–240, 312) and Marx and Engels (2002, 219–33). See Ashton (in Hayek 1954b, 127–59) and George (1925, 8, 63–107) for the discussions of London housing and also Macaulay's (1965) response to Southey Ashton (1948, 11) contrasts Ireland and England. See also Hartwell (1959). For a detailed analysis of long-term trends in income distribution in the United States, see Williamson and Lindert (1980). For a series of essays on the general history of capitalism, see Neal and Williamson (2014).

20. Davis and Huttenback (1986). See also Lebergott (1980).

21. For the transatlantic slave trade, see Eltis and Richardson (2010); for European war deaths, see Wright (1965, 625–72).

22. Kiernan (1969). On wars in general, see Wright (1965), who argues that the post-1860 years saw a decline in the number of wars from earlier periods. Hirschman (1977, 132–35) notes that a key earlier argument in favor of capitalism was as a substitute for the destructive forces created by military activities. Hirschman also repeats Schumpeter's arguments from his essay on *Imperialism* (1951) that it was the survival of a precapitalist mentality that explained imperial

ambitions as well as the "warlike spirit." In an introduction to an edited volume on European warfare from c. 1280 to c. 1780, Contamine (2000, 1) points out that "it would probably be difficult to find a single year . . . wholly without war or without an open demonstration of hostility in one corner of the continent or another, or indeed outside it." Parker (1996, 118) distinguishes between wars to enslave enemies, which characterized the non-European world, and the absence of a desire to acquire slaves by warfare among Europeans in the seventeenth and eighteenth centuries. The frequency of wars and of high military mortality for northwestern Europeans at the time when their armies would not enslave citizens of other nations was roughly comparable to that of the non-European world. For a detailed collection of data relating to long-term trends in deaths in military actions and homicides, see Pinker (2011). See also Keeley (1996) and Wright (1965) on wars and war deaths in Native American and European societies.

23. See Engerman (2007b). Voluntary slavery was important when needed to obtain subsistence at low levels of income and also when there was a need to obtain protection in times of chaos.

24. For a discussion of early famines, see O'Gráda (2009, 25–39, 92–93). See also Walford (1879). On the decline in population in the Americas with the arrival of Europeans, see Livi Bacci (2008).

Similar points about famines were made by both Mill (1895) and Marshall (1949). Mill (1895) commented that "we may observe, however, that rich and refined countries can ever be secure against the devastation of famines," while Marshall (1949) stated that "in all ages of the world except the present, want of food has caused wholesale destruction of the people. . . . But gradually the effects of increased wealth and improved means of communication are making themselves felt nearly all over the world; the severity of famine is mitigated even in such a country as India; and they are unknown in Europe and the New World."

25. See also Gemery, Hogendorn, and Johnson (1990).

26. See the *Oxford English Dictionary*. The term "capitalist," however, was utilized earlier. See the discussion in Pryor (2010, 7–10) and earlier works by Pryor on the nature of capitalism, as well as Williams (1985, 50–52).

27. See the discussion in Cardoso (2014) on the role of Smith and other classical economists.

28. There were arguments made about the projected ending of the system of Southern slavery based on a declining land-labor ratio. These contentions were also applied to the Northern system of agriculture. See Fox-Genovese and Genovese (2005). The belief in what has been called the Domar-Nieboer argument was the standard nineteenth-century model used to explain economic change in the world at that time.

29. See William Stanley Jevons (1865: ix, 215, 316, 349) for a prediction echoed several years later by his son, H. Stanley Jevons (1915), with a different time horizon. For a more recent defense of Jevons, see Bardi (2011, 64–65). He dates the first geological argument for the finite nature of fossil fuel to John Williams in 1789. Bardi (2011, 13) argues that *The Limits to Growth* was a warning to be acted on, not a prediction. A recent book by Kolbert (2014) has described the probability of the sixth large-scale extinction, but the first due to faulty human behavior. The previous five, over a period of about 450 million years, had apparently occurred before the arrival of humankind, let alone capitalism. This does not, of course, mean that the threatened reoccurrence will not take place, but it again points to some complexity in blaming contemporary society for all the world's evils. In the seventeenth century, British economic growth was expected to decline due to the shortage of timber used for construction, heating, and shipbuilding. See Flinn (1958) and Hammersley (1973). This timber shortage was overcome by imports of timber from Sweden and the British North American colonies.

30. The classic starting point here is, of course, Smith. A major source of anticapitalistic rhetoric in the first part of the nineteenth century was found among US Southern slaveholders and British slaveholders and British proslavery advocates. The defense of slavery compared important aspects of the treatment of individuals and the social and economic behavior in slave societies with so-called free labor societies. See the works of Fox-Genovese and Genovese (2005, 2008, 2011). Frequent mention was made in these arguments of the better long-term care and provisioning of slaves than of the free workers. These points were also made by the members of the British and American working classes.

31. See Hume (1963), who commented that "necessity, hunger, want, stimulate the strong and courageous. Fear, anxiety, terror, agitate the weak and infirm."

32. Schumpeter (1950, 61–71). Rosenberg (2000, 7, 11) states that Schumpeter believed that although innovation may create monopolies, these will, by the dynamics of capitalism, be "only temporary" due to the "incentive mechanisms of capitalism."

33. See Friedman (1962); Friedman and Friedman (1990). Somewhat more outspoken and popular advocacy of capitalism can be found in Ayn Rand et al. (1967), which includes two short essays by Alan Greenspan, later chairman of the Federal Reserve Board. There seemed, however, little apparent relation between Greenspan's monetary policy and his objectivist beliefs.

34. Increased leisure has been a major benefit of economic growth that is not usually considered part of the customary GNP measures. It has been achieved by reductions in hours worked per day, days worked per week, weeks worked per year, and years worked per lifetime. In addition, there have been changes in the nature of work routines, reducing the actual time at work and the intensity of work. Laborers now enter the labor force at older ages, which permits a longer time for education, and they also retire and leave the labor force earlier. This means that much of the potential increase in consumption is taken in the form of nonworking rather than in more goods and services and also that it is probable that all levels of income have received such benefits.

35. As Rosen (2004, 28) pointed out, "Markets value diversity. Individuals, using their respective talents and different preferences, respond to these valuations and create important induced differentiation in consumption patterns, earnings, and occupational choices."

36. For the argument that the money economy (capitalism) will increase "individual liberty," see Simmel (1990, 283–354). On the civilizing effect of capitalism, see also Hirschman (1977). For a differing view, see Engels (1968, 31, 81–85, 236).

37. An argument is often made that the search for economic progress should cease, since further progress cannot lead to any increase in human happiness. The argument about limiting progress is often supported by showing that this belief has had numerous adherents over time and place. It is not obvious, however, at what point in time progress should have been halted, given the changes in the type of goods and of health institutions during the time since this argument was first made. See Schui (2014).

38. See the German and English historical Schools as described in Schumpeter (1954, 307–24); Hayek (1954, 33–63); and Gide and Rist (1947).

39. Polanyi (2001, 3, 130) also drew upon in an earlier critic of capitalism, Robert Owen, claiming that "Robert Owen's was an insight; market economy if left to evolve according to its own laws would create great and permanent evils." For a quite different discussion of the twentieth century, see Williamson (1998).

40. Among the aspects of Smithian economics criticized by Polanyi is the belief in, and acceptance of, the consumer's rationally seeking to maximize consumption. To Polanyi, this belief

was not inevitable, and society would do better by seeking a different set of influences, such as altruism, communalism, or a limited desire for goods influencing individual utilities. Polanyi's argument that African societies were characterized by nonmarket transactions has been disputed by many scholars who point to the frequent fluctuations in slave prices and the basically rising trends in prices paid by Europeans to Africans to acquire slaves.

41. Bell (1976) and Appleby (2010, 423) point to three types of criticisms of capitalism: those purely about what is regarded as the vulgarity and ugliness of the pursuit of property, those opposed to globalization, and finally the view that capitalism has no sensitivity to its misery and injustice. In general, however, Appleby is more favorable to the accomplishments of capitalism than are many other of its critics. See also Wood (2002). Mises (1972, 73–105) points to a number of noneconomic objections that have been made to capitalism but finds them all somewhat doubtful.

42. There had been, for example, long-term sustained inflations in Europe in the period 1180–1320 and during the price revolution of 1520–1640, as well as several in the ancient world, including in Greek times after the conquest of Persia and in the Roman Empire under Diocletian, who introduced an edict in 301 to limit price increases. See Schwartz (1973, 243–69) and Temin (2013, 77–79). Bubbles and financial collapses also have a long history. This can be seen at or near the onset of capitalism in England with the South Sea Bubble of 1720. This was described by the pamphleteer Cato (Trenchard and Gordon 1969: I, 12) as causing severe losses to individuals and the state who had a right to be vengeful toward the directors and certainly should not attempt to cover their losses. When asked what to do, they stated "let them only be hanged, but hanged speedily."

References

Acemoglu, Daron, Johnson, Simon, and Robinson, James A. 2002. "Reversal of Fortune: Geography and Institutions in the Making of the Modern World Income Distribution." *Quarterly Journal of Economics* 117 (4): 1231–94.

Appiah, Kwame Anthony, and Bunzl, Martin, eds. 2007. *Buying Freedom: The Ethics and Economics of Slave Redemption*. Princeton, NJ: Princeton University Press.

Appleby, Joyce. 2010. *The Relentless Revolution*. New York: W. W. Norton.

Ashton, T. S. 1948. *The Industrial Revolution*. Oxford: Oxford University Press.

Ashton, T. S. 1954a. "The Treatment of Capitalism by Historians." In Hayek, F.A., ed. *Capitalism and the Historians*. Chicago: University of Chicago Press.

Ashton, T. S. 1954b. "The Standard of Life of the Workers in England, 1790–1830." In Hayek, F.A., ed. *Capitalism and the Historians*. Chicago: University of Chicago Press.

Backhouse, Roger E., and Bateman, Bradley W. 2011. *Capitalist Revolutionary: John Maynard Keynes*. Cambridge, MA: Harvard University Press.

Bardi, Ugo. 2011. *The Limits to Growth Revisited*. New York: Springer.

Bell, Daniel. 1976. *Cultural Contradictions of Capitalism*. New York: Basic Books.

Blackstone, William. 1979 (1765). *Commentaries on the Laws of England*. 4 vols. Vol. 1, *On the Rights of Persons*, 410–54. Chicago: University of Chicago Press.

Blum, Jerome. 1978. *The End of the Old Order in Rural Europe*. Princeton, NJ: Princeton University Press.

Boyer, George. 1998. "The Historical Background of the Communist Manifesto." *Journal of Economic Perspectives* 12: 151–74.

Burbank, Jane, and Cooper, Frederick. 2010. *Empires in World History: Power and the Politics of Difference*. Princeton, NJ: Princeton University Press.

Cardoso, José Luís. 2014. "The Political Economy of Rising Capitalism." In Neal and Williamson 2014, 574–99.

Carey, Henry Charles. 1852. *The Harmony of Interests: Agriculture, Manufacturing, and Commercial*. 2nd ed. New York: M. Finch.

Chang, Ha-Joon. 2002. *Kicking Away the Ladder: Development Strategy in Historical Perspective*. London: Anthem.

Cohen, Jon S. 1988. "Was Italian Fascism a Developmental Dictatorship? Some Evidence to the Contrary." *Economic History Review* 41: 95–113.

Contamine, Philippe, ed. 2000. *War and Competition between States*. New York: Oxford University Press.

Crouzet, François. 1985. *The First Industrialists: The Problem of Origins*. Cambridge: Cambridge University Press.

Davis, Lance E., and Huttenback, Robert A. 1986. *Mammon and the Pursuit of Empire: The Political Economy of British Imperialism, 1860–1912*. Cambridge: Cambridge University Press.

Davis, Robert C. 2003. *Christian Slaves, Muslim Maters: White Slavery in the Mediterranean, the Barbary Coast and Italy, 1500–1800*. Basingstoke: Palgrave Macmillan.

Drescher, Seymour. 2002. *The Mighty Experiment: Free Labor versus Slavery in British Emancipation*. Oxford: Oxford University Press.

Eltis, David, and Richardson, David. 2010. *Atlas of the Transatlantic Slave Trade*. New Haven: Yale University Press.

Engels, Friedrich. 1968 (1845). *The Condition of the Working Class in England*. Stanford, CA: Stanford University Press.

Engerman, Stanley L. 1984. "Reflections on 'The Standard of Living Debate': New Arguments and New Evidence." In James and Thomas 1984, 50–79.

Engerman, Stanley L. 2007a. *Slavery, Emancipation and Freedom*. Baton Rouge: Louisiana State University Press.

Engerman, Stanley L. 2007b. "Slavery, Freedom, and Sen." In Appiah and Bunzl 2007, 77–107.

Engerman, Stanley L., and Sokoloff, Kenneth L. 2012. *Economic Development of the Americas since 1500. Endowments and Institutions*. Cambridge: Cambridge University Press.

Feinstein, Charles H. 1990. "What Really Happened to Real Wages? Trends in Wages, Prices and Productivity in the United Kingdom, 1880–1913." *Economic History Review* 43: 329–55.

Flinn, Michael. 1958. "The Growth of the English Iron Industry, 1660–1760." *Economic History Review* 11: 144–53.

Fogel, Robert William. 2000. *The Fourth Great Awakening and the Future of Egalitarianism*. Chicago: University of Chicago Press.

Fox-Genovese, Elizabeth, and Genovese, Eugene D. 2008. *Slavery in White and Black: Class and Race in the Southern Slaveholders New World Order*. Cambridge: Cambridge University Press.

Fox-Genovese, Elizabeth, and Genovese, Eugene D. 2011. *Fatal Self-Deception: Slaveholding Paternalism in the Old South*. Cambridge: Cambridge University Press.

Fox-Genovese, Elizabeth, and Genovese, Eugene D. 2005. *The Mind of the Master Class: History and Faith in the Southern Slaveholders' World View*. Cambridge: Cambridge University Press.

Friedman, Milton. 1962. *Capitalism and Freedom*. Chicago: University of Chicago Press.

Friedman, Milton, and Friedman, Rose. 1990. *Free to Choose*. San Diego: Harcourt Brace Jovanovich.

Gemery, Henry A., Hogendorn, Jan, and Johnson, Marion. 1990. "Evidence of English-African Terms of Trade in the Eighteenth Century." *Explorations in Economic History* 27 (2): 157–77.

George, M. Dorothy. 1925. *London Life in the Eighteenth Century*. London: Kegan Paul.

Gide, Charles, and Rist, Charles. 1947. *A History of Economic Doctrines from the Time of the Physiocrats to the Present Day*. 2nd English ed. Boston: D. C. Heath.

Hacker, L. M. 1954. "The Anticapitalist Bias of American Historians." In Hayek, F.A., ed. *Capitalism and the Historians*. Chicago: University of Chicago Press.

Hammersley, G. 1973. "The Charcoal Iron Industry and Its Fuel, 1540–1750." *Economic History Review* 26: 593–613.

Hansen, Alvin. 1939. "Economic Progress and Declining Population Growth." *American Economic Review* 29: 1–15.

Hartwell, R. Max. 1959. "Interpretations of the Industrial Revolution in England: A Methodological Inquiry." *Journal of Economic History* 19: 229–49.

Hartwell, R. Max. 1970. "The Standard of Living Controversy: A Summary". In Hartwell, R. Max, ed. *The Industrial Revolution*. Oxford: Blackwell.

Hartwell, R. Max. 1995. *A History of the Mont Pèlerin Society*. Indianapolis: Liberty Fund.

Hartwell, R. Max. 1961. "The Rising Standard of Living in England, 1800–1850." *Economic History Review* 13: 387–416.

Hayek, F. A., ed. 1954. *Capitalism and the Historians*. Chicago: University of Chicago Press.

Hayek, Friedrich A. 1944. *The Road to Serfdom*. Chicago: University of Chicago Press.

Hirschman, Albert O. 1977. *The Passions and the Interests*. Princeton, NJ: Princeton University Press.

Hobsbawm, E. J. 1958. "The British Standard of Living, 1790–1850." *Economic History Review* 10: 46–68.

Hoffman, Philip T. 2015. *Why Did Europe Conquer the World?* Princeton, NJ: Princeton University Press.

Hollander, Samuel. 2011. *Friedrich Engels and Marxian Political Economy*. Cambridge: Cambridge University Press.

Hume, David. 1963 (1752). "Of Commerce." In *Essays: Moral, Political and Literary*, 259–74. Oxford: Oxford University Press.

Imlah, Albert H. 1958. *Economic Elements in the Pax Britannica: Studies in British Foreign Trade in the Nineteenth Century*. Cambridge, MA: Harvard University Press.

James, John A., and Thomas, Mark, eds. 1984. *Capitalism in Context: Essays on Economic Development and Cultural Change in Honor of R. M. Hartwell*. Chicago: University of Chicago Press.

Jevons, H. Stanley. 1915. *The British Coal Trade*. New York: E. P. Dutton.

Jevons, William Stanley. 1865. *The Coal Question*. London: Macmillan.

Keeley, Lawrence H. 1996. *War before Civilization*. New York: Oxford University Press.

Kiernan, V. G. 1969. *The Lords of Human Kind: Black Man, Yellow Man, and White Man in an Age of Empire*. Boston: Little, Brown.

Kolbert, Elizabeth. 2014. *The Sixth Extinction: An Unnatural History*. New York: Henry Holt.

Kuznets, Simon. 1955. "Economic Growth and Income Inequality." *American Economic Review* 45: 1–28.

Lebergott, Stanley. 1993. *Pursuing Happiness: The American Consumer in the Twentieth Century*. Princeton, NJ: Princeton University Press.

Lebergott, Stanley. 1980. "The Returns to U.S. Imperialism, 1890–1929." *Journal of Economic History* 40: 229–52.

List, Friedrich. 1956 (1841). *The National System of Political Economy*. Philadelphia: J. B. Lippincott.

Livi-Bacci, Massimo. 2008. *Conquest: The Destruction of the American Indios*. Translated by Carl Ipsen. Cambridge: Polity.

Macaulay, T. B. 1965 (1830). "Southey's Colloquies." In *Critical and Historical Essays*, 25–69. New York: McGraw-Hill.

Malthus, Thomas R. 1993 (1789). *An Essay on the Principle of Population*. New York: Oxford University Press.

Marshall, Alfred. 1949 (1890). *Principles of Economics: An Introductory Volume*. New York: Macmillan.

Marshall, Alfred, and Marshall, Mary Paley. 1888 (1871). *The Economics of Industry*. London: Macmillan.

Marx, Karl. 1936 (1906). *Capital*. New York: Modern Library.

Marx, Karl, and Engels, Friedrich. 1968. *On Colonialism*. Moscow: Progressive.

Marx, Karl, and Engels, Friedrich. 2002 (1848). *The Communist Manifesto*. London: Penguin Books.

McCloskey, Deirdre. 2010. *Bourgeois Dignity: Why Economics Can't Explain the Modern World*. Chicago: University of Chicago Press.

McCulloch, J. R. 1830 [1825]. *Principles of Political Economy*. 2nd ed. London: Longman, Rees, Orme, Brown and Green.

Meadows, Danella H., et al. 1974. *The Limits to Growth: A Report for the Club of Rome's Project on the Predicament of Mankind*. 2nd ed. New York: New American Library.

Mill, John Stuart. 1895 (1848). *Principles of Political Economy*. 5th ed. New York: D. Appleton.

Mises, Ludwig von. 1972. *The Anti-Capitalist Mentality*. South Holland: Libertarian Press.

Mueller, John. 1999. *Capitalism, Democracy, and Ralph's Pretty Good Grocery*. Princeton, NJ: Princeton University Press.

Muller, Jerry Z. 2010. *Capitalism and the Jews*. Princeton, NJ: Princeton University Press.

Musgrave, Richard. 1959. *The Theory of Public Finance: A Study in Public Economics*. New York: McGraw-Hill.

Neal, Larry. 2014. "Introduction." In Neal and Williamson 2014, 1:1–23.

Neal, Larry, and Williamson, Jeffrey G., eds. 2014. *The Cambridge History of Capitalism*. 2 vols. Cambridge: Cambridge University Press.

Neal, Larry, and Williamson, Jeffrey G., eds. 2014. *The Cambridge History of Capital, Vol. I, The Rise of Capitalism: From Ancient Origins to 1848*. Cambridge: Cambridge University Press.

Ó Gráda, Cormac. 2009. *Famine*. Princeton, NJ: Princeton University Press.

Olson, Mancur. 1982. *The Rise and Decline of Nations: Economic Growth, Stagflation, and Social Rigidities*. New Haven: Yale University Press.

Parker, Geoffrey. 1996. *The Military Revolution: Military Innovation and the Rise of the West, 1500–1800*. 2nd ed. Cambridge: Cambridge University Press.

Piketty, Thomas. 2014. *Capital in the Twenty-First Century*. Cambridge, MA: Belknap Press.

Pinker, Steven. 2011. *The Better Angels of Our Nature: Why Violence Has Declined*. New York: Viking.

Plato. 1970 (360 B.C.E.). *The Laws*. Translated by Trevor Saunders. Harmondsworth: Penguin.

Polanyi, Karl. 2001 (1944). *The Great Transformation*. Boston: Beacon Press.

Polybius. 2009. *The Complete Histories of Polybius*. New York: Digireads.

Pryor, Frederick L. 2010. *Capitalism Possessed*. Cambridge: Cambridge University Press.

Rand, Ayn, et al. 1967. *Capitalism: The Unknown Ideal*. New York: New American Library.

Robbins, Lionel. 1952. *The Theory of Economic Policy in English Classical Economy*. London: Macmillan.

Rodinson, Maxime. 1973. *Islam and Capitalism*. New York: Pantheon.

Rosen, Sherwin. 2004. *Markets and Diversity*. Cambridge, MA: Harvard University Press.

Rosenberg, Nathan. 2000. *Schumpeter and the Endogeneity of Technology: Some American Perspectives*. London: Routledge.

Rubinstein, W. D. 1993. *Capitalism, Culture, and Decline in Britain, 1750–1990*. London: Routledge.

Schui, Florian. 2014. *Austerity: The Great Failure*. New Haven: Yale University Press.

Schumpeter, Joseph. 1950 (1942). *Capitalism, Socialism, and Democracy*. 3rd ed. New York: Harper and Brothers.

Schumpeter, Joseph. 1951 (1918). "The Sociology of Imperialism." In *Social Classes and Imperialism: Two Essays*, 3–98. New York: New American Library.

Schumpeter, Joseph. 1954. *History of Economic Analysis*. New York: Oxford University Press.

Schwartz, Anna. 1973. "Secular Price Change in Historical Perspective." *Journal of Money, Credit, and Banking* 5 (1): 243–69.

Simmel, Georg. 1990 (1900). *The Philosophy of Money*. 2nd ed. London: Routledge.

Smith, Adam. 1937 (1776). *The Wealthy Nations*. New York: Modern Library.

Sombart, Werner. 1913. *Jews and Modern Capitalism*. London: T. F. Unwin.

Tanzi, Vito. 2011. *Government versus Markets*. Cambridge: Cambridge University Press.

Temin, Peter. 2013. *The Roman Market Economy*. Princeton, NJ: Princeton University Press.

Toynbee, Arnold. 1956 (1884). *The Industrial Revolution*. Boston: Beacon Press.

Trenchard, John, and Thomas Gordon [Cato]. 1969 (1733). *Cato's Letters: or Essays on Liberty, Civil and Religious, and Other Important Subjects*. 4 vols. New York: Russell and Russell.

Walford, Cornelius. 1879. *The Famines of the World: Past and Present*. London: E. Stanford.

Weber, Eugen. 1964. *Varieties of Fascism: Doctrines of Revolution in the Twentieth Century*. Princeton, NJ: Van Nostrand.

Weber, Max. 1961 (1927). *General Economic History*. New York: Collier.

Weber, Max. 1968. *Economy and Society: An Outline of Interpretive Sociology*. 3 vols. Edited by Guenther Roth and Claus Wittcich. New York: Bedminster Press.

Weber, Max. 1952 (1904). *The Protestant Ethic and the Spirit of Capitalism*. Translated by Talcott Parsons. New York: Scribner.

Williams, Raymond. 1985. *Keywords*. Rev. ed. New York: Oxford University Press.

Williamson, Jeffrey. 1998. "Globalization, Labor Markets and Policy Backlash in the Past." *Journal of Economic Perspectives* 12: 51–72.

Williamson, Jeffrey. 1985. *Did British Capitalism Breed Inequality?* Boston: Allen and Unwin.

Williamson, Jeffrey, and Lindert, Peter H. 1980. *American Inequality: A Macroeconomic History*. New York: Academic Press.

Wood, Ellen Meiksins. 2002. *The Origin of Capitalism: A Longer View*. London: Verso.

Wright, Quincy. 1965. *A Study of War: Second Edition, with a Commentary on War since 1942*. Chicago: University of Chicago Press.

4

Following in the Path of Deirdre McCloskey: The Lutheran Ethic and the Nordic Spirit of Social Democracy

ROBERT H. NELSON

From mid-nineteenth-century thinkers such as Karl Marx through much of the twentieth century, the dominant way of explaining events in the historical and social sciences was in material—in economic—terms. It was thus a great intellectual surprise when attention in the last few decades of the twentieth century began to shift to the explanatory power of ideas and culture. More recently, religion's central role in shaping society has been rediscovered. The importance of religion has been further magnified by a growing recognition that the scope of "religion" extends well beyond traditional forms of faith—most importantly, now incorporating a developing scholarly understanding that "secular religion" is an actual form of religion. Marxism can then be understood (as is now widely accepted) to have been an actual religion that imaginatively transformed key Christian themes to outwardly secular—economic—disguises. Indeed, Marxism was only one of a much wider category of all "economic religion"—the diverse set of modern belief systems offering the hope and expectation that continuing rapid economic progress will lead to heaven on earth and thus save the world (Nelson 2001; Nelson 2010b). In recognizing and contributing to this major intellectual shift of the late twentieth century, now continuing into the early twenty-first century, Deirdre McCloskey has been a leading figure.

I first became aware of McCloskey's work when she published a 1983 article in the *Journal of Economic Literature* titled "The Rhetoric of Economics" (McCloskey 1983). The theme of the article was that economics is not what it seems. It pretends to be doing a version of science, but it is actually engaged in making disguised philosophical arguments that involve deep value judgments, fundamental worldviews, and other large nonscientific elements. By claiming the mantle of science, however, economists were engaged in an imperialistic claim for special authority for their own value judgments and worldviews against more honest presenters of normative beliefs who did not try to dress their arguments in false scientific clothing.

It was not difficult for McCloskey to convince me in 1983 that this was an accurate description of much of the activity occurring within the economics profession. I had already become skeptical about formal economics as a result of my graduate school experiences in economics at Princeton University in the late 1960s. McCloskey, however, organized and stated my concerns more clearly. I was impressed at the time that the *Journal of Economic Literature* would give so much space to such heretical thinking. It encouraged me to publish my own small piece of heresy, "The Economics Profession and the Making of Public Policy," in 1987, also in the *Journal of Economic Literature* (Nelson 1987). I argued there, similarly to McCloskey, that the most important role of economists in the public policy arena was as strong advocates for the powerful values of a shared ideology, derived originally in the American case from the Progressive Era "gospel of efficiency," restated in more scientific-sounding language in post–World War II economics.

McCloskey followed with a 1985 book of the same title, *The Rhetoric of Economics*, in which she further developed the view that economics was a form of philosophical argument masquerading rhetorically as science. As the author now of her own book, she was freer to make stronger criticisms and to use more colorful language. It was of special interest to me that a number of the metaphors she used to describe economics portrayed it in religious terms. McCloskey (1985, 6) wrote, for example, that economics was a leading branch of the modern "church of science." Its rise could be understood as part of a general social trend whereby "as religious faith retreated among the intelligentsia in the nineteenth and twentieth centuries, a modernist faith flowed in" as a secular substitute (6). Economics, McCloskey observed, also had its "Ten Commandments and Golden Rule" (7). Its rituals included "modernist chanting, supported by hooded choruses," that could be "good for the soul" (9). Indeed, at the core of modern professional economic belief was a "trinity of fact, definition and holy value" (6). The history of economics since the 1930s showed it passing through three stages, from a young and vigorous "crusading faith" that with time "hardened into ceremony" and had now reached an institutional status with its own officially recognized "nuns, bishops, and cathedrals" of the economics profession (4).

Again, it was not difficult for McCloskey to persuade me that such religious elements were in fact present in professional economics. She used more colorful language, but I had already been thinking along similar lines in my daily work as an economist in the Office of Policy Analysis within the Office of the

Secretary of the Interior (where I worked from 1975 to 1993 before coming to the School of Public Policy at the University of Maryland; Nelson 1989; Nelson 2015b). I was struck there in particular by the strong sense that the public land and environmental policy conflicts that were being waged all around me had a deeply religious character. I had already concluded during my first few years in the Interior Department that the environmental movement was grounded in a fundamentally religious—if nominally secular—belief system. It took me somewhat longer to reach the same conclusion with respect to economics. This recognition began with the empirical observation that economists and environmentalists around me often talked past one another in mutual incomprehension; the worldviews of each were so different and they held to them so fervently, not showing much introspective awareness of their own powerful value assumptions, that they had little basis even to begin a rational discussion. Since I had already concluded that environmentalism was a secular religion, it gradually dawned on me—an understanding that I was coming to recognize more explicitly by the time of McCloskey's 1985 book—that the same must be true of economics. Simply put, it takes a religion to engage in a fierce clash of values with another religion (Nelson 1990).

I was further encouraged in this direction of thought by the recognition that McCloskey and other scholars that I was increasingly encountering were characterizing economics as having the behavioral features and performing the social functions of a religion. I then took a further radical step that would not find many followers in the economics profession—even to the present day. I decided to analyze economics as a religion not only in a metaphorical and functional sense but in a literal sense; in other words, I would examine economics from a lens of "secular theology," a novel concept then that for most contemporary economists is still unfamiliar. McCloskey had said that economics offered actual philosophy in the scientific rhetoric of economics; I now extended this critique to argue that economics also offered actual theology in a scientific rhetoric.

This required me to begin reading in theological literature, where I was especially interested to discover that many theologians regarded the term *religion* more broadly than economists normally understand it. Of particular importance to me, Paul Tillich had famously defined a religion as a deeply held belief system that dealt with matters of "ultimate concern"—and thus did not have to have a god (Brown 1965). With this understanding as expressed by one of the leading theologians of the twentieth century, and by many other scholars of religion I was increasingly encountering, I felt more confident in my decision to examine economics as literally a secular form of actual religion—

as was characteristic of many of the most influential belief systems of the modern age.

It took some time, but in 1991 I published *Reaching for Heaven on Earth: The Theological Meaning of Economics* (Nelson 1991). As the title suggests, I argued in the book that there was an implicit transcendent message underlying economics. Indeed, while few professional economists thought in these terms, economics was a central part of the modern discussion of the sources of "immoral" behavior—of "sin"—in the world. Christianity had traditionally attributed the presence of sin to the fall in the Garden of Eden, but this belief was fading in the seventeenth and eighteen centuries, increasingly regarded as mythological. Rather, from the Enlightenment onward, a much different explanation for the widespread presence of socially reprehensible actions—of sin—was increasingly advanced: the features of the environment in which a person grew up and then lived as an adult. In other words, increasing numbers of people were coming to believe that it is actually bad environments that make people do bad things. In many of the most widely held modern versions of this understanding, the most important thing about the environment is its economic character—for many in the modern age, dire poverty became the true source of the most sinful behavior in the world. The logical corollary was that abolishing poverty—and in the end all economic scarcity—held out the prospect of ending evil in the world and thus arriving at a new earthly paradise. Economics, in other words, had the critical knowledge to bring about the salvation of the world, and economists as the holders of this knowledge would become the new leading priesthood in modern society.

As I argued in *Reaching for Heaven on Earth*, American progressivism from 1890 to 1920, the early years in which the American economics profession was conceived and took shape in the progressive spirit, had been one important form of a wider rise of such economic modernism in Western civilization since the Enlightenment. The core assumptions, the central elements of faith, were that the world was advancing rapidly on a path of economic progress; that society would be capable of maintaining and even increasing the rate of progress by effective governmental actions; that rational social and economic planning would provide the necessary expert guidance for such actions; and that this continuing process of economic advance would in the long run transform—save—the world. As I increasingly wrote in publications continuing up to the present, this was the dominant belief system of professional economics, and it also provided much of the wider social legitimacy for the development of the American welfare and regulatory state in the twentieth century. Many working economists in the government, and some in academia as well, made basic practical contributions, but a significant number of the professional economists in the university world (along with some inside government) mostly added to the economic religious grace notes. McCloskey tried but mostly failed to embarrass them.

I devoted one chapter in *Reaching for Heaven on Earth* to American economic progressivism, covering as leading examples the early American economist Richard Ely, who was a founder of the American Economic Association in 1885; Thorstein Veblen; the prominent New Dealer Thurman Arnold; and John Kenneth Galbraith, all of whom I characterized as twentieth-century apostles of the American progressive gospel of efficiency. The next chapter, however, was devoted to the rise of a strong "postmodernist" strain of thinking among a minority of American economists after World War II that rejected main elements of the progressive vision. The five leading apostles of such economic postmodernism that I chose for illustrative purposes were Charles Lindblom (best known as a political scientist but also a professor emeritus of economics at Yale), Mancur Olson, Deirdre McCloskey, James Buchanan, and Kenneth Boulding. As I wrote in 1991 of McCloskey's writings about economics and rhetoric up to then, in rejecting progressive economic scientism and instead advocating a new pluralism of true economic belief,

> theologically, McCloskey is moving in the direction of a shift potentially as momentous as the shift from the medieval Roman Catholic church, possessed of the one truth and the one priesthood, to the conversations within and among the denominations of the Protestant Reformation, each of the Protestant faithful now possessing freedom of individual religious conscience. If each Protestant still believed in principle that there was a single divine message, in actuality there was a pluralism of faiths, often disagreeing sharply in the answers given to basic questions of the divine purpose and the rules for living on earth. The consequences were hardly limited to debates among theologians. In the modern era it has been economic theology that has served for many men as the guide to salvation, the valid revealer of a path to heaven on earth. The conflicts among communist, fascist, socialist, and other gospels of economic theology have yielded consequences for the world no less momentous than those experienced in the Reformation era [and its violent aftermath]. (Nelson 1991, 287–88)

I had trouble finding a publisher for a book with such an ambitious scope that went so far beyond the subject matter of the mainstream economics in which I had been trained and had achieved some professional recognition as at least a sound policy analyst (the manuscript was initially rejected by about fifteen publishers). Here again, McCloskey played a significant role in my professional life. Late in the process, she was asked to provide a review for

Indiana University Press. The review was positive, but I had already signed a contract by then with another publisher, Rowman & Littlefield (whose commitment to the book was heightened when I promptly sent them the favorable McCloskey review). Rowman & Littlefield then recruited McCloskey to write the foreword to *Reaching for Heaven on Earth*, to which she agreed, helping significantly to boost the book's prospects.

I can think of few other economists who would have done the same given the actual theological character (not, of course, in a biblical sense) of much of the book's analysis and the challenge it posed to the typical self-image of economists. McCloskey continued to be supportive with blurbs and other ways in my continuing efforts as I went on to write two sequels, publishing *Economics as Religion: From Samuelson to Chicago and Beyond* in 2001 and *The New Holy Wars: Economic Religion versus Environmental Religion in Contemporary America* in 2010. The help she has given me with these and other related projects is testimony to her willingness to think about fundamental economic questions that fall well outside the conventional boundaries of mainstream economic discussion and also to her personal generosity in offering strong support for the work of other heretical economists.

By the twenty-first century, McCloskey was writing less about the rhetorical meaning of economics and had returned to her original deep interest in the study of economic history. She now approached the subject, however, from the broader perspective of an economic philosopher. In this respect, she was following in the spirit of an Adam Smith, John Stuart Mill, or Karl Marx—and also in the footsteps of Max Weber in that she was now examining the normative roots within Western civilization of the rise of capitalism. In bringing together a vast array of information and incorporating large normative elements, she has done this with a depth of insight virtually unique among the economists of her generation. Again, I found myself following a few years after her. McCloskey's writings helped encourage me to pursue a growing interest on my own part in a broader historical analysis of economic and policy history informed by philosophy and religion.

In 2010, I published an essay titled "Max Weber Revisited," in which I argued that despite the many criticisms of Weber in the twentieth century, his basic conclusion that the Protestant Reformation played a key role in the rise of capitalism had held up well, even as the exact reasons may not have been the ones Weber emphasized (the Protestant encouragement of literacy in order to read the Bible, for example, was probably among the strongest contributing factors; Nelson 2010a). In 2012, I published another essay, "Is Max Weber Newly Relevant? The Protestant-Catholic Divide in Europe Today," in the *Finnish Journal of Theology*, concluding that the widely noted "north-south" divide in Europe at that time might be better understood as a historically Protestant-Catholic divide (a controversial interpretation, admittedly; Nelson 2012). Most recently, while spending seven months of my 2013–14 sabbatical year at the Collegium for Advanced Study of the University of Helsinki, I began work on a new book manuscript that is now titled *A Second Protestant Ethic: The Lutheran Ethic and the Spirit of Social Democracy in the Nordic Countries* and finished a full draft in the fall of 2015 at the University of Maryland. I will be discussing some of my main findings in this chapter.

Max Weber wrote famously about the role played by the "Protestant ethic" in encouraging the rise of capitalism, but he really meant a "Calvinist ethic." It has received less attention among economic historians, but there was also a "Lutheran ethic" with its own Lutheran view of an appropriate calling, one that differed in significant ways from the Calvinist viewpoint. The Lutheran ethic, for example, had a much more negative view of the role of commerce and market transactions based on self-interest. Instead of worldly success, the Lutheran ethic emphasized social solidarity, fulfilled through a calling serving the biblical Golden Rule of "do unto others as you would have them do unto you" and thereby the whole community.

Weber was on the whole less impressed by Lutheranism, writing of the "relative moral helplessness of Lutheranism" in contrast to Calvinism and that "the differences of conduct, which are very striking, have clearly originated in the lesser degree of ascetic penetration of life in Lutheranism as distinguished from Calvinism" that resulted in Lutheranism's significantly lesser contribution to the rise of capitalism (Weber 2003, 126–27). In this chapter, I will argue that Weber, however, did not do Lutheranism full justice. A "Lutheran ethic," largely neglected by Weber, also played a large part in European social and economic history. This Lutheran ethic, grounded in a distinct Lutheran concept of a calling and then reinforced by institutional features of the Lutheran state churches established after the Reformation, contributed to the origins of the welfare state in of Germany and was even more important in the Nordic countries. By the twentieth century, a secularized Lutheranism provided a critical value foundation and other cultural supports to shape and sustain the development of the five Nordic social democracies of Denmark, Finland, Iceland, Norway, and Sweden.

Indeed, the Lutheran ethic has had as large an impact on the history and economic systems of the Nordic world as the Calvinist ethic had on the history and economic systems of England, Scotland, Holland, Switzerland, the United States, and other countries with Protestant Anglo-American roots in which Calvinism played a major role. Although the number of people living in historically Nordic and Lutheran countries has been relatively small, the worldwide impact of Nordic social democracy has been greater than the total size of the Lutheran populations of these countries (today about twenty-five million) would suggest. In recent years, the Nordic countries, shaped by their Lutheran origins, have often been leading players in defining the collective moral principles and other values of the evolving world social and economic order.

In dealing here with a different part of the European Protestant world outside the Calvinist orbit (I might note that my own heritage traces to Finnish and Swedish immigrants more than one hundred years ago), I again find myself following in the path of McCloskey's much more extensive and grander exploration of the normative background of capitalism in *The Bourgeois Virtues: Ethics for an Age of Commerce* and its sequel, *Bourgeois Dignity: Why Economics Can't Explain the Modern World* (McCloskey 2006 and 2011).

Although having a much smaller historic place in Roman Catholicism, the idea of having a "calling" to some type of activity in this world is central to Protestantism in general, including both Lutheranism and Calvinism.[1] Finnish social historian Pirjo Markkola writes, for example, that in late nineteenth-century Finland, the application of the Lutheran "concept of 'woman's calling' became central in women's organizations and new female occupations." For Cecilia Bloomquist, "her work was vocation, a calling given by God, and she repeatedly reflected on her insufficiency as God's servant. . . . However weak she might have felt herself, the calling led her to a remarkable career in the service not only of Christian social work but also health care in Finland." For Lutherans as well as other Protestants, the importance of pursuing a religious calling extends to all members of society, another radical implication of the Protestant emphasis on a "priesthood of all believers." As Markkola puts it, in Finland and elsewhere in the Nordic world, "according to the Lutheran concept of calling everybody was called to serve in his or her daily life" (Markkola 2000, 115, 121, 122).

A Contrasting Calvinist Ethic

The distinctive character of the Lutheran ethic is revealed in part by its contrast with the Calvinist ethic. Calvin had suggested that only a minority of people could expect to be saved (even among the outwardly Christian faithful), a matter predestined by an all-powerful God and therefore outside any human ability to influence by individual actions (such as "good works") in this world. God's thinking in matters of salvation, Calvin had emphasized, must remain a great and inscrutable mystery, known only to God Himself. Weber argued, however, that such a view, whatever its theological merits in emphasizing the total omnipotence of God, was psychologically untenable for many ordinary members of the human species. If one literally believed, so that nothing whatsoever within human control made any difference in matters of salvation and all eternal fates were already predestined even before a person was born, this might easily lead to a deep fatalism, a lack of moral commitment, or a withdrawal from the world—or perhaps instead to a selfish hedonism in an unrestrained pursuit of worldly pleasures.

The later Calvinist response in practice (if not that of Calvin himself), as Weber argued, was to regard success in a calling as a good "sign" of God's favor. For the Calvinist devout, as they came to think, those who were actually among the saved would have an inner peace of mind and grace that would manifest itself in worldly accomplishments in the pursuit of a calling—even as this could have no true long-run significance for salvation. In a great paradox, the actual religious impact of Calvinism as perceived by its later followers may have lain significantly in the fact that its popular reinterpretation brought back a new form of salvation by good works—including prominently in a business calling.

For Calvinists, achieving a high level of profit might therefore in practice serve as a promising indicator of a heavenly future. High profits, however, could also pose a grave new threat. If a successful businessman began to use his monetary gains to live a life of pleasure and luxury, the prospects for his eternal soul might be gravely endangered—as had happened to many ex-Calvinists. It was not necessary, however, for the businessman to live in poverty. A devout Calvinist whose calling was in business could be successful—could make as large a profit as possible—within the bounds of living within modest pleasures and acting ethically in his personal relations with others.

As Weber emphasized, regarded from a modern utilitarian point of view of maximizing personal happiness and enjoyment—indeed, perhaps the outlook of most people in the history of the world—the Calvinist businessman was behaving "irrationally." Calvinism produced, one might say, a new kind of human "ascetic entrepreneur and businessman." As Weber wrote of the "Protestant" (really Calvinist) ethic, it "acted powerfully against the spontaneous enjoyment of possessions; it restricted consumption, especially of luxuries. On the other hand, it had the psychological effect of freeing the acquisition of goods from the inhibitions of traditionalist ethics. It broke the bonds of the impulse of acquisition in that it not only legalized it, but . . . looked upon it as directly willed by God. The campaign against the temptations of the flesh, and the dependence on external things, was . . . not a struggle against rational acquisition, but against the irrational use of wealth" (Weber 2003, 171).

The Calvinist drive to fulfill a worldly calling persisted even long after devotion to the original Christian faith of Calvin had waned. The American Benjamin Franklin, in the second half of the eighteenth century, was prominently mentioned by Weber as an example of the powerful motivating influence of a Calvinist calling, even though Franklin by then was skeptical about traditional Christianity. In the later nineteenth century, another person with skeptical tendencies, Andrew Carnegie, raised in Calvinist Scotland before immigrating to the United States, offered another such example. As he wrote in 1889 about "the gospel of wealth,"

> It becomes the duty of the millionaire to increase his revenues. The struggle for more is completely freed from selfish or ambitious taint and becomes a noble pursuit. Then he labors not for self, but for others; not to hoard but to spend [his wealth for public benefit]. The more he makes, the more the public gets. His whole life is changed from the moment that he resolves to become a disciple of the gospel of wealth, and henceforth he labors to acquire that he may wisely administer for others' good. His daily labor is a daily virtue. (Quoted in Nasaw 2006, 361)

Carnegie actually did as he preached, eventually giving away almost the entirety of his vast accumulated fortune for a wide variety of public causes, including the establishment of many nonprofit institutions (such as Carnegie Mellon University in Pittsburgh and the Carnegie Institute for International Peace in Washington), the building of more than two thousand community libraries across the United States, and the construction of seven thousand church organs, as well as Carnegie Hall in New York City, thus touching the lives of millions of ordinary Americans. As a good Calvinist, if now of a newly secular mold, Carnegie's purpose was not to provide charity for the poor but to make education and other useful tools available to them to empower their lives on their own.

Few American professional economists in the twentieth century studied Weber and the Protestant ethic; Weber was taken seriously only in the field of sociology and among intellectual historians. As an early indication of changing attitudes among American economists, however, a leading contemporary American macroeconomist, Bradford De Long, reported in 1988 that his statistical research into the historical causes of the relative economic progress of the more advanced nations of the world had shown little support for the most commonly offered explanations. But to his surprise, there was "one striking ex ante association between growth over 1870–1979 and a pre-determined variable: a nation's dominant religious establishment." Indeed, the historical presence in a nation of "a religious establishment that is Protestant" or that even contained a significant mixture of Protestants and Catholics, as opposed to predominantly Catholics, "is significantly correlated with growth" (De Long 1988, 1146).

A growing number of such writings appeared over the next twenty-five years. A 2003 study of the economic impact of Calvinism describes it as having brought about a "disciplinary revolution" in early modern Europe. In comparing Catholicism, Lutheranism, and Calvinism, Philip Gorski notes that "while all three confessions advocated discipline—both religious and social—it was the Calvinists who did so with the greatest fervor and consequence" (Gorski 2003, 20–21). With their frequent involvement in worldly affairs and fierce commitment to the pursuit of their various callings, individual Calvinists and indeed whole Calvinist societies were more likely to prosper economically and otherwise—including in another area of religious importance to the Calvinist faithful, the early development of modern science as a way of understanding God's plan for the structure of the universe (Harrison 2001).

Indeed, by 2010 it was becoming increasingly common among American economic historians to conclude that Weber had been broadly correct, that there was a significant association of Protestantism with national economic success but that many other things were at work besides the Calvinist way of thinking about a calling (Becker and Woessmann 2009). By 2013, two economic researchers would find that "going beyond the 'work ethic' hypothesis, we show that Weber's classic can be seen to argue that the different religions will also lead to different political preferences, and our empirical results [in Switzerland] confirm this"; in addition, the existence of political differences inevitably leads to economic differences (Basten and Betz 2013, 89). Another 2013 article in the *Journal of Economic Literature* explains that, as seen in the 2000s economic historical writings of Deirdre McCloskey, for example, "the recent literature on economic growth and development has increasingly focused on very long-run effects of geographic, historical, and cultural factors on productivity and income per capita"—long run factors that, geography aside, historically have been much influenced by a nation's historic religion, such as Lutheranism in the Nordic countries.(Spolaore and Wacziard 2013, 361). A historic Protestantism, whether in Calvinist, Lutheran or other forms, goes far to shape whole societies even today. In the most recent 2015 World Happiness Report, all of the top-ten ranked nations in the world were historically Protestant, including all five of the Nordic countries among the ten (Helliwell et al. 2015). If the goal of an economic system is utility maximization, the citizens of historically Protestant nations, it would appear, have a special knack.

Lutheran Salvation by Good Works

As noted above, the idea of a calling from God was prominent in Lutheran as well as Calvinist theology. Like all Protestants, Luther taught that good works in a calling could themselves do nothing to advance an individual's prospects for salvation—that this was a matter of "faith alone," and the very existence of personal faith, and thus salvation, was ultimately in the hands of God alone. Luther taught, however, that those who had faith would also surely do good works—even as it was not the good works themselves that produced the ultimate salvation but necessarily the other way around. As he wrote, the "just have faith and every work will flow from you naturally" (Wannenwetsch 2003, 128). As it says in the Lutheran Augsburg Confession of 1530, "In the power of the Spirit, faith renews the heart, and the renewed heart is clothed with new affects which, in turn, enable good works" (Wannenwetsch 2003, 129).

In his understanding of the Ten Commandments, Luther emphasized that it was the first commandment—"I am the Lord your God, you shall have no other Gods except me"—that stood before all the others, because the following of this commandment would by itself mean that a person had a full faith in God, and obedience to the remaining commandments would follow directly as a matter of course. As Bernd Wannenwetsch explains, "Luther's emphasis on the First Commandment is the strongest possible guard against the temptation that fulfilling the [other] commandments would be an achievement" expected to influence God's judgments favorably. Rather, even if all the other commandments were obeyed, as God had revealed these laws to Moses at Mt. Sinai, it would not mean justification in the eyes of God for the believer. Once faith exists (i.e., the first commandment is followed), however, "the very way in which the [remaining] individual commandments are followed, by individual acts of hand and mouth and body, is merely a mechanical and formal obedience to God." A true Christian's life must be "in the first place, a matter of the heart (i.e. of faith). This is why the Christian life does not fall apart into a 'spiritual' sphere on the one hand and a 'worldly' sphere on the other" (Wannenwetsch 2003, 123). In contrast to so much modern thinking about religion, for the Lutheran faithful, there can be no separate realms of the private religious conscience and the individual's actions in the outside political and economic world.

Scott Hendrix, the Princeton Theological Seminary professor of Reformation history, similarly explains that for Lutherans, "good works were expected from believers because beneficial deeds always followed genuine faith." He observes that "Luther wrote that faith was 'a living, busy, active mighty thing' that was incessantly doing works without asking whether they should be done or not. 'It is impossible,' he said, 'to separate works from faith, quite as impossible as to separate heat and light from fire." The devout understood Luther as saying, "'You are saved by faith alone and not by good works, but you should be doing good works nonetheless. They do not [assure] salvation but they are necessary for living as a Christian.' That was the first nuance: good works were necessary [to right living], but not necessary [or sufficient] for salvation" (Hendrix 2010, 50).

This way of thinking created, however, a difficult balancing act for a good Lutheran. If a person performed good works, it could well mean that this person first had true faith and thus was among the saved in the eyes of God, and the good works then necessarily followed. It could also mean, however, that the person simply wanted to be convinced of his own faith and thus of his own salvation, the actual motive for performing the good works. But if the good works were done as an expedient meant to bring about a confident expectation of salvation (and not simply as a spontaneous personal expression of human love and friendship as the natural outcome of true faith), this would mean turning back to the Roman Catholic falsehood that good works actually could contribute to salvation and that human actions thus can influence the actions of God, detracting from His total grandeur and omnipotence. If the very theological essence of the Reformation was to be upheld, faith therefore must come first, and its existence for each person must remain in the hands of God alone, predestined prior to his or her birth.

On closer logical inspection, however, it could not be this simple. A deep desire for personal salvation, even if first expressed in the performance of good works for this purpose, could in itself be taken as a good indication of a true faith in God (otherwise, why worry about salvation?). From this perspective, the devoted Lutheran pursuit of good works might easily be taken to mean the prior existence of faith. But there is a virtual contradiction arising here: good works in themselves cannot assure salvation, but devoutly doing good works in itself can be taken to demonstrate the presence of genuine faith, and thus the good works can actually assure salvation, contradicting the original premise. It has often been said of Luther that he was a less logical and systematic thinker than Calvin. Much of his vast body of writings was for polemical purposes at the height of theological and political controversies. Diarmaid McCulloch, professor of the history of the church at Oxford University, writes that "Luther was a passionate, impulsive man, who felt his theology rather than beginning with logical questions and answers about God, resulting in a theology full of paradoxes and even contradictions" (MacCulloch 2004, 115).

Lutherans were not exempt from the existential dread experienced by Calvinists with respect to their potentially slim prospects for salvation;

Luther was equally committed to full predestination and to a doubt that the saved will be among the majority. For many Lutherans as well as Calvinists, however, it was difficult to live with the idea that they might simply have been predestined to eternal damnation independent of the lives they lived and for reasons of which they could have no knowledge. How could a loving God be so seemingly harsh and arbitrary? Luther himself had no good explanation, other than that God was all powerful and His ways were known to Himself alone. This must necessarily be true according to the longstanding Jewish and Christian understanding of God in the book of Job and elsewhere—but by emerging modern standards of thought, it was difficult to accept.

Weber had conjectured that devout Calvinists would therefore have found it psychologically necessary to look at least for signs that they were among the saved, as could be indicated by success in a worldly calling, even if such signs could not offer any guarantees. One might expect that a similar psychological dynamic would be at work in the lives of the Lutheran faithful as well. Luther had, after all, declared that the saved would be naturally impelled to perform good works. So, probabilistically, some percentage of those performing good works would in fact be among the Lutheran saved, even if this exact percentage and the ultimate fate of each specific individual in the hereafter remained known only to God. Equally important, and going in this respect beyond Calvinism, if a Lutheran did not perform good works, it logically followed from Luther's teachings that he could not have true faith and thus could not be among the saved. So the psychological and religious imperative for a good Lutheran—even greater than for a good Calvinist—was overwhelmingly in favor of pursuing a calling that involved doing good works.

Lutheran Ethical Challenges to Capitalism

Despite this common element, there remained, however, a large area of difference between the Calvinist and Lutheran ethics and related concepts of a valid calling that might have large political and economic consequences. Calvinists were encouraged to find their callings in worldly matters, such as the conduct of business affairs, even though they should not immorally spend any large profits resulting from business success in the pursuit of their own luxurious living. Luther's view of the world of business was much more fundamentally skeptical and even antagonistic. Indeed, Luther was often outwardly hostile to the commercial developments of his own times that were setting the stage for the rise of capitalism in Europe. As Carter Lindberg, the Boston University professor of church history, writes, "Luther found the calculating entrepreneur extremely distasteful. He was convinced that the capitalist spirit divorced money from use for human needs and necessitated an economy of acquisition." As a result, Luther routinely "preached and wrote against the expanding money economy as a great sin" (Lindberg 2003, 172–73). Success in business for a good Lutheran thus was unlikely to be seen as a promising sign for salvation; indeed, it might more likely portend the opposite.

As he describes Luther's thinking, Lindberg comes close at times to finding an outlook characteristic of modern socialism with its past historic antagonism toward capitalism. Lindberg finds that "Luther's concern was not only about an individual's use of money, but also the structural social damage inherent in the idolatry of the 'laws' of the market." Any ideas of an "impersonal market" or "autonomous laws of economics"—such as long found at the heart of capitalist apologetics—would have been "abhorrent to Luther." For Luther, long before the 2008 financial crisis, the community was "endangered by the rising power of a few great financial centers; their unregulated economic coercion would destroy the ethos of the community." This mean that "early capitalism was doubly dangerous because it not only exploited people but also strove to conceal its voracious nature and to deceive people" behind various false claims of public benefit such as Adam Smith would later advance. Hence governments should be wary of such claims and should learn how to recognize them; this led Luther to appeal "for government regulation of interest rates and business practices" (Lindberg 2003, 173).

Luther rejected any basic assumption that self-interest could play a legitimate role as a main organizing force in society. He thus would have strongly objected to a main premise of the *Wealth of Nations*—the pursuit of self-interest as an "invisible hand" that worked to advance the human condition in the world. Indeed, the invisible hand is increasingly seen by contemporary historians of economic thought as actually having implicitly meant for Smith an invisible hand of God (Oslington 2012). By contrast, concerning one of Luther's early writings on commercial ethics, Sean Doherty (2014) writes that for Luther, "self-interest is always wrong. Luther eschews all syntheses of self-love and neighbor-love," even as this blending of the two remains at the heart of mainstream economics today. Doherty explains that Luther condemns "many economic practices" of his own day as masking "vested interests and avarice" that violate God's commands. While there is no grand conspiracy, it is nevertheless the case that for Luther, those who write about "financial matters tend to be *deliberately* obscure, and this opacity is a camouflage for duplicity"—not unlike McCloskey's assessment of the scientifically camouflaged writings of the present-day economics profession, although she has a much more favorable assessment of the results of capitalism than Luther did.

The apologists for the private marketplace, Luther thought, follow a convoluted "logic which justifies greedy behavior," all the while ignoring the contrary "commands of Jesus [that] are refreshingly clear." As Luther thus considers, "trust in the gospel may appear naïve, but true naivety would be an uncritical acceptance of economic claims" as put forth by those who rationalize the economic system (Doherty 2014, 67). It all sounds rather similar to public debates today (think of current economic policy differences within the Democratic Party in the United States) and also to attitudes widely held in the Nordic world in the twentieth century. The language has changed radically, but the content may be surprisingly little altered even over five hundred years, reflecting the fact that the core issues dealt with by contemporary economics are normative and religious and often do not change in their essential character, even as they have frequently been disguised implicitly in more recent times in scientific economic language. We encounter again what has been a familiar refrain in the career of Deirdre McCloskey.

A Lutheran Ethic of Social Welfare

What was most radical about Luther was thus not the importance of doing good works but his transformed concept of the character of good works. Good works not only differed among Lutherans and Calvinists, but the good works of the Catholic Church had typically focused on things that would serve the church itself. In one extreme case that incurred Luther's particular wrath, the payment of indulgences, one form of good works, was designed to fill the coffers of the Roman church. But more broadly, the Catholic Church had long promised the faithful that their prospects of salvation could be enhanced (or perhaps even guaranteed) by making monetary donations, performing services, and making contributions of many other kinds to the church. Hendrix describes a range of such longstanding forms of Catholic good works, including "collecting relics and depositing them in local shrines, promising miracles and indulgences to believers who made pilgrimages to those shrines, adding alters to specific saints that attracted more devoted worshippers than the main alter where Mass was celebrated, endowing fraternities in the name of saints and hiring priests to say special Masses for themselves and their relatives" (Hendrix 2010, 50). The practice of confession offered numerous avenues for encouraging the faithful to perform acts of penance in ways that would be practically beneficial to the church.

The Reformation, however, meant the abolition of most of this. For a good Lutheran, good works should be actively done by all people and should aim to serve all people, not be performed especially for the benefit of the church itself. Luther thus called for the faithful to devotedly serve the welfare of their fellow human beings, beginning with the villages and other communities where they actually lived. The monastic orders of monks and nuns also showed their devotion to God—and contributed to their own prospects of salvation—by building church structures and living in ways that kept them separate from the main body of the community. Here again, Luther's revolution in theology and church practice, with its new emphasis on the priesthood of all believers, swept this aside. Luther's efforts were admittedly abetted by the possibility created for rulers such as Henry VIII in England and Gustaf Adolphus in Sweden to confiscate large amounts of church property—the products of past Catholic acts of good works—for their own use and benefit. In England, by some estimates a third of the land in the nation had been owned by the Catholic Church prior to Henry's secession from Rome in 1534; this fact is itself a testimony to centuries of lay donations and other historical offerings to the church in fulfillment of the longstanding religious obligations expected of good Catholics.

For Luther in his time, as Hendrix explains, "the opposite of faith was idolatry," as seen in worship of "other gods of any stripe—idols made with hands, other human beings, noble ideals, or material goods," much as modern life today seems to offer in abundance. Those who had true faith in God, however, would surely pursue "all the genuine good works that were directed outward toward the neighbor in obedience to the remaining [nine] commandments. These good works were not religious activities," as was the common understanding in the Roman Catholic Church, but involved "the dedication of one's public and private lives to charity, honesty, sympathy, encouragement, aid, and justice" to the benefit of the full community itself (Hendrix 2010, 51). Doherty sums this up well: "Based on this theological account of [civil] authority, Luther argues that it has a pro-active role in actively assisting the needy. Government's role is not construed minimally or solely negatively (to restrain wickedness). It also carries responsibility for doing and promoting good. Hence, care for the needy is not a private affair left at one's personal discretion, but a public, collective responsibility" of civil government (Doherty 2014, 69). For Luther, this must be achieved not by any forceful or revolutionary means but by the continuing spread in society of faith in God to more and more people in each nation and, in the end, throughout the world.

A further important Catholic form of good works was charity—almsgiving—to the poor. As Lindberg remarks, the many biblical messages declaring "God's preferential option for the poor gave them a decided edge in the pilgrimage to salvation (the rich can no more squeeze through the eye of a needle into heaven than can a camel). On the other hand, the [Catholic] church had long emphasized that almsgiving atones for sin." This form of good works created a symbiotic relationship, as "almsgiving provided the poor with some charity, enabled the rich to atone for their sins, and blessed the rich with the intercessions of the poor." It was said that "God could have made all men rich, but he wanted poor men in this world, so that the rich might have an opportunity to redeem their sins" (Lindberg 2003, 171).

The Calvinist ethic, by contrast, encouraged the poor to escape poverty, to improve themselves by the pursuit of an individual calling that, one could hope, would frequently result in some form of worldly success. In one respect, the Lutheran ethic was closer to the Catholic understanding in that it encouraged direct support for the poor, but this assistance should be the responsibility of the entire community, not a special responsibility of the rich themselves. For Luther, being poor was not a desirable state in and of itself; indeed, it was a condition to be overcome with hard work. The differing Catholic expectation of charity from the rich to benefit a permanent class of the poor has led in many Catholic nations to a lasting greater social stratification of rich and poor (Castles 1994). It was in Protestant nations that general public education was first introduced in the nineteenth century; even today, the nations of Catholic Latin America lag well behind in the quality of public education provided for the broad masses of the people.

In Argentina, Juan Perón built a lasting political movement based in significant part on pursuing policies of public charity and other government assistance for the masses. In the Lutheran welfare states of the north, by contrast, an emphasis was placed on education, good health care, job training, and other means of improving the future prospects of the poor. While the Nordic countries achieved some of the lowest levels of income inequality in the world in the twentieth century, Latin American countries had some of the highest (Nelson 2007).

Luther himself not only preached a message of communal care for the needy but was involved locally in its practical application. In Wittenberg, beginning in 1522, he helped establish a "common chest" for welfare work. Lindberg writes that it "was a new creation of the Reformation that transformed theology into social praxis," including the assumption in Wittenberg of responsibilities for "care of the sick and elderly in hospitals, a medical office for the poor whose doctor, Melchior Fendt, established prophylactic measures in times of hunger and inflation, and support of communal schools" (Lindberg 2003, 172). Such ideas and methods soon spread beyond Wittenberg to other Reformation cities. While Luther preached a religious ethic of greater concern for others than oneself, he was also well aware that trust could not be unlimited and that helping others required disciplined efforts to ensure that poverty did not become a permanent condition. As Doherty explains,

> It is worth noting the effective practical implications of this aspect of Luther's thought in the common chest arrangements which he supervised. These reflect his so-called realism. Contributions were personal but mandatory. Recipients of disbursements were vetted to ensure that they were genuinely impoverished. Money from the chest was usually given to alleviate short term need, for example, if crops had been poor. Newcomers were given money to launch themselves in trade, or to tide them over while seeking employment. Recipients could not become perpetually dependent, unless they could not work for a strong reason such as age or illness. The intention was to foster a culture of local accountability, preventing abuses. (Doherty 2014, 69)

Luther himself, as Doherty elaborates, does not press for the actual "enactment of the Sermon on the Mount" by means of the public measures of the civil authorities. Nevertheless, "his vision of the integrity of earthly justice yields far broader and higher standards than his disapproval" in other contexts of the German princes "ruling the world with the gospel" might have suggested. For civil rulers, as Luther sees it, their "purpose and calling are to govern in accordance with God's will, to secure justice, and to provide for the needy" (Doherty 2014, 66–68). Although many German princes and their subjects failed to live up to such ideals, following after Luther's teachings and example, this would become at least in concept a guiding principle of the Lutheran state churches of the Nordic countries that followed the Reformation—and thus a future guiding principle for all of Nordic society.

As Pirjo Markkola and Ingela Naumann explain, "For many centuries, the Lutheran churches had a hegemonic status and the clergy represented both the state and the church in local communities"—functioning as local Nordic theocracies in which the normative values of the Lutheran clergy were the values of the state as locally present (Markkola and Naumann 2014, 1). Five hundred years later, Luther's original teaching of using the state to advance the interests of one's neighbors, not of oneself, remained a prominent feature of the culture of the Nordic social democracies, with their unusually powerful sense of the social solidarity of all the people of the nation.

In 1998, Harvard University sociologist Aage Sorensen thus found that in the twentieth century, the Nordic social democratic ethic could be traced to Lutheran influences centuries earlier. As he wrote, "The generosity of the welfare state system" in the Nordic countries depended in the twentieth century on "the prevalence of beliefs in the efficacy of rules and intentions." In many other non-Nordic societies, they were characterized by higher levels of "opportunism," "rule-violation," and "rent-seeking." If such ways of thinking had prevailed in the Nordic countries, the unusually generous Nordic welfare state would have rapidly broken down under the pressure of a growing popular tendency to exploit it for individual private gain (something Sorensen fears may now actually be a growing danger even within the Nordic world itself; Sorensen 1998, 364–65).

Seeking to trace the origins of Nordic social solidarity, Sorensen examines how "basic elements were created in 18th century absolutism and its spiritual support system Lutheran Pietism." It was the "conflation of autocratic and militaristic regimes with Pietism that created an emphasis on education, and support for the poor, orphaned and infirm that is quite consistent with the objectives and concerns of the modern welfare state." Pietism in the Nordic countries typically saw itself as a new Reformation, amounting to a "Second Reformation," within the Lutheran church itself, a revival of the true message of Luther that had been frequently lost in the intervening centuries to be replaced by an increasingly arid—indeed, often a scholastic—version of Lutheranism. As Sorensen writes, it was the newly Pietistic eighteenth-century Lutheran state church "model for the relationship between king and subject that was to become the model for the relationship between state and citizen in the modern Scandinavian welfare state. It is a relationship of obedience and respect for the good intentions of the ruler and his agents, who want to help and support those in need" (Sorensen 1998, 364).

Unlike the Calvinist ethic of individual worldly success, the Lutheran ethic thus substitutes adherence to the Golden Rule in the daily affairs of life. This Lutheran ethic was still alive and well in the reformed Lutheranism of the eighteenth-century Nordic world and continued to be influential throughout the nineteenth century in its explicitly religious forms. By the mid-twentieth century, however, it had been transformed at least outwardly to become a secular belief system; the Lutheran ethic was still present and providing the requisite normative glue for Nordic society, but it now was implicit. Officially, social science and especially economics guided the public and private course of Nordic social democracy, reflecting a Nordic climate of increasing skepticism and even antagonism toward traditional religious beliefs. But this popular distancing of Nordic culture from religion was an illusion; the powerful Lutheran values underlying Nordic social democracy had instead been camouflaged, disguised in various forms of ostensibly more "scientific" thinking. McCloskey had similarly argued in 1983 that economics offers powerful social values and a guiding social philosophy (a secular religion, if you will) disguised as science (McCloskey 1983).

Recently, the continuing presence of a special Nordic ethic of trust and compassion toward others was illustrated in one specific case by a journalistic experiment in which 192 wallets containing money and identifying information were intentionally dropped in 2013—as though they had been lost—in sixteen cities around the world. In Helsinki (the only Nordic city studied), eleven out of the twelve dropped wallets were returned to the owners, the highest such rate in the world. In total, about half the dropped wallets were returned worldwide; when people were asked why they had done so, a common answer was a strong sense of personal sympathy for the individual wallet owner—a modern application of the Golden Rule. In societies apparently not sharing that sentiment as widely, at the bottom of the list were such cities as Lisbon (1 of 12 wallets returned); Madrid (2 of 12); Prague (3 of 12); and Rio de Janeiro, Bucharest, and Zurich (4 of 12)—none in historically Lutheran countries (Readers' Digest 2013). Some of the Finns returning the wallets expressed pride in serving a national culture of honesty and trustworthiness. It is a common view recently expressed by the winner of the Nobel Peace Prize in 2008 for his efforts to resolve international conflicts in Kosovo and elsewhere, former Finnish president Martti Ahtisaari. He believes and preaches to his fellow citizens that "the Finnish attribute [that] is the most conducive to generating personal and professional success . . . is Finnish honesty and trustworthiness" (quoted in Chaker 2011, 216).

The Lutheran Roots of Nordic Social Democracy

In her more recent books, *The Bourgeois Virtues: Ethics for an Age of Commerce* and *Bourgeois Dignity: Why Economics Can't Explain the Modern World*, Deirdre McCloskey explores the normative foundations of capitalism. What she is examining in significant part are the "bourgeois virtues" and the "bourgeois dignity" associated with the evolution of the Calvinist ethic. Calvinism, however, had much less of an impact on the Nordic world than it had on much of the rest of the Protestant world. In the Nordic world, it was the Lutheran ethic that shaped the Nordic version of the modern world. It is equally true in this particular case that economics "can't explain the Nordic world," but the actual driving "virtues" and the actual driving sense of "dignity" of the Nordic world are Lutheran, not Calvinist.

Nordic scholars have been acknowledging more frequently in recent years that powerful normative forces were necessary to sustain the Nordic welfare state of the twentieth century. This partly reflects a new level of introspection in light of a perceived waning of Nordic public confidence in the long-run future of its welfare states. As the normative foundation of the Nordic welfare state has been threatened, it has created a new awareness of its existence and core values—previously simply taken for granted—and of its vital importance for the healthy functioning of the welfare state. In 2005, for example, an edited book collection appeared, titled *Normative Foundations of the Welfare State: The Nordic Experience*. The Norwegian editors, Nanna Kildal and Stein Kuhnle, explain that "the current external and internal challenges to the moral structures of welfare states have given normative analyses and normative theory in welfare research a more important role than has so far been the case" in the mainstream scholarship of the Nordic welfare state. They recall that in the past, "normative analyses did not swell the ranks of welfare research publications during the Nordic 'golden age' of public welfare expansion" from the 1940s to the 1970s. Over the past two decades, however, "publications on welfare issues have been increasingly raising questions about the norms and values that are embedded in welfare policies." This is becoming more urgent in the twenty-first century because in the "assessment of several minor and larger, more or less incremental or casual, welfare reforms during recent decades, studies of the more or less hidden governing values and principles in welfare policies are crucial for any interpretations, justifications or rejections of them" (Kildal and Kuhnle 2005, 2–3).

Kildal and Kuhnle thus acknowledge that key values underlying Nordic social democracy and the welfare state have often been unacknowledged or "hidden." As a result, as one might say, key welfare state values remained for the most part "implicit values." It was in a way like Christianity in medieval Europe, where there was little perceived need to examine closely the relevance or applicability of Christianity to the great issues of the time; that was simply automatic. The most influential religions of the twentieth century—the various forms of secular religion—often had a similar character. With their core values taken as virtual givens, secular religions were not even recognized explicitly as religions; they were regarded simply as core modern truths requiring little further elaboration or justification. For many of these secular religions of the twentieth century, the central article of faith was that humanly guided scientific and economic progress—not the Christian God of old—will save the world.

Here again, times have been changing. The British Anglican vicar Edward Bailey launched a scholarly movement in the 1970s to study what he labeled as "implicit religion"—a term he preferred to the similar "secular religion" that he regarded as an oxymoron. As interest spread in his efforts, he founded the Centre for the Study of Implicit Religion and Contemporary Spirituality in 1995, began publishing the journal *Implicit Religion* in 1998, and held annual meetings in England for many years, where international scholars with related interests assembled (he died in 2015; Bailey 1990, 2009, 2010). Partly due to Bailey's efforts, there is now a chair in implicit religion at Cambridge

University. Bailey wrote in 2012 that "there is much to be gained if we recognize the presence of actual religions in modern life whose true religious tenets are mainly expressed in hidden and thus implicit ways" (Bailey 2012). Hence we may advance significantly in our understanding of the workings of modern society if we "apply something of what we now know about [traditional] religious life, to [study] ordinary secular life," where actual religion is often still powerfully present in disguised forms (Bailey 2012, 196). As McCloskey would say, the real religious message is hidden in the rhetoric.

Yet the strong tradition in the social sciences in the twentieth century of seeking to do "value-free" analysis has proven a large obstacle to doing careful research on the implicit religious values of the welfare state. When the driving historical role of values and culture is studied, these factors are typically regarded as important "inputs" (hence the term "social capital") into social outcomes. But with a few exceptions—almost none of them economists—social scientists mostly have lacked experience in the study of how the core values of a society are actually formed. This would require inquiry into the internal dynamics of the creation and evolution of religions, a subject that economists seemingly see as mainly for a theologian.

For much of the twentieth century, moreover, social science did not take religion very seriously at all, believing that its role in society was fading and might well disappear altogether in the longer run. In *Normative Foundations of the Welfare State* (Kildal and Kuhnle 2005), the subject of the possible large importance of religion in sustaining the Nordic welfare state seldom comes up, except in a chapter by Bo Strath. It is mostly taken for granted that the key powerful values underlying the Nordic welfare state are secular values such as social "equality" and the "universalism" of the provision of benefits by the Nordic state. Remarkably in light of the central role of Lutheran religion in shaping the Nordic world for many centuries, the historical fact of this pervasive Lutheran presence is rarely discussed (again, with the Strath chapter excepted). There are no entries for "Martin Luther" or "Lutheranism" in what is generally a comprehensive index.

To give another example of the continuing blind spot of surprisingly many Nordic social scientists when it comes to religion, it was still possible in 2013 for three Norwegian political scientists—Nik Brandal, Oivind Bratberg, and Dag Einar Thorsen—to write an intellectual history of Nordic social democracy, beginning with developments in the nineteenth century, and include only a brief mention of Nordic religion and essentially nothing about the large influence of Lutheranism itself. Ironically, their book, *The Nordic Model of Social Democracy*, is itself a strong implicit religious statement, in this case of the secularized Lutheranism that was the actual religion of twentieth-century social democracy (Brandal et al. 2013).

As one might conjecture, the Nordic scholarly neglect of the large role of Lutheranism in the rise and functioning of social democracy in the twentieth century may well have been deliberate, an implicit way of effectively saying that social democracy is built on a newly modern foundation of objective scientific truth that has transcended the past ignorance and biases of traditional religion. Since the implicit religion of social democracy seeks the secular salvation of the world in "progress," it is important to be able to assert that the forward march of progress extends to matters of religion as well—that the new social democratic understanding of society has left the old religions behind as it marches forward into a glorious new progressive future. To explicitly acknowledge the continuing powerful presence of the Lutheran heritage might be disconcerting if not distressing.

Brandal et al. describe how in the early history of Nordic social democracy there was often a large element of "socialist utopianism"—what Bailey would call an implicit religion (Brandal et al. 2013, 107, 180). This was partly a reflection of the significant Marxist influence on the development of European social democracy in the first decades of the twentieth century. Many millions were attracted to the idea that the class struggle would lead to a perfect world under a state of true communism; it would be heaven on earth, a secularization of longstanding millennial hopes and expectations of Christianity. Indeed, Luther in his own time was firmly convinced that the last days with Christ finally returning to earth would be arriving soon. The millennial expectations among many of the communist—and early social democratic—faithful were almost as optimistic with respect to the near-term prospects for a new heaven on earth.

As has happened to many previous millennial expectations, the bleak history of the first half of the twentieth century dashed any such hopes. Brandal et al. thus warn that social democrats today should be careful to avoid their old mistake in their earliest days of tending "to err on the side of naïveté rather than cynicism" (Brandal et al. 2013, 123). But the underlying economic determinism of Marxism and other "economic religions" survived in less utopian forms, perhaps nowhere more so than in the social democracies of the Nordic world, outwardly among the most "secular" of societies. While cautioning against excessive optimism, Brandal et al. write that for both the left and right "ends of the political spectrum, it is imperative that the economy, by historical necessity, constitutes the driving force behind societal developments" toward a much better future. Having shed their Marxist roots, Nordic social democrats believed from the 1930s onward that "democratically elected parliaments could and should regulate the economy, in order to create an improved society and a better world" (Brandal et al. 2013, 183). Political management of the economy, following the advice of economic experts, and a large role for private enterprise under tight state oversight would be key to a continuing Nordic march of progress.

Instead of the old naïve utopianism, Brandal et al. thus suggest that Nordic social democrats should present themselves to the world as "moderate optimists who—in spite of everything—believe that it is possible to work systematically for a better world in gradual steps, thinking through how the world works at the moment, and how it could be improved and better organized." There should nevertheless be no abandoning of the fundamental "social democratic perception of the world [that it] is one of continuous progress," even if no culminating end state to progress can be specified in any detail. Yet since World War II, Brandal et al. find that, as experience has shown, there is "no doubt that the world is a better place . . . as a result of systematic and consistent work for a better future." We can expect continuing progress to further advance "basic values that point out the direction in which we ought to be headed. The pursuit of democracy and decent living conditions for all regardless of status and background is perhaps the clearest example" of the social democratic values whose realization will—seemingly more slowly than once expected—in the long run triumph and transform the world (Brandal et al. 2013, 122–23).

As Brandal et al. sum up, in such a social democratic vision for the future, "war, dictatorship, poverty and hunger are evils which will continue to be sources of human misery for the foreseeable future. But the struggle against these evils has merely just begun." Here their language does come close to the moral judgments of Luther, who also saw the world as filled with "evil" actions, and for Luther as well, we could expect a much better future in heaven if not on earth. As Brandal et al. write further, "Progressive ideas have been met with fierce resistance and great obstacles before." But there is no reason to abandon hope now; "the development of welfares states and democratic citizenship rights in Northern Europe in the years after the Second World War"—the years of Nordic social democratic political triumph—offers "a powerful reminder that people can through peaceful [democratic] means change their own lives and the world for the better, even under quite unfavorable circumstances," such as the continuing tensions of the Cold War and the harsh northern climate (Brandal et al. 2013, 123, 116).

Brandal et al. proclaim that Nordic social democrats must today spread the progressive word of past Nordic successes as an example to other parts of the world. Indeed, the encouragement and support for such a global progressive faith will be a necessary element in the long-run worldwide success of the progressive cause. Without this core faith, it will be impossible to sustain the national solidarity in other parts of the world that has been so essential to the Nordic model of social democracy. Indeed, at times Brandal et al. come surprisingly close to suggesting that the progressive heaven on earth will be attained "by faith alone." Without faith in its values and methods, the social democratic cause is hopeless; with faith, the future is assured. The Nordic progressive God of the twentieth century apparently still bears some important resemblances to the God of Martin Luther five hundred years ago.

Brandal and his two fellow Norwegian political scientists thus write that social democracy is "an *international* movement because it believes that its most basic ideas and demands are of a universal nature." As a result, its "values therefore ought to be equally appreciated across the globe." This reflects the social democratic conviction "that solidarity across borders, and between different people and cultures, is a necessary precondition for the development of a better and more peaceful world." Although the final goal is a true international solidarity of all peoples everywhere—in which national boundaries would be minimized or abolished—the practical realities today have meant that social democrats have "accepted and adopted the nation state as a useful and indeed necessary arena for the exercise [and spread] of democracy in the modern world" (Brandal et al. 2013, 109). The long-run objective nevertheless remains "supranational and intergovernmental cooperation" among all nations. Modern history has shown that nationalism all too easily leads to large divisions and excesses among human beings that were among the leading causes of the many evils of the twentieth century.

Despite their disavowals, it is apparent that an implicit utopianism still lies behind the hopes of Brandal et al. for a future perfection of human life on earth. (Like most earlier socialists and other progressives, they have little to say about nonhuman life.) Here again, the actual roots of Nordic social democracy are to be found in the Lutheran heritage of the Nordic countries. Indeed, it is not only Lutheranism but all of Christianity that seeks to offer universal truths for all human beings. Christianity must transcend national aspirations to serve the community of the world. It shares this missionary zeal with Islam—another Abrahamic religion—but otherwise such a goal has not been typical of religions outside the West. China, for example, has never exhibited a powerful drive to perfect the rest of the world in a Chinese mold. Following the Enlightenment, however, the missionary tradition of Christianity would often be absorbed by new implicit forms of Christianity such as Marxism and socialism—and in the Nordic countries, a new state church of social democracy in which Brandal et al. are true believers.

Some "McCloskeys" of the Nordic World

As elsewhere, however, change is in the air in the Nordic world. They have not been as systematic in their efforts as Deirdre McCloskey, but some students of Nordic history and society have been seeking to move beyond the disciplinary boundaries of the contemporary university to include religion in its diverse forms as an important historical factor and in general to escape the tight limitations of conventional secular modes of thought that dominated Nordic intellectual discourse for much of the twentieth century.

As recently as 2008, it was possible for the German sociologist of religion Michael Opielka to write that "little research exists reflecting the religious foundations of welfare states." The usual view of students of the welfare state—including the Nordic social democracies—had long been "to avoid treating religion as an external variable of decision makers or national cultures, or even as an independent variable belonging at the centre of social policy analysis." As a result, "cultural or religious factors have seldom played a role in comparative research on the welfare state" (Opielka 2008, 98). This began to change, however, about twenty-five years ago, around the same time that McCloskey's work began to receive growing attention.

In calling for change, Opielka argues, moreover, that the impact of religion on the welfare state goes well beyond that of traditional Catholic and Protestant religions, reflecting a "growing awareness of the complexity and plurality of religions in the sociology of religion and in the sciences of religion" that has expanded the concept of "religion" beyond "the traditional quintet or septet of world religions—Christianity, Islam, Judaism, Buddhism, and Hinduism, plus Confucianism and Daoism." Opielka agrees with the 1970s understanding of the American sociologist Talcott Parsons that "religion is the social subsystem which organizes, through 'ultimate values,' the society's relations to an 'ultimate reality" (Opielka 2008, 100–101). This is partly because a closer analysis almost invariably shows that "behind elaborated [contemporary] political and ideological values one always finds a realm of religious values" of some kind or another—often misleadingly described by twentieth-century writers as "secular" (Van Oorschot et al. 2008, 14).

The appearance in 1997 of *The Cultural Construction of Norden* was something of an intellectual breakthrough in Nordic history (Sorensen and Strath 1997). A chapter by the Finnish historian Henrik Stenius was titled "The Good

Life Is a Life of Conformity: The Impact of Lutheran Tradition on Nordic Political Culture" (Stenius 1997, 162). Opening up new avenues for social inquiry, the editors Oystein Sorensen and Bo Strath write that "it is not particularly difficult to imagine the social democrats as a secularized Lutheran movement"; indeed, as they summarized matters, a main conclusion of the book was that in the Nordic world of the twentieth century, "social democracy [is] a continuation/transformation of Lutheranism" (Sorensen and Strath 1997, 13, 5). In another chapter, the Norwegian theologian Dag Thorkildsen writes that "the two pillars of the welfare state have been full employment and social security. These two pillars correspond with two central ideas in Lutheranism: daily work as the fulfillment of God's vocation, and a priesthood of all believers. The idea of full employment may be seen as [a Nordic] secularization of the [traditional Lutheran] emphasis on the importance of daily work, which was reinforced during the periods of Pietism and revivalism" in the eighteenth and nineteenth centuries (Thorkildsen 1997, 159).

University of Helsinki sociologist Risto Alapuro wrote a year later that "after the Reformation . . . there was no rivalry between the state and the church and no protest movement from below," as all the Nordic nations ended up with top-down Lutheran state churches. This continued into the twentieth century to a surprising extent as "the role of the Lutheran tradition in the development of the welfare state" continued in new ways. As Alapuro writes, "A new 'secularized Lutheranism' in the form of the social democratic parties continued the Lutheran tradition in the construction of the welfare state" (Alapuro 1998, 377).

The Nordic scholars Jon Kvist, Johan Fritzell, Bjorn Hvinden, and Olli Kangas wrote in 2012 that two core social values were central to the functioning of the Nordic welfare states in the twentieth century. One is a "passion for equality" that lies behind the Nordic commitment "to provide uniform income protection and access to high-quality services and to a considerable extent, even for the system of [nationally conducted] collective bargaining about wages and occupational benefits." A second core Nordic value has been "a passion for work," which "is broadly seen as a goal in itself. . . . Having a job is understood as being the key to achieving autonomy and emancipation" (Kvist et al. 2012, 6–7). These are not, to be sure, new values in the Nordic world. As Thorkildsen writes, Lutheranism "promoted a culture of equality, where obvious wealth and large social differences were not acceptable because fundamentally all individuals are equal and have the same worth" in society (Thorkildsen 1997, 159). The powerful Nordic sense of social solidarity has its roots in the Lutheran ethic.

In *Religion, Class Coalitions, and Welfare States*, the Dutch political scientist Kees Van Kersbergen and the German political economist Philip Manow examine how the European welfare state has taken characteristically different forms according to whether the historic religion of a nation is Roman Catholic, Lutheran, or Reformed Protestant (Van Kersbergen and Manow 2009). American political scientist Karen Anderson observes in the same volume that "religion as an explanatory variable is conspicuously absent in most accounts of the historical development of the Scandinavian welfare states," a gap she now seeks to help fill in a chapter titled "The Church as Nation? The Role of Religion in the Development of the Swedish Welfare State" (Anderson 2009, 210). As Sigrun Kahl sums up in the concluding chapter, the different forms of historic religion of a nation in Europe have "generated political consensus and affected the emergence of different welfare states—through the institutionalization of [different] religious doctrines into countries' poor relief systems, and the secularization of these institutions" in the development of national welfare states in correspondingly different ways according to the historic religion of a nation (Kahl 2009, 267; Kahl 2005). In another 2009 book, Anders Backstrom and Grace Davie conclude that Lutheranism offers the strongest form of religious support for the establishment of an all-encompassing welfare state, as reflected in the fact that "the Lutheran countries of Northern Europe, including Germany, were the first to develop systems of welfare and social insurance" in the late nineteenth and early twentieth centuries (Backstrom and Davie 2009, 5–6).

Roman Catholicism, by contrast, has often perceived the national welfare state as a secular challenge to its own longstanding history of church provision of social services, thus causing it to offer resistance and to seek to limit the process of welfare state expansion. If perhaps to a lesser degree, Calvinism has also been less congenial to the welfare state for similar reasons. This was much less of a factor in the Lutheran Nordic world, however, because the social democracies of the Nordic welfare state could easily step into the shoes of the former Lutheran state churches that date to the sixteenth century. All this lent support to the conclusion that "modernity does not necessarily entail the displacement of religion, but is more likely to mean a change in its form, function and content. 'Religious change' is therefore a more helpful label than 'secularization' when describing the position and role of religion and religious organizations in late modern European societies" (Pettersson 2009, 15).

Finally, and most recently, an important collection of writings on "Lutheranism and the Nordic Welfare States" came from a surprising source: a 2014 special issue of the American *Journal of Church and State* (published at Baylor University in Texas) guest edited by Ingela Naumann from Edinburgh University in Scotland and Pirjo Markkola from the University of Jyväskylä in Finland. The various articles, they write, affirm that "the Lutheran inheritance" has provided a key "cultural backdrop of welfare state development" in the Nordic countries (Markkola and Naumann 2014, 8–9). This growing body of scholarship, however, has thus far been read mainly by a limited number of professional specialists. The central role of the Lutheran heritage in shaping Nordic social democracies has not penetrated widely into Nordic public discussion or even into mainstream Nordic intellectual life—perhaps because it might have heretical implications for the religion of social democracy itself.

The new scholarship has also been long on descriptions of the mounting empirical evidence for a strong continuing Lutheran influence in the twentieth century and short on study of past and present Lutheran theology and the specific ways that the Lutheran theological heritage has been secularized in the twentieth century in forming Nordic social democratic thought and practice. In describing a "Lutheran ethic" and showing how it contrasts with a "Calvinist ethic," seeking to follow in the spirit of Max Weber, this chapter—and my forthcoming book—hope to move that discussion forward (Nelson 2015b).

Conclusion

Even as a greater recognition of the historical social and economic importance of religion began to develop toward the end of the twentieth century, few (if any) American economics, sociology, or history departments introduced the routine study of Christian religion as a part of their curricula. (A few individual students did, of course, enter into such studies for their own professional purposes.) Indeed, there might not have been any faculty members in these areas with the knowledge to teach theological history as a basis for examining its past and continuing important consequences for all of society. Within theology schools, it is the opposite: they have mostly focused on the history and conceptual issues within religion itself, seldom seeking to explore the profound political and economic consequences for contemporary America and Europe of historic religious beliefs and events—in earlier centuries and now continuing into our own time. Breaking down the artificial separations between the historical and social sciences and religious studies will be a large challenge to the strict disciplinary specializations (even theology has now become a "professional" field of its own) that today characterize the university world.

Although she has not entered deeply into the study of theology as part of her own investigations into economic history, the research and writings of Deirdre McCloskey provide an exemplary case of transcending disciplinary boundaries. She has also sought vigorously to penetrate surface appearances such as the pervasively overstated scientific claims (outside the area of the study of the natural world) of the modern era. McCloskey's career offers us a model that should now be more widely followed among economists, sociologists, historians, and others who wish to delve at the deepest level into modern political and economic history.

Notes

1. The remainder of this chapter is adapted from portions of Nelson (2015b).

References

Alapuro, Risto. 1998. "Comments on Sorensen's 'On King's, Pietism and Rent-Seeking in Scandinavian Welfare States.'" *Acta Sociologica* 41: 4.

Anderson, Karen M. 2009. "The Church as Nation? The Role of Religion in the Development of the Swedish Welfare State." In Van Kersbergen and Manow 2009.

Backstrom, Anders, and Davie, Grace (with Edgardh, Ninna, and Pettersson, Per), eds. 2009. *Welfare and Religion in 21st Century Europe: Volume 1, Configuring the Connections*. Burlington: Ashgate.

Backstrom, Anders, and Davie, Grace. 2009. "The WREP Project: Genesis, Structure and Scope." In Backstrom and Davie 2009.

Bailey, Edward. 1990. "Implicit Religion: A Bibliographical Introduction." *Social Compass* 37 (4): 483–98.

Bailey, Edward. 2009. "Implicit Religion." In Clarke 2009.

Bailey, Edward. 2010. "Implicit Religion." *Religion* 40 (4): 271–78.

Bailey, Edward. 2012. "Implicit Religion? What Might That Be?" *Implicit Religion* 15 (2): 195–207.

Basten, Christoph, and Betz, Frank. 2013. "Beyond Work Ethic: Religion, Individual and Political Preferences." *American Economic Journal: Economic Policy* 5 (3): 67–91.

Becker, Sascha O., and Woessmann, Ludger. 2009. "Was Weber Wrong? A Human Capital Theory of Protestant Economic History." *Quarterly Journal of Economics* 124 (2): 531–96.

Brandal, Nik, Bratberg, Oivind, and Thorsen, Dag Einer. 2013. *The Nordic Model of Social Democracy*. New York: Palgrave Macmillan.

Brown, Mackenzie D., ed. 1965. *Ultimate Concern: Tillich in Dialogue*. New York: Harper and Row.

Castles, Frances D. 1994. "On Religion and Public Policy, Does Catholicism Make a Difference?" *European Journal of Political Research* 25: 19–40.

Chaker, Andre Noel. 2011. *The Finnish Miracle*. Helsinki: Talentum.

Clarke, Peter B., ed. 2009. *The Oxford Handbook of the Sociology of Religion*. New York: Oxford University Press.

De Long, J. Bradford. 1988. "Productivity Growth, Convergence, and Welfare: Comment." *American Economic Review* 78: 5.

DeMartino, George, and McCloskey, Deirdre N., eds. 2015. *Oxford Handbook of Professional Economic Ethics*. Oxford: Oxford University Press.

Doherty, Sean. 2014. *Theology and Economic Ethics: Martin Luther and Arthur Rich in Dialogue*. Oxford: Oxford University Press.

Gorski, Philip S. 2003. *The Disciplinary Revolution: Calvinism and the Rise of the State in Early Modern Europe*. Chicago: University of Chicago Press.

Harrison, Peter. 2001. *The Bible, Protestantism and the Rise of Natural Science*. New York: Cambridge University Press.

Helliwell, John F., Layard, Richard, and Sachs, Jeffrey, eds. 2015. *World Happiness Report 2015*. New York: Sustainable Development Solutions Network.

Hendrix, Scott H. 2010. *Martin Luther*. Oxford: Oxford University Press.

Kahl, Sigrun. 2005. "The Religious Roots of Modern Poverty Policy: Catholic, Lutheran and Reformed Protestant Traditions Compared." *European Journal of Sociology* 46 (1): 91–126.

Kahl, Sigrun. 2009. "Religious Doctrines and Poor Relief: A Different Causal Pathway." In Van Keesbergen and Manow 2009.

Kildal, Nanna, and Kuhnle, Stein, eds. 2005. *Normative Foundations of the Welfare State: The Nordic Experience*. Oxford: Routledge.

Kildal, Nanna, and Kuhnle, Stein. 2005. "Introduction." In Kildal and Kuhnle 2005.

Kvist, Jon, Fritzell, Johan, Hvinden, Bjorn, and Kangas, Olli. 2012. "Changing Social Inequality and the Nordic Welfare Model." In Kvist, Fritzell, Hvinden, and Kangas 2012.

Kvist, Jon, Fritzell, Johan, Hvinden, Bjorn, and Kangas, Olli, eds. 2012. *Changing Social Inequality: The Nordic Welfare Model in the 21st Century*. Bristol: Policy Press.

Lindberg, Carter. 2003. "Luther's Struggle with Social-Ethical Issues." In McKim 2003.

MacCulloch, Diarmaid. 2004. *Reformation: Europe's House Divided, 1490–1700*. London: Penguin.

Markkola, Pirjo. 2000. "The Calling of Women: Gender, Religion and Social Reform in Finland, 1860–1920." In Markkola 2000.

Markkola, Pirjo, and Naumann, Ingela K. 2014. "Lutheranism and the Nordic Welfare States in Comparison." *Journal of Church and State* 56:1.

Markkola, Pirjo, ed. 2000. *Gender and Vocation: Women, Religion, and Social Change in the Nordic Countries, 1830–1940*. Helsinki: SKS/FLS.

McCloskey, Deirdre N. 2006. *The Bourgeois Virtues: Ethics for an Age of Commerce*. Chicago: University of Chicago Press.

McCloskey, Deirdre N. 2011. *Bourgeois Dignity: Why Economics Can't Explain the Modern World*. Chicago: University of Chicago Press.

McCloskey, Donald N. 1983. "The Rhetoric of Economics." *Journal of Economic Literature* 21 (2): 481–517.

McCloskey, Donald N. 1985. *The Rhetoric of Economics*. Madison: University of Wisconsin Press.

McKim, Donald K., ed. 2003. *The Cambridge Companion to Martin Luther*. New York: Cambridge University Press.

Nasaw, David. 2006. *Andrew Carnegie*. New York: Penguin.

Nelson, Robert H. 1987. "The Economics Profession and the Making of Public Policy." *Journal of Economic Literature* 25 (1): 49–91.

Nelson, Robert H. 1989. "The Office of Policy Analysis in the Department of the Interior." *Journal of Policy Analysis and Management* 8 (3): 395–410.

Nelson, Robert H. 1990. "Unoriginal Sin: The Judeo-Christian Roots of Ecotheology." *Policy Review* 53: 52–59.

Nelson, Robert H. 1991. *Reaching for Heaven on Earth: The Theological Meaning of Economics*. Lanham, MD: Rowman & Littlefield.

Nelson, Robert H. 2001. *Economics as Religion: From Samuelson to Chicago and Beyond*. University Park: Pennsylvania State University Press.

Nelson, Robert H. 2007. "The Philippine Economic Mystery." *Philippine Review of Economics* 44: 1.

Nelson, Robert H. 2010a. "Max Weber Revisited." In Pyysiainen 2010.

Nelson, Robert H. 2010b. *The New Holy Wars: Economic Religion versus Environmental Religion in Contemporary America*. University Park: Pennsylvania State University Press.

Nelson, Robert H. 2012. "Is Max Weber Newly Relevant? The Protestant-Catholic Divide in Europe Today." *Finnish Journal of Theology* (University of Helsinki) 5: 420–45.

Nelson, Robert H. 2015a. "Confessions of a Policy Analyst." In DeMartino and McCloskey 2015.

Nelson, Robert H. 2015b. *A Second Protestant Ethic: The Lutheran Ethic and the Spirit of Social Democracy in the Nordic Countries*. Unpublished manuscript.

Opielka, Michael. 2008. "Christian Foundations of the Welfare State: Strong Cultural Values in Comparative Perspective." In Van Oorschot, Opielka, and Pfau-Effinger 2008.

Oslington, Paul, ed. 2012. *Adam Smith as Theologian*. New York: Routledge.

Pettersson, Per. 2009. "Majority Churches as Agents of European Welfare: A Sociological Approach." In Backstrom, Davie, Edgardh, and Pettersson 2009.

Reader's Digest, press release, Reader's Digest online, September 14, 2013, http://www.rda.com/news/reader%E2%80%99s-digest-reveals-the-most-and-least-honest-cities-in-the-world-with-the-wallet-drop-project.

Pyysiainen, Ilkka, ed. 1010. *Religion, Economy, and Cooperation*. Berlin: Mouton de Gruyter.

Sorensen, Aage B. 1998. "On Kings, Pietism, and Rent-Seeking in Scandinavian Welfare States." *Acta Sociologica* 41 (4): 363–75.

Sorensen, Oystein, and Strath, Bo, eds. 1997. *The Cultural Construction of Norden*. Oslo: Scandinavian University Press.

Spolaore, Enrico, and Wacziard, Roman. 2013. "How Deep Are the Roots of Economic Development?" *Journal of Economic Literature* 51 (2): 325–69.

Stenius, Henrik. 1997. "The Good Life Is a Life of Conformity: The Impact of Lutheran Tradition on Nordic Political Culture." In Sorensen and Strath 1997.

Thorkildsen, Dag. 1997. "Religious Identity and Nordic Identity." In Sorensen and Strath 1997.

Wannenwetsch, Bernd. 2003. "Luther's Moral Theology." In McKim 2003.

Weber, Max. 2003 (1958). *The Protestant Ethic and the Spirit of Capitalism*. Translated by Talcott Parsons. Mineola, NY: Dover.

Van Kersbergen, Kees, and Manow, Philip, eds. 2009. *Religion, Class Coalitions, and Welfare States*. New York: Cambridge University Press.

Van Oorschot, Wim, Opielka, Michael, and Pfau-Effinger, Birgit, eds. 2008. *Culture and Welfare State: Values and Social Policy in Comparative Perspective*. Cheltenham: Edward Elgar.

5

Economics with Varying Values: McCloskey's Humanism and Fundamental Insights

JACK A. GOLDSTONE

Deirdre McCloskey is a remarkable scholar—a humanist in the social sciences, a true heir to Adam Smith, and a longtime friend. We have taken parallel journeys with some twists and turns but have ended up in a remarkably similar place in regard to our academic findings. That is a place of opposition to conventional economics—an insistence that ideas, liberty, and social relationships matter more than the accumulation of human or material capital in explaining long-term economic growth and, in particular, in explaining the onset of exponential economic growth that arose in nineteenth-century England and continues to transform the world.

It All Started in Chicago

It all started in Chicago, of course. I had just come to Northwestern University as an assistant professor in, of all places, the sociology department. Yet I had already come to realize that truth and wisdom, if they resided anywhere at all in the social sciences, were emerging in economic history. It was there that the rigorous reconstruction of the past was being undertaken, using both formal models and enormous efforts to wring witness from previously unexamined data. I had already been relying on new findings in demographic history and price history to fuel my understanding of long-term social change in Europe and Asia, so I joined Jonathan Hughes and Joel Mokyr, with students such as Avner Greif and John Nye, in the Northwestern Economic History Seminar.

Early in my first year, a young economist from Chicago named McCloskey came to talk about property rights in the medieval English village. Through data and theory he persuaded me that English peasants in the thirteenth and fourteenth centuries were perfectly rational utility maximizers and that the division of common fields and much else could be explained by using modern economics. I was both stunned and inspired to see, once again, the power of modern economics to explain even distant history. I have to say I think that both Deirdre and I have never let go of the fundamental belief that of all of modern economics, price theory and the "laws" of supply and demand remain the best guide to understanding material behavior in just about any time or place. Or, I should say, as long as the time and place of the economy or subunit examined is near equilibrium. Once we start trying to explain sharp departures from equilibrium or sustained out-of-equilibrium behavior, one has to expand the explanatory tool kit beyond price theory. It is in making that leap that McCloskey has been particularly insightful.

That introduction to McCloskey led to my being invited to one of the first "cliometrics" conferences in Iowa City, where Deirdre brought me to her home and we began our conversations about economics and history. And it was at that cliometrics meeting that I first developed my own ideas on price history and the link between urbanization and monetary velocity (Goldstone 1984) that fueled my lifelong interest in the meaning of prices and their relation to social life.

I should say that I started my intellectual life studying physics, where the use of mathematics and abstraction to explain reality is taken for granted. This was true to such an extent that I learned that imagining infinitely tall triangles with two ninety-degree angles at their base is how you analyze the light from incoming stars; that any sphere could be treated for examining electrical or gravitational forces as a dimensionless point; and that electrical circuits are best modeled in the imaginary number space, not the "real" one. So the idea that human beings and their interactions are best understood by models based on abstract utility maximization was never a stretch.

But there was a fundamental difference between economists and physicists, at least circa the 1980s. That is that physicists never lost sight of the need to constantly test their mathematical tools against their ability to predict and match reality; the mathematical elegance and sophistication of their tools was always a means to an end, never an end itself (well, perhaps string theory excepted). But in economics, the beauty of mathematical results was starting to take over, even if resting on flimsy, partial, or "stylized" facts. For example, mathematically, at equilibrium, the workers' wages should reflect their productivity, and if labor receives the bulk of income, the mean wage per person should reflect the gross domestic product per capita (GDP/capita). And so it was in the data in the United States from the 1950s through the 1970s. Then in the 1980s, things changed, and the link between productivity (which continued to grow) and wages (which stagnated) disappeared (Mishel and Gee 2012).

A physicist would look for a new model. Sociologists were quite clear about what happened; in the 1980s, unions were dismantled, supply chains became global, and thus changes in *social relationships* shifted the leverage from labor to capital, and the rewards of economic growth shifted likewise. A few economists noted the shift, of course, and started thinking of wages in terms of global disequilibrium, with workers in low-wage countries now competing directly with workers in high-wage countries for many kinds of work, holding down wages in the latter even as the highest-productivity work preferentially remained where there were higher wages.

Nonetheless, the belief that wages reflect productivity and GDP/capita, rather than an interaction between these economic factors and social relationships and bargaining power, remained—so much so that even in economic history, people were willing to look at real wage estimates for different places in the sixteenth to eighteenth centuries and read them off directly as indicating differences in the productivity and GDP/capita of entire societies (Allen 2001; Allen et al. 2011; Goldstone 2014). In my own work on the origins of revolutions in preindustrial societies, I, too, began looking first at material issues: real wages, urbanization, changes in social mobility, state fiscal dilemmas. Yet it became clear to me in the course of my research that however important these issues were, material factors alone could not explain why people would seek to overturn the entire social order of the societies in which they lived. That depended on *how* elites and rulers responded to these material issues and whether those responses were viewed as truly fair and compassionate or as hypocritical and unjust. Values, in other words, made the great difference, and so I argued that once social order had begun, in material terms, to break down and shift out of accustomed patterns, the solutions and changes that people would seek would be shaped by their ideas of justice, their values regarding on what basis social hierarchy should be constituted, and their beliefs about the nature of man's history and future. The forces making Robespierre, Napoleon, Lenin, and Stalin into world-historical figures were not their concern for the poor (largely lacking) or the economic crisis of their societies (a mere opportunity) but their desire to reshape the world according to certain values (Goldstone 1991a, 1991b).

What economists set aside, or took as unproblematic, was that people do not merely maximize their utility—an easy process to model assuming an abstract utility function—they maximize *subject to constraint*. Those constraints are their choice set as they perceive it and as they are able to effectively make those choices. In relatively stable equilibrium conditions, these constraints can largely be assumed to be constant, and therefore irrelevant to solving the problems of maximizing by choice within constraints. But if there is an extremely large shift in conditions, from one equilibrium set to an entirely different one, it is essential to ask, *What has changed the constraints*?

Values and Growth

Prior to 1800, for thousands of years, growth in GDP/capita in even the most advanced places in the world was generally from 0.2 percent to 0.5 percent per year, interrupted by decades or centuries of zero or negative growth. Then, between 1850 and 1950, this rate increased to a new steady state of first 1.0 percent and then 2.0 percent per year (Broadberry et al. 2015: fig. 11.02). This was not, as the long-term unified growth theorists would have it, a single, long-term process of accelerating growth (Galor 2011; Vries 2015). The data simply do *not* fit that model, as growth rates in GDP/capita before 1850 and after 1950 were fairly constant. Rather, what occurred was a change in equilibrium conditions, from an early equilibrium of very little growth in GDP/capita to one in which there obtained stable growth rates of GDP/capita that were about an order of magnitude greater.

Such a sudden change very clearly calls for an analysis of *how the constraints on choice changed*. Realizing this is what has led McCloskey, me, and a few other social scientists to focus on what values lay behind the choices people were making during this shift and how they could have changed in a way that would create an order-of-magnitude change in per capita growth rates (Mokyr 2002; Jacob 2014; Goldstone 2012).

The answer is laid out in spellbinding detail in McCloskey's trilogy on bourgeois values (McCloskey 2006, 2010, forthcoming 2016). She shows how between 1600 and 1800, in a slow but accelerating process, driven by reading, Reformation, revolt, and revolution (as she now puts it), bourgeois values shifted from being seen as petty, mean, and insignificant—by comparison with the aristocratic values of honor, generosity, military prowess, service to the monarch, and physical valor—to being seen as worthy and virtuous, and even providing much greater benefit to society as a whole.

There is, of course, a risk in this project of being badly misunderstood. McCloskey has always been a staunch defender of capitalism for the benefits it has brought to man- and womankind. The risk is being seen as the defender of "Gordon Gecko capitalism"—the individual accumulation of personal wealth regardless of the cost to other people or society as a whole. That is not at all what McCloskey intends. She is a true heir to Adam Smith in understanding capitalism as a system to produce wealth for "*the nation*," for what Smith would identify as the commonwealth as a whole.

Indeed, the essence of the power of capitalism driven by bourgeois values, as opposed to aristocratic systems or capitalist systems degraded by autocracy and oligarchy, is its ability to empower, tap, and reward the creativity and effort of *all* its members (citizens, in the bourgeois value mode). This is *not* just democracy—an exercise in voting whereby otherwise-powerless individuals and groups weigh in, at lengthy intervals, on who among the elites will exercise ultimate power. Rather, it depends on maintaining a liberal order in society, in which the powers of elites and government are constantly held in check and in which the exercise of free choice to create new products, new companies, and new sources of wealth, as well as access to the necessary ideas, information, and capital, are almost universally available.

The bourgeois values, as their history and character are developed by McCloskey, are not simply the individual pursuit of material wealth. That is greed—one of the cardinal sins and not a virtue. Rather, the bourgeois virtues are rooted in respect for the abilities and dignity of the common people, compassion for their faults, and a willingness to work together to overcome institutional and social obstacles to individual liberty. These values praise contracts and the law as a means to sustaining social order and thus as sacrosanct, not merely (as in aristocratic values) a means to control the poor and thus inapplicable to those in power. These values praise credit and property as means to improve efficiency, output, and social well-being over time, not (as in aristocratic values) as means to demonstrate one's prodigality and superiority over others. Perhaps most importantly, bourgeois values carry a belief in the possibility of continuous improvement, both of the individual's moral character and material well-being and of society's capacity to move toward ever-higher levels of health, welfare, and happiness for all, as opposed to the aristocratic, zero-sum worldview that values securing ever-larger portions of existing wealth and amassing (and denying others) positional goods.

As bourgeois values diffused throughout societies, those societies shifted their core activities from providing for the wealth and power and glory of a narrow elite to developing the abilities and opportunities of all citizens (through measures for public education and public health); from valuing war and display as primary goods, and production and improvement as secondary and merely necessary for the former, to valuing production and improvement as primary and war and display as regrettable and distasteful; and from disdaining innovation as costly and threatening to the social order and the established elites to valuing innovation as the fulfillment of humanity's destiny for ever-greater improvements in the human condition. In short, the adoption of bourgeois values changed everything and made the modern world possible.

Yet economists generally do not like to deal with values. They are hard to quantify and thus hard to model. Where quantification and modeling have become ends in themselves and the test of the validity of theory, resistance to a theory of social change rooted in values is understandable. But that does not make it right—especially when the quantification and modeling by itself offers little toward understanding the cause of the order-of-magnitude change in the growth of GDP per capita.

Humanism Plus Economics = Something More

So how did McCloskey manage to arrive at the answer to this riddle and sustain a three-volume analysis of a shift in values as the key to modern economic growth? The answer is that she is not just a sterling economist but a learned humanist. I do not much like her coinage for this combination—"humanomics." But something new and special does emerge from this combination. A scholar who can analyze Austen and Shakespeare and the history of innovation and production is rare and often difficult to understand. I think it is for this reason that Adam Smith is so often misunderstood or reduced to a caricature, for he too was a scholar of both moral philosophy and literature and the history of production. It was this rare combination that led to Smith's breakthrough understandings of how changes in the social division of labor led to a new era in the production of material wealth; and I believe it is this combination that also enabled McCloskey to achieve breakthrough understandings in how changes in social values led to a new era of innovation and exponential per capita growth.

Aside from the identification of the impact of bourgeois values, I believe McCloskey's bridging of humanities and social sciences has broader lessons. Putting the "social" back into "social sciences" is badly needed. The emphasis in both political science and economics on the "science" part—especially when this is wrongly understood as quantification and formal modeling (and the cult of statistical significance in particular, as McCloskey has pointed out; Ziliak and McCloskey 2008) rather than as the real testing of theory against hard reality and changing theory accordingly—has been harmful. Both political science and economics have become less useful and less interesting, telling us less and less about the real world, albeit more elegantly and formally. The inability of economic theory to account for the recent Great Recession, much less foresee it; our inability to leverage economic science to restore wage growth in America or economic growth in Europe; the inability to forewarn of either the collapse of the Arab dictatorships or the renewed vitality of authoritarian regimes elsewhere in the world; and the dysfunction of America's political system and the sharp rise in political and economic inequality and decline in opportunity throughout the developed world all make a mockery of any claims of powerful breakthroughs in political and economic science. The contention between neo- and anti-Keynesian economists and between realist and Wilsonian political scientists seems rooted far more in fashions and personal preferences than in scientific analysis and rigorous theory testing.

To be sure, most economics and politics take place in open systems rather than the closed or controlled conditions of the laboratory or parts of the natural universe. Thus theory testing cannot always discriminate tightly between competing views. But that is all the more reason to inquire into and understand the conditions that *do* act as constraints in social systems as we find them, and those are the values and ideas that constrain and guide choice.

Deirdre McCloskey is not just a champion of liberal values, although in her work and her life she has been that, too. Rather, she has shown, like Adam Smith and John Stuart Mill and Friedrich Hayek and others, how to analyze those values and demonstrate their role in enabling material progress. She has shown that there is, and should be, no barrier between the scholarly analysis of values and meanings and the scholarly analysis of economic processes, including innovation and economic growth. The trick—and this is one that few pull off—is to do both equally well!

Let me close by saying that for half a lifetime, Deirdre has always shown me the bourgeois values of respect, criticism, and search for improvement. My own work and understanding of values and history would be far poorer without her example, her insights, and her friendship.

References

Allen, Robert C. 2001. "The Great Divergence in European Wages and Prices from the Middle Ages to the First World War." *Explorations in Economic History* 38: 411–447.

Allen, Robert C., Bassino, Jean-Pascal, Ma, Debin, Moll-Murata, Christine, and Luiten van Zanden, Jan. 2011. "Wages, Prices, and Living Standards in China, 1738–1925: In Comparison with Europe, Japan, and India." *Economic History Review* 64 (1): 8–38.

Broadberry, Stephen, Campbell, Bruce M. S., Klein, Alexander, Overton, Mark, and van Leeuwen, Bas. 2015. *British Economic Growth 1270–1870*. Cambridge: Cambridge University Press.

Galor, Oded. 2011. *Unified Growth Theory*. Princeton, NJ: Princeton University Press.

Goldstone, Jack A. 1984. "Urbanization and Inflation: Lessons from the English Price Revolution of the 16th and 17th Centuries." *American Journal of Sociology* 89: 1122–1160.

Goldstone, Jack A. 1991a. "Ideology, Cultural Frameworks, and the Process of Revolutions." *Theory and Society* 20: 405–453.

Goldstone, Jack A. 1991b. *Revolution and Rebellion in the Early Modern World*. Berkeley: University of California Press.

Goldstone, Jack A. 2012. "Divergence in Cultural Trajectories: The Power of the Traditional within the Early Modern." In Porter 2012, 165–192.

Goldstone, Jack A. 2014. "Quantity versus Quality: Population, Productivity, and Growth in the 'Great Divergence.'" Paper presented at the 50th anniversary meeting of the Cambridge Population Group, Downing College, Cambridge.

Jacob, Margaret. 2014. *The First Knowledge Economy: Human Capital and the European Economy, 1750–1850*. Cambridge: Cambridge University Press.

McCloskey, Deirdre N. 2006. *Bourgeois Virtues: Ethics for an Age of Commerce*. Chicago: University of Chicago Press.

McCloskey, Deirdre N. 2010. *Bourgeois Dignity: Why Economics Can't Explain the Modern World*. Chicago: University of Chicago Press.

McCloskey, Deirdre N. 2016. *Bourgeois Equality: How Ideas, Not Capital, Enriched the World*. Chicago: University of Chicago Press.

Mishel, Lawrence, and Gee, Kar-Fai. 2012. "Why Aren't Workers Benefiting from Labour Productivity Growth in the United States?" *International Productivity Monitor*. http://www.csls.ca/ipm/23/IPM-23-Mishel-Gee.pdf.

Mokyr, Joel. 2002. *The Gifts of Athena: Historical Origins of the Knowledge Economy*. Princeton, NJ: Princeton University Press.

Porter, David, ed. 2012. *Comparative Early Modernities 1100–1800*. New York: Palgrave-Macmillan.

Vries, Peer. 2015. *Escaping Poverty: The Origins of Modern Economic Growth*. Vienna: V&R UniPress.

Ziliak, Stephen T., and McCloskey, Deirdre N. 2008. *The Cult of Statistical Significance: How the Standard Error Costs Us Jobs, Justice, and Lives*. Ann Arbor: University of Michigan Press.

6

Liberal Advocacy and Neoliberal Rule: On McCloskey's Ambivalence

STEPHEN G. ENGELMANN

Introduction: Neoliberalism and McCloskey's *Oeuvre*

Arguments for liberal freedom today are dominated by a strain of libertarianism that is armed with a science of economics. Economic libertarianism argues that market exchange is the sine qua non of a free society and that politics—in particular, the state—is a threat.[1] This rhetorical move has helped close public space in liberal societies in a way that endangers the project of freedom itself. It might seem that as a virtue ethicist Deirdre McCloskey recognizes and laments political decline while as an economist she contributes to it. But the genius of McCloskey's work is that on her terms her ethics and her economics are perfectly consistent with one another. They are joined, as they are in the work of Adam Smith, by a humanist perspective that puts rhetoric front and center; for McCloskey, rhetoric constitutes and reconstitutes the moral and economic practices of a polite, commercial society that promotes a virtuous circle of wealth-enhancing liberty and liberty-enhancing wealth.

For better and worse, we have come a long way from eighteenth-century Scotland and Smith's thought of a system of natural liberty. Today, the rhetoric of economic freedom plays a constitutive role in multiple schemes of government. And economic language—for example, the language of investment and return on investment—has shaped everything from natural-scientific discourse to pillow talk. The neoliberal project is not a project of government only narrowly speaking—one exercised through the state alone—but instead includes reform and realignment of self-government, family government, and the government of various intermediary associations: consider the surprisingly rapid reform and restructuring that is roiling our universities. Lecturing at the Collège de France in early 1979, Michel Foucault, as part of a series of reflections on government, had the following to say about the neoliberalisms that had shaped postwar West Germany and that were surging in think tanks in the United States and elsewhere: "The problem of neo-liberalism was not how to cut out or contrive a free space of the market within an already given political society, as in the liberalism of Adam Smith and the eighteenth century." Instead, "the problem of neo-liberalism is rather how the overall exercise of political power can be modeled on the principles of a market economy." This requires "taking the formal principles of a market economy and . . . projecting them on to a general art of government." And in order to do this, "the neo-liberals had to subject classical liberalism to a number of transformations" (Foucault 2008, 131). Following and extending Foucault's insights, we can say that rather than simple political decline, neoliberalism involves a kind of political substitution: the substitution of particular arts of economic rule for the plural arts of democratic deliberation, cooperation, contestation, and struggle.

Most critiques of neoliberal transformation are focused on neoliberalism as an apology for an especially unstable and unjust kind of capitalism. That is not what this more narrowly political-theoretical chapter is about. My concern here is neoliberal theory's frontal attack on, displacement of, and substitution for the art of politics, which goes well beyond the wariness of despotism—what Judith Shklar called the "liberalism of fear"—that marks much classical liberalism. Shklar's liberalism, in its insistence on institutional pluralism, countervailing power, and the rule of law, was political in its orientation, even as its politics was no republican or democratic end in itself but instead had "only one overriding aim: to secure the political conditions that are necessary for the exercise of personal freedom" (Shklar 1989, 21). This classical liberalism is perfectly compatible with markets, as it is with perfectionist doctrines of virtue and a scientific worldview; the liberalism of fear recognized, however, that either a moral theory of the self or an economic theory of society could threaten the conditions of freedom when elevated to a ruling political principle.

The irony of McCloskey's work is that a genuinely freedom-loving project effectively contributes to the erosion of freedom. This is because it is insistently evasive about politics and the political conditions that, according to Shklar and the long tradition of which Shklar speaks, secure the freedom McCloskey prizes. McCloskey is nervous about what she calls "demoralization." She is nervous that the monistic prudence-only discourse that dominates her discipline, and perhaps even capitalism itself as currently practiced with the encouragement of that discourse, is contributing to a kind of disenchantment: to the draining of meaning from our practices through the denigration of rhetoric and lack of attention to what she calls the bourgeois virtues. But her rhetorical theory is in some tension with her virtue theory; her rhetoric is all about worldly publicity and audience, and her ethics is all about morality and the scene of the self. Because of this tension between a worldly rhetoric and a psychologized ethics, McCloskey repeatedly recognizes only to recast political problems as moral problems, and this recasting suits the monism, individualism, and antipolitical politics of neoliberal theory and practice. Combining this moralism as she does with a full-throated promotion of the market mechanism, McCloskey unwittingly contributes to neoliberal rule. Despite her classically liberal political intentions, she contributes to what is for her anathema: she contributes to our contemporary romance with economic government.

Although "neoliberalism" is a contested term that is today used mostly by critics, it circulated among Friedrich Hayek's Mont Pèlerin group as part of that group's political reaction against early twentieth-century social liberal and antiliberal developments (Mirowski and Plehwe 2009). The triumph of neoliberalism has been the triumph of the core, if not the whole, of McCloskey's own argument: the argument that we owe the bulk of whatever freedom and prosperity we enjoy to the phenomenon of trade-tested betterment. The rise of neoliberalism has demonstrated the truth of McCloskey's insight that rhetoric can remake a world: over the past few decades, neoliberal rhetoric has moved from the margins to the center to remake our world in ways that would be bewildering to many classical liberals. Classical liberals tended to think that they owed freedom and prosperity to rights-based justice and to the civil society secured by it. Neoliberalism has come to emphasize efficiency and choice.

McCloskey's work worries about and warns against the baneful influence of the clerisy, against intellectuals eager to use law and other institutional tools to disrupt the competitive play of the market for what their expertise takes to be scientifically informed corrective ends. A predominant means through which neoliberal rhetoric continues to remake our world is through just such an attack on expertise: an attack based in an economic science that sees groups of self-styled experts as using institutions for rent-seeking ends. (These experts are said to restrict our choices, too.) Ironically then, McCloskey's allies in the anticlerisy launching this attack also use law as a policy instrument, even as they do so in the name of competitive ends; Hayek himself was criticized for precisely this contradiction by the political theorist Michael Oakeshott, who noted long ago that Hayek's *Road to Serfdom* was, perversely, an exercise in antiplanning planning (Oakeshott 1962, 21). Neoliberal rhetoric has been enormously influential in the internal reform of state and nonstate entities alike, as it has been for the ethos of everyday life.

Think about it: the vast majority of plans to improve our condition involve the implementation of schemes invoking trade-tested betterment at the heart of them: so-called deregulation, privatization, and public/private partnerships for a range of formerly public and private industries and services with new markets and market-like entities appearing in areas as diverse as school choice, pollution credits, and legacy securities. This has produced peculiar new hybrids in areas as diverse as developer-regulated housing, workfare, and mandatory health insurance markets. We have seen a proliferation of decentralized budgets and contracting-out in all kinds of organizations. And many of the most obvious changes have tended toward the consumerization and casualization of everything: the redefinition of a range of products, services, institutions, and employments as driven by the inner-directed choices of enterprising individuals, justifying an array of restructurings, some of which necessarily remain at the level of pure fantasy (a personal favorite of mine was the US military's short-lived "Army of One" recruiting campaign). The experts who have designed and implemented many of the more enduring schemes tend to be either professional economists or those schooled in their rhetoric.

"Neoliberalism" has become a term of art, and even abuse, for leftist political economy, but my interest here is to elaborate a political-theoretical rather than strictly political-economic perspective on it: to consider neoliberalism more fundamentally as a grammar for the government of souls and cities (Brown 2015, 21–28 and passim). I suggest that neoliberal rhetoric, and the practices it informs, hollows out the republican political framework that classical liberalism took for granted (Engelmann 2014). One consequence for liberalism is that an architecture of rights and law is steadily eroded by a turn to choice and policy (Engelmann 2003, 1–3).

My analysis in this essay is informed at a distance by Hannah Arendt's worries about the loss of the public realm and the rise of the social (Arendt 1998) and more proximately by William Davies's concerns about the "the disenchantment of politics by economics" (Davies 2014, 1–34). Davies, a UK think-tank veteran turned sociologist, notes in a recent book that "the key institution of neoliberalism is not a market as such, but particular market-based (or market-derived) forms of economization, calculation, measurement, and valuation" (Davies 2014, 21). And although there is a theoretical divide between minority Austrians and majority non-Austrians over the basis and uses of economic science, Davies demonstrates the ways in which this divide has been effectively bridged in practice. Davies's conventionalist approach is broadly compatible with McCloskey's rhetorical sensibilities. But he came to his project wanting to understand "how the economic critique of the state can be employed precisely so as to legitimate, empower, and expand the state" (Davies 2014: x). As Foucault already hinted, the state, whatever we mean by that slippery term, is at least a bit of a red herring (Foucault 2007, 109). Attention to disenchantment confirms that the argument has never been about the state per se but instead about politics, the grounds of freedom, and the art and science of government.

In political-theory speak, we might say that neoliberalism has evacuated much of the republican tradition from liberalism; one consequence of this transformation is that, for the plural arts of government accommodated by liberal democracy, it has substituted a single kind of administrative expertise. And as Arendt well understood, what might otherwise look like an unrelated rhetorical turn to the interior of the self—the substitution of inner-directed morality for engaged ethos—is historically a key indicator and promoter of this kind of political change.

My argument that McCloskey contributes to neoliberal government despite her best intentions begins and ends with a mix of historical and contemporary political and political-theoretical analysis, but it relies more centrally on an immanent critique of her work in the Bourgeois Era volumes. The immanent critique, which includes a close reading of a revealing chapter on institutions in *Bourgeois Dignity* (McCloskey 2011, 296–309), notes how McCloskey makes us aware of political conditions and problems only to construe them as moral conditions and problems. For example, the McCloskey chapter concludes with a surprising, on her part, embrace of the neorepublican theory of liberty. This theory defines freedom not in familiar market-liberal terms as nonintervention but instead as nondomination; rather than focusing on noninterference, republican liberty is attentive to worldly conditions and to relations of subordination and dependency. Such a theory of liberty is subversive of neoliberal hierarchies and their free-choice justifications unless it is redefined in moral and psychological terms. Lamentably, after introducing and endorsing republican liberty, McCloskey performs just this redefinition, illustrating nondomination in terms of the interior of the self and its attitude. It is by way of this kind of feat of psychologization and moralization, a product of the gravitational pull of subject-centeredness (Mihic 2010), that McCloskey is able throughout recent work to assimilate Machiavelli and Hobbes together as prudence-only theorists when these theorists are opposites from the worldly vantage point of the republican tradition. Thus my contribution to this volume learns from and complements John Nelson's appreciation of McCloskey's *oeuvre* in chapter 9; Nelson, also a political theorist, is similarly dismayed by McCloskey's treatment of Machiavelli as part of her general tendency to convert political virtuosities into moral virtues.

I proceed in four stages. In what follows, I first offer a reconstruction of the main argument of the Bourgeois Era volumes and its broad relationship to liberal and neoliberal political theory and political history. Then I turn to a kind of contradiction, or at least tension, in McCloskey's thought regarding her concerns about demoralization. Next, I turn to the chapter on institutions and its implications. Finally, I return again to a broader canvas, with special attention to neoliberal education reform, before concluding the piece as a whole. My purpose throughout is to build on the strengths of McCloskey's humanism in order to showcase and challenge her work's ambivalent contribution to neoliberal rule.

Understanding the Bourgeois Era

McCloskey's Bourgeois Era volumes are a sustained reflection on capitalism (McCloskey 2006: xiv and passim), or innovation (McCloskey 2011: xii and passim), or trade-tested betterment (McCloskey 2016: table of contents and passim). (I will use all these terms in what follows, keeping in mind why McCloskey has rejected first "capitalism" then "innovation" for "trade-tested betterment.") The argument of these volumes is that modern capitalism is ethical and that it arose from and is sustained by rhetoric. In the first volume, we learn that capitalism relies not on prudence alone but on the six other bourgeois virtues as well—faith, hope, love, justice, courage, and temperance—and that it meets their sometimes demanding criteria besides, and not only because of, the wealth it generates. In the second volume, we learn that the Great Fact—the amazing enrichment generated by modern capitalism, originally in northwestern Europe but now in several parts of the world—is owed in large part not to accumulation, or to institutions, or to technology, but to rhetoric. Rhetoric made our world and continues to make it, and the most important rhetoric for the Great Fact was and remains the support of the dignity and liberty of the virtuous bourgeoisie. The third volume argues that capitalism is born from and contributes to equality. McCloskey continues to show the importance of virtue, rhetoric, the Great Fact, and dignity. But trade-tested betterment is not only grounded in equal dignity; it also produces equality through the enrichment of the poor—that is, it doesn't produce equality in wealth or income, but it does produce a measure of equality in consumption, and thus it contributes to the equality of genuine comfort.

The trilogy as a whole is determined to defend capitalism from its critics on the right and the left, to defend it from an often well-meaning but always wrongheaded clerisy that has condemned it for its supposed destructiveness, injustice, immorality, and so on. The main argument of the trilogy seems to be that all is for the most part well as long as we don't continue to say all is not well.

Thus McCloskey is in fact ambivalent about whether all is well, as is evident from her sense that it is not only critics but also many fans who are demoralizing capitalism—demoralizing it, that is, in both senses of the word: draining capitalist practice of moral meanings by at least misdescribing it in disenchanting prudence-only terms and in this way and perhaps others causing participants in the bourgeois era to act differently, at least by doubting themselves and one another. I will explore this ambivalence and read it as an encounter less with demoralization than with misrecognized depoliticization, a depoliticization that is symptomatic of neoliberal disenchantment.

McCloskey describes herself as follows on her website, in response to the characterization of her as a "conservative" economist: "I'm a literary, quantitative, postmodern, free-market, progressive Episcopalian, Midwestern woman from Boston who was once a man. Not 'conservative'! I'm a Christian libertarian." And indeed, progressive free-market libertarianism seasoned with Christian charity (i.e., love) is what comes through in all of her work. In this chapter, I don't have anything to say about love, but I do have something to say about progressive market libertarianism, or neoliberalism. That neoliberalism would be progressive will strike some leftist ears as strange. But of course it is in important senses progressive, especially in its effective conversion and assimilation of the liberating rhetorics of the movements of the New Left (Fraser 2009), which have done so much to attack and sometimes redress status hierarchies of domination and to mobilize and mainstream formerly submerged and marginalized identities. McCloskey's work is unusual for how frankly and fully it embraces the whole neoliberal spectrum, dispensing with narrow utility-maximizing (what she disparagingly calls "Max U") thinking to service a range of self-actualizing agents of choice. Yet neoliberalism often mobilizes rhetorics of freedom and choice for projects the consequences of which are, among other things, illiberal. Neoliberals—and McCloskey here is no exception—are understandably scandalized by this suggestion, inspired as they are by a proud classical liberal tradition that puts liberty at the center of its concerns and reflections.

But how did the classical liberals put liberty at the center of their reflections? The first people to call themselves and to be called liberals in Britain were progressive Whigs and Radicals who attacked what one of their number, Jeremy Bentham, called the "sinister interests" of religious and political establishments (Bentham 1989; Schofield 2006, 109–36). Political economy, the ancestor of economics, was still largely at this time a relatively limited science of wealth and population, and it was only one of many tools used in the reform effort. Liberals were continuing an eighteenth-century project to clear the way for civil society and its institutions, including the market. They were often allied with radical republicans but did not share the latter's love for popular self-government for its own sake; instead, classical liberals generally supported democratization as an instrument rather than as an end in itself, as one of many reforms that would better secure the autonomy of civil society with its liberties and interests of (eventually all adult) individuals.

This instrumental view of democracy was shared by opponents such as Bentham's ally James Mill and Mill's liberal critic Thomas Babington, Lord Macaulay (Mill 1992), who otherwise disagreed dramatically over political-theoretical foundations (reason versus history) and institutional recommendations (extensive versus limited political reform). Fervent republicans, by contrast, agreed with Thomas Paine that the people should rule not just because they are the ones who will know and defend their own best interests but also simply because they are the people and are the only legitimate source of rule (Paine 1986).

You can see this tension between liberalism and republicanism on the American side in the friendly differences between James Madison and Thomas Jefferson. Jefferson drafted the revolutionary Declaration and Madison became known as the "father" of the arguably counterrevolutionary Constitution. Jefferson thought it would be good if each generation could rule itself in its own way (how else can we be said to be free?), and Madison, more attentive to the Humean insight that there are no generations, only different individuals entering and exiting life every day, questioned "whether it be possible . . . without subverting the foundation of civil Society" (Madison, 4 February 1790). Still, Madison and Jefferson were allied in the mission to guard the guardians so as to secure *both* popular sovereignty and individual liberty.

Thus we mustn't exaggerate the divide; arguably, liberalism is republicanism adapted for a commercial world (Kalyvas and Katznelson 2008). In his famous speech of 1819 comparing ancient and modern liberty, Benjamin Constant tallied losses and gains from this adaptation in favor of the moderns: housed as we are in large commercial empires, we can no longer be self-governing in the way the ancients were, but now more importantly we enjoy rights and find fulfillment in private life. Constant reminds us, however, of the common, public source of our rights and their security: it is absolutely essential, according to this classical liberal, that we exercise at least a measure of ancient republican liberty through vigilant representative government; without politics, we will soon find ourselves dominated by those who encourage us to mind our own business, and we will be less than fully human to boot (Constant 1988, 309–28).

Constant was a political theorist with no developed political economy. Whereas only some of the great (nineteenth-century) classical liberals were political economists, most of the great (twentieth-century) neoliberals are economists. There is a connection here, because it is very difficult to be an economist and to join classical liberals in putting liberty—as opposed to, say, efficiency—at the center of one's reflections. McCloskey tries, fierce critic of utilitarianism and its Max U assumptions that she is. Economics as we know it is the child of utilitarianism, and its mathematical utilitarianism has historically been less concerned with liberty than even its most systematically utilitarian predecessors were, such as the classical liberal Jeremy Bentham.

When William Stanley Jevons—who dropped "political economy" in favor of "economics" in the second edition of *The Theory of Political Economy*—launched one strain of the neoclassical tradition in 1871, he helped begin the slow conversion of liberalism's grounding in rights and other political and juridical conditions into neoliberalism's emphasis on the desiring and choosing self, which was taking on enhanced importance as the ground of a new science of value (Jevons 1888). Meanwhile, many classical liberals, such as Bentham's protégé John Stuart Mill, had recognized that the expansion of liberty they urged and celebrated was in danger of hitting a wall or going into reverse: it required sustained attention to new hierarchies. If more wasn't done to ameliorate the condition of the poor, now known as the working class, then not only would they remain in a state of practical unfreedom, but their growing political power could lead to despotism for all (see, e.g., Mill 1981, 239 on democracy and socialism).

This turn in liberalism reached its apogee in the New Liberalism of Leonard Hobhouse. In his 1911 treatise on liberalism, Hobhouse argued that liberals needed to address the domination experienced by those who were dependent on employment. The expansion of freedom required the expansion of rights (such as the right to a living wage—that is, one sufficient for "full independence"; Hobhouse 1964, 85) as well as a range of institutions and expertises of civil society and state, some of which were unknown to older liberals, but none of which were necessarily anathema to them (a case can always be made, of course, but many of these rely on anachronistic thought experiments—"What would Adam Smith think of X?"). It is misleading simply to characterize this emerging complex as "the rise of the welfare state," as that is for the most part a later development and because, of course, the transformation I'm describing involved the development of numerous private-sector as well as public-sector agencies. Instead, we should probably speak of the "rise of the social" (Donzelot 1979), which involved, among other things, the rise of the professions, especially the new feminine ones that emerged with the political emancipation of women. Consider the example of the social worker, distrusted or even hated by many neoliberals and new leftists alike—is she a figure come to smother or to enhance liberty? Influenced as I am by the criticisms, I have some real ambivalence, but there is certainly a strong emancipatory case to be made on her side.

Professions are constituted by the institutional organization of expertise; they are sustained in large part by the distinctive rhetorics that these institutions nurture and promote. I return to the question of the professions in a brief discussion of markets, metrics, and the university below. For now, it should be noted that McCloskey is softer on the professions and professionalization than most neoliberals are; she appreciates, in an argument that goes back to Plato, that the practice of medicine is distinct from the practice of earning income from medicine and that the difference is a vitally important one (McCloskey 2006, 111). This can, of course, be said of any craft, as certainly the more Knights-of-Labor-leaning of early unionists would remind her. I would add that maintaining a distinction between the craft of earning and the crafts by which one earns can be very important to the freedom of practitioners, as it can be to their customers or clients. It can also be vitally important to nonmarket forms of competition and to eventually enriching innovation. McCloskey notes that the difference between money making and other crafts is not one readily evident to most economists, even as, ironically, economists live the difference, not confusing getting it right with getting paid (McCloskey 2006, 411). Classical liberals were generally friendly to expertise in all its burgeoning forms. Neoliberal economists, experts in the science of competitive market tests, tend to be hostile to noneconomic forms of expertise; the institutions that nurture such expertise are simply seen as anticompetitive. Denigrated externally for "rent-seeking" behavior, institutions are also disenchanted internally, redescribed by economistic social scientists as reducers of transaction costs. McCloskey celebrates trade-tested betterment and indulges in frequent criticisms of "regulation," yet she is hesitant to attack the professions, except as a sharp and able critic of her own profession (McCloskey 1990; McCloskey 1998; McCloskey 2002). And in her heterodoxy, she takes her fellow economists to task for badly misconstruing institutions, for missing that they are spaces and sources of meaning.

So, scandalous as it is already to accuse economists of illiberalism, it can seem doubly wrong to accuse McCloskey herself of economistic illiberalism. And perhaps it is, because there is definitely ambivalence here. On the one hand, McCloskey's rhetorical blasts at the ranks of the market-wary clerisy follow in the footsteps of decades of fierce and often successful neoliberal attacks on the social institutions of New Liberalism. On the other hand, McCloskey's break from neoliberal orthodoxy extends beyond qualified support of the professions to moments of support for unionism (amid many swipes at unions) and even friendliness to some forms of social democracy. She writes that social democracy done right does good things and that Scandinavia illustrates that we can afford it without killing the golden goose, but just don't forget you owe everything to that golden goose—that is, to the bourgeoisie, to their dignity, their liberty, and their virtues (see, e.g., McCloskey 2011, 356, 445).

My critique of McCloskey's ambivalent neoliberalism primarily engages the first two volumes of her work on the bourgeois era. And it will zero in on one fascinating chapter in particular—to my mind, McCloskey's most consistently antineoliberal writing—chapter 33 in the *Bourgeois Dignity* volume, which is titled "Institutions Cannot Be Viewed Merely as Incentive-Providing Constraints" (McCloskey 2011, 296–309). The chapter comes close to a genuinely political reading of institutions and ends with a surprisingly republican discussion of liberty. Paired with much of *The Bourgeois Virtues*, it might seem that chapter 33 completes an attack on Bentham and Benthamism; *The Bourgeois Virtues* is all about the shortcomings of the prudence-only ethical framework pioneered by Bentham (see also McCloskey 2005), and this chapter from *Bourgeois Dignity* is all about the shortcomings of viewing institutions as nothing but bundles of (dis)incentives for the prudential actor. But Bentham was a classical liberal, even if a strange one, and the views McCloskey is criticizing are distinctly neoliberal Max U views.[2] Although she is right to see a strong affinity between Bentham's work and the views she is criticizing, the chapter on institutions reveals just how far the new institutionalists are from Bentham. Bentham was not a moral philosopher or an economist in our sense; he was a theorist of the art and science of government. And although he saw laws and institutions primarily as organizers of sanctions and rewards—of disincentives and incentives—he would see as weird nonsense any view that began with the maximizing actor and built up to institutions as reducers of transaction costs, any view that in its abstraction or utopianism didn't appreciate that we are always already governed. Thus even Bentham, that most protoneoliberal and economistic of classical liberals, saw institutions as given rather than as products of iterated games. And political economy was only one of many sciences relevant to his struggle for institutional reform (Engelmann 2005).

The world of classical liberalism is long dead, and whether born of rhetoric or not, I suspect that it was killed as much by circumstance as by rhetoric. But there is substantial evidence that the subsequent rise of neoliberalism is a story of rhetorical triumph; its history fits very well a set of claims McCloskey makes that are at the center of her work (the claims that name this anthology, of humanism challenging materialism). Even as dedicated a materialist as the Marxist geographer David Harvey acknowledges that the neoliberal revolution was driven in large part by ideas (Harvey 2005). According to Harvey, the crisis of the 1970s in the United States and elsewhere—marked as it was by a historically high labor share of income, oil shocks, stagflation, and a period of negative real interest rates—did produce a kind of material revolutionary situation, but it was the rhetorical work of busy think tanks and others that won the day for neoliberalism as opposed to other alternatives. In their fascinating anthology on neoliberalism, Philip Mirowski and Dieter Plehwe (2009)—who decidedly do not confuse neoliberalism with classical liberalism—understand the neoliberal revolution as the eventual success of a program that was self-consciously ideological, in the broad and generic sense of the word, from its beginning decades earlier (their subtitle is *The Making of a Neoliberal Thought Collective*). There is a surprising degree of consensus that the victory of neoliberalism has been a rhetorical victory above all.

As I have already suggested, this victory has followed the core of McCloskey's own argument, that we must accept a political-economic argument she calls the Bourgeois Deal (McCloskey 2011, 70): give the bourgeoisie free reign for their practices of trade-tested betterment, give them the freedom to get rich and manage their riches in their own way, and they will make the rest of us rich and free too. McCloskey is well aware that this deal is not the same as "let the bourgeoisie run things," which Smith noted already in the late eighteenth century would be a terrible mistake, because their interests as a class are so often not in accord with those of the public (Smith 1981a, 266–67; McCloskey 2016: final chapter). She is also well aware that the Deal is not the same thing as "let the neoliberal economists run things," because unlike most of her colleagues, she is rightly wary of the governmental aspirations of all social science and denies the possibility that any social science, including economics, can be predictive (McCloskey 1990). But the problem of the rich and rich-friendly economists running things, in a context marked by the erosion of countervailing power and by a lack of significant contestation by competing orthodoxies, is a significant part of the problem of our disenchanted neoliberal politics. Consider how all the loudest talk about urban development or public education or other matters of common concern is dominated by the *haute* bourgeoisie and conducted in their economic terms; the only other mission or metric that appears with any great frequency relates to the preservation and enhancement of life qua life—that is, security and health. Yet McCloskey's awareness that economic rule is the road to ruin is cast almost entirely in moral rather than political terms. Thus it is helpless against the consequences of continual neoliberal appropriations of the more directly political argument of her Bourgeois Deal.

In a discussion of disenchantment and economic politics, in a discussion of the draining of meaning from public life and its displacement by economics-generated governmental arts and sciences, it seems patently unfair to target McCloskey. Her work of the past few decades has after all been animated by a desire to reenchant economics and our view of economic life; her writing is aimed against the positivist attack on meaning and against social science as policy science, against social science that furnishes the tools for "social engineering." And whereas most neoliberal economists are happy to launch the latter sort of critique selectively against other social scientists and against competing economists, McCloskey has written extensively against this approach even to what she judges to be good economic science itself. In this, she seems to follow in the footsteps of the great neoliberal theorist Hayek, who went so far as to call for the abolition of "the economy" as a label, reflecting as it does its etymological roots in household management, which he thought confused his colleagues and others into thinking that society is something to be managed. Hayek's alternative, "catallaxy," is not any kind of organization but instead a spontaneous order produced as an unintended effect of the myriad trade-tested and retested activities that constitute it. These activities occur within the confines of a rule of law that, à la Oakeshott, is supposedly "nomocratic" rather than "telocratic"—that is, it does not itself manage, because it does not promote any social purpose but only puts bounds on how individual purposes can be pursued (Hayek 1967, 160–77). What directs on this view is only the price system, which Hayek and Milton Friedman and other neoliberals celebrate as a kind of alternative to politics: marvelously coordinating the actions of vast numbers of individuals within and across borders through consent rather than coercion.

It would seem then that for Hayek, as for McCloskey, the use of the state as a kind of policy instrument is a violation of (neo)liberal principle. But a close reading of Hayek confirms that politics is to be disenchanted to make way for good economic science—that in fact the orientation of neoliberalism is decidedly not laissez-faire and amounts instead, as Oakeshott noted, to a kind of antiplanning planning or more. The telocratic and utilitarian orientation of Hayekian law is confirmed by its mission to "maximize the fulfilment of expectations as a whole" (Hayek 1982, 103). And for lesser neoliberals, especially of the common Max U variety, the critique of social engineering is little more than a prelude to what I call "skeptical engineering" (Engelmann n.d.). That is to say, the social scientist remains a practical rather than a theoretical scientist, like a physician, examining a social world of cause and effect for the purpose of identifying and therapeutically activating causal levers.

The contemporary skeptical engineer feints with a tale about the resistances to social engineering inherent in human nature or human systems as a prelude to recommending how to govern people in accordance with what the scientist takes to be their own (e.g., Max U) laws. Hayek himself was fond of Smith's "man of system" quotation from *A Theory of Moral Sentiments*, warning that the man of system attempts to govern without attention to the propensities of subjects (Smith 1982a, 233–34). For Hayek and all the neoliberal skeptical engineers, this is a spur to study the principles of motion of "the great chess-board of human society" through endeavors like economic science. In this way, for example, a doctrine that speaks of the spontaneity of markets can see its way to engineering them into existence where they are not yet to be found.

McCloskey is no skeptical engineer. But then she is silent on politics and government generally, except for the occasional resort to neoliberal commonplaces about state coercion and inefficiency in contrast to market freedom and efficiency (e.g., McCloskey 2006, 35). It is primarily this silence that I will explore here. She is quite vocal about virtue, but virtue understood in Smithian and not Machiavellian terms, in terms of the moral sentiments. McCloskey is concerned, unlike her neoliberal colleagues, about disenchantment. Attention to demoralization and moral virtue is the primary form that her attempt at reenchantment takes. It is my contention that McCloskey's concern with morality represents a kind of misrecognized or suppressed politics. And the moral avoidance and suppression of politics, in combination with heavy doses of rhetorical advocacy for trade-tested betterment, sadly ends up serving the disenchanted economic politics of McCloskey's skeptical engineering neoliberal colleagues.

The Politics of Demoralization

McCloskey's blind spot for politics should be brought into focus. How does her work on the bourgeois era generally acknowledge only to recast the political disenchantment wrought by neoliberalism on liberal societies—that is, how does she treat neoliberalism's displacement of the republican standpoint, the standpoint of the public, of the political commons and its virtues or virtuosities? McCloskey's treatment takes the form of a concern on her part with demoralization. It is not always clear what the concern is. And this is not surprising, because the concern, so central to her work on the bourgeois era—beginning as it does with *The Bourgeois Virtues*—is haunted by a tension, by something very close to a contradiction. The tension, which I argue is a symptom of her evasion of politics, goes like this. According to McCloskey, rhetoric matters tremendously; rhetoric changed the world and brought us wealth. The rhetorics of utilitarianism (as morality and as philosophy of action) and of a good part of economics (both in their grounding in prudence-only utilitarianism as well as in their flawed methods) are wrong—in the case of ethics, they are deeply wrong. Yet these misguided rhetorics can't have mattered all that much; if they had, there might be grounds for the kinds of concerns about contemporary market society that McCloskey wants to keep at bay. So how have they mattered at all? Capitalism has not demoralized itself—she rejects the Polanyian thesis (McCloskey 2006, 410)—but it has been at least somewhat affected by prudence-only rhetoric, such that some kind of remoralization is called for. Or so McCloskey occasionally suggests: "If the economy were understood as more than Prudence Only, then we could remoralize it" (2011, 448).

But it is not at all clear what this demoralization really amounts to and whether the project of remoralization is a matter of convenience or of necessity (as the early moderns would put it), whether or not it is needed for system survival. In the final chapter of *Bourgeois Dignity*, McCloskey addresses the tension head-on with regard to one strain of misguided rhetoric: the supposed anticapitalism of the clerisy. If rhetoric can make or unmake us, how has this rhetoric not destroyed us? It seems there is a split between elite and popular opinion that has made anticapitalist elites relatively ineffective, except in those instances in the last hundred years when they have been able to perpetrate destructive fascist or communist experiments. But also, "once the cat of dignity and liberty was out of the bag, she was hard to stuff back in." We need to be on guard against the rhetoric of the anticapitalist clerisy, but they are on the losing side of history, and there is good reason for guarded optimism (McCloskey 2011, 439–50).

Notice, though, how this just covers the misguided antimarket folks. Perhaps the faulty neutral or promarket science of much of economics wedded to statistical significance is bad because it costs us "jobs, justice, and lives": this then requires nothing more than replacing bad science with good (Ziliak and McCloskey 2008). And bad science is not just a matter of bad statistical method. Indeed, part of what is needed for better science is more comprehensive scientific accounting for ethics: when we ignore *S* (solidarity, service, soul, . . . sacred) variables and attend only to *P* (prudence, price, payment, . . . profane) variables, we get stuff wrong (McCloskey 2006, 407–15). So far so good. But we are still left in some mystery about bad ethics talk and its effects. What is so bad about the mistaken rhetoric of materialism and Max U? What is so bad about the misguided prudence-only prattle of what has become, in the last few decades at least, a generally promarket crowd? This is less clear.

In an article titled "The Demoralization of Economics," published a year before the first of the Bourgeois Era volumes, McCloskey acknowledges that Smith, in addition to his praise for the morality of commercial society, was concerned "'over the impoverishing effects of commercial society in eroding standards of public decency as well as private morality,'" and she acknowledges that "such concern is merely what one would expect from a serious discussion of bourgeois virtue. . . . Smith was not Ronald Reagan in knee britches" (McCloskey 2005, 22). But what are the demoralizing effects of commercial society and its partisans? We never quite find out. *Bourgeois Equality* contains a discussion of the dangers of bad rhetoric, but this amounts to little more than another criticism of the anticapitalist clerisy, warning that since good rhetoric made us, bad rhetoric could still undo us (McCloskey 2016: part 10). What besides inaccuracy could be wrong about especially Max U thinking, which these days is the work of the people who would seem to have *rescued* us from the clerisy in the postwar era, culminating in the 1970s (Amadae 2003)? Max U was favored by many of McCloskey's former colleagues in the neoliberal revolution, centered in the United States at the University of Chicago (see, e.g., Becker 1992). If these people rescued us by getting us to a new consensus of appreciation for markets, accompanied by some equally misguided contractarians and Kantians, what does it matter how they did it? Aren't all these people, even if wrong, the opposite of dangerous? Could they not instead be purveyors of a kind of noble lie?

No, for McCloskey there is a real problem of some sort: perhaps not only in vulgar appreciative descriptions of capitalism but more broadly in the moral-rhetorical course of capitalism itself. The unmooring of contract, Kant, and Bentham from their grounding in virtue ethics that McCloskey narrates in *The Bourgeois Virtues* was "an ethical catastrophe" (strong rhetoric! McCloskey 2006, 497). We could say again that the ethically misguided promarket views are clerisy centered—that most people don't think this way, so there is no problem really. But then "catastrophe" would be a kind of lie; catastrophes are consequential, and McCloskey from time to time suggests that this catastrophe is from a more generalized corrosive demoralizing that calls for a remoralizing through the bourgeois virtues. It is a problem, isn't it, when the car mechanic in big Chicago, unlike the one in little Iowa city, is unmoored enough from the virtues to see each new customer as a potential sucker (McCloskey 2011, 408)? But then this kind of example coming from her is deeply puzzling. Does McCloskey think, with the Jefferson whom she oddly praises (McCloskey 2011, 400, 433), that the urbanization she generally celebrates is also somehow dangerous and corrupting (Jefferson 2015)? It seems not. It seems that for the most part she needs to ridicule such talk, which she associates with the anticapitalist clerisy: "We are always already lamenting becoming urban and selfish and alienated. The years when our parents were children are seen as blessed times of familial and social solidarity, the clerisy's version of a Norman Rockwell world" (McCloskey 2011, 67).

What catastrophe, then? She offers some hints. At the beginning of *Bourgeois Dignity*, written in the wake of a global financial crisis, we learn that "ethical (and unethical) talk runs the world. . . . Perhaps economics and its many good friends should acknowledge the fact." Why? "When they don't they get into trouble, as when they inspire banks to ignore professional talk and fiduciary ethics, and to rely exclusively on silent and monetary incentives such as executive compensation." We are left to draw the conclusion that it can be highly consequential that "the theorists of prudence forbid ethical language, even in the word-drenched scene of banking" (McCloskey 2011, 6).

McCloskey is a virtue ethicist (McCloskey 2006); her virtue talk is part of a "rhetorical investment in renewal" (McCloskey 2011, 374). Many contemporary liberals would argue that she is playing with fire. With John Rawls, a good number of liberal political theorists today would join most market libertarians in warning of the dangers of perfectionist theories of human excellence, which might pose a threat to the equal liberty that contract theory enshrines (Rawls 1999, 22). But of course, as McCloskey teaches us, virtue ethics is no stranger to especially classical liberalism (McCloskey 2016, chapter 20). She could tell a virtue-centered story based in concerns that classical liberals learned from a tradition of politically inflected virtue talk from Plato to Rousseau. Such a story would defend and speak directly to her libertarian priorities. The story, which I use with my undergraduates to illustrate this tradition of thought—that is, to illustrate how prudence only as a virtue can have devastating effects—goes like this. Look at the US tax code. Why is it so big? Put aside for a moment your knowledge and insights about powerful lobbies and rent seeking, as relevant as they no doubt are, and consider simply this: Here is a body of law that guides the commission of a civic duty. Firms of any reasonable size, and most wealthy and some merely well-off citizens, employ people *whose job it is—that is, whose duty it is*—to find ways to meet the letter of the law while evading its spirit. Their creativity in doing end runs around the law as it stands in turn provokes more laws and more sanctions, which provoke new innovations, and so on, and so on. If people simply saw it as their duty to uphold the spirit of the law, they could live with a lot less law. This and any number of analogous cases illustrate how prudence-only behavior can undermine liberty.

McCloskey could tell this kind of story, but she doesn't. She will take the first step, that law has to be supplemented by virtue to be effective, that it has to be more than law and sanction to function as law (McCloskey 2016: exordium). But she won't take the next step, that trying to function as law sans virtue is liable to undermine liberty. The reason, I think, is that such a story gets uncomfortably close to validating moral-political critiques from the right or legal- and institutional-political critiques from the center and left of aspects of trade-tested betterment. So it needs to remain somewhat mysterious how trade-tested betterment is demoralized in our time of its celebration and how it needs to be remoralized away from Max U.

This contradiction or at least tension regarding rhetorical effect is connected with another McCloskeyian trait: like any good economist or moralist, she is fundamentally averse to thinking politically, and her main way of thinking about politics when compelled to think about it is to think, like any good libertarian, that politics is a necessary evil at best and deadly at worst. Note that this antipolitics is at least logically consistent with the virtue libertarianism I just outlined—it's just that if the problem of demoralization is at all serious, the suggestion is likely to follow that a political response of some sort is warranted, that such a response would be necessary, however risky it might prove to be.[3]

As McCloskey emphasizes and celebrates rhetoric, or the broadly linguistic art of persuasion, throughout the Bourgeois Era volumes and beyond, the political theorist will remind her of the political dimension of the classical humanist tradition in which she writes. It is the "faculty of language" and its ability "to declare what is just and what is unjust" that, according to Aristotle (1946, 6), makes us political animals, which, as Arendt and others never tired of reminding us, is not even the same as a social animal, much less an economic or moral animal (Arendt 1998). How can we distinguish these? All kinds of animals in addition to us are social animals; unlike politics, we don't need speech to be social. Economics, alternatively, is originally mostly about our necessary household (*oikos*) relations with unequals. Economics is about management, although it does have a public and rhetorical if not quite political element in our exchange relations (Arendt 1998, 160). As Smith noted, "Nobody ever saw a dog make a fair and deliberate exchange of one bone for another with another dog," as they and other nonhuman animals lack the requisite "means of persuasion" (Smith 1981a, 26).

Neoliberalism has made exchange, this classically public and comparatively egalitarian and free feature of economic life—Karl Marx's "very Eden of the innate rights of man" (Marx 1976, 280)—absolutely foundational not only for its political economy but for life in general. For most neoliberals, this feature is no longer public but instead reduced to its psychological dimension, to Smith's "propensity in human nature . . . to truck, barter, and exchange" (1981a, 25), stripped of the latter's attention to rhetoric and stripped of his much richer moral psychology. From this antipolitical and antirhetorical foundation, inattentive to both classical and Enlightenment antecedents, neoliberalism rhetorically feeds the increasingly hierarchical and securitized worldly context that it theoretically suppresses. McCloskey joins neoliberals in elevating one aspect of economics over others and in making it a foundational object of theoretical solicitude; she doesn't begin, as Smith does, with labor (Smith 1981a), much less with jurisprudence (Smith 1982b). But she follows Smith in reminding her colleagues of the crucial rhetorical dimension of economic exchange and of the virtues that sustain it, and this attention to virtue and to rhetoric necessarily refers beyond exchange and beyond economics altogether.

Note, however, that we can read shelves of neoliberal literature, and McCloskey's work is unfortunately no exception, and almost never be reminded of a simple political-economic fact: most people in capitalist societies don't do the bulk of their work and earning directly in and through the marketplace. We are instead, in classical terms, masters or servants; the vast majority of us, even those of us in management and the professions, earn by working for others. We may not truck or barter, but we do a lot of truckling for our pay, and even our ideally free and public exchanging is not really that: it consists mostly of spending wages and salaries (that we make from our contractual participation in hierarchical organizations) when we're off the clock, exchanging with others who are usually on the clock while we're not. There are exceptions, of course. I have a wonderfully McCloskeyian virtuous, dignified, and egalitarian experience with the couple that owns the dry cleaning establishment down the street whenever we do business together. But I'm very glad that I don't work for them, and it's not the case that they work for me, and getting my shirts laundered is not even a necessary thing for me to do. Thus our sometimes rhetorically rich exchange is not structured or haunted by any element of coercive managing or being managed. (I imagine that theirs is a cooperative and collaborative relationship, which from all appearances it is.) These moments of mutual market-stall encounter, these flashes of commercial Eden, are the exception and not the rule in the relatively despotic economic lives that the vast majority of us lead.

In classical terms, what we call morality can look outward and play a crucial rhetorical and even political role as ethos, but it is generally more about our souls, or for the secular among us, about our inward-looking relationship with what we call our consciences, our second-order desires, our wills, our essential identities, and so on. Politics, on the other hand, is about our relationship to others in the common, in the public realm, in that encompassing "completion of associations existing by nature" (Aristotle 1946, 5), an association of citizens (*politai*), and so its virtues are not exclusively or even fundamentally social, or economic, or moral. The rhetorical tradition from which McCloskey draws, unlike McCloskey herself, sees politics not as a necessary evil but instead as the noble art of human living-together among equals.[4]

The contradiction, then, is that McCloskey is continually reminding us that we are political animals, in the sense that it is the rhetoric with which we maintain or transform our common life that counts; yet she is, for various understandable if not sustainable reasons, going to do everything she can to avoid recognizing this politics *as* politics. Instead, she repeatedly construes political phenomena as moral phenomena. It is this fundamental misrecognition of politics that allows her work to so easily contribute to the neoliberal transformations of our commons, despite what I take to be its best intentions.

Institutions, Agency Theory, and Republican Freedom

A close look at chapter 33 of *Bourgeois Dignity* confirms that McCloskey's demoralization critique uncovers only to suppress the political dimension disenchanted by neoliberal rhetoric. McCloskey's moralized reading of the political-theoretical grounds of freedom and obligation contributes to neoliberal rule even as this reading is motivated by worries about the consequences of that rule. My study of this chapter informs a reflection on McCloskey's conflation of Machiavelli and Hobbes in the earlier *Bourgeois Virtues*, a conflation that further dramatizes her political blind spot.

Chapter 33—on what institutions are not—is for the argument of *Bourgeois Dignity* a kind of aside. In the preceding chapters, McCloskey has been criticizing flawed accounts of the Great Fact of enrichment; she argues in the chapter following that institutions—for example, property rights and parliamentary supremacy—will not explain it. But she pauses in chapter 33 to take swipes at an increasingly dominant understanding of what institutions *are*. This understanding is captured in Douglass North's claim that institutions are "the humanly devised constraints that structure political, economic, and social interaction" (quoted in McCloskey 2011, 297). Institutions can do this as manipulators of humans understood on a view that always sees us as "Max U, that unlovely maximizer of Utility, *Homo prudens*, the prudent human—never *Homo ludens* . . . or *Homo faber* . . . and *Homo hierarchus* . . . or, as I and most non-economist social scientists would claim, *Homo loquens*, the speaking human" (McCloskey 2011, 297). Again, *Homo loquens* is certainly familiar to political theorists in her role as *Homo politikos*. And in chapter 33, it is *Homo politikos* that McCloskey sidles up to only to push away again.

The argument takes a political turn with a discussion of corporate governance and its teaching in business schools, with an account of how the former managerial ideology, with its ideas of stewardship and the common good, was undermined by Max U agency theory assumptions. McCloskey agrees that a watershed moment for the agency theory revolution was the appearance of a popular article by Milton Friedman, yet she insists on defending her former colleague: "Friedman says that managers should increase the stock value of the firm *subject to the norms and laws of the society*—which is a rather different principle than 'the public be damned'" (McCloskey 2011, 305, emphasis in text). Friedman's article, however, is itself a powerful polemic aimed at dismantling established norms and legal interpretations: it targets the whole Berle-Means school of corporate governance, the then-still-dominant framework for coming to terms with the peculiar kind of restricted commons that is a business corporation and with its place in liberal-democratic society (Berle and Means 1932; see also Davis 2011). In 1970, Friedman was insistent, against decades of theory and practice in a society that understood itself as free, that to understand the large business corporation in even a limited way as the political creature that it is, rather than as a purely economic creation of consenting adults, is the road to tyranny (Friedman 1970). What Friedman means by the qualification emphasized by McCloskey is "subject to the norms and laws of society as I see them and as I hope and trust that you will too after reading this." Perhaps the greatest irony of Friedman's attack on managerial ideology is that an argument based in the principal-agent problem (managers are duty-bound to serve owners, not "society") probably helped undermine the effective fiduciary responsibility of managers to owners in subsequent years ("Friedman and B-school told me I'm all about profit for individuals rather than about any imaginary institution, and so long as I am, then why not . . . ?").[5]

To her credit, McCloskey sees this. She concedes that "the tendency in the Chicago School of the 1970s cannot be doubted," and she bundles Friedman's attack on extant corporate governance with attacks from the left and right on the professions and with economic theories of regulation, the "human capital"–centered new labor economics, and the older Buchanan/Tullock public-choice school and Coasian and other law and economics (McCloskey 2011, 305–6). But she retreats to a moral and moral-psychological from a political interpretation of these tendencies: "All the Chicago economists strode past meaning—love, temperance, courage, justice, faith, hope—and fixed on the individual agent's prudent self-interest, like a prudent blade of grass" (McCloskey 2011, 306). This is not to say that her own understanding of the virtues is ultimately psychological—she is saying that rather than a blade of grass or other atom of mere life, we should be attentive to actual people and their conversations and conventions—the problem is that her reading of her opponents is at best methodological; they proceed from incorrect assumptions. And so we are left somewhat mystified about the constitutive effects of this wrongheaded rhetoric, with only occasional hints slipping out as in the Friedman and business school example—which I am arguing, and McCloskey is strongly hinting, was quite politically consequential for US practices of corporate governance.

In the last part of the chapter, however, McCloskey's political slips get bigger. Returning to and mocking corporate agency theory, she writes, "Align the incentives of managers with the interests of the stockholders. That is all ye know on earth, and all ye need to know. The Great Recession gave us all some perspective on how agency theory works" (McCloskey 2011, 307). Alan Greenspan's remarks during what he called the "credit tsunami" of 2008 could be a target here, as Greenspan expressed the kind of shock from on high that no mere mortal would feel regarding the behavior of financial managers (Andrews 2008). But of course—despite the probable role of legal and other institutional changes urged by Greenspan, among others—a psychological rather than structural account is favored by both McCloskey and Greenspan (McCloskey's "commitment" and Keynesian "animal spirits," Greenspan's "animal spirits" and "euphoria"), neatly replicating what Anna Kornbluh has identified in the Victorian turn away from critical financial journalism toward the new discipline of psychology (Kornbluh 2014). The upshot is that the crisis mustn't be viewed primarily as a political or institutional problem; what is missing according to McCloskey and Greenspan is sufficient virtue (Greenspan, unlike McCloskey, needs to translate the *S* variable of honor into the *P* variable of "'concerns for reputation'" [Goodman 2008]). But, anti-Keynesians that both McCloskey and Greenspan are, even this psychological and moral critique is potentially too much. Neither is going to want to give any justification for any meddling; Greenspan will suggest at least a partial fix from the deployment by market actors themselves of better actuarial science, and McCloskey will be reluctant to suggest anything at all for fear again of giving ground to critics of innovating spontaneous-ordering markets. Of course, this aversion to meddling didn't prevent Greenspan and the vast majority of his anti-interventionist colleagues from endorsing massive state action in support of collapsing financial markets (on "contingent neoliberalism," see Davies 2014, 148–87).

McCloskey continues her critique of agency theory with an acute insight regarding its fundamental contradiction: agency theory is all about obligation—the obligation of agents to principals—and at the same time, it dissolves the foundation for obligation with its prudence-only, Max U approach (McCloskey 2011, 307). She views this problem, however, in moral-philosophical and phenomenological rather than political-theoretical terms as the simultaneous need for and nonrecognition of a meaning-making creature who feels ethical responsibility. But from a political-theoretical point of view, she is getting at a deep problem of authority and the foundations of law. The problem goes like this: even Thomas Hobbes, a *P*-only adversary in *The Bourgeois Virtues*, has what H. L. A. Hart called a "peremptory" theory of legal obligation (Hart 1982, 253). I must obey the law not merely because it is in my interest or our interest to do so but because it is the law, because it issues from the sovereign, who has authority, whom in the final analysis I have authorized. It is Bentham, another and more strictly appropriate *P*-only adversary from *The Bourgeois Virtues*, who does away with this ground of legal obligation; for Bentham, my obligation to obey the law is actually nothing other than the interest I have in obeying it. This is why sanctions must outweigh benefits, as they construct the interest that is my obligation to obey (Bentham 1997, 158–60; Engelmann 2001). Again, McCloskey is not wrong to view this as a problem for moral agency, but she is silent on the prior problem of its transformation of political order: what happens to the character of rule and to the conditions of freedom when we thus convert the meaning of law by reconfiguring it as policy? The mainstream of the law-and-economics movement—not just its Posnerian extreme—has done a lot to systematize this reconfiguration, such that the practice of rights is transformed, with consequences that go well beyond fiduciary duty to basics of civil and criminal law and justice: breach of contract is just another cost for the rich, and plea-bargaining is a much more efficient way than trial to manage the poor.

Finally, McCloskey turns in this chapter to a surprising discussion of liberty (McCloskey 2011, 307–9). She shows appreciation for the neo-Roman theory revived by Quentin Skinner among others. Skinner was frustrated with the way liberty was being talked about within twentieth-century liberalism; too many discussions took their cues from Isaiah Berlin's 1958 account of positive versus negative liberty, a brilliant (if transformatively postclassical) analytical reprise of Constant's "The Liberty of Ancients Compared with That of the Moderns." Skinner argues in *Liberty before Liberalism* that the positive/negative dichotomy obscures a more political idea of liberty of crucial importance in the early modern era. If positive liberty asks "who rules" (answer: my best self) and negative liberty asks "how much rule" (answer: as little as possible), then what about that which is more fundamental to liberty: the quest for independence, especially freedom from arbitrary power (Berlin 1969, 118–72; Skinner 1998)? Dependence is unfreedom; freedom is, in McCloskey's words, about "whether you are under the orders of some other mortal" (McCloskey 2011, 308). If you are, you're not free; freedom is a condition. If we think of freedom as rational self-control (positive) or as noninterference (negative), we can't adequately account for how a continent and mobile slave is unfree. But of course he or she is.

On this neo-Roman conception of freedom, "dependency itself was a scandal—even though a potential rather than an exercised impediment" (McCloskey 2011, 308). And here McCloskey delivers a most surprising line, showing her affinity for the classical political-theoretical package I outlined above: all kinds of people who have historically been treated by liberals and neoliberals alike as free consenters are basically slaves of a sort, including not only many wives but also those "employ[ed] in a corporation" and even assistant professors (McCloskey 2011, 309). Others have used this insight in the service of wholesale opposition to the system of wage labor (see Gourevitch 2015), among other political upshots. But McCloskey has at this point already pivoted and translated this resolutely political conception of freedom into a feature of individual identity: "An actual impediment is a constraint, à la Max U. A potential impediment is a symbol and a shame. . . . It would often show itself, for example, through internalized self-contempt" (McCloskey 2011, 308).[6]

Again, I am not saying that this translation is simply wrong; it no doubt gets at important truths about the moral consequences and the phenomenological experience of dependence. But it leads to a misunderstanding of what might be at stake here from a political point of view. The misunderstanding is evident from McCloskey's closing discussion of the death of the republican martyr Algernon Sidney in 1683. "Sidney dared to refuse to plead when faced with charges of treason before Charles II's pet judges, and died for it. He died for meaning and morality, not for Prudence Only and incentives" (McCloskey 2011, 309). But did he die for meaning and morality? Isn't this a weirdly reflexive and unparsimonious way of putting it? Why not take Sidney at his word and simply say that he died for the "*lawes of this land*" (Sidney 1772: X.3)—that is, for the *res publica*, for the public thing, for the freedom of it, which is inseparable from freedom within it?

McCloskey's affinity for the nondomination thesis is no doubt sincere, but as formulated, in terms of meaning and morality, it is in danger of echoing a dominant strain of our neoliberal zeitgeist—the rage against the supposed inefficiency and unfreedom of Fordism and Fordist institutions, against the expense and rigidity of structures associated with the labor/capital pacts of twentieth-century liberalism and social democracy. Austerity and labor flexibility have been continually imposed on workers in the name of their freedom. Consider the questioning in recent decades of the value of unions and lifetime employment, and recall the enumerating of ways that welfare benefits harm the unemployed themselves by fostering the scandal of dependency. Notice how often we are exhorted to free ourselves from dependency (on drugs, relationships, etc.) through a new orientation to ourselves; notice how often we are called upon to exercise exit rather than voice (Hirschman 1970) to alter our circumstances of possible dependency through alert individual initiative. "Be your own boss!" "Brand yourself!" "Stuck? Don't just sit there; today's the day; visit Monster.com." In the neoliberal imaginary, all employment and even unemployment are always already self-employment; we are investors in and purveyors of our "human capital," a postwar economic category promoted by McCloskey. Classical political economy and New Liberalism acknowledged that class was a requisite of capitalism; human capital, among other things, turns class standing and power from a relationship with others and a product of political-economic order into a feature of the enterprising self and its development.

When the neo-Roman critique of dependency is taken up in the way that McCloskey does—mainly in terms of identity, meaning, morality, and new technologies of the self—a profound translation is performed. To put the matter in starkly political terms, imagine Frederick Douglass escaping from Maryland to Massachusetts not to work for Abolition but to get a new life and call it a day, or perhaps to serve meaning and morality by exhorting slaves to run away or by running free webinars advising them how to run away. For the liberal and republican Douglass, the lack of a *political* response to slavery is unthinkable. McCloskey's engagement with Sidney reminds us of the still-central place of a republican imaginary in the liberal tradition. But her moral interpretation, in light of its family resemblance to neoliberal uptakes of freedom-as-nondependence, likely contributes to the contemporary disenchantment of politics.

Sidney and Douglass are political creatures attentive to worldly conditions: they think ultimately from the outside of the self, not from the inside. Through her study of the history of the moral sentiments, McCloskey teaches us that the kind of virtue displayed by Sidney and Douglass is not about unselfishness versus selfishness, about "altruism" versus "egoism." She clearly conveys how the modern cant about altruism misunderstands the virtues and is just as problematically psychological as egoism; this is why Gary Becker's self-styled ecumenism (his Max U accommodation of "altruistic preferences") is nothing of the sort (Becker 1992 and McCloskey 2006, 109–12; see also Dixon 2008). But even a sophisticated understanding of the virtues can confuse political and moral problems and political and moral solutions. Sidney's martyrdom was first and foremost a political act, both in its intent and in its meaning for contemporaries.

McCloskey's misrecognition and translation of politics, her conflation of politics and morality, is evident from her conflation of Hobbes and Machiavelli as prudence-only thinkers in *The Bourgeois Virtues* (McCloskey 2006,

372). A moral perspective can indeed see them allied as dangerous theorists of expediency. But from a political-theoretical point of view, Hobbes and Machiavelli are virtual opposites. Sidney's republican martyrdom is the kind of orientation that Hobbes, three decades earlier, had identified as a serious threat to political order, along with the willingness to die for God (the two often went hand in hand during the English Civil Wars of the 1640s). Prudence-only wasn't so much a universal assumption about human behavior for Hobbes as it was a solution to the problem of intestinal political conflict; a regime that would institutionalize prudence isn't the whole solution—that requires additionally a political science that constructs authority—but it goes a long ways toward solving the problem. According to Hobbes, we need to look to human nature rather than to history for politically relevant knowledge. The whole framing of *Leviathan* is quite deliberately introspective (Hobbes 1968, 82–83); if we can get individuals focused on their own passions—most prominently the passion of fear that undergirds all prudence—perhaps we can get them off of thinking about history, of thinking about the examples of great cities and the great deeds that made and maintained them (Hobbes 1968, 267–68). In this way, we can tug people away from their temptation to think to the common, to the world they inhabit and reshape with and against others and in which they both act in concert and strive for distinction.

Machiavelli is no Hobbes. First, just as Hobbes supplements prudence with authority in *Leviathan*, Machiavelli, even in *The Prince*, reminds us of how imprudent prudence can be for the purpose of building and maintaining political power and order in a contingent world. Calculating prudence must be more than supplemented by impetuosity and glory seeking, hence chapter 25's notorious "fortune is a woman" passage (Machiavelli 1950, 94). But more important, Machiavelli in all his writings denigrates the care of the interior of the self in favor of an orientation toward the outside, toward rule of the kingdom or care of the city. He goes so far as to express his wariness of Christianity, which he sees as dangerously unpolitical in its orientation toward the soul (Machiavelli 1950, 285). This couldn't be further from the introspection of Hobbes. The difference manifests itself methodologically in Machiavelli's elevation of history and experience as sources of knowledge in *The Prince* and manifests itself politically in the praise of republican freedom in *The Discourses*. Machiavelli goes so far as to praise the very sort of factional political strife, for example, between the Roman Senate and the people, that Hobbes will condemn; it is this strife, according to Machiavelli, that preserves the mutually supportive virtue, power, and freedom of the Roman political order (Machiavelli 1950, 118–21). For Hobbes, of course, faction starts one on the slippery slope to ruin (Hobbes 1968, 236–37).

In their disenchantment of politics, neoliberals are not at all heirs to Machiavelli; they are heirs to Hobbes. Although they get tools of disenchantment—their economics—from a refinement of Bentham, they get their politics from Hobbes: they are antipluralists through and through (pluralism begets rent-seeking). The class politics of classical liberalism and the group politics of social liberalism are replaced by an antipolitical scene of all and one. Nascent in the liberal discovery of society but fully developed by neoliberalism is what Arendt, following Gunnar Myrdal, calls the "'communist fiction'" of economics, its positing of "'the interest of society as a whole'" (Arendt 1998, 44n). Thus pluralism and countervailing power give way to economic rule. The disenchantment of politics by economics is more consequential than any Max U moral disenchantment. McCloskey, in her emphasis on moral disenchantment and her understandable skittishness about arguing its effects, goes so far as to convert political questions into moral ones. And this, in turn, wittingly or not, contributes to the neoliberal (antipolitical) political project.

Conclusion: Value, (In)Equality, and the Disenchantment of Politics

A good part of McCloskey's critique of demoralization and effort at remoralization consists in singing the praises of capitalism, or innovation, or trade-tested betterment. Thus even as she works rhetorically to protect moralized virtues from reduction or erasure by neoliberal economics, she at the same time joins the neoliberal political battle against organized attempts to protect institutionalized virtues from market tests. In her advocacy of trade-tested betterment, McCloskey is quite happy to dismiss such demands for protection as the work of an at best misguided and at worst nefarious market-interfering or market-distorting politics. This is typical of her writing on the bourgeois era, and yet this approach sits in some tension with her appreciation of the value of rhetoric and of professional and other politically salient virtues.

Consider an example close to home: the political economy of the contemporary university (an institution that, like the church, predates modern capitalism). If my continued employment at my public university depended on my meeting market or market-like rather than professional tests, I might be out of a job very quickly. So might many of us throughout the academy: physics, philosophy, and many other core disciplines are not great commanders of any market share, and they are in danger of losing quasi-market "customer satisfaction" or "workforce development" tests being instituted by some administrators and policy makers. McCloskey could, however, pass basic market tests with ease, and considering the quality and quantity of her work, I can only applaud this from a professional-test standard. But this coincidence of test results would be a mere coincidence; she would do well for what we professionals think are the wrong reasons. She would do well because of her production of a product enjoying significant effective demand—to be precise, the production of trade-tested-betterment boosterism for deep-pocketed think tanks whose funders have a strong and sometimes direct financial interest in promoting it. As a political theorist with some knowledge of the history of political economy (rather than, say, a classicist or a set theorist), I could of course start producing lesser but quite passable products too and probably make a living at it from these same think tanks. Why? I know how to make what I take it are false or at best radically insufficient arguments defending the justice and utility of capitalist society. If I did this, however, McCloskey would agree that my practice would be vicious rather than virtuous: it would be corrupt. To be a bit grandiose about it, we are both seekers after truth: she, on the market-test alternative, would still be practicing her craft; I, on the other hand, would be practicing the craft of money making at the expense of my craft.

If McCloskey is correct in her Bourgeois Era argument about the centrality of rhetoric to the Great Fact, then her own work of "rhetorical investment in renewal" (McCloskey 2011, 374) might be fantastically valuable—potentially productive of far more wealth than any market reward she would ever receive for it. But if McCloskey is correct, then my work might be pretty valuable too. This skeptical essay and some of the other material I have published might be a bit destructive of wealth, but not very destructive, not only because of its relatively innocuous political character, but because, as with most of us, hardly anybody reads the stuff anyway. My nondoctrinal teaching, on the other hand—which I try as best I can to do in the grand liberal arts tradition—could do far more than counterbalance the effects of my research. On McCloskey's account, if I teach just a few people to be far more effective trade-tested betterment promoters than they already are, I might earn my keep many times over in future tax receipts alone. If, on the other hand, I'm tossed out or retire and my position is turned over to a donor and the donor's market test needs to be met—something like this is happening in some parts of the academy, where donors have actively participated in hires (see, e.g., Hundley 2011)—then who knows? Maybe my replacement would be less valuable on McCloskey's account of value. This scenario is only one of many ways by which, extrapolating from McCloskey's account, the introduction of market tests might degrade the system of trade-tested betterment as a whole in a way that only an economic historian years later could ever possibly confirm.

Yet McCloskey thinks of state university professors as a protected class living at others' expense (McCloskey 2011, 431). Now retired, she quipped before retirement that she would quietly and happily go if and when she were replaced by a machine. But if the invention of the book didn't replace the classroom and instructors, then why should the web, even Web 2.0, do so? Shedding educators is less likely to be a function of betterment in education than it will be a capitulation to managerial rhetorics of innovation and efficiency and to the erosion of a public commitment to postsecondary education. If present trends continue and higher education is radically transformed in the years ahead, I risk a prediction for you: the rich will continue to send their children to traditional colleges and universities for face-to-face learning, no matter how expensive. This doesn't mean that more innovative institutions will have failed any market test. Demand might be quite high for their cheaper product; effective demand is, after all, a matter of willingness to pay, which presupposes ability to pay. McCloskey was right to abandon the faddish "innovation" of *Bourgeois Dignity* for the "trade-tested betterment" of *Bourgeois Equality*, because innovations don't necessarily make life any better, even in the long run. But it is not clear which successful market tests and background conditions do either.

The future of the university is only one small concern about the fate of institutional pluralism in the face of neoliberal rule with its love of markets and market-ish metrics. New Liberal and socialist architects of and agitators for the institutions of social liberalism were motivated in part by the project of politically constructing conditions for widespread economic prosperity and independence; they were motivated by the project of constructing what they saw as conditions for universal freedom. In acknowledging neo-Roman freedom-as-independence, McCloskey acknowledges an inescapably political phenomenon even as she suppresses it with a moral interpretation. But how can I properly attend to our independence or to my independence if I am not aware that that condition is not really a function of my or our beliefs or intentions (in the way that my or our identity at least partially is) but instead has everything to do with the world between, with the public thing? The public thing is politically constituted. And as many advocates for social liberalism recognized, the problem of dependence illustrates the intimate link between freedom and equality, between my freedom as a nondependent and my equal station among others. The link between freedom and equality continues to be a subject for liberal reflection, as evidenced by the title of McCloskey's third Bourgeois Era volume (*Bourgeois Equality*, 2016). Here her historical work acknowledges that this equality is in large part a political matter. But in her commentary on contemporary (in)equality, she conceives of this (in)equality in neoliberal and unpolitical rather than liberal republican terms.

In Arendt's influential discussion of the rights of man in *The Origins of Totalitarianism*, she notes the political constitution of equality: "The public sphere is as consistently based on the law of equality as the private sphere is based on the law of universal difference and differentiation. Equality, in contrast to all that is involved in mere existence, is not given us, but is the result of human organization insofar as it is guided by the principle of justice. We are not born equal; we become equal as members of a group on the strength of our decision to guarantee ourselves mutually equal rights." Arendt goes on to remind us that a politically free commons is necessarily constituted by, and is constitutive of, equality: "Our political life rests on the assumption that we can produce equality through organization, because man can act in and change and build a common world, together with his equals and only with his equals" (Arendt 1973, 301). These reminders are crucial in a chapter that explains the paradoxes and limits of a doctrine of human rights; equal rights are constituted and guaranteed by political orders, and global humanity is not a political order.

In their ventures into political theory, the great neoliberals of the twentieth century, such as Hayek and Friedman, do accommodate a residue of the public and its political equality (Mihic 2009): witness Hayek's stated love for the rule of law and Friedman's similar embrace of common rules and impartial judges. But even these more political of the neoliberal thinkers see the state as a sovereign that should serve competition: Hayek wants to make "the best possible use of the forces of competition as a means of co-ordinating human efforts" (Hayek 1944, 36), and Friedman similarly wants to "foster competitive markets" (Friedman 1962, 2). They don't see the contradiction here with their views on the antitelocratic character of liberal justice because they see the market as serving the plurality of human purposes in all their grand diversity. The Hayek/Friedman state is not about itself and the dynamic maintenance of the equality it forges; its technocratic appropriation, already in their own work, marks a big step on the way to "how the overall exercise of political power can be modeled on the principles of a market economy" (Foucault 2008, 131). This journey is complete when the state is conceptually built back up from market processes, as it is in the neoinstitutionalism criticized by McCloskey and its public choice and law-and-economics predecessors. Here politics is not just shrunk and instrumentalized; it is fully disenchanted and displaced (see also Coleman 2013).

Although McCloskey rejects any reductionist approach to institutions, her avoidance of political theory has her even less prepared than Hayek or Friedman to appreciate the importance of the political organization of equality. Her discussion in *Bourgeois Equality* is decidedly world-historical; in this way, she tries as best she can to depoliticize the problem of inequality, to move it out of its institutional settings. She mostly explores several variations on a prominent argument about absolute versus relative enrichment that dates back at least to Mandeville, who remarked how "the very Poor Liv'd better than the Rich before" (Mandeville 1988, 26, 169), and "if the Ancient *Britons* and *Gauls* should come out of their Graves, with what Amazement wou'd they gaze on the mighty Structures every where rais'd for the Poor!" (Mandeville 1988, 171). McCloskey follows in a long line of theorists who encourage us not to worry about inequality as such—for example, the yawning wealth gap between rich and the rest of us—but instead to consider the Great Fact of increasing enrichment and its contribution to a kind of equality of genuine comfort that she argues remains on the rise.

But whether or not we accept her history and her prognosis, this approach of hers ignores a serious problem resulting from the subordination of the political conditions of freedom to market logics. Against McCloskey and other economists, a long republican tradition warns of the political dangers of material inequality. McCloskey claims to share the concern this tradition has that "those who have the gold, rule" (McCloskey 2006, 45), but she is at the same time fairly hostile to the various forms of collective action that have traditionally kept plutocrats in check (McCloskey 2006, 42–53). We don't have to agree with Machiavelli that freedom requires that we periodically get together and kill some gentlemen (Machiavelli 1950, 254–55), but surely Ben Bernanke is right that not getting together to jail some bankers after 2008 was a big and perhaps even catastrophic mistake (Page 2015). McCloskey is out of touch in thinking that the gold is with the median voter (McCloskey 2006, 45–46). The median voter would have been happy to jail some bankers. That this and many others of that voter's policy preferences aren't exercised says something about the relationship between increasing economic inequality and increasing political oligarchy, a relationship that is getting a new wave of attention from mainstream American political science (see, e.g., Winters and Page 2009). But the political challenge posed by neoliberalism is more than the challenge of plutocrats and their policy preferences. By disenchanting politics with economics, neoliberalism has produced a distinctive grammar of rule, one that has been steadily corroding liberalism's resources of rights, pluralism, and countervailing power. McCloskey's hostility toward collective action is unfortunately reflected in developments like the growing substitution of private arbitration for public class-action civil justice in US consumer and employment law (Silver-Greenberg and Gebeloff 2015). Yes, this is a plutocrat-driven policy change. But its success is related to the continuous deployment of rhetorics of efficiency, flexibility, and individual choice that have steadily undermined our sense of the common and its conditions of freedom. It has become increasingly clear that we no longer need a liberal-democratic order to sustain some form of trade-tested betterment, or capitalism. We can do it with other forms of organization—witness the Chinese state, and witness our own oligarchic national-security surveillance state.

The neoliberal law professor Eric Posner has wondered aloud what exactly the objection is to recently exposed NSA surveillance programs. After all, we trade information for benefits on a regular basis, and knowing of these programs might give us a "sense of creepiness," but what real harm do they do to our freedom or anything else (Foust, Jaffer, and Posner 2013)? Posner's position is hardly mainstream, but that it is as thinkable as it is today is telling. In our leading capitalist societies, it is generally only fringe right- and left-wing rhetoric that even raises the problem of republican freedom, as the ends of our common life are assumed rather than examined in a public discourse dominated by the economists' rendering of utility. McCloskey's advocacy for market tests unfortunately gives aid and comfort to the myriad consultants who use the rhetoric of economics to advise governments and other public and private institutions. Yes, she thinks that many of these consultants are peddling snake oil. But that their advice might be bad or at best useless is less serious, in my view, than their disenchantment of politics by economics.

McCloskey does write against disenchantment. But her emphasis is on moral disenchantment, and she is reluctant to name any worldly consequences of that disenchantment. She is reluctant to name consequences, I suggest, because of the political implications of naming them. She comes closest to such naming in her discussion of freedom. When it comes to freedom, neoliberal economists are generally satisfied with the consent theory that undergirds and justifies their emphasis on the centrality of choice and voluntary exchange as the route to the good life. McCloskey, however, recognizes in her discussion of neo-Roman freedom that choice-as-consent can lead us astray and even underwrite a kind of slavery. Political theorists tend to think it vital that we have a continuing public conversation about the conditions of freedom, which is necessarily a conversation about our common life and our own and others' standing in it. To even have this conversation requires working at the continuing project of organizing equality; it requires struggling to maintain the space for the preservation of old or the arrival of new claims of right.

McCloskey is absolutely right that a good part of what constitutes and reconstitutes the common is rhetoric. She might find my political-theoretical rhetoric irritating and potentially destructive: "There goes another misguided member of the clerisy, sowing doubts about capitalism and the bourgeoisie." I have tried to show, however, how rhetoric like mine here—a republican concern with the conditions of freedom, wary of both the bourgeoisie and their economists—springs up in her own work, if only to be suppressed by a moral interpretation. This moral interpretation, turning the focus away from the common and toward the self's relationship to itself, abets the very forces that are effectively undermining conditions of freedom in part by displacing our attentiveness toward them, which in turn helps disenchant what sustains them. Thus neoliberal political disenchantment stands out as an unintended consequence of Deirdre McCloskey's generally virtuous and enchanting intellectual practice.

Notes

1. Although my criticisms of economics are by no means restricted to this economic libertarianism, they are aimed at a limited range of historical and contemporary argument. Many economists—especially those who draw on more heterodox traditions in the field—will not recognize themselves in what follows.

2. In fact, as I have tried to persuade her in conversation, her (moral) nemesis Bentham is a (political-historical) McCloskeyian ally of the first order: his 1787 *Defence of Usury* attacks Smith's ceiling on interest rates in a paean to the dignity and liberty of moneylenders and projectors, two particularly despised wings of McCloskey's heroic bourgeoisie (Bentham 1952, 121–207).

3. I call the view that politics is potentially deadly and at best a necessary evil "libertarian" rather than neoliberal because this view of politics has strong classical liberal antecedents; Thomas Paine, for example, writes in *Common Sense* of how society arises from our virtues and government from our vices (Paine 1986, 65). This view is a particularly pronounced and at times paranoid strain of Shklar's liberalism of fear. But in the late eighteenth and early nineteenth centuries, this state-phobic view was more prevalent, ironically, among those thinkers who at the same time leaned more republican and who, like Paine, Jefferson, and the Jacksonian democrats, celebrated the people and their collective self-rule. Smith was not state-phobic, as illustrated by book 5 of the *Wealth of Nations* (Smith 1981b, 689–947). In the American context especially, the bulk of Madison's "most considerate and virtuous citizens" (Madison 2015b)—the Hamiltonian Federalists and their successors—leaned more liberal; they were advocates of the strong state they thought necessary to build and maintain a commercial empire. Recent histories of American political development have recognized again how much of a Leviathan was intended from the beginning and for what purposes (Edling 2003, 2014). Contemporary libertarians remain oblivious to this history and to the contradictions it implies for their thinking. This is the case even though some of the history relevant to this contradiction between their conception of liberty and their state-phobia is relatively recent; for example, the expansion of individual rights in the twentieth century and beyond has entailed the expansion of claims on others to respect those rights, which is connected, for better and worse, to the growth of a judicial and security apparatus that enforces such claims.

4. Political theorists might object that I am blending what the literature distinguishes as "civic humanist" and "civic republican" notes in the course of my critique (see, e.g., Lovett 2014). But these distinctions, like those between these and liberalism, can be overdrawn as historical matters (after all, Constant's 1819 lecture combines moments of all three); my emphasis here is the contrast between any properly political perspective and a disenchanting and disempowering economic alternative.

5. In the course of making his 1970 argument, Friedman reiterates the bracingly antipolitical market/state binary of *Capitalism and Freedom* (1962, 22–23): the more we can do collectively through what he calls "unanimity," the better. We can't do away with the state altogether, but we should do away with it as much as possible, because one can only dominate or be dominated through the state—be a winner or a loser—whereas in the market we all have our way through transactions freely chosen. Note how this completes and purifies classical liberalism's reversal of priority between Aristotelian *polis* and *oikos*; economy and the private are for Aristotle the place of life and necessary hierarchy, and politics and the public are the place of the good life and free equality (Aristotle 1946, 1–38).

6. Critical upshots from McCloskey's "slavery of a sort" are toward the end of *Bourgeois Dignity* actually mocked by her in a takedown of the rhetoric of wage slavery that defends even "terrible" jobs as the choice of the poor (McCloskey 2011, 424–25).

References

Amadae, Sonjae M. 2003. *Rationalizing Capitalist Democracy: The Cold War Origins of Rational Choice Liberalism.* Chicago: University of Chicago Press.

Andrews, Edmund L. 2008. "Greenspan Concedes Error on Regulation." *New York Times*, October 23. http://www.nytimes.com/2008/10/24/business/economy/24panel.html.

Arendt, Hannah. 1973. *The Origins of Totalitarianism.* New York: Harcourt Brace & Company.

Arendt, Hannah. 1998. *The Human Condition.* 2nd ed. Chicago: University of Chicago Press.

Aristotle. 1946. *The Politics of Aristotle.* Edited and translated by Ernest Barker. Oxford: Clarendon.

Becker, Gary S. 1992. "The Economic Way of Looking at Life." Nobel Lecture in Economics. http://www.nobelprize.org/nobel_prizes/economic-sciences/laureates/1992/becker-lecture.pdf.

Bentham, Jeremy. 1952. *Jeremy Bentham's Economic Writings.* Vol. 1. Edited by W. Stark. London: George Allen and Unwin.

Bentham, Jeremy. 1989. *First Principles Preparatory to Constitutional Code (The Collected Works of Jeremy Bentham).* Edited by Philip Schofield. Oxford: Clarendon.

Bentham, Jeremy. 1997. *De l'ontologie et autres textes sur les fictions.* Edited by Philip Schofield. Paris: Éditions du Seuil.

Berle, Adolf, and Means, Gardiner. 1932. *The Modern Corporation and Private Property.* New York: Macmillan.

Berlin, Isaiah. 1969. *Four Essays on Liberty.* Oxford: Oxford University Press.

Brown, Wendy. 2015. *Undoing the Demos: Neoliberalism's Stealth Revolution.* New York: Zone Books.

Coleman, William. 2013. "What Was 'New' about Neoliberalism?" *Economic Affairs* 33: 78–92.

Constant, Benjamin. 1988. *Constant: Political Writings.* Edited by Biancamaria Fontana. Cambridge: Cambridge University Press.

Davies, William. 2014. *The Limits of Neoliberalism: Authority, Sovereignty and the Logic of Competition.* London: Sage.

Davis, Gerald F. 2011. "The Twilight of the Berle and Means Corporation." *Seattle University Law Review* 34: 1121–38.

Dixon, Thomas. 2008. *The Invention of Altruism: Making Moral Meanings in Victorian Britain.* Oxford: Oxford University Press.

Donzelot, Jacques. 1979. *The Policing of Families*. Translated by Robert Hurley. New York: Pantheon.

Edling, Max. 2003. *A Revolution in Favor of Government: Origins of the U.S. Constitution and the Making of the American State*. Oxford: Oxford University Press.

Edling, Max. 2014. *A Hercules in the Cradle: War, Money, and the American State, 1783–1867*. Chicago: University of Chicago Press.

Engelmann, Stephen G. 2001. "Imagining Interest." *Utilitas* 13: 289–322.

Engelmann, Stephen G. 2003. *Imagining Interest in Political Thought: Origins of Economic Rationality*. Durham, NC: Duke University Press.

Engelmann, Stephen G. 2005. "Posner, Bentham and the Rule of Economy." *Economy and Society* 34: 32–50.

Engelmann, Stephen G. 2014. "Neoliberalism." In *The Encyclopedia of Political Thought*, edited by Michael T. Gibbons. Chichester: Wiley Blackwell.

Engelmann, Stephen G. n.d. *Skeptical Engineers: Evolution, Character, and the Pursuit of Social Science*. Manuscript in progress.

Foucault, Michel. 2007. *Security, Territory, Population: Lectures at the Collège de France 1977–78*. Translated by Graham Burchell. New York: Palgrave Macmillan.

Foucault, Michel. 2008. *The Birth of Biopolitics: Lectures at the Collège de France, 1978–79*. Translated by Graham Burchell. New York: Palgrave Macmillan.

Foust, Joshua, Posner, Eric, and Jaffer, Jameel. 2013. "Is the N.S.A. Surveillance Threat Real or Imagined?" *New York Times*, June 9. http://www.nytimes.com/roomfordebate/2013/06/09/is-the-nsa-surveillance-threat-real-or-imagined.

Fraser, Nancy. 2009. "Feminism, Capitalism and the Cunning of History." *New Left Review* 56: 97–117.

Friedman, Milton. 1962. *Capitalism and Freedom*. Chicago: University of Chicago Press.

Friedman, Milton. 1970. "A Friedman Doctrine: The Social Responsibility of Business Is to Increase Its Profits." *New York Times Magazine*, September 13. http://query.nytimes.com/mem/archive-free/pdf?res=9E05E0DA153CE531A15750C1A96F9C946190D6CF.

Goodman, Peter S. 2008. "Taking Hard New Look at a Greenspan Legacy." *New York Times*, October 8. http://www.nytimes.com/2008/10/09/business/economy/09greenspan.html.

Gourevitch, Alex. 2015. *From Slavery to the Cooperative Commonwealth: Labor and Republican Liberty in the Nineteenth Century*. Cambridge: Cambridge University Press.

Hart, Herbert L. A. 1982. *Essays on Bentham: Jurisprudence and Political Theory*. Oxford: Oxford University Press.

Harvey, David. 2005. *A Brief History of Neoliberalism*. Oxford: Oxford University Press.

Hayek, Friedrich A. 1944. *The Road to Serfdom*. Chicago: University of Chicago Press.

Hayek, Friedrich A. 1967. *Studies in Philosophy, Politics and Economics*. London: Routledge.

Hayek, Friedrich A. 1982. *Law, Legislation, and Liberty: A New Statement of the Liberal Principles of Justice and Political Economy*. 1 vol. ed. London: Routledge.

Hirschman, Albert O. 1970. *Exit, Voice, and Loyalty: Responses to Decline in Firms, Organizations, and States*. Cambridge, MA: Harvard University Press.

Hobbes, Thomas. 1968. *Leviathan*. Edited by C. B. Macpherson. New York: Penguin.

Hobhouse, Leonard T. 1964. *Liberalism*. Oxford: Oxford University Press.

Hundley, Kris. 2011. "Billionaire's Role in Hiring Decisions at Florida State University Raises Questions." *Tampa Bay Times*, May 9. http://www.tampabay.com/news/business/billionaires-role-in-hiring-decisions-at-florida-state-university-raises/1168680.

Jefferson, Thomas. 2015. "From Thomas Jefferson to James Madison, 20 December 1787." Founders Online, National Archives. http://founders.archives.gov/documents/Jefferson/01-12-02-0454 (last update: December 30, 2015). Source: Boyd, Julian P., ed. 1955. *The Papers of Thomas Jefferson*. Vol. 12, *7 August 1787–31 March 1788*, 438–43. Princeton, NJ: Princeton University Press.

Jevons, William S. 1888. *The Theory of Political Economy*. 3rd ed. London: Macmillan. http://www.econlib.org/library/YPDBooks/Jevons/jvnPE.html.

Kalyvas, Andreas, and Katznelson, Ira. 2008. *Liberal Beginnings: Making a Republic for the Moderns*. Cambridge: Cambridge University Press.

Kornbluh, Anna. 2014. *Realizing Capital: Financial and Psychic Economies in Victorian Form*. New York: Fordham University Press.

Lovett, Frank. 2014. "Republicanism." In *The Stanford Encyclopedia of Philosophy*, edited by Edward N. Zalta. http://plato.stanford.edu/archives/win2015/entries/republicanism/.

Machiavelli, Niccolò. 1950. *The Prince and the Discourses*. Translated by Luigi Ricci. New York: Modern Library.

Madison, James. 2015a. "From James Madison to Thomas Jefferson, 4 February 1790." Founders Online, National Archives. http://founders.archives.gov/documents/Madison/01-13-02-0020 (last update: September 9, 2015). Source: Hobson, Charles F., and Rutland, Robert A., eds. 1981. *The Papers of James Madison*. Vol. 13, *20 January 1790–31 March 1791*, 18–26. Charlottesville, VA: University Press of Virginia.

Madison, James. 2015b. *The Federalist* Number 10, [22 November] 1787. Founders Online, National Archives. http://founders.archives.gov/documents/Madison/01-10-02-0178. Last updated December 30, 2015. Source: vol. 10 of Robert A. Rutland, Charles F. Hobson, William M. E. Rachal, and Frederika J. Teute, eds., *The Papers of James Madison, 27 May 1787–3 March 1788*, 263–70. Chicago: University of Chicago Press, 1977.

Mandeville, Bernard. 1988. *The Fable of the Bees: or Private Vices, Publick Benefits*. Indianapolis: Liberty Fund. Reprint of the 1924 Oxford University Press edition.

Marx, Karl. 1976. *Capital: A Critique of Political Economy, Vol. 1*. Translated by Ben Fowkes. New York: Penguin.

McCloskey, Deirdre N. 1990. *If You're So Smart: The Narrative of Economic Expertise*. Chicago: University of Chicago Press.

McCloskey, Deirdre N. 1998. *The Rhetoric of Economics*. 2nd ed. Madison: University of Wisconsin Press.

McCloskey, Deirdre N. 2002. *The Secret Sins of Economics*. Chicago: Prickly Paradigm Press.

McCloskey, Deirdre N. 2005. "The Demoralization of Economics: Can We Recover from Bentham and Return to Smith?" In *Feminism Confronts Homo Economicus: Gender, Law, and Society*, edited by Martha Albertson Fineman and Terence Dougherty, 20–31. Ithaca, NY: Cornell University Press.

McCloskey, Deirdre N. 2006. *The Bourgeois Virtues: Ethics for an Age of Commerce*. Chicago: University of Chicago Press.

McCloskey, Deirdre N. 2011. *Bourgeois Dignity: Why Economics Can't Explain the Modern World*. Chicago: University of Chicago Press.

McCloskey, Deirdre N. 2016. *Bourgeois Equality: How Ideas, Not Capital or Institutions, Transformed the World*. Chicago: University of Chicago Press.

Mihic, Sophia Jane. 2009. "Penumbras of Publicity: A Distinction Between Liberalism and Neoliberalism." Paper presented at Kurrents, "What Is the Common?," Gothenburg, Sweden, October 10–11.

Mihic, Sophia Jane. 2010. "Interpretation, Political Theory, and the Hegemony of Normative Theorizing." In *Democracy and Pluralism: The Political Thought of William E. Connolly*, edited by Alan Finlayson, 96–113. New York: Routledge.

Mill, James. 1992. *James Mill: Political Writings*. Edited by Terence Ball. Cambridge: Cambridge University Press.

Mill, John Stuart. 1981. *The Collected Works of John Stuart Mill, Vol. I: Autobiography and Literary Essays*. Edited by Paul Robson and Jack Stillinger. Toronto: University of Toronto Press.

Mirowski, Philip, and Plehwe, Dieter, eds. 2009. *The Road from Mont Pèlerin: The Making of the Neoliberal Thought Collective*. Cambridge, MA: Harvard University Press.

Oakeshott, Michael. 1962. *Rationalism in Politics and Other Essays*. New York: Basic Books.

Page, Susan. 2015. "Ben Bernanke: More Execs Should Have Gone to Jail for Causing Great Recession." *USA Today*, November 13. http://www.usatoday.com/story/news/politics/2015/10/04/ben-bernanke-execs-jail-great-recession-federal-reserve/72959402/.

Paine, Thomas. 1986. *Common Sense*, edited by Isaac Kramnick. New York: Penguin.

Rawls, John. 1999. *A Theory of Justice*. Rev. ed. Cambridge, MA: Harvard University Press.

Schofield, Philip. 2006. *Utility and Democracy: The Political Thought of Jeremy Bentham*. Oxford: Oxford University Press.

Shklar, Judith. 1989. "The Liberalism of Fear." In *Liberalism and the Moral Life*, edited by Nancy L. Rosenblum, 21–38. Cambridge, MA: Harvard University Press.

Sidney, Algernon. 1772. *The Works of Algernon Sydney*. New ed. In *Eighteenth Century Collections Online*. London: Gale.

Silver-Greenberg, Jessica, and Gebeloff, Robert. 2015. "Arbitration Everywhere, Stacking the Deck of Justice." *New York Times*, October 31. http://www.nytimes.com/2015/11/01/business/dealbook/arbitration-everywhere-stacking-the-deck-of-justice.html?_r=0.

Skinner, Quentin. 1998. *Liberty before Liberalism*. Cambridge: Cambridge University Press.

Smith, Adam. 1981a. *An Inquiry into the Nature and Causes of the Wealth of Nations*. Vol. 1. Indianapolis: Liberty Fund. Reprint of the 1976 Oxford University Press edition.

Smith, Adam. 1981b. *An Inquiry into the Nature and Causes of the Wealth of Nations*. Vol. 2. Indianapolis: Liberty Fund. Reprint of the 1976 Oxford University Press edition.

Smith, Adam. 1982a. *The Theory of Moral Sentiments*. Indianapolis: Liberty Fund. Reprint of the 1976 Oxford University Press edition.

Smith, Adam. 1982b. *Lectures on Jurisprudence*. Indianapolis: Liberty Fund. Reprint of the 1976 Oxford University Press edition.

Winters, Jeffrey A., and Page, Benjamin I. 2009. "Oligarchy in the United States?" *Perspectives on Politics* 7: 731–51.

Ziliak, Stephen T., and McCloskey, Deirdre N. 2008. *The Cult of Statistical Significance: How the Standard Error Costs Us Jobs, Justice, and Lives*. Ann Arbor: University of Michigan Press.

7

Economics as the Conversation about the Conversation of the Market

PETER J. BOETTKE AND VIRGIL HENRY STORR

Introduction

The connection between the Austrians' and McCloskey's understanding of economics and the economy is a deep one. In *The Rhetoric of Economics* (1985) as well as in *Knowledge and Persuasion in Economics* (1994), McCloskey has highlighted the scientific limits of modern approaches to economics and has made us attuned to the literary aspects of economic science. Economics, she explained, is a conversation and, even at its most positivistic and formalistic, economic science is an effort to persuade. As she (1990, 5) writes, "Economists are tellers of stories and makers of poems, and from recognizing this we can know better what economists do." Arguably, this view of the science not only makes apparent the unsatisfactory rhetoric of modernist methods (as she discusses) but also recommends the more literary and self-consciously rhetorical approaches adopted by Austrian economists. McCloskey's rhetorical turn is consistent with the Austrian insistence that economics is a science that attempts to explain and understand human action and with its recognition that making sense of human action means focusing on what people think and believe.[1]

Similarly, McCloskey has recommended that economists think of the economy as a conversation and so pay attention to the importance of all talk that involves efforts at persuasion in the market. As McCloskey (1994, 30) writes, "Economists specialize in knowing costs and benefits. But someone—maybe even a specialized economist—might want to learn about the speech by which people construct their stories of the cost and benefit." And, as she (1994, 30) explains, "The economy does a great deal of talking. . . . The faculty of speech deserves some analytic attention, even from economists." Also, as she writes with Klamer, "Economists view talk as cheap and culture as insignificant. Yet humans are talking animals, talking in their markets. The talk probably matters" (Klamer and McCloskey 1995, 191). Additionally, she has pointed out that at least a quarter of national income is persuasion (ibid.). McCloskey's recommendation that we view the economy as a conversation of conversing individuals is consistent with the Austrian view that the market is a spontaneous order brought about by the action of individuals who have found ways to coordinate their actions with each other.

Our point is simple—methodologically and analytically—the strong affinity between the intellectual tradition of the Austrian school (especially as practiced by Mises, Hayek, Kirzner, and Lavoie) and the work of Deirdre McCloskey should be very evident for all to see. Moreover, McCloskey is a liberal in the classical sense just as Mises, Hayek, and Kirzner were (and Knight and Buchanan, but of course it all traces back to Adam Smith and David Hume); perhaps one might even suggest that she is a *radical* liberal in the same sense that Lavoie and we are. So the affinity also has an ideological component as well. And this methodological, analytical, and ideological connection was not just an abstract intellectual friendship.

There are also personal connections between McCloskey and the Austrians that are worth noting. She has, for instance, visited the Austrian economists based at George Mason University on a regular basis since the mid-1980s. And, many an Austrian economist (including both authors) consider her a friend and mentor. McCloskey's imprint on the contemporary generation of Austrian economists is profound as seen in (1) the rejection of the modernist method and the broad acceptance of multiple sources of data including ethnography, narrative history, and even cultural reference points; (2) the analytical focus on the multiple margins of adjustment that economic actors engage in during the market process and the role that the entrepreneur plays in propelling that process; and (3) the broad social philosophical perspective on the legitimating ideology of the market system that evolved during the bourgeois era and must be recalibrated for the politics and history of our time.

This chapter therefore explores the deep connections between the Austrians' and McCloskey's understanding of economics and the economy.

Storytelling in Economics: The Rhetorical and Interpretive Turns

McCloskey has argued that "modernism" is the official method within economics but that, ultimately, it is an impoverished method. As she (1985, 18) summarizes, "Economists follow a modernist line in their official methodology." Mainstream economists tend to embrace positivism, to stress prediction, and to champion formalism when they (albeit rarely) write and speak of their approach to their science. "Modernism," McCloskey (1985, 6) explains, "views science as axiomatic and mathematical, and takes the realm of science to be separate from the realm of form, value, beauty, goodness, and all unmeasurable quantity." This way of thinking about the science, however, is more likely to harm the scientist than to assist her in her efforts to pursue her science or to understand her discipline. As McCloskey (1985, 7) bemoans, "Notwithstanding its gleams of steely brilliance, it has produced by now many crippled economists. Many are bored by history, disdainful of other social scientists, ignorant of their civilization, thoughtless in ethics, and unreflective in method."

Specifically, McCloskey has complained that "modernism" is a poor method because (1) it demands falsification, and falsification is not really possible; (2) it purports to be predictive, but true prediction is impossible in economics; and (3) positivism is not philosophically defendable, nor is it particularly fruitful.

Modernist economists demand that economic propositions be subjected to empirical tests that either refute or fail to refute them. Often, economists utilize more or less sophisticated econometric techniques and employ statistical significance for hypothesis testing. But, as McCloskey (1985, 13) explains, "Philosophers have long recognized . . . that the doctrine of falsification . . . runs afoul of a criticism made by the physicist and philosopher Pierre Duhem in 1906." Duhem explained that there are innumerable explanations for any empirical observation and that it is impossible to construct what would be a critical test for any hypothesis because every test requires the adoption of ancillary assumptions. Empirical "tests" are simply not the conversation stoppers that they pretend to be. And, as McCloskey (1985, 14) explains, much of the body of knowledge that economists rely on has not been subjected to falsification but instead has simply been accepted as true. Rather than using new facts to test theories, economists attempt to force new data into their preferred theories. "At the level of broad scientific law," McCloskey (1985) writes, "the scientists simply use their theories. They seldom try to falsify them."[2]

In addition to falsification, modernist economists also stress the importance of prediction. Any science worthy of the name, according to this view, is a predictive science, and this goes for economics as well. As such, the realism of the assumptions that economic models rely on is not at all important in judging their usefulness, and instead the models' predictive power is what matters. But, as McCloskey (1985, 15) writes, "Prediction is not possible in economics." Economists simply do not know the future. There are very real limits to economic forecasting. This is evidenced by the reluctance of most economists "to put their money where their mouths are," or as she puts it, "If economists are so smart about the future why aren't they rich" (i.e., the circumstantial ad hominem argument). As McCloskey (1992, 34) points out, "Notice that the reason it is difficult to forecast is not merely that humans are too complicated or too changeable or too free. The humanistic criticisms of social science may be true but they are not telling; they are easy to make and easy to answer." Additionally, "the circumstantial ad hominem puts more fundamental limits on what we humans can say about ourselves. It puts a limit on mechanical models of human behavior. It does not make the mechanical models useless for interesting history or routine forecasting; it just makes them useless for gaining an edge about the future" (1992). And, "human scientists and critics of human arts . . . write history, not prophecy" (1992).

According to McCloskey, economic modernism, with its insistence on falsification and prediction, is simply not philosophically defensible, nor is it particularly useful. As McCloskey (1985, 12) explains, "The philosophical arguments for [modernism in economics] have long been known to be unpersuasive." Moreover, "if taken at its word the methodology is impossible. . . . If economists (or physicists) confined themselves to economic (or physical) propositions that literally conformed to such steps, they would have nothing to say." The objective science composed entirely of propositions that have been subjected to falsification is not possible. As McCloskey (1985, 19) summarizes, "A modernist methodology consistently applied . . . would probably stop advances in economics. . . . There is nothing to be gained and much to be lost by adopting modernism in economics." Happily, the modernist methodology that most economists espouse is rarely the methodology that they practice.

Indeed, many economists are only hiding behind a veil of modernism.

Arguably, the most "successful" texts written under the guise of modernism use and, in fact, depend on rhetoric. "Economic science," McCloskey (1985, 87) reminds us, "must use rhetoric and might as well be aware that it must." Stated another way, the style of argumentation that a particular economist employs is not and cannot be disconnected from the substance of her economic argument. In fact, style and substance work together in an attempt to persuade the reader to the economist's point of view. To recognize that we, as academic economists, are ultimately engaged in an effort to persuade moves us away from fetishizing particular mathematical representations and statistical techniques and moves us toward accepting that we resort to mathematical formulations, statistical tests, or scholarly traditions as rhetorical devices to make our case. This recognition cannot help but make us better scientists. And, in so doing, it will no doubt improve our science and the conversations between economic scientists. "It is people, not intellectual devices," McCloskey (1985, 37) points out, "that are good or bad. Good science demands good scientists—that is to say, moral hardworking scientists—not good methodologies."

Austrian economists have anticipated or echoed each of the critiques of modernism in economics that McCloskey advances.

Mises, for instance, has rejected the notion that theory can be falsified by history.[3] Arguably, Mises's insistence on the aprioristic status of economic theories can be read as an acceptance of the Duhem-Quine thesis about the impossibility of devising empirical tests to falsify particular hypotheses in isolation (Boettke 1998). As Mises (1960, 28–29) explains, "New experience can force us to discard or modify inferences we have drawn from previous experience. But no kind of experience can ever force us to discard or modify a priori theorems. They are not derived from experience; they are logically prior to it and cannot be either proved by corroborative experience or disproved by experience to the contrary." And, also (Mises 1960, 30), "A proposition of an aprioristic theory can never be refuted. Human action always confronts experience as a complex phenomenon that first must be analyzed and interpreted by a theory before it can even be set in the context of an hypothesis that could be proved or disproved; hence the vexatious impasse created when supporters of conflicting doctrines point to the same historical data as evidence of their correctness. . . . Whoever is convinced a priori of the correctness of his doctrine can always point out that some condition essential for success according to his theory has not been met." Rather than viewing history as being valuable primarily as a way of refuting or confirming theories about the world, Mises views theory as being useful insofar as it helps us make sense of history. Stated another way, theory is valuable for Mises because it allows us to tell better stories about what has happened, what might have happened, and what might happen.

Similarly, Austrians have advocated pattern prediction over point prediction. Hayek (1967, 1978), for instance, has carefully distinguished between point predictions of the sort most economists pretend are possible and pattern predictions that Hayek believes correctly capture what the social sciences can offer. As Hayek (1967, 8) explains, "By a scientific prediction we mean the use of a rule or law in order to derive from certain statements about existing conditions statements about what will happen. . . . Its simplest form is that of a conditional or 'if then' statement combined with the assertion that the conditions stated in the antecedent are satisfied at a particular time and place." And, also (1967, 9), "'Explanation' and 'prediction' of course do not refer to an individual event but always to phenomena of a certain kind or class; they will always state only some and never all the properties of any particular phenomenon to which they refer. In addition, each property stated will be expressed not as a unique value or magnitude but as a range, however narrow, within which the property will fall."

Of course, identifying all the conditions that might matter for the application of the rule or law is difficult to do with regard to complex phenomena. And, consequently, while it is possible to describe the range of events that might or might not happen when it comes to human affairs, it is impossible to predict what will happen. Stated another way, the range of predicted possibilities is likely to be larger the more complex the phenomena. There are, simply, very real limits to the degree of prediction possible in the human sciences. As Hayek (1967, 18) explains, predictions within the social sciences do "not tell us what particular events to expect at a definite moment, but only what kinds of events we are to expect within a certain range." While pattern predictions are possible within the human sciences, point predictions are not possible. Pretending otherwise does violence to empirical projects within the social sciences (Hayek 1974).

Additionally, Austrians have been very critical of modernism and especially its scientistic thrust. Hayek (1952, 24), for instance, distinguished between being scientific (i.e., adopting a "general spirit of disinterested inquiry") and embracing scientism (i.e., the "slavish imitation of the method and language of Science" and "an attitude which is decidedly unscientific in the true sense of the word, since it involves a mechanical and uncritical application of habits of thought to fields different from those in which they have been formed"). McCloskey and the Austrians agree that scientism in the end kills science.

Admittedly, the Austrians would go further in their critique of modernism than McCloskey does, at least in her *Rhetoric of Economics* (1985). It is not just that modernism is an impossible ideal to achieve, as McCloskey (1985) stresses, but that attempts to live up to the ideal have come at a high cost (Boettke 1988).[4] Knowledge that we once possessed has been lost. Knowledge that we might have already discovered has not yet been discovered. As Boettke (1988, 7) argued elsewhere, "The opportunity cost of modernism has been huge. We, as economists, are no longer interesting or appealing. Our interpretive skills have deteriorated and, as a result, we are incapable of illuminating the human condition."

Polanyi's rendering of the humanistic critique of modernism perhaps captures the Austrian critique best when he argues that modernism's emphasis on formalism and empirical tests has reduced the social sciences to a collection of uninteresting facts. "If the scientific virtues of exact observation and strict correlation of data are given absolute preference for the treatment of a subject which disintegrates when represented in such terms," Polanyi (1962, 139) writes, "the result will be irrelevant to the subject matter and probably of no interest at all." Modernism fails not only because we can never live up to its ideals but because under its influence, the human sciences have nothing of interest to say.[5]

Because of these shortcomings of modernism, McCloskey (1990, 61) has argued that economists would do well to recognize that they "are tellers of stories and makers of poems." As she explains, economists are concerned with both explanation and understanding, with both *erklaren* and *verstehen*. We are, she writes (1990, 63), not just in the business of devising models of how the world works; we are also in the business of describing and interpreting actual historical happenings. As such, we use metaphors and tell stories. "There seem to be two ways of understanding things," McCloskey (1990, 61) explains, "either by way of a metaphor or by way of a story, through something like a poem or through something like a novel." These two modes of making sense of phenomena are connected. As she (1990, 61) writes, "The metaphorical and the narrative explanations answer to each other. . . . A story answers a model. Likewise a model answers a story." According to McCloskey (1990, 62), the "best economics" combines and balances the use of metaphors and stories. Interestingly, she points to Mises's work on the impossibility of economic calculation under socialism as being an exemplar in this regard. There are, indeed, several advantages to recognizing that economists are storytellers and there is an important relationship between metaphors/models and stories/histories. First, if we are more self-conscious about our role as storytellers, we might better understand what we are, in fact, up to and recognize the limits of our efforts. As McCloskey (1995b, 219) complains, "Economists and other scientists are unselfconscious about their metaphors. They suppose that because they can speak an economic metaphor, it simply is. Economists are poets / But do not know it." Second, we might avoid writing the kinds of fiction that no one wants to read and "come back into the conversation of mankind" (1990, 73). We might, for instance, elevate the use of narrative compared to other types of economic argument. Economists might, as McCloskey (1990, 73) writes, stop "practicing a physics-worship that misunderstands physics and themselves." Instead, as she recommends, "economists could get their gods from poetry or history or philology and still do much the same job of work, with a better temper." The benefit of doing this is nowhere more obvious than when discussing the conversation of the market.

The Market as a Conversation

Interestingly, although much of economic theory is concerned with market phenomena, the market is more often in the background of economic analysis than in the foreground. Several prominent economists have noted that the market is not a central concern for economists. For instance, as Stigler (1967, 291) observed, "economic theory is concerned with markets much more than with factories or kitchens. It is, therefore, a source of embarrassment that so little attention has been paid to the theory of markets." Similarly, as North (1977, 710) has stated, "it is a peculiar fact that the literature on economics . . . contains so little discussion of the central institution that underlies neo-classical economics—the market." Likewise, as Coase (1988, 7) notes, "although economists claim to study the working of the market . . . in the modern textbook, the analysis deals with the determination of market prices, but discussion of the market itself has entirely disappeared." James Buchanan, strongly influenced by Mises and Hayek, championed the idea that economics is about exchange and the institutions within which exchange takes place. In "What Should Economists Do?" (1964, 42), Buchanan states emphatically that economists "should be 'market economists,' but only because I think they should concentrate on market or exchange institutions, again recalling that these are to be conceived in the widest possible sense. This need not bias or prejudice them for or against any particular form of social order. Learning about how markets work means learning more about how markets work."

Several noneconomists have also noticed this strange place that the market occupies within mainstream economic thought. As the economic sociologist Lie (1997, 342), for instance, has argued, "The market is [supposedly] a central category of economics. . . . It is then curious that the market receives virtually no extended discussion in most works of economic theory or history. . . . The market, it turns out, is the hollow core at the heart of economics." Similarly, as Swedberg (1994, 257, 255) observed, "astonishingly little work has been done" on the market within mainstream economic thought, and where it does factor into the analysis, it is discussed as an "abstract price-making mechanism" and not a "social phenomenon in its own right."

Mainstream economists are simply not much interested in the market. As Storr (2008, 135–36) argued,

> The market occupies a peculiar position in mainstream economic thought. It is in one sense ever-present. The market is the site where buyers and sellers meet, prices emerge, and resources change hands. As such, it is the scene where all the action in contemporary economics occurs. On the other hand, the market is more often in the background of economic analysis than in the fore. If the entrepreneur is the forgotten man in mainstream economic theory, then the market is certainly the forgotten place. Its existence is often assumed. . . . The market as a system of social rules/norms and a stable pattern of relationships embedded within a broader social context rarely enters into the calculus.[6]

This criticism of mainstream economic thought, however, does not apply to Austrian economics. The market "as a system of social rules/norms and a stable pattern of relationships" is a key focus within Austrian economics, as are the political, social, and cultural institutions that are necessary for markets to function correctly.

Indeed, the market occupies a central place within Austrian economics. For Austrians, the market has always been a central concern. Austrian economics, as Kirzner (1963) explains, is composed not only of economic theory but also of market theory. And, moreover, for Austrians, market theory represents the core of economic theory. "Economic analysis," Kirzner (1963, 13) explains, "reveals chains of cause and effect linking together the mass of transactions taking place in the market. Market theory investigates these chains of cause and effect. . . . Market theory provides the general framework for the analysis of the market system." Austrian economics, then, is interested not only in the nature of economic laws but in the manifestation of these laws in the interplay of market forces and the interactions of individuals within a market system (1963, 5).

Additionally, Austrians have always argued that the market is a social structure. "The market," Mises (1949, 312) has stated, "is a social body; it is the foremost social body. The market phenomena are social phenomena. They are the resultant of each individual's active contribution." In addition, Mises (1949, 258) has explained that "the market is not a place, a thing, or a collective entity. The market is a process, actuated by the interplay of the actions of the various individuals cooperating under the division of labor." For Austrians, then, the market is a social structure or a spontaneous order that emerges as the result of the interactions of multiple individuals who are simultaneously competing against other individuals for resources and cooperating with one another in the provision and distribution of goods and services (Ikeda 1994, 29). This view of the market acknowledges the key role that institutions and social structures play in shaping economic activity.

Austrians have profitably compared the interplay of actions that occur within markets to a conversation. Hayek (1948, 86), for instance, has argued that "we must look at the price system as . . . a mechanism for communicating information if we want to understand its real function." Market participants possess unique bits of information that they must communicate to one another if they are to coordinate their activities and attain the goods and services that they desire and can afford. The price system assists them in this effort. In particular, it allows them to communicate with one another when some particular good or service has become scarcer or more abundant. It does so without requiring that they share a great deal of information about their situations or the circumstances surrounding the change in the scarcity of the particular good in question. As such, while economizing on what market participants have to say to one another in order to communicate useful information, it nonetheless facilitates their communicating a great deal of useful information to one another. In functioning markets, price changes are meaningful utterances that communicate to individuals that the world has changed in some way and signals to them that they might want to adjust their activities accordingly. As Hayek (1948, 87) has explained, "It is more than a metaphor to describe the price system as a kind of machinery for registering change, or a system of telecommunications."

Austrians believe that market participants can and do use prices to "speak" to one another and that the market is a particular kind of extended social discourse. Lavoie (1994) has, for instance, described the market as a procedure for the "conveyance of inarticulate knowledge." Similarly, Lavoie (1990a, 77–78) has described the market as a "dialogical learning process" like "verbal conversation." Ebeling (1990), likewise, has argued that prices are mechanisms for communicating desires but has stressed that the messages conveyed by market prices must be interpreted. And, as Horwitz (1995) points out, there are several connections between money and language. Both money and language, he writes, "mediate social processes. . . . Money is the 'medium of exchange' . . . while language is the 'medium of experience'" (1995, 164). Also, "if money is the analog to language, then price is the analog to word. A market price embodies knowledge made available through the medium of money, just as word is knowledge made available by speaking or writing in language" (1995, 166).

Austrians also recognize that market participants communicate with each other using more than prices and that they say more to each other than how much they want to buy/sell and the price that they are willing to pay/accept. Mises, Hayek, and Kirzner all have discussed the vital role that advertising plays in persuasively alerting potential buyers about the opportunities for mutual gain that lurk right around the corner throughout the marketplace (locally and globally). There has also been an effort within Austrian economics to explore the nature of conversations that occur within the market. Storr (2008, 137), for instance, has noted that "meaningful conversations . . . happen in markets; conversations that express more than bid-ask; conversations that are not just bartering and negotiations; conversations between socially bonded market participants concerned with more than simply making a deal." In addition to being the site of cooperation, competition, and exchange, markets are also a space where meaningful social relationships can and do develop.

McCloskey shares this concern and has stressed that the market is properly viewed as being peopled by human beings (not *homo economicus*) and that conversation in the market is rightly viewed as being concerned with persuasion.

McCloskey (2010) has roundly criticized approaches to economics that treat human beings as prudence-only figures, lacking in other virtues or vices for that matter.[7] She has derisively called *homo economicus* "Max U." As she (2010, 297) explains,

> "Max U," you see, is a man with the last name "U" who has peopled the arguments of economists since Paul Samuelson in the late 1930s elevated him to a leading role. The joke is that the only way that an economist knows how to think about life after Samuelson is to watch Mr. Max U coldly *Max*imizing a *U*tility function, U(X,Y). Ha, ha. Max U is a pot-of-pleasure sort of fellow. He cares only for the virtue of prudence, and "prudence" defined in an especially narrow way, that is, knowing what your appetites are and knowing how to satisfy them.

To do "modernist" economics is to do Max U. The problem is that Max U just does not work in the study of human action in the real world. Max U is indistinguishable from a robot or rather an early science-fiction model of a robot. He does not reason. He does not act. He merely responds in a predictable way to the stimuli that he is programmed to recognize. He does not belong to any social groupings, nor does he forge any relationships. In short, Max U is not a human being. Thus any economies peopled by Max Us are at best toy economies. Samuelsonian economics (whether practiced at MIT or Chicago) is the economics of toy economies, not the economics of real economies that exist in time and in particular places.

Actual economies are peopled by real, reasoning, and acting human beings. Human beings form friendships, forge political alliances, and develop and adopt worldviews. As Boettke (2012b, 755) noted, "It is human actors that are free and responsible beings, who participate and try to prosper in a free market economy, and who strive to live within and be actively engaged in caring communities. It is human actors that come up with new ideas, recognize the gains from trade and the gains from innovation, and act upon the opportunity for those gains by engaging in enterprise." Any economics that strives to be an economics of human economies rather than toy economies must rely on models of the economy that are peopled by human beings and not robots. It is telling that McCloskey has pointed to Austrian economics as evidencing the approach within economics that recognizes that its subjects are actually humans.

Importantly, those human beings, McCloskey reminds us, must have the faculty of speech. Max U does not speak; human beings do. And, sometimes—

quite often, in fact—they have important things to say to one another. Recall that McCloskey has argued that economists should pay attention to all the talk that goes on within markets including efforts at persuasion. As McCloskey (1994, 30) has explained, "The economy does a great deal of talking. . . . The faculty of speech deserves some analytic attention, even from economists." And, as she writes with Klamer, "Economists view talk as cheap and culture as insignificant. Yet humans are talking animals, talking in their markets. The talk probably matters" (Klamer and McCloskey 1995, 191).

According to McCloskey (2010), it was a change in talk that led to the Industrial Revolution. In *Bourgeois Dignity*, McCloskey (2010) examines and critiques the dominant explanations for the emergence of the modern world. As she explains, almost all of the world's population (with very few exceptions) lived off three dollars a day until the nineteenth century. In the last two hundred years, however, there has been a tenfold increase in average daily income in some countries. But, McCloskey (2010) complains, traditional economic explanations (e.g., ones that emphasize thrift and capital accumulation or the adoption of liberal institutions or that point to an extension of trade, slavery, or imperialism) cannot explain this dramatic increase in income. As McCloskey (2010, 6) argues, "Economics . . . can't explain the rise in the whole world (absolute) advantage from $3 to $30 a day. . . . Economics can't explain the onset or the continuation, in the magnitude as against the details of the pattern, of the uniquely modern." McCloskey (2010) argues that the Industrial Revolution was triggered by a change in the dignity afforded to the innovative entrepreneur and that this change in dignity was reflected in the way that people in seventeenth-, eighteenth-, and nineteenth-century Western Europe and the United States talked about the entrepreneur and about her activities. "Free innovation led by the bourgeoisie," McCloskey (2010, 386) writes, "became . . . respectable in people's words." Merchants, for instance, came to be described as "gentlemen," a term once reserved for the aristocrat, and "honest," a term that came to mean upright rather than of high social rank. "The initiating changes" of the Industrial Revolution, McCloskey (2010, 403) summarizes, "were sociological and rhetorical—that is to say, they were about habits of the lip, what people thought and said about each other." The change in talk was economically significant and led to real and significant changes in the economy.

McCloskey's rejection of Max U and her recognition of the importance of talk not only is consistent with but has influenced and is being influenced by the Austrian view that the market can be viewed as a conversation between actual human beings who have found ways to coordinate their actions with each other.

Conclusion

At a methodological, analytical, and ideological level, the affinity between McCloskey and the Austrian school of economics is strong. Deirdre McCloskey has been widely celebrated throughout the classical liberal intellectual community for her pioneering work on the *Bourgeois Era*, but the attention paid by the Austrian school subset of that broader intellectual community dates back much further, to her pioneering work on the methodology of economics and to her microanalytic work in market theory and the price system. As she used to remark in the mid-1990s, she was an economist in transition (pause), from a Chicago economist to an Austrian economist. But while we have not shown this here, it is important to stress that the influence has not been only in one direction. Her towering achievements in methodology, analytical economics, social philosophy, and political economy have influenced the youngest generation of Austrian school economists. McCloskey's influence can be seen throughout their work and in particular in the focus on multiple forms of evidence, the attention to the multiple margins of adjustment in the market process, and the emphasis on the liberalism in classical liberalism. McCloskey is one of the grand contributors to what Boettke (2012a) has called the "mainline" of economic and political economy thought. That mainline tradition, from Adam Smith to Vernon Smith and everyone in between, strove for what McCloskey now dubs "humanomics." Menger, the founder of the Austrian school, wrote in his *Principles of Economics* (1871) that man and his relationship with other men is the alpha and the omega of economic analysis. McCloskey has advanced that agenda more than any other contemporary thinker. Let us hope the reorientation in thought she demands of economists and political economists continues to gain acceptance.

Notes

1. See Hayek, "The Facts of the Social Sciences" (1943), for a discussion of the "knowledge from within" that is the analytical starting point for meaningful economic analysis. Also see Storr (2010) for a further elaboration of this point.

2. McCloskey has also criticized the dominance of statistical significance for empirical testing within economics. That a result is statistically significant, Ziliak and McCloskey (2008) explain, is not necessary or sufficient grounds to conclude that the variable in question is scientifically important.

3. It has been argued that Hayek was more enamored with falsification than was Mises (see Hutchinson [1981]), but see Caldwell (1992) for a compelling argument against this view.

4. Hayek's Nobel Lecture "The Pretence of Knowledge" can be read as an explicit indictment of modernist economics along these lines and that the discipline has in fact been corrupted by a wrong view of what constitutes science.

5. A classic McCloskey essay that pushes this point is her "Kelly Green Golf Shoes and the Intellectual Range from M to N" (1995).

6. See also chapter 2 in Storr (2012).

7. To link McCloskey's concerns back again to Buchanan's "What Should Economists Do?" (1964), it might be useful to note that Buchanan first argues that a strict maximizing paradigm is not the appropriate way to engage in economic analysis. First, "if the utility function of the choosing agents is fully defined in advance, choice becomes purely mechanical. No 'decision,' as such, is required; there is no weighing of alternatives." There would not in this sense be a human actor dealing with the agony of choice, but only robots being strictly obedient to decision rules. Second, this concentration on decision science as opposed to exchange relations closes off the ability of economists to properly understand Adam Smith's "invisible hand." As Buchanan stresses, revolutions in thought begin in dictionaries. Right now, our scientific talk is about optimizing behavior and not human action, and the market is talked about in terms of allocation and not exchange relations. This results, Buchanan states, in "nonsensical social science" where all the social content of the economic process is squeezed out.

References

Boettke, Peter J. 1988. "Story-Telling and the Human Sciences." *Market Process* 6 (2): 4–7.

Boettke, Peter J. 1998. "Ludwig von Mises." In Davis, Maki, and Hands 1998.

Boettke, Peter J. 2012a. *Living Economics: Yesterday, Today, and Tomorrow*. Oakland: The Independent Institute.

Boettke, Peter J. 2012b. "A Behavioral Approach to the Political and Economic Inquiry into the Nature and Causes of the Wealth of Nations." *Journal of Socio-Economics* 41: 753–56.

Boettke, Peter J., and Prychitko, David L., eds. 1994. *The Market Process: Essays in Contemporary Austrian Economics*. Aldershot: Edward Elgar.

Boettke, Peter J., and Sautet, Frederic, eds. 1963 (2011). *The Collected Works of Israel M. Kirzner*. Indianapolis: Liberty Fund.

Boettke, Peter J., ed. 2010. *Handbook on Contemporary Austrian Economics*. Northampton: Edward Elgar.

Boettke, Peter. J., ed. 1994. *The Elgar Companion to Austrian Economics*. Northampton: Edward Elgar.

Buchanan, James M. 1964. "What Should Economists Do?" *Southern Economic Journal* 30 (3): 213–22.

Caldwell, Bruce J. 1992. "Hayek the Falsificationist? A Refutation." *Research in the History of Economic Thought and Methodology* 10: 1–15.

Coase, Ronald. 1988. *The Firm, the Market, and the Law*. Chicago: University of Chicago Press.

Davis, John, Maki, Uskali, and Hands, Wade, eds. 1998. *The Handbook of Economic Methodology*. Aldershot: Edward Elgar.

Ebeling, Richard. 1990. "What Is a Price? Explanation and Understanding (with Apologies to Paul Ricoeur)." In Lavoie 1990.

Chamlee-Wright, Emily, ed. 2011. *The Annual Proceedings of the Wealth and Well-Being of Nations, Volume III: Entrepreneurship and the Market Process*. Beloit: Beloit College Press.

Hayek, F. A. 1943. "The Facts of the Social Sciences." *Ethics* 54 (1): 1–13.

Hayek, F. A. 1948. *Individualism and Economic Order*. Chicago: University of Chicago Press.

Hayek, F. A. 1952. *The Counter-Revolution of Science: Studies on the Abuse of Reason*. Glencoe: Free Press.

Hayek, F. A. 1967. *Studies in Philosophy, Politics and Economics*. London: Routledge and Kegan Paul.

Hayek, F. A. 1974 (1989). "The Pretence of Knowledge." *American Economic Review* 79 (6): 3–7.

Hayek, F. A. 1978. *New Studies in Philosophy, Politics, Economics and the History of Ideas*. London: Routledge and Kegan Paul.

Horwitz, Steven. 1995. "Monetary Exchange as an Extra-Linguistic Social Communication Process." In Prychitko 1995.

Hutchinson, Terence. 1981. *The Politics and Philosophy of Economics: Marxians, Keynesians and Austrians*. Oxford: Basil Blackwell.

Ikeda, Sanford. 1994. "Market Processes." In Boettke 1994.

Kirzner, Israel M. 1963 (2011). *Market Theory and the Price System*. In Boettke and Sautet 1963 (2011).

Lavoie, Don. 1990a. "Computation, Incentives, and Discovery: The Cognitive Function of Markets in Market Socialism." *Annals of the American Academy of Political and Social Science* 57: 72–79.

Lavoie, Don, ed. 1990b. *Economics and Hermeneutics*. New York: Routledge.

Lavoie, Don. 1994. "A Political Philosophy for the Market Process." In Boettke and Prychitko 1994.

Lie, John. 1997. "Sociology of Markets." *Annual Review of Sociology* 23: 341–60.

McCloskey, Deirdre N. 1985. *The Rhetoric of Economics*. Madison: University of Wisconsin Press.

McCloskey, Deirdre N. 1990. "Storytelling in Economics." In Lavoie 1990.

McCloskey, Deirdre N. 1992. "The Art of Forecasting: From Ancient to Modern Times." *Cato Journal* 12 (1): 23–43.

McCloskey, Deirdre N. 1994. *Knowledge and Persuasion in Economics*. New York: Cambridge University Press.

McCloskey, Deirdre N. 1995a. "Kelly Green Golf Shoes and the Intellectual Range from M to N." *Eastern Economic Journal* 21 (3): 411–14.

McCloskey, Deirdre N. 1995b. "Metaphors Economists Live By." *Social Research* 62 (2): 215–37.

McCloskey, Deirdre N. 2006. *The Bourgeois Virtues: Ethics for an Age of Commerce*. Chicago: University of Chicago Press.

McCloskey, Deirdre N. 2010. *Bourgeois Dignity: Why Economics Can't Explain the Modern World*. Chicago: University of Chicago Press.

McCloskey, Deirdre N. 2011. "A Kirznerian Economic History of the Modern World." In Chamlee-Wright 2011.

McCloskey, Deirdre, and Klamer, Arjo. 1995. "One Quarter of GDP Is Persuasion." *The American Economic Review* 85 (2): 191–95.

Menger, Carl. 1871 (1976). *Principles of Economics*. New York: New York University Press.

Mises, Ludwig von. 1949. *Human Action: A Treatise on Economics*. New Haven: Yale University Press.

Mises, Ludwig von. 1960. *Epistemological Problems of Economics*. Princeton, NJ: D. Van Nostrand.

North, Douglass C. 1977. "Markets and Other Allocation Systems in History: The Challenge of Karl Polanyi." *Journal of European Economic History* 6 (4): 703–16.

Polanyi, Michael. 1962. *Personal Knowledge: Towards a Post-Critical Philosophy*. Chicago: University of Chicago Press.

Prychitko, David L., ed. 1995. *Individuals, Institutions, Interpretations: Hermeneutics Applied to Economics*. Burlington: Ashgate.

Smelser, N., and Swedberg, R., eds. 1994. *The Handbook of Economic Sociology*. Princeton, NJ: Princeton University Press.

Stigler, George J. 1967. "Imperfections in the Capital Market." *Journal of Political Economy* 75 (3): 287–92.

Storr, Virgil Henry. 2008. "The Market as a Social Space: On the Meaningful Extraeconomic Conversations That Can Occur in Markets." *Review of Austrian Economics* 21: 135–50.

Storr, Virgil Henry. 2010. "The Facts of the Social Sciences Are What People Believe and Think." In Boettke 2010.

Storr, Virgil Henry. 2012. *Understanding the Culture of Markets*. New York: Routledge.

Swedberg, R. 1994. "Markets as Social Structures." In Smelser and Swedberg 1994.

Ziliak, Stephen T., and McCloskey, Deirdre N. 2008. *The Cult of Statistical Significance: How the Standard Error Costs Us Jobs, Justice, and Lives*. Ann Arbor: University of Michigan Press.

8

Rhetoric and Public Policy: Pathos, Ideology, and the Specter of Health Care

PAUL TURPIN

The purpose of this chapter is to make the case that a rhetorical perspective continues to be the best resource for assessing public policy arguments. Contentious policy disagreements are most often disagreements about value priorities and, as such, are imbued with intense emotional commitments. Because a rhetorical perspective is alert to the embedding of value commitments and their associated emotional attachments in policy arguments, it is an incisive tool. This chapter attempts to illustrate these value commitments by locating ways in which metaphor can be understood to identify emotional resonances that help us articulate what is important to us.

A modern lowest-common-denominator concept overshadows civic discussion now: cost-benefit analysis. In one sense, this is the *summum bonum* of economic thought's contribution to civic discourse: a clear-eyed look at trade-offs in policy decisions. In another sense, cost-benefit analysis can turn public policy issues into arithmetic problems by converting all values into monetary values and, by implication, mishandling values that resist quantification. Controversial public policy argument is controversial in the struggle over which values will become assumptions in cost-benefit analysis.

The perennial problem in policy argument is how to articulate public policy amid the struggles among different and competing value orientations. The rhetorical problem on all sides is how to identify and communicate the values that matter most in order to clarify the limits of cost-benefit analysis.

The challenge of the persuasive promotion of values is the ever-present risk that rhetoric poses: that emotional appeal will swamp good sense and reasoned discourse, leading to a debased public sphere. Such was Plato's view in the *Gorgias* (1990), for example, which has saturated so much of Western thinking.

The corrective to this view, which this chapter pursues, is to adopt Aristotle's treatment of emotion as an essential aspect of persuasion that provides the attitudinal frame in which practical reasoning achieves its full power. In this reading of Aristotle, emotion is the complement of reason, and its function is to reveal to us, through emotional response, what our value commitments actually are. This is how the persuasive dynamic of *pathos* works, contextualizing the reasoned argument of *logos*, together with the emotional response of trust in the persuader that constitutes the closely allied emotional dynamic of *ethos*.

Viewed in this light, pathos is about putting values in relation to each other, which is to say arranging them in a coherent structure to help guide decisions about action. To examine how pathos is at work in a policy issue like health care, an initial survey of differing prioritizations helps demarcate the field of investigation. In rhetorical terms, a given viewpoint can be understood as having a set of expectations about relevant topics—that is, expectations about what counts as relevant and important to say or hear. Rhetoric organizes such sets of topics and expectations into three genres—deliberative, epideictic, and forensic. Deliberative and epideictic rhetoric concern us most here. Policy argument is typically a search for which action is best and is a natural product of deliberative rhetoric. Epideictic rhetoric, as the genre that articulates values and can be recognized by its language of praise and blame, is also important because of its intimate connection with deliberation. A course of action is always motivated by a value, though the value may be implicit rather than explicit. The rhetorical genres compose the contexts in which the modes of persuasion—logos, pathos, and ethos—operate. A given set of value commitments focus the general form of a genre into a specialized discourse characteristic of *ideological* perspectives, so I now turn to taking up ideological perspectives in terms of how their worldviews shape their sets of values and beliefs.

Ideological Perspectives and Political Economy

To say that the field of public discourse is fragmented today is to say more than that there are many conflicting interests that bog down efforts at formulating policy. Framing the extent of differing worldviews as conflicts of interest misleadingly suggests that politics is simply a matter of bargaining among interest groups. While the institutional processes of politics certainly do include elements and episodes of bargaining, the larger disagreements are driven by disagreements at the level of worldviews—in short, by ideological differences. While the end result appears to be a fragmented stalemate, the ideological differences themselves are not arbitrary. They have grown out of the historical development of political-economic understandings of the world that are intimately attached to the value commitments by which their priorities are ordered.[1]

The dominant ideological perspective in the modern era in the West has been political liberalism, understood as the ideology initially organized around a theory of individual rights. The customary account of the development of political liberalism begins somewhere around the late seventeenth century with John Locke's *Second Treatise on Government* (1824) and its emphasis on the protection of property, the separation of powers in government, and a voice in legislation. The Lockean view of government becomes supplemented by Adam Smith's view of a market economy in the late eighteenth century. The combination of Locke's political theory, including its definition of property through a labor theory of value, with Smith's argument for the independent, self-regulating market through the operation of trade marks the foundations of the political economy of Classical Liberalism.

By Smith's time in the late eighteenth century, and then increasingly so into the nineteenth century, the figure of the Classical Liberal was starting to emerge: an individualist, usually urban figure, impatient with tradition followed for its own sake, interested in trade and the activity of an increasingly less-controlled market—dismantling the favoritisms of Mercantilism, for example—and in favor of measuring worth in terms of personal achievement, especially in the market, rather than inherited rank. Deirdre McCloskey's *Bourgeois* volumes (2010, 2006) are strongly devoted to these developments.

Barry Clark expands on this developmental narrative in *Political Economy: A Comparative Approach* (1998) by providing a broad account of the development of different schools of political-economic thought from the early modern period into the twentieth century, producing a richer account of ideological perspectives than the usual left-right political spectrum offers. Clark accounts for the ways in which the emergence of Classical Liberalism was perceived as a disruption or, perhaps more properly, a *further* disruption of a traditional view of society as an ordered set of social ranks and roles, the remains of which still persisted in the early modern period in the gradually eroding feudal structures. Adam Smith, for example, felt the need to deploy a lengthy critique of the rule of primogeniture and entailments as economically inefficient ([1776] 1976: III:2). This disruption becomes characteristic of the evolution of modernity: the calling of tradition and custom into question at the historical moment the individual comes to occupy the foreground of attention and an increasingly productive economy creates both great wealth and great stresses of dislocation.

The social and economic disruption of emerging Classical Liberalism, in Clark's narrative, in turn provoked two oppositional critiques—one from Conservatives and one from Radicals. What Conservatives and Radicals shared was the observation that Classical Liberalism was in the process of putting an end to traditional forms of social relationships in an abrupt and disruptive fashion. For Conservatives like Edmund Burke, the loss of tradition meant the dissolution of the bonds of loyalty that held society together, especially in terms of dismantling the hierarchies of authority. The Conservative response was to look back, to restore some lost former time of social harmony. For Radicals, the changes wrought by developing technologies and economic models, as well as the persistence of historical injustices, meant there was no turning back; for Radicals, the only solution lay in constructing a new form of social relationship, deliberately and consciously rather than by the accretion of tradition.

This triad of conflicting perspectives was in place by the early nineteenth century, even before Marx's writings, on the cusp of the acceleration of the Industrial Revolution in the mid-1800s: uneasy frictions punctuated by abortive revolutions, reactionary revivals of tradition, and the increasing development of markets and trade.

A fourth perspective, Modern Liberalism, emerges in Clark's narrative in the late nineteenth century as a compromise of sorts between Classical Liberal defenses of individual liberty and market economies on one side and Radical critiques of the social disruptiveness of market economies and the desire to correct for problems of individualism through collective action on the other. The Modern Liberal sided with Classical Liberals on the issue of individual liberty but worked to correct market disruptions through a combination of government regulation, to put limits on behaviors in the market, and welfare measures, to compensate for market inequalities of impoverishment.

Each of these four ideological positions had economic and corresponding political positions made up of their beliefs and value commitments. For Modern Liberals, for instance, the question of market failure loomed large, while Classical Liberals considered actual cases of market failure to be rare. The nineteenth century was a period of great booms and busts, with plenty of economic misery and its attendant social unrest as well as economic growth. For Modern Liberals, problems of externalities beset economic thinking. Negative externalities, in which harms impacted third parties who were not part of the transaction that produced the harm, were taken by Modern Liberals to be a sign that markets could not be left entirely to themselves. For Modern Liberals, this created a warrant for regulation by government. Classical Liberals, on the other hand, considered most claims about market failures and externalities to be overblown, at worst requiring legal remedies of tort rather than government regulation.

From Historical Explanation to Conceptual Model

Following his account of the historical development of value-laden political-economic perspectives, Clark develops a conceptual model for the four ideological positions. Starting from the values of liberty and equality, Clark argues that each of these is not only in tension with each other, which is a fairly common staple of modern political philosophy, but each is also in tension with another value. Liberty, identified with valuing freedom of the individual, is at one pole of a tension with the relative value of community at the other pole. That is, freedom of the individual is conceived in relation to connection to a community along a spectrum of degrees of commitment to one end of the pole or the other. In theory, an even commitment to values of individual liberty and community cohesion would lie at the middle of the tension, balancing between the two.

Equality, similarly, lies at one pole of a tension with hierarchy. Equality here refers to a type of status or standing and is primarily political in nature, as against being a descriptor of attributes or possessions like equal or unequal wealth or endowments. Hierarchy, as equality's polar opposite, refers to an order established by rankings, where standing is determined by place in the rankings. As with the individual and the community, a balance could conceivably be struck between the two.

Clark's conceptual model arranges these two polar tensions in a matrix as a way of visually indicating the primary value commitments of the four major ideological perspectives he has identified from the historical development of modern theories of political economy. Each perspective corresponds to the values more important to them: Classic Liberals, to the individual and to hierarchy, and so on.

Because the polar tensions are matters of degree, the model is not strictly a two-by-two binary model but rather a gradient, representing the degree of commitment to the values at the ends of the poles. In theory, the center point is one that balances each tension evenly. Because the model is a gradient organized around general, yet-to-be-specified terms, it can function as a fairly flexible heuristic, which points to its compatibility with the rhetorical notion of genres as sets of topoi with coherent interconnections.

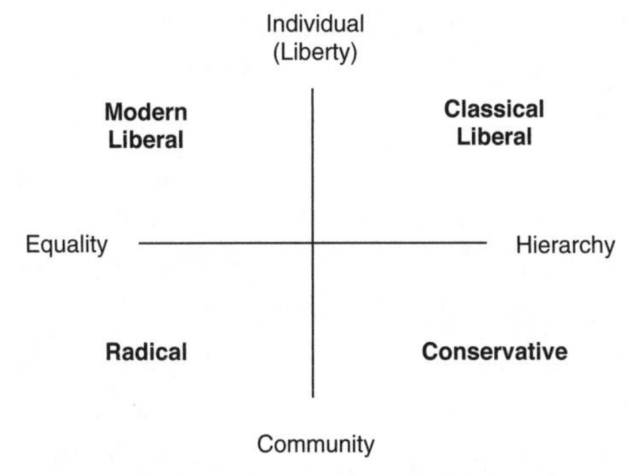

FIGURE 8.1 Clark's conceptual model. Figure from Clark (1998, 35).

Positions sharing a value have a potential for alliance—Modern Liberals with Classical Liberalism with respect to individualism, or Classical Liberals with Conservatives with respect to hierarchy, for example. Similarly, perspectives diagonally positioned have less potential for alliance because of the relative lack of shared primary values. As a gradient, the model also allows for greater and lesser degrees of commitment to particular values. Libertarians—a strongly individualistic type of Classical Liberal—are typically wary of communitarian constraints, for instance, putting them further away from conservatives than, say, a Classical Liberal like economist Milton Friedman (1962), who foregrounded individual choice but argued that individuals should be free to live the traditions set out by their ancestors—which is a decidedly Conservative sentiment.

Aside from these features of Clark's conceptual model, its heuristic rhetorical usefulness lies in what the key terms may actually mean in practice for a given perspective. Each ideological position can and will have its own definitions for each key term that refine a generic understanding of the term in different directions. While not exhaustive, the following examples should serve to indicate the wide range of possible interpretations.

For Classical Liberals, the hierarchy that matters most lies in the differences of meritorious effort, particularly in the market. Some people are better—smarter, more talented, more hardworking, more willing to defer gratification, and so on—than others in the market. Individual achievement, in this view, establishes a natural hierarchy of worth, so liberty of the individual is a natural component in structuring a social order based on market achievement. Equality, for Classical Liberals, is typically equality before the law, meaning, in contradistinction to feudalism, for instance, that the law does not recognize differences of class privilege in legal matters ("privilege," after all, meaning "private law"), hence the strong Classical Liberal aversion to affirmative action programs of any stripe as the reintroduction of privilege into legal relations.

Conservatives, on the other hand, tend to view hierarchy in terms of a defining characteristic of community. The usual identifiers range among family, ethnicity/race, and/or religion, any or all of which are identified with custom and tradition.[2] Individuals are their own persons, but their identity is made up of all their entwinement with their community fellows. Equality is usually defined in terms of group memberships, social roles, and cultural practices; while an individual family's status, say, may be determined by the status of ancestors, such that families fall into rankings, equality would be a concept that applied among members of a given ranking. A similar standard would apply within a religious framework, where equality (within the constraints of roles) obtained among fellow believers. In the Christian tradition, for instance, the basis for equality is that everyone is equal in the eyes of God. Theologically, all are equally sinners in need of redemption, but all are also loved by God.

Modern Liberals, while generally favoring markets and individual achievement but wary of market instabilities and social barriers, tend to identify equality with equal opportunity for individuals. Differences among people regarding talent, hard work, and so on will produce hierarchical structures, but those structures must not be arranged to play favorites and refuse membership on grounds other than achievement—hence a strong aversion to cronyism as a distortion of a genuinely free market, and hence also a concern that social barriers can become obstacles to genuine equality of opportunity.

Radicals tend to view equality in substantive terms related to membership in a collective; substantive equality at a minimum would mean support as needed for the necessities of life but also an insistence on an equality of standing. In this respect, Radicals tend to view community as a collective—that is, a willed or at least conscious association—that leaves nobody out, while Conservatives tend to view community as a naturally occurring organic relationship that develops through families.[3]

Because of these possible differences in interpretation of the key value terms, the rhetorical usefulness of Clark's model lies precisely in the work of identifying what is meant in an articulation of a given ideology's position, not only in what it says for itself, but also in how it identifies itself as different from the other positions. Rendering Clark's account of ideological perspectives into rhetorical terms, those perspectives are materials for rhetorical criticism in the service of mapping value priorities in policy debates.

Clark's model of ideology is useful because it helps make sense of the apparent fragmentation of the modern era. The fragmentation is not random, in the sense of being accidental or arbitrary; it is purposeful, in the sense that each ideological perspective is an attempt to diagnose the ills of the world and propose solutions for them. The model's heuristic nature also suggests that any possible rendering of common ground would most likely occur through articulating a way to find a balance among competing values.

As remote as the prospect of common ground might seem, its possibility suggests that rhetorical criticism is a necessary process in making sense of the ground of the appeals of conflicting perspectives. A primary way criticism makes sense of such appeals is by assessing their emotional resonances. With that in mind, I now turn to my reflections on pathos and figuration.

Rhetorical Criticism and Ideological Perspectives

The essential purpose of criticism is the communication of a perception; this suggests that rhetorical criticism is the communication of a perception of how persuasion is at work in a given situation. The value of rhetorical criticism lies partly in helping detect bad arguments, but even more so its value lies in being able to discern the play of emotional force as it makes itself felt in arguments that rely on appeals to values. A rhetorical analysis is aware that values involve more than propositional articulations; they are also *commitments*, whence their visceral importance comes.

From a rhetorical view, the differences among potential political audiences indicated by Clark's assessment of ideological perspectives as being constructed around differing value commitments mark a fractured rhetorical landscape, which is to say an *agonistic* rhetorical landscape; different viewpoints struggle with each other not only across ideological borders but also within them. In undertaking an examination of persuasion in policy argument, the task of rhetorical criticism is to track the struggles.

The central place of value commitments in ideological perspectives points to the need to analyze the role of epideictic rhetoric—the genre concerned with the articulation of values through the language of praise and blame. At first glance, this may seem wrongheaded because public policy is so clearly a deliberative process. Epideictic rhetoric is essential to deliberation, however, because epideictic topics are where the values that guide action are expressed. Epideictic and deliberative rhetoric have a reciprocal relation to each other, as do the uses of emotion and reason in *pathos* and *logos*. I turn now to consider these dynamics in relation to the operation of metaphor, the better to frame the subsequent analysis of the operation of metaphor in public policy discourse.

Emotion and Figuration in Rhetoric: The Role of Pathos

In undertaking this reflection on how evoking emotion works in a public policy controversy like health care, this essay does not attempt a systematic account of the various health care debates or a chronicle of their development. Rather, my purpose is to consider what may be discerned about how differing audiences may be moved by an argument or an event. Being moved is sometimes tidal in nature, as in being carried out with the tide, which we know is an occult phenomenon of the moon's invisible but irresistible influence; that is, it may be felt but not immediately recognized. The task of this essay is to account for a movement that may not be explicitly conscious but nonetheless exerts cognitive power in the sense of influencing the audience's perceptions, perhaps less in being anticipated before the fact than in recognizing or resonating in the moment. The tensions that characterize the different ideological perspectives, fragmenting our common ground, are also susceptible to different recognitions and resonances.

The immediate conundrum is, how can cognition happen without conscious awareness? Some cognitive response can clearly be habitual and hence unreflective. The preliminary answer is that feeling emotion supplies an intuitive "knowing" that can be revealed in consciousness by being claimed. Recognizing—coming to an awareness—that you love someone is that kind of movement, and its fulfillment, its full actualization, lies in claiming and owning it, in declaring oneself. Values are like that; they are claimed and declared as commitments after the fact of their being felt. Such recognition is also necessarily situational and thereby inevitably carries an accompanying judgment about appropriateness. A judgment of appropriateness is a claim about rightness of attitude in a given situation, and so values, as personal commitments, also contribute to the formation of social connection.[4]

As a rhetorician, I defend the idea that feeling is a way of knowing and therefore has a cognitive dimension, and so I argue that the effort of persuasion is to interest relevant audiences in taking on a view of the world and a view of how to relate to each other that is fully alive as well as thoughtful. Not that all persuasion reaches such a high mark, but even its failures can be instructive.

In everyday parlance, the way rhetoric works is primarily through words—though, of course, images and other signs also carry meaning—so, technically, *signification* is the process of persuasion: a structuring of meaning. Rhetorical tropes have been part of the basic toolkit of persuasion from the start. The ability of figures of speech and thought to turn attention—that is, to *direct*, not just attract, attention—indicates their value in the cognitive work of persuasion.

But rhetorical tropes, like emotion, have a long history of being criticized. Figurative language has been castigated as distracting, irrelevant, subject to the abuses of flattery and deception, and at best ornamental and flowery, mere grace notes. The Enlightenment's reaction against Renaissance humanism is nowhere more noticeable than in the abjuration of flowery language by figures like John Locke, a central influence on Enlightenment political theory.

Attitudes such as Locke's toward figurative language[5] are in keeping with the tendency in Enlightenment thinking to "purify" reasoned argument—that is, to maximize its cognitive power—by keeping it free from distortion, whether emotional distortion or fanciful distraction, which has only become more intensified by the transformation of Enlightenment reason into modern science.

But even this way of speaking generally about rhetoric and figures of speech leaves open the implication that a given rhetorical usage speaks to all, as if language is aimed at a unitary audience. This is the case only in the most abstract sense, so a second dimension of Aristotelian rhetorical principles is needed to correct the misapprehension of a unitary audience: the centrality of the judgment of the audience. The deployment of logos, pathos, and ethos—taken together, the modes of persuasion—is the work of the person who wants to persuade, but that persuasive effort has to take account of its audience, who are the final arbiters of the persuasive effort. Real audiences are not uniform. Their differences exceed even the parameters that Aristotle acknowledged, such as age or station in life, because of the enormously greater variety in worldviews today than in the classical world, as I argued above with Clark's model of ideologies.

While the modes of persuasion compose Aristotle's psychology of persuasion, the genres compose persuasion's social ground. Rhetorical genres are where topics for discussion meet the expectations of audiences. The basic Aristotelian genres still provide a point of departure: deliberative rhetoric concerns future action (and thus policy); epideictic, that which is to be celebrated or condemned; and forensic, questions of past fact. Two features stand out: first and most generally, Aristotle implicitly posits a connection between the value promotion of epideictic rhetoric and the action orientation of deliberative rhetoric. Whatever we decide to do, we rely on an important value. The urging of the action invokes, even if only implicitly, the rightness of the value.[6]

Clark's assessment of ideology makes the issue of audience expectations more complex than Aristotle's original social psychology. To address the question of how audiences can be theoretically conceived in a time of multiplying worldviews, I developed the concept of "discourse community" as a way to identify the commonality available to those who share in common discursive resources.[7] Because sets of discursive resources abound, all of us are members of multiple discourse communities rather than being members of a single unitary audience. Some of those discourse communities appear in our avocations and may cut across many other discourse communities, such as being a dedicated reader of Jane Austen, while other discourse communities compose the resources through which we ground our identities in culture, religion, and similar worldviews, including political-economic ideologies.

Understanding ideological perspectives as discourse communities makes it possible to appreciate their rhetorical nature, not simply in *that* they seek agreement and adherence, but in *how* and *why* they seek agreement—in what their values and priorities are, in short. The value commitments of an ideology are the source of the power of their appeals that take the form of pathos, so the use of figures in persuasion faces the need to resonate with the values at stake. When audiences are not unitary, they will have differing responses to a given figure. To explore those differences, I now turn to an account of ideological perspectives.

Four Ideological Discourse Communities

First, a caveat: my adaptation of Clark's model of ideology is not intended as prescriptive or definitive so much as heuristic, as a way of searching for explanatory usefulness in examining our historical and current political circumstances. Nor are his categories exhaustively precise; indeed, they are general categories, as are the values he names as the poles of tension in his model, and there are many specific political organizations and parties that would take issue at being lumped together with another they disagree with. Taking Clark's ideological categories as discourse communities also implicitly takes them as historical interactions rather than static concepts. The argumentative struggle to articulate values always happens in particular times and places. That said, I do find the major ideological positions that Clark identifies to be fruitful as a rhetorical heuristic in looking at political discourse as something that happens within as well as between discourse communities.

What follows, then, is an exploration of how ideological discourse communities can be identified by how figuration through metaphor works as a register of pathos. My purpose here is not to engage in analysis of policy positions or to analyze debates[8] but rather to look for metaphors that resonate—that is, metaphors that produce feeling through a harmony with experience, which is to say with a cultural memory. Such resonance is part of the always-ongoing process of interpreting and connecting present experience with an understanding of the past. To explore this, I have selected the figure of "specter" to look at pathos in policy debate around the Affordable Care Act.

Classical Liberalism

A spectre is haunting Europe . . .

KARL MARX AND FREDERICK ENGELS, *The Communist Manifesto*

The specter at work in the Classical Liberal perspective is not Marx and Engels's call for revolution but its ironic afterlife in the wake of the twentieth century's experience of state socialism, especially as embodied in the USSR. In the debate over US health care policy, Classical Liberalism's major objection to single-payer proposals and to the eventual Affordable Care Act (ACA, a.k.a. "Obamacare") was the charge that it was "socialism!" This charge is distinct from the argument over the ACA's constitutionality but in harmony with charges that the ACA was a form of collectivism. The charge of "socialism!" (exclamation point included), as typically used by both Classical Liberals and Conservatives, works metaphorically to invoke the specter of totalitarianism that haunted Europe and Asia in the twentieth century, roughly encompassing not only Nazism and the death camps but more especially the variations of communism: Bolshevism, Stalinism, Maoism, the gulags and re-education camps, and the millions of lives lost in the world wars. From this perspective, socialism in the twentieth century haunts Europe with its millions of ghosts; the irony of the opening line from the *Communist Manifesto* is the transposition of its call to break chains into the chains of totalitarianism.

This train of associations, which itself is far from exhaustive, taken to the end of the line depicts the entire history of socialism of all types as unrelenting tyranny, usually murderous, and always the enemy of liberty understood as individual freedom. This is the resonance for Classical Liberalism in particular.

Conservatism

"Death panels . . ."

SARAH PALIN ON THE ACA

The specter at work in Sarah Palin's 2009 coinage of the term "death panels" in the health care debate is the prospect of becoming haunted by injustice codified into a bureaucratic scheme. While harmonious with the Classical Liberal charge of tyranny, Palin's charge evokes something slightly different. Used to evoke the Nazi eugenics schemes as a criticism of proposed health care legislation, Palin's coinage actually had a nearer-to-hand resonance in the case of Terri Schiavo. The Schiavo case was not directly about medical care coverage, being more directly about the right to die by refusing extreme measures of resuscitation, but its relevance for cultural memory comes from its emotional resonance as a tragedy embedded in medical failure that became enmeshed in governmental decisions.

Terri Schiavo suffered a heart attack in 1990 and never recovered consciousness after her resuscitation. First diagnosed as being in a coma, Schiavo received a variety of medical treatments to no avail. Schiavo's diagnosis was changed to that of a persistent vegetative state about a year after the heart attack. Her husband, Michael Schiavo, eventually in 1998 sought to have her feeding and hydration tubes removed, citing her previously stated desire not to continue a life with no hope for recovery. Her parents, Mary and Robert Schindler, staunch Catholics who considered such an act euthanasia, objected, leading to a series of court cases that were finally settled in 2005, but not before drawing political intervention, with the Florida legislature authorizing Governor Jeb Bush in 2003 to reinstate the feeding and hydration process and ultimately leading Congress and President George W. Bush in 2005 to attempt to block the Florida court decisions.

The political intervention was a clear sign that the Schiavo case occasioned much mobilization among conservatives. The Schindlers, who had argued all along to keep her on life support, termed the result of their eventual loss in court a form of "judicial murder" (2006).

While a core of the conservative audience translated their distress over the Schiavo case directly into political terms, there was a broader cultural resonance beyond conservatism in which the Schiavo case served as an emblem of family tragedy. Terri Schiavo's condition, first thought to be a coma and then revised into persistent vegetative state (which her parents contested), became a story of family conflict and distress as her husband's and parents' grief and disagreement became a recurring staple of family distress over the seven years of the legal dispute over whether her feeding tube could be legally removed.

The case revealed the tension between Classical Liberal and Conservative perspectives over the value of individual choice, a high priority for Classical Liberals but secondary to a moral order for Conservatives. Michael Schiavo argued that Terri had expressed the wish not to be kept alive under conditions where there was no hope, which Terri's diagnosis of persistent vegetative state represented. Still, the Schiavo family tragedy resonated even beyond conservatives' distress because there was no happy ending for anybody. Though the conservative anger at the court was not shared broadly across the population, Schiavo's death was nevertheless widely perceived as a sorrow.

Terri Schiavo finally died in 2005, after the final court decisions led to her life support being disconnected. Schiavo's case remains an important cultural landmark because it illustrates a specific kind of family disaster: a long and ultimately futile medical problem. This is a specter from the future that haunts everyone: the possibility of a long, painful, expensive, and ultimately futile battle against disease.

Modern Liberalism

The Ghost of Christmas Yet to Come . . .
CHARLES DICKENS, *A Christmas Carol*

The specter of Dickens's ghost is a haunting from the future: the prospect not only of a long, painful, expensive, and ultimately futile battle against disease but also of one that brings financial ruin in its wake. The most universal part of the fear stems from mortality itself, but another significant part stems from the worry of being unable to obtain what appears to be increasingly expensive medical help. The prospect of ruin was not just of health but also financial; not just of the possibility of losing a loved one but of bankrupting the family. Recall that in Dickens's novel, Tiny Tim's foreshadowed death follows from his father's loss of employment. The combination of increasing medical costs, increasing insurance costs, and most recently, increasingly precarious employment on which insurance depended finally generated the conditions under which the Affordable Care Act was able to pass Congress.[9]

There were, to be sure, a multiplicity of factors that led to favorable legislative conditions, not least of which were Democratic electoral victories in 2008. There was also considerable disagreement between Modern Liberals and Radicals over whether a single-payer health system (similar to European systems) should replace the health insurance market currently in place, a change that would have had a dramatic effect on the business models of doctors, hospitals, and pharmaceutical and medical equipment manufacturers, not to mention insurance companies themselves. The victory of the health insurance system overhaul in the Affordable Care Act was, in effect, a compromise between the Modern and Classical Liberal positions to the extent that it left the medical infrastructure of fee-for-service generally in place. This increased tensions between Modern Liberals and Radicals. In effect, the ACA took the route that making insurance available to everyone was the best compromise to achieve some equity in access to health care.

Has the ACA laid to rest the Ghost of Ruin Yet to Come? Partly it is too soon to tell, not least because the prognosis for the ACA itself is still undetermined. Critics cite increasing percentages of disapproval from polls, but other polls indicate the disapproval has to do more with the ACA's implementation and less with its principle of wider insurance support. What does seem to be the case is a growing legitimacy of government taking on support for health coverage as one of its duties.

Radicalism

I am invisible, understand, simply because people refuse to see me.
RALPH ELLISON, *Invisible Man*

The Radical metaphor of specter takes the form of transparency, or invisibility, as in a ghostly figure that can only be seen by some.

In the United States, progressivism is the largest variant of Radicalism. Some explicitly socialist or communist parties do exist, but they exert no influence on policy and generally stand solely as external critics rather than as participants in the political process. Progressives are vocal proponents as well as critics and are sometimes participants in the political process itself, though their electoral participation can be uneven. Progressives generally favor European-style welfare state policies, and their opposition to the ACA was that the preferable route to true health care reform would have overturned the existing model of health insurance and converted it to single-payer, or "Medicare for all" as it was sometimes called.

Progressives share the Radical commitment to substantive equality. In the issue of health care, this would mean equal access to health care, which at a minimum would mean national financing of health care if not also national administration (illustrated by the difference, for example, between Medicare and the Veterans' Administration Hospitals). What haunts Progressives is that a failure of equal access is a failure of the community. Those who do not have access to health care because of unemployment or poverty become invisible to the community and become lost; they become invisible.

Metaphorically invisible, as the line from Ralph Ellison's *Invisible Man* indicates, they are ignored to the point of not being seen, of being looked through rather than looked at. Some of this is racial exclusion, as Ellison's story recounts, but much of it is also about economic class and especially about poverty. This kind of invisibility puts Radicals in the position of being the only ones who can see those who are left out, who are marginalized to the point that they are "disappeared" from awareness. This haunts Radicals because they become the only ones in society who can see "ghosts," specters or spirits that are invisible to everyone else. This cuts off Radicals from society as not quite right in the head—they see ghosts, after all, and there are no such things as ghosts—yet leaves them with the burden of being unable to look away.

Conclusion

The point of rhetorical analysis is not to find a magic bullet of common ground when there is serious disagreement. That can often be manipulative, if not coercive, when there are real differences at stake. The real point of rhetorical analysis in a controversy is to be clear-eyed about what the different stakes actually are—and they are always values, which is to say commitments. This essay has attempted to explain how the field of public argument over health care is fractured in terms of the differences between ideological perspectives.

So this essay ends with a reflection on the significance of a series of associations springing from the metaphor of specter: hauntings from pasts or futures, ghosts, spirits of the age. Our mortality inevitably attaches these associations with issues of health care, giving weight to the pathos of policy argument. These sets of associations filter through ideological perspectives to shape conflicting arguments, and our ideological differences lend themselves to a contentious state of moral argument, of feeling set against feeling. The moral of *this* story is that the only route to anything approaching common ground in a fractured world of conflicting ideologies is to begin to recognize the real differences that divide us; only after that can it be possible to acknowledge the burdens of suffering, requiring the moral imagination to follow out the implications of hauntings.

Notes

1. See Daniel Rodgers (2011) and Barry Clark (1998). Taking Clark's analysis, the four major ideological perspectives are Conservative, Classical Liberal, Modern Liberal, and Radical.

2. An interesting instance of the attempt to unify Classical Liberalism with Conservatism is Neoconservatism, which promulgates its conception of American exceptionalism by grounding it on the historical touchstone of the founding of the United States. It thus combines a claim to historical heritage (conservatism) with a claim to the primacy of individualism and liberty of human choice (classical liberalism). The emphasis on the American founding as a *choice*, the argument goes, makes it different from other nations founded on shared language, ethnicity, and so on.

3. Clark's model of ideology is historical-conceptual, but its structure has some empirical reflection in the Pew Research Center's Political Typology (http://www.people-press.org/2014/06/26/the-political-typology-beyond-red-vs-blue/) in its categories of Business Conservatives versus Steadfast Conservatives, which map well onto Clark's Classical Liberal versus Conservative dynamic.

4. See my discussion of decorum in Turpin (2011), starting at p. 14 with the discussion of discourse communities.

5. See Locke (1824, 41): "But yet if we would speak of things as they are, we must allow that all the art of rhetoric, besides order and clearness; all the artificial and figurative application of words eloquence hath invented, are for nothing else but to insinuate wrong ideas, move the passions, and thereby mislead the judgment; and so indeed are perfect cheats."

6. Aristotle (1954) *Rhetoric*, bk. 1, ch. 9: "To praise a man is in one respect to urge a course of action. . . . Consequently, whenever you want to praise any one, think what you would urge people to do; and when you want to urge the doing of anything, think what you would praise a man for having done" (1367b, l.36f.).

7. Turpin (2011, 15–16):

> Understanding audiences as discourse communities is a way to think concretely about what audiences think and care about. I include here both communities of face-to-face interaction as well as those that exist through writing or other symbolic communication. Discourse communities acknowledge both the similarities and sympathies we may share as well as real differences we may have; we experience those phenomena because we share some discourse communities but not others. . . . We become members by participating, by learning and practicing, and one of the important lessons we learn is how to speak and act appropriately—we learn our community's decorum.
>
> The concept of membership in a discourse community helps to keep in mind the embeddedness of individual identity within social structures.

8. For an account of policy debates about health care, see Zompetti (2015: chapter 4).

9. Steven Brill's (2015a) book was a detailed examination of the cost structures of US medical care, distilled from his *Time* magazine series on the topic from 2013 to 2015.

References

Aristotle. 1954. *Rhetoric*. Translated by W. Rhys Roberts. New York: The Modern Library.

Bizzell, Patricia, and Herzberg, Bruce. 1990. *The Rhetorical Tradition: Readings from Classical Times to the Present*. Boston: Bedford Books.

Brill, Steven. 2013a. "Bungling the Easy Stuff." *Time*, December 16, 18.

Brill, Steven. 2013b. "Goodbye to the Surgical Mask." *Time*, May 20, 17.

Brill, Steven. 2013c. "Bitter Pill." *Time*, March 4, 16–55.

Brill, Steven. 2014a. "How Kentucky Got It Right." *Time*, August 18, 20–25.

Brill, Steven. 2014b. "The Hidden Cliffs in Obamacare." *Time*, June 9, 18–19.

Brill, Steven. 2014c. "Code Red." *Time*, March 10 26.

Brill, Steven. 2014d. "Hate Obama, Love Obamacare." *Time*, January 27, 18.

Brill, Steven. 2015a. *America's Bitter Pill: Money, Politics, Backroom Deals, and the Fight to Fix Our Broken Healthcare System*. New York: Random House.

Brill, Steven. 2015b. "What I Learned from My $190,000 Surgery." *Time*, January 19, 34–43.

Clark, Barry. 1998. *Political Economy: A Comparative Approach*. 2nd ed. Westport, CT: Praeger.

Dickens, Charles. 1843. *A Christmas Carol and Other Stories*. Online.

Ellison, Ralph. 1995. *Invisible Man*. New York: Vintage International.

Friedman, Milton. 1962. *Capitalism and Freedom*. Chicago: University of Chicago Press.

Locke, John. 1824. "An Essay concerning Human Understanding." *The Works of John Locke in Nine Volumes*. Vol. 2. London: Rivington.

Marx, Karl, and Engels, Friedrich. 1964. *The Communist Manifesto*. New York: Monthly Review.

McCloskey, Deirdre N. 2006. *The Bourgeois Virtues: Ethics for an Age of Commerce*. Chicago: University of Chicago Press.

McCloskey, Deirdre N. 2010. *Bourgeois Dignity: Why Economics Can't Explain the Modern World*. Chicago: University of Chicago Press.

Plato. 1925 (1990). *Gorgias*. In Bizzell and Herzburg 1990, 61–112.

Rodgers, Daniel T. 2011. *Age of Fracture*. Cambridge, MA: Belknap Press.

Schindler, Mary, and Schindler, Robert. 2006. *A Life That Matters: The Legacy of Terri Schiavo—a Lesson for Us All*. New York: Warner Books.

Smith, Adam [1776]. 1976. *An Inquiry into the Nature and Causes of the Wealth of Nations*. Edited by Edwin Cannan. Vols. 1 and 2. Chicago: University of Chicago Press.

Turpin, Paul. 2011. *The Moral Rhetoric of Political Economy: Justice and Modern Economic Thought*. London: Routledge.

Zompetti, Joseph P. 2015. *Divisive Discourse: The Extreme Rhetoric of Contemporary American Politics*. San Diego: Cognella.

9

Humanism, Materialism, and Epistemology: Rhetoric of Economics as Styles in Action

JOHN S. NELSON

> A change in rhetoric *about* prudence, and about the other and peculiarly human virtues, exercised in a commercial society, started the material and spiritual progress . . . [of] the Industrial Revolution, and then the modern world.
>
> DEIRDRE N. MCCLOSKEY (2010, xi)

"Whence the bourgeoisie and capitalism? Indeed whence modernity?" inquires Deirdre McCloskey. Here I propose as a political theorist and epistemologist to explore whence human sciences, especially of epistemics, economics, and politics. The interest is in not only how they arise but especially where they might go in our emerging postmodern, incipiently post–Western world. I proceed by taking McCloskey's inquiries into rhetoric of economics, economic history, and virtue theory as inspirations, grists, and targets. I argue that McCloskey's work can help us appreciate how human sciences can improve by recognizing and refining their political projects.

In addition to their acuity and style, McCloskey's writings are particularly good cases in point for me because we both pursue rhetoric of inquiry as a kind of practical epistemology and because I've been able to talk at length with McCloskey about her virtue theory. There are many virtue theorists lately, so my secondary target is Alasdair MacIntyre. This is due to his influence and, again, the opportunity to speak with him in some detail. McCloskey's virtues are bourgeois and MacIntyre's are neo-Aristotelian, but both feature philosophical concepts more than practical politics. I argue that this misses an opportunity, at least for McCloskey and possibly for MacIntyre too, because the attention to rhetoric points to a republican-rhetorical tradition with a much more substantively political take on virtues. A strong illustration is Niccolò Machiavelli's republican virtues as what I call "virtue-osities." I argue that they suit McCloskey's bourgeois culture better than her (or MacIntyre's) modernized Aristotelian idea of characters as psychological structures. Republican virtue-osities fit the entrepreneurial energy, practical realism, and drive to succeed that McCloskey shows emerging from the capitalist emphasis on inventions tested by markets (McCloskey 2010, 1–9).

Human sciences such as economics have sought inspiration, precision, and profundity in doctrines of methodology, epistemology, and ontology. These have included materialism, idealism, realism, individualism, behaviorism, and more. The deconstruction of metaphysics in the nineteenth and twentieth centuries could have discredited any need for such grounds, along with their spurious authority, but too few social scientists noticed this. One way to appreciate the economic humanism in McCloskey's writings is to specify how her economic history can resist reductive metaphysics. Another track is to explore how her rhetoric of economics can suggest that materialism and other foundational creeds serve as political and aesthetic styles more than as ontologies, methodologies, or other guarantees of certainty for the social sciences, including economics. A third path is to consider how McCloskey's rhetoric of economics can lead from a practical take on disciplinary epistemology into a novel political economy of the bourgeoisie.

All three are routes worth taking at one time or another, for one group or another. For me, for now, the third route has several advantages. It helps explain how epistemology can be political theory. Not only should this demystify epistemology and bring it down to earth, but it should clarify how McCloskey's rhetoric of economics helps inform her argument for bourgeois virtues. In turn, that can help us recognize how the virtues of McCloskey's humanist economics emerge in important part from her virtuoso styles of communication in political economy, along with what often is regarded as her "more substantive" contributions to economics and history.

For McCloskey and me, all these are lessons in rhetoric of inquiry (Nelson, Megill, and McCloskey 1987). It is a humane and practical take on what has been pursued more narrowly as epistemology, philosophy of science, methodology of research, or logic of discovery and testing. Another advantage of the third path is its illumination for rhetoric of inquiry. As McCloskey's contributions often show, rhetoric of inquiry is an immanent and comparative epistemology. Within specific fields of study, it proceeds to direct and reflect on detailed inquiries, even as it learns also by relating those to substantive inquiries in other fields (Nelson 1987b, 407–34). Hence its project is to rhetorize one network of inquiry after another in order to improve the learning in diverse fields. How do economists or historians, for example, actually persuade themselves about what to study and what to say about it? There are differences among, but also within, such inquiries. Yet there are commonalities too. Rhetorical attention to our own practices of inquiry and others can help all of us improve how and what we know. As the third route lets us glimpse, this is why McCloskey comes to do rhetoric of inquiry as rhetoric of economics—and especially as economic history interested in the virtues of the bourgeoisie.

The explanation here is that McCloskey's epistemic pivot from economical materialism to historical humanism, as fulfilled in her defense of bourgeois virtues and dignity, readily arises from her rhetoric of economics. This is because, as epistemology, rhetoric of inquiry arises from the rhetorical tradition long associated with realist-republican principles of politics. McCloskey rightly indicts most economic materialism for monism, whereas the republican epistemology of rhetoric insists on plurality (of principles, tropes, virtues, etc.) unified by participation in shared publics. In fact, McCloskey's kind of humanism traces at least to Renaissance republicans, if not to their classical inspirations in Cicero, Aristotle, or even the ancient Sophists, who invented the discipline of rhetoric as the first systematic study and practice of politics. When we apprehend the politics in epistemologies, we can see humanism, materialism, realism, and the like as styles of politics and inquiry. As styles, these conventionally get characterized with aesthetic, ethical, and rhetorical markers, whereas philosophical doctrines usually get specified as canons of belief or rules of method. When we apprehend McCloskey's epistemic humanism as innovations in a family of political styles, therefore, we can appreciate her striking styles of inquiry and writing as intriguing gestures toward reviving the republic of science as a humanist ideal. This testifies to the politics in economics and the political theory in epistemology.

Epistemics as Politics

As the study of how we know, epistemology can do and be many things. But just as economics began as political economy and never truly did or could leave behind all politics, epistemology began as aspects of political inquiry by ancient Sophists and philosophers. By asking what to learn, how, and why, the ancient Greeks and Romans tried to clarify what to do with one another in making homes for people in the world (Gunnell 1968: esp. 40). Epistemology remains an exercise in political theory. Yes, I say this as a scholar whose attention to epistemology led into studies of politics, inclining me to special pleading for the epistemic importance of politics. Moreover, I concede (even insist) that we have reason to see epistemology also as cultural, psychological, economic, aesthetic, and more. Nonetheless, there are at least three further reasons to lead with a recognition of epistemology as political theory in particular.

One is historical. At its major turning points, as at its beginning, epistemology has kept eyes peeled for political implications. Renaissance and Enlightenment innovators in epistemics often contributed theories of politics as well as knowledge, sometimes entangled (even unified) in the same works. Cases in point include Machiavelli (1992), Bacon (2002), Hobbes (1962), Locke (1996), Vico (1948), Hume (1955), and Bentham (1952). Nineteenth-century philosophers such as Kant (1956), Hegel (1977), Marx (1977), and Nietzsche (1972, 1982) linked accounts of knowledge and politics. The same goes for key epistemologists and philosophers of science in the nineteenth and twentieth centuries. Thus Husserl (1965), Heidegger (1972), Russell (1962, 1965), Popper (1963), Hempel (1965), Merleau-Ponty (1962), Foucault (1984), Derrida (1974), and company cited high political stakes for their epistemologies: facing crises in Europe, seeking survival for the West, protecting the open society, or resisting terror, totalitarianism, and other perversities. Thomas Kuhn (1970), Imre Lakatos and Alan Musgrave (1970), and Paul Feyerabend (1975, 1978) made the dynamics of politics especially overt in their treatments of scientific inquiry. Even Ludwig Wittgenstein's epistemics (1958; Winch 1958; Louch 1966; Pitkin 1972; Danford 1978; Rorty 1978) for forms of life turn out to provoke—if not exactly provide—theories of politics later developed by Stanley Cavell (1979), Richard Rorty (1982), and others (Temelini 2015). So far, epistemology and political theory have been highly interdependent—often indistinguishable—endeavors. Principles for how we can or should know have been proposed and received as accounts of how we can and should organize ourselves and act in communities.

A second reason to begin by appreciating epistemology as political theory is that this can clarify the sources and stakes for epistemic principles, especially in the human sciences. Edicts of epistemology and method lose Olympian luster when seen as political arguments (at best) or power plays (at worst). Take methodological individualism, which says that good explanations must be in terms of individual beings. Whatever plausibility it has comes from considerations of ontological, biological, moral, romantic, and other individualisms that rely in important part on arguments about the awful consequences when our politics don't respect human individuals (Krimerman 1969, 585–688). Similarly, the behaviorism that limits good evidence to observations of bodily appearance and movement was meant from the start to counter politics that make room for misleading words (Nelson 1987a, 198–220; Nelson 1998, 102–4). This holds also for the logicism that confines good inference to axiomatic or analytic systems (Janik and Toulmin 1973, 120–238). Such individualism, behaviorism, and logicism are epistemological projects of liberal politics (Nelson 1998, 147–53). By different connections, so are the falsificationism and significance testing that Stephen Ziliak joins McCloskey in criticizing for overuse and other forms of misuse (McCloskey 1998, 154–73; McCloskey

1996, 21–59; Ziliak and McCloskey 2008; Beardsley 1974, 27–40). Likewise, the methodological holism more attuned to cultures, institutions, and emergent properties often ties concomitantly to traditionalist, fascist, socialist, or communitarian politics.

To respect epistemology as political theory, third, is to highlight the politics that inform rhetoric of inquiry. These politics propel McCloskey's criticism of key aspects of neoclassical economics. Rhetoric of inquiry decenters the logic of science claimed to regulate behaviorists, positivists, falsificationists, and their fellow travelers in twentieth-century social sciences. Instead, rhetoric of inquiry pursues a more encompassing, avowedly humanistic version of epistemology. As the name implies, rhetoric of inquiry stems in important part from the republican-rhetorical tradition of politics. Rooted in sophism and Aristotle, the republican-rhetorical tradition has flowered repeatedly in the West: in classical antiquity, the Renaissance, the Enlightenment, and after World War II (Nelson 1993, 78–100; Nelson 1998, 3–33).

Politics as Rhetorics

Rhetoric is the practice and study of persuasion. Learning is the persuasion of ourselves and others by presentations of experiences in claims, evidence, arguments, principles, theories, and criticisms. The republican-rhetorical tradition long concentrated on persuasion in or about public life, often regarded as politics. Gradually, we recognized other places of shared speech-and-experience as strongly similar to publics: markets, galleries, societies, and eventually sciences as sites of learning. Thus the Royal Society of London for Improving Natural Knowledge came to be seen as a model for "the republic of science," to which we'll return. Academic disciplines and their sponsoring multiversities are more recent versions. To practice rhetoric of inquiry is to analyze and improve how we persuade ourselves and others as we learn in communities, whether in disciplines or elsewhere.

Rhetoric of inquiry is immanent and comparative epistemology (Nelson and Megill 1986, 20–37). It does not pursue the logos and topos of inquiry alone but also the ethos, mythos, pathos, and tropos of inquiry (Nelson 1998, 99–114 and 135–49). We who launched it did not envision a standing field of scholarship separate from ongoing inquiry in myriad disciplinary and interdisciplinary endeavors. The project is to rhetorize one network of inquiry after another to improve the learning in diverse regions of research. Nobody should expect this to proceed by some revolutionary avalanche sweeping down the steep stairs of the ivory tower. Nobody should neglect the fact that the goals are better practices and products of inquiry in many fields. And nobody should forget that rhetoric of inquiry addresses what it recognizes to be territories of scholarship, science, art, and action that remain immensely diverse yet intensely resistant to the rhetorical turn away from modern quests for certain foundations of knowledge.

The epistemology is immanent because it proceeds within specific, substantive inquiries. This is exactly what McCloskey does in tracing the importance of persuasion in economics and especially economies (McCloskey 1998, 54–153; McCloskey 1990). It is what McCloskey does in challenging the plausibility of materialist, rationalist, and spiritualist explanations of modernity (McCloskey 2006, 2010). Attending to the epistemics of biology as rhetorics of evolution is likewise what Stephen Jay Gould did in framing detailed arguments for "punctuated equilibrium" through fossil records and analysis of peculiar cases (Gould 1987, 1989; Gould and Lewontin 1993; Gould 1977, 1980). Gould did much the same for epistemic rhetorics of "intelligence" in psychology and anthropology, as well as biology (Gould 1981). Records of inquiry in the natural and social sciences, the humanities, the arts, and the learned professions feature many a major contributor whose innovative accounts of subject matters at hand arise and proceed as reconsiderations of the field's earlier rhetorics of inquiry.

The epistemology is comparative, keeping eyes on other fields of inquiry and sometimes crossing into them, because uncertain researchers need to learn from each other as communities and modes of argument. Otherwise, they lack key perspectives and resources for refining their methods, evidence, and explanations. Even before attending to rhetoric as a learned discipline, McCloskey was working in economics and history. Her works after *The Rhetoric of Economics*, especially her inquiries into the characters and origins of bourgeois life, weave together these two endeavors to the benefit of both. They link also to literary criticism and theory, philosophy, and political theory. This is another way of saying that McCloskey's studies of bourgeois life continue to advance and learn from doing rhetoric of inquiry as comparative epistemology.[1]

Still, the epistemology is political too. However widely this might hold for epistemology in general, rhetoric of inquiry grows specifically from rhetoric as the first systematic study and practice of politics (Aristotle 1992; Cicero 2001, 2014; Nelson 1983b; Nelson 1990, 258–89). Almost from the start, rhetoric sustains a strong affinity for the politics of republics (Arendt 1958, 1963, 1968a, 1972; Pocock 1975; Dolan and Dumm 1993; Rahe 1994; Pettit 1997; Skinner 1998). By modernity, it promotes the "republic of letters," and its dream-unto-practice of "the republic of science" continues into the twenty-first century (Polanyi 1962). Its concerted, self-conscious exercise as rhetoric of inquiry targets organized practices of persuasion in human communities of learning. This examines the boundary work of organizational constitution and development. It encompasses the sociology of everyday conduct in disciplinary and additional professional settings. It parses the politics of discourse in scholarly publishing, grantsmanship, and so on (Friedrichs 1970; Crane 1972; Collins 1982; Gilbert and Mulkay 1984; Collins 1985; Mulkay 1985; Clifford 1986; Latour and Woolgar 1986; Bazerman 1988; Ashmore 1989; Bazerman and Paradis 1991; Crosswhite 1996; Condit 1999). Its potential implications differ from one scholar to the next. But for McCloskey, it began with criticizing the "modernism" of economic research.

Rhetorics as Economics

Deirdre McCloskey's turn to rhetoric in economics began as an acute attention to the talk by economists in their methods of inquiry. Typically, McCloskey applauded what economists had been learning about sales, resources, regulations, prices, markets, finances, firms, entrepreneurs, advertising, and such. Often she prized the economic explanations that some of her colleagues were propounding for apparently noneconomic activities like government, marriage, religion, science, traffic, and war. As a distinguished practitioner of economic history, McCloskey came to suspect that many economists had been writing and teaching woefully incorrect accounts of how they learned about economic phenomena of all sorts. Initially, the inference seemed to be fed by McCloskey's participation as an advocate of Chicago-style economics in debates among the several schools of economic theory and practice that continue to this day. Rhetorical analysis (informed by republican politics) helped McCloskey refine the symptomatology, the diagnosis, and eventually the therapy that she has come to pursue for modernist diseases of economics.

So McCloskey was edging into what philosophers call epistemology. The devices and limits for economic learning could be clarified by considering general principles for learning—as well as the resources and troubles for other sciences or fields of knowledge. Soon McCloskey was also working to clarify our scholarly devices and challenges for communicating with each other on methods, questions, results, criticisms, and the like. Such issues of communication are traditionally the province of rhetoric, first produced for comprehending and improving talk in politics but since available for other arenas too. Moving for a time from Chicago to Iowa City, McCloskey helped stitch together a diverse, extensive network of colleagues there and beyond. They have shared enthusiasm for exploring the dynamics of community learning. Especially, they have been keen to pursue practical devices for improving diverse, substantive inquiries.

McCloskey herself has moved through a series of colorful and widely persuasive studies of the ways economists talk. These illuminate how economists persuade themselves personally and collectively. They even investigate how economists sometimes persuade businesspeople, politicians, and wider publics. These analyses emphasize the use by economists of rhetorical devices such as examples, exigencies, metaphors, plots, genres, stories, and characters. They specify how esteemed economists use such "scientific" methods as cases, counts, experiments, models, proofs, puzzles, and statistics in ways that persuade more by literary power than any mathematical or observational warrant (Klamer, McCloskey, and Solow 1988; McCloskey 2000b, 2002).

A principle from rhetoric of inquiry is that academicians often fail to explain or even conceive adequately how their research actually proceeds (Nelson 1998, 47–71). So some economic studies are better than the modernist accounts they often receive. A take on finance, labor, or trade might explain its economic phenomena with more acuity than its own arguments. Yet rhetoric of inquiry also teaches that no grand dichotomy of form and content or of method and substance can be sustained or extended for long. From the beginning, I have thought that McCloskey's criticism of modernism in economics cuts far too deep and wide for *The Rhetoric of Economics* to remain complacent about the Chicago school or most other economic schools on the present scene.

The trouble with somebody like me making such criticisms of McCloskey or modernist economics is that outsider comments usually lack the ethos for attention within the discipline, where most of the work is done. Rhetoric of inquiry departs from logic of science in important part by resisting the disastrous temptation to dictate from an epistemological high horse above the detailed conduct of research.[2] Yet many economists, too, regard the paradox that emerges from *The Rhetoric of Economics* as its claims that neoclassical economics in the Chicago mode are mostly sound in substance, even though dysfunctionally modernist in methodological talk. To be sure, some of these economists are Austrians (Horwitz 1992, 2000), Marxians (Polanyi 1944; Piketty 2014), or feminists (Ferber and Nelson 1993; Folbre 1993, 1994, 2001) who dissent from the neoclassical consensus of the major schools of economics. Others are economic historians, philosophers and historians of economics, or economic methodologists who work in fields often on the fringes of the discipline (Fogel and Elton 1983; Fogel 1994; Sen 1970, 1987, 1997, 2002; Mirowski 1988, 1989, 1994, 2002, 2004). Such interests consign more than a few to departments outside elite universities. Like other social scientists in recent decades, economists practice "normal science" with a vengeance so that rhetorizing the tiniest parts of economics must mimic the "strong and slow boring of hard boards" that Max Weber saw as the lamentable lot of politics responsible for most changes against the grain (Weber 1946, 128).

McCloskey, on the other hand, has plenty of visibility and more than a little credibility among mainstream economists. If most economists ignore most of her rhetorizing criticisms, well, there is no special liability or deficiency to be overcome. After all, most disciplinarians in any social science ignore most of the words and works other than the ones tied most tightly to their subfield's studies. This obstacle, virtually structural, impedes McCloskey's evangelism less than most. McCloskey is a considerable celebrity in economics, and its disciplinary culture of weekly research talks by visitors from departments around the world puts her repeatedly in a position to reinforce her writings in the semiconversational settings where she persuades with flair. Even so, McCloskey's effort faces powerful forces for active ignorance among economists.

In early work, McCloskey has held that the results and methods analyzed rhetorically are mostly good economics. She has been cogent on how our many inquiries, including our sciences, vary appropriately in their methods and modes of argument. So it is not surprising that some of her rhetorical treatments make us even more impressed with the plausibility—at times even the virtuosity—of the economics analyzed. In other cases, however, McCloskey's rhetorical analysis has eroded our respect for the methods and findings of specific inquiries in neoclassical economics. Full acknowledgment of these implications has not come readily or rapidly to McCloskey. This befits a disciplinary insider. Still of late, McCloskey's continuing exercises in rhetoric of economics have begun to persuade her to look differently at her home discipline of economics. First, she argues directly that some prominent methods and results of neoclassical economics are wrong: "The problem [with current economics as a field of study] is that its methods are wrong, and produce wrong results" (McCloskey 1996, 13). Second, she traces many mistakes to poor epistemology, methods, education, and rhetorical self-awareness by economists in her time. And third, she is pursuing some radical alterations in the style and substance of disciplinary economics. My aim, again, is to evoke how all three contributions by McCloskey grow from rhetoric of economics as epistemology that taps political theory from the republican-rhetorical tradition. Then I hope to show how this recommends a more political, specifically republican, substance for McCloskey's bourgeois virtues.

A persistent example is the assault on statistical significance as mistaken for substantive significance. As McCloskey and colleagues have been showing, this calls into question *many* a microeconomic study. But it might sweep away some of the empirical support for *most* of the macroeconomic work in recent decades. As an in-house critic of disciplinary argumentation, McCloskey has been explaining how a wide range of specific inquiries mishandle several uses of statistics in ways that undermine claims about economic realities: not only significance tests but also standard error in regressions, R^2 as "explanations of variance," and so on. But another implication from rhetoric of inquiry covers when criticisms mean that normal scientists would have to abandon much of what they know how to do. If they are not being shown much about plausible alternatives, including practical ways to pursue careers with them, most scientists are apt to ignore the bearers of bad news about normal inferences or awkward truths about familiar statistics. An irony is that McCloskey's pieces on statistical significance, especially, are staples of early instruction in "social-science methods" for graduate students in several disciplines. Still, it is not the least surprising that the next waves of professional scholars follow in the footsteps of their mentors in continuing to disregard cautions like McCloskey's.

McCloskey's ample appreciation for economics in general and many of its recent classics in particular surely has made her criticisms easier for economists to applaud in general but ignore in particular. Had McCloskey's version of rhetorized economics developed little in subsequent writings, her advantages in ethos would have had scant opportunity to change the discipline. Since *The Rhetoric of Economics* (1998), however, McCloskey's criticisms and amendments to modernist economics have been growing more substantive and adventurous. *If You're So Smart* (1990) emphasizes metaphors and stories in economics, so it operates primarily within the literary take on economics promoted by the previous book. Still, the title essay enhances the early rhetorical turn on neoclassical economics into a logical turn on the neoclassical notions of sales, markets, and information (McCloskey 1990, 111–22). It scolds uneconomical marks like me who get others rich quick by buying unreflectively into their get-rich-quick schemes, especially recipes for gaming the stock market. Economic reasoning shows how low-cost information spreads fast in markets and changes their dynamics so that it cannot reliably deliver big returns for long. The last pronoun's referent is ambiguous: "it" could be low-cost information or economic reasoning. Lurking in McCloskey's insistence on fundamentally unsettling dynamics of reflexivity and recursivity for information in markets is a lesson for rhetorically unsophisticated practitioners of economics. They do well to learn the rhetorizing move of turning their principles on their own practices of inquiry (Carlston 1987). If not, they fall into the rhetorical fallacy of self-exception: they do not recognize that information in economics as a set of disciplinary markets must suffer the same limits.[3] By the next chapter, McCloskey explains how informational limits can keep economists from predictions accurate enough for directing economic decisions (McCloskey 1990, 123–34).

In terms implicitly aligned with chaos mathematics, she has demolished a pillar crucial for the plausibility of most economics in a modernist mode. It defends "unrealistic" models of economic man and the free market as narrowly economic calculators of expected—which is to say, predicted—utilities. Milton Friedman and others have argued that these false figures can be good tools for economics in helping generate good predictions. At the macroeconomic level, of course, the predictions somehow never get all that good. Few economists would dwell on an awkward detail like that when the beautiful mathematics of microeconomics remains; yet the McCloskey take suggests, at least to me, that such practical failures of macroeconomics imply a principled limit on microeconomics. If so, McCloskey is toppling a tower in a gleaming city on the hill. But does the utopian glow keep most citizens from noticing? The further question we know from trees and forests: if the tower falls unseen, does it count as falling at all? As the title character and his friend murmur in *Gladiator* (2000), a republican movie, "Not yet. Not yet."

Knowledge and Persuasion in Economics (1994b), the second sequel, is a little less literary and a bit more specifically rhetorical in its treatments of modernist economics. After touring many of the same territories as the earlier books, it is ready to end with "The Economy as a Conversation" (McCloskey 1994b, 367–78; McCloskey and Klamer 1995, 191–95). It is no surprise that neoclassical economists slight talk in favor of more conventionally material goods when they analyze economies. McCloskey and colleagues have begun to count the ways that talk (such as advertising and information itself) can figure in recent economies. They even reckon monetary amounts and proportions of the language products that comprise something like an economic sector of talk. This is another step by McCloskey in rhetorizing economics by supplementing the neoclassical apparatus in some of its own terms. Again, "the supplement" may become Derridean and deconstructive, or even rhetorical and reconstructive. At least from my vantage, McCloskey's twists on neoclassical figures like the economic sector, the economic man as "Max U" then "Maxine," the market price, and the economics of information turn the initial concepts somewhat against themselves. Remembering strictures on prediction, we must not pretend to say for sure what will follow from these rhetorical innovations. But we can see them as potentially far-reaching tropes that spring from practicing the rhetoric of economics.

Economics as Virtues

One of the latest turns for neoclassical economics to come from McCloskey's repertoire as a rhetorician is her exploration of bourgeois virtues and dignity (McCloskey 1996, 2006, 2010). She argues that the world benefits from a capitalist code of bourgeois, commercial, middle-class conduct—by contrast with the three virtues of Christian, plebeian morality and the four virtues of pagan, patrician aristocracy. The bourgeois virtues synthesize these older seven into a better (code of) ethics.[4] Thus bourgeois virtues add hope, faith, and love to justice, courage, temperance, and prudence.

As an exercise in rhetoric of economics, this is highly immanent and comparative. It is comparative in learning from studies of ethics, literature, and rhetoric—as well as history. It is immanent in challenging important aspects of neoclassical economics with supplements such as bourgeois virtues. These might decenter the maximization of expected utilities or transmute an explicitly materialist discipline. In other words, McCloskey's analysis of economic rhetoric has become emphatically and predominantly substantive in its detailed contributions.

As an exercise in rhetoric of economics, McCloskey's proposal of bourgeois virtues is also shrewd and subtle. Alasdair MacIntyre has argued that modern cultures in general and economics in particular start by homogenizing classical *virtues* in the plural into *virtue* in the singular. This soon becomes *value* of a singular, commensurated, unidimensionablized sort that gets subjectivized into preference then monetarized into dollars and cents (MacIntyre 1984, 1988). McCloskey's arguments are related. Especially, they rebut Immanuel Kant's priority for prudence as *the* rational virtue in the maximized singular (McCloskey 2006, 263–69 and 353–60). The protest is against epistemic and ethical monism, especially in modernist economics.

To these accounts, let us add that modernist economics makes singular value as possibly rational into sometimes plural but strictly nonrational *preferences*. As personal, undebatable senses of usefulness or desirability, preferences often differ from one human and one moment to the next. Some economics respect such preferences as specifiable in words, but most know and measure preferences by behavior, especially in market transactions. More or less rational estimations of probabilities for fulfilling specific preferences then make them into the *expected utilities* that emerge as crucial for neoclassical economics in recent decades.

To join in explaining how economics is ethics is bound to please most economists and businesspeople alike, as long as McCloskey can reassure both constituencies that the ethics are prudently, hardheadedly "realistic" (2006, 332–36). It might even spur support from scholars in the human sciences who take talk of "business ethics" to be oxymoronic and "economic realism" to defend corruption. To promote the bourgeoisie and, by extension, capitalism as "virtuous" is likely to delight the first two constituencies. And the glow rises if the bourgeois virtues—the capitalist ethics—can be presented as surpassing earlier efforts, which McCloskey labors mightily to do.

On the other hand, it is apt to seem strange, extreme, even perverse to many economists for McCloskey to abandon the advantages of a unified measuring stick for value (as preference as expected utility) in favor of seven separate, incommensurable virtues. Even if the bourgeois virtues evoke an admirable life available to us in capitalist economies, McCloskey's proposal could seem to comprise something of an "eternal return" to our roots—or to an earlier genius that requires what Friedrich Nietzsche called a "revaluation of values," even a "transvaluation of value" (1968; Conway 1997). Furthermore, people often dismiss such radical ambitions as impossible attempts to turn back the clock by retrieving earlier cultures now long gone.

In recent work, McCloskey doubles down. She rejects the epistemological materialism of economics as monistic (2006, 263–69). She could advance the same complaint against methodologies of behaviorism and individualism in the social sciences. The monism of any singular explanatory principle—even any cardinal principle that supposedly trumps all others in all cases—implies a God's-eye-view omniscience to comprehend everything and in exactly the same terms. Short of divine revelation, we finite humans cannot hope to transcend limitations of perspective. Yet even those graced by it concede that divine revelation is intrinsically personal and unsharable, as Thomas Hobbes observed in explaining why divine revelation cannot ground community (Nelson 2015, 69–81).

The epistemic monism of neoclassical economics makes its linear mathematics plausible, and the same goes for other social sciences of late. Without the monism, their reliance on linear regression and calculus would be less widely appropriate. Perhaps political economy attempts to pluralize its epistemology when Marxians try to make their materialism "dialectical." It is no accident that another form of the word is "dialogical," for talk among several parties. After all, talk as immaterial or duplicitous is just what other materialists would exclude. But even when Marxians do not follow the master in seeking "iron laws" or a singular, omnicompetent science, their economic explanations too often smack of determination of a cultural "superstructure" by a materialist "substructure." (The "dialectical idealism" of Hegelians faces parallel challenges.) Dialectics seem difficult to sustain scientifically or even philosophically. Thus

McCloskey has a point in faulting Plato for monism—that very Plato who invented philosophy in dialogues (McCloskey 2006, 361–68).

McCloskey's alternative is not dialectics but humanism. It is more often taken as ethics than epistemology.[5] But either way, humanism is anthropocentric: putting humans and their perspectives in the middle of the action. Erupting in the European Renaissance and Reformation and gaining momentum in the Enlightenment, humanism can be regarded as a modern version of the sophistic principle that "man is the measure." Ideological doctrines of human nature can be ways to homogenize humanity into a single body and viewpoint. But Renaissance humanism was emphatically pluralist: note the *five* points where Leonardo da Vinci's famous drawing of a standing human intersects the not-quite-enclosing circle that can indicate aspiration, excellence, health, wholeness, and community. From the first, in fact, humanism has been mostly a project of modern initiatives in the republican-rhetorical tradition.

For McCloskey, humanism in economics includes attending to numerous characters and stories of production, distribution, consumption, and such. It means accounting for their many motives, virtues, and vices. It involves accounting for their diverse histories, institutions, and situations. It implies investigating their distinct discourses as well as the investigative rhetorics themselves. And it requires resistance to reducing such dimensions and dynamics of economics to some master variable or another. Arguably game theories, institutional economics, and other innovations toward the discipline's edges have been moving some economists in at least a few of these directions. But by McCloskey's recent accountings, the discipline still has leagues to go.

Epistemologically, therefore, McCloskey's humanism is primarily pluralism. It protects against reductive monism by materialists, behaviorists, and others. To do this, it draws on the plurality implicit in recognizing many tropes at the heart of the republican-rhetorical tradition, whence humanism stems. Yet like MacIntyre, Richard McKeon, and Wayne Booth, McCloskey treats the ethics of virtues as primarily Aristotelian and secondarily rhetorical (McKeon 1987, 1990; Booth 1961, 1970, 1974a and b, 1979, 1988). Thus her take on virtues is moral rather than political, as Stephen Engelmann explains in the third and fourth parts of chapter 6 of this book. That makes decent sense for many a neoclassical economist. But notice how Aristotle—and later Aristotelians or even neo-Aristotelians such as Booth and MacIntyre—have not been notably humanist. Aristotle and his followers incline more toward naturalism than humanism. For epistemological and ethical humanists, better versions of virtues are available from specifically republican contributions to the republican-rhetorical tradition. These are more amply public and political.

Virtues as Virtue-osities

What *are* virtues? McCloskey defines *virtues* as *aspects of character manifest in practice.*[6] She writes, "A 'virtue' is a habit of the heart, a stable disposition, a settled state of character, a durable, educated characteristic of someone to exercise her will to be good" (2006, 64). Like the Victorians, however, the bourgeoisie have been inclined to treat character as a structure ("settled state") of mind or personality. This account informs the nineteenth-century *Bildungsroman* as well as the Marine training to "build character." This take on character is eminently practical, but it is not entirely behavioral. Nor is it especially rhetorical, either. McCloskey's virtues strike this tone, resonating with her significant attention to religion and psychology for morals (Hauerwas 1974, 1975, 1981, 1989, 1995, 1997; Bennett 1993, 1995).

Modern republicans, by contrast, get their senses of character from how ancient Greeks and Romans got to know one another politically through words and deeds in public places such as the marketplace and the forum. For Greeks, including Aristotle, *character* is *ethos*: *who* the individual is for the rest of the community as it interacts with him in public.[7] (Nelson 1998, 2015). For Machiavelli and other modern republicans, character is likewise manifest in public behavior, and ethical or political character is only achieved in public performance (Fleisher 1972; Hariman 1995, 95–140).[8] What we might call the republican cultivation of *virtues* as *virtue-osities* arguably begins with Machiavelli, and it extends into many presentations and practices in our world. It has considerable potential to improve McCloskey's arguments for the bourgeois virtues as rhetorical supplements for neoclassical economics.

By *virtue-osities*, I mean *talents for good realized in practice in public.* Our synonyms for *talents* have ranged from *knacks* cultivated in crafts to *skills* developed by trainers. Especially for Machiavelli, nothing can be virtuous without practical attainment. Virtues unrealized are not virtues at all. Moreover, virtuosity requires not only some success (as survival and succession in results) but also agreed excellence in performance. (The ancient Greek word for any specific excellence, *arētē*, is often translated as *virtue.*) This republican emphasis on public performance recognized by other participants as particularly good or excellent makes *virtues* into *aspects of character* only when *character* is *ethos*: publicly defined by responses to someone's words and deeds. Thus republican virtues as virtue-osities are more public, political, practical, and performative than McCloskey has been pursuing so far.

By *public*, though, we need not mean a classical, encompassing *place or population with every member taking part in managing the commonwealth.* This strictest sense of *public* seldom happens anywhere. Nor need we feature with liberalism, capitalism, and most of their offshoots a supposedly sovereign state. Then *public* means *the government, its policies and electorate, as well as open discourse by or about them*; so that *politics* are *activities within, by, or with respect to government*. Recent economists usually assume this, so that *private* means "nongovernmental." Yet to call for a more specifically public and substantively political sense of virtues need not be to exclude conduct and character in everyday life. It can include the social sense of *public* developed by the likes of Erving Goffman (1959, 1963, 1971), Richard Sennett (1974 [1992]), and Michael Warner (1990, 2002). Thus it can cover the bourgeois, "private" interest in social or economic fulfillment by individuals and their families. This was not Machiavelli's mission, but his "public" virtue-osities can adjust to it.

Machiavelli gets short shrift from McCloskey. Presumably because she is trying to spare the bourgeois virtues any taint of association with Machiavellian conniving or realist defense of awful results by noble ambitions, McCloskey attacks Machiavelli's realism as monist. Although I do not share much of Machiavelli's realism, McCloskey's criticism seems to me implausible, even perplexing. Machiavelli's virtues are plural: ambition as aspiration to glory, audacity as boldness, courage as perseverance in the face of fear, critical intelligence as skill in questioning, performance as skill in self-presentation, and prudence as realism. McCloskey complains that Machiavelli precedes Kant in making prudence into the singular, master virtue. But his realism is a far cry from the reductive consequentialism of Jeremy Bentham or the overarching wisdom of Kant's categorical imperative. Machiavelli's virtues do not boil down to prudence, and even his ethical realms are plural (Berlin 1971, 20–32).

McCloskey also claims that nowhere do Machiavelli or Thomas Hobbes as realists "take the virtues seriously as a system. They were early in that strange belief that a serious political philosopher had no need to be serious about ethics" (2006, 372). Oh my. 'Tis not true about Machiavelli, Hobbes, or most other realists among political thinkers (Hariman 1995, 13–49; Beer and Hariman 1996, 31–165). Overtly or covertly, the people who are altogether anti-ethics are mostly cynics rather than realists. Realisms are kinds of politics, ethics, epistemics, and so on (Nelson 2013). Perhaps only in the caricatures of realism promoted by a few idealists would a "realist" oppose all ethics, moralities, virtues, and so forth. And perhaps only in the caricatures of idealism promoted by a few realists would an "idealist" oppose taking any and all realities into decent account. Unfortunately, it is in such an unsophisticated, unpolitical, pejoratively rhetorical sense that McCloskey finds her ethics of bourgeois virtues to be "realist," because "realism is a social, that is, a rhetorical, that is, an ethical necessity for any science" (2006, 334). The word definitely gets used this way at times, but the meaning is too thin to engage ethical idealists, political realists, or any epistemologists in productive discussion.

Arguably Machiavelli's *Prince* and *Discourses on Livy* (1970) epitomize the modern republican "system" of civic education in virtues. This rhetorical tradition treats publics as story spaces for lessons in the glorious virtues and inglorious vices evident in a community's words and deeds. It monumentalizes great moments of history into the gestures of statues, the postures of paintings, and the faces of busts presented in public places. It teaches citizens telling words by inscribing them in public places and reciting them in settings of education or commemoration. It informs virtue-ous acts by sloganizing rules of thumb into practical maxims, then imparting them as punch lines for anecdotes, myths, and other tales that evoke meanings, uses, and limits of the deeds directed. Through strenuous exercises of body-and-mind, it makes these resources second nature to citizens who are to act prudently, audaciously, courageously, critically, and so on—often on the spur of the moment in the surprising situations that pop up in modern times (Nelson 2003, 229–57).

Much of this translates readily from Machiavelli's neoclassical publics into (shall we say) social, everyday publics. Moreover, a public turn can complement McCloskey's (and Engelmann's) criticism of social scientists who would reduce institutions to incentives (or even rules) for individuals (2006, 296–324). McCloskey explains some inadequacies of such reductions, but then she talks again about virtues rather than providing a fuller, more substantive view of institutions. In the republican-rhetorical tradition of Machiavelli and the American founders, *institutions* are (as the Latin etymology implies) "stitches in space-and-time" (Nelson and Nelson 1998, 641–53). Put more prosaically, institutions are sustained associations that *stitch into* the public characters of participants their distinctive aims, rules, virtues, vices, and more. Typically, they use maxims, myths, and rituals to do so.

(Dis)missing the republican kind of maxim (or precept or principle) as a practical rule of thumb, McCloskey proposes to articulate a system of bourgeois virtues by dumping maxims in favor of stories (2006, 270–78). This is odd at best, because bourgeois life features many a maxim that there seems little reason to trash, if often some reason to refine: "A penny saved is a penny earned"; "Pass on your values, not just your assets"; "Earn your first dollar by your labors: get up early, work late"; "Smile at challenges, curse at idleness"; "Be true to your dream: don't stop until you achieve it."[9] So that saving is not confused with hoarding, for example, this initial maxim needs a memorable little story (or two or three) that it can summarize but that can contextualize it. If a myth of ant and grasshopper gets the third precept as a punch line, we might remember both better when the time comes to act like an ant. Why pit stories against maxims for a system of virtues? Indeed, the republican-rhetorical tradition repeatedly finds principles, precepts, and maxims to be better than one- or two-word concepts at specifying and communicating virtues (Arendt 1968b, 143–71). So the republican-rhetorical tradition that informs rhetoric of inquiry shows how these ethical elements gain from—even need—each other: characters, maxims, stories, virtues, and more.

The republican-rhetorical tradition typically treats virtues as politics, encompassing ethics and spurring epistemologies, rather than as standing to the side of them. This is usual, too, for epistemological and ethical humanisms. Humanisms can go readily enough with idealisms of ethics, politics, or epistemology; but humanisms also can go with realisms. Thus it can make good sense to recognize Machiavelli as a humanist in some or all of these ways. Merleau-Ponty (1964b, 211–23) portrayed Machiavelli as a "new humanist," and others (Wolin 2004, 175–213) sketch him as an anguished humanist. Albeit in different ways, McCloskey and Machiavelli could agree to promote virtues as aspects of character and guides to ethical action. My hope, accordingly, is that we can learn from seeing bourgeois virtues as virtue-osities in the republican, especially the Machiavellian, sense.

Whatever we do with Machiavelli and his notorious realism, though, we need to notice that both Aristotelianism and the republican-rhetorical tradition bring obnoxious baggage with their rosters and practices of *virtues*. By linguistic roots, the very word is masculine unto sexist; the lists of specific virtues are sometimes more so; and Aristotelian and republican practices of virtues have been downright patriarchal. These two virtues traditions also share other troubles by standards ascendant in capitalist societies of the twenty-first century: heteronormativity, humanist insensibility to environmental challenges, ignorance of "sovereign" states, and undue deference by individuals to authorities, for starters. McCloskey acknowledges that bourgeois culture has shared much of this baggage, and it probably brings some of its own. What should virtues ethics of public character do to accommodate the psychological individualism and inner subjectivism of bourgeois culture? Such commonalities and differences might ease or trouble development of bourgeois virtues in disciplinary economics or our larger cultures. Either way, though, it is a priority to consider strategies for dealing with these actual or potential issues.

There might be further troubles too. Are republican virtue-osities intrinsically militarist, expansively imperialist, implicitly patriarchal, or excessively glory seeking? Again, these are reasonable worries that also hold for Aristotelian virtues and bourgeois cultures (Straub 1979; Kann 1998; Nelson 2002; Nelson and Nelson 1998). MacIntyre makes his neo-Aristotelianism attractive in part through mere, quick stipulations that classical Aristotelian virtues now should and would simply set aside their long-standing associations with aristocracy, patriarchy, plutocracy, racism, sexism, and such. What MacIntyre and McCloskey write about our cultures, practices, and systems makes this seem implausible. Yes, McCloskey brings feminist projects to economics and bourgeois virtues, but there remains much more to be done in adjusting any tradition of virtues to postmodern conditions and priorities. The hope must be that McCloskey and others will address in substantial, political detail how to refine bourgeois virtues for our times. As for republican virtue-osities, the work of needed cultural adjustments is far from done, but it's been proceeding with some success since the Second World War (Walzer 1983; Brin 1985; Etzioni 1995, 1999; Sandel 1996). This includes adapting republican maxims from Machiavelli to everyday action in social publics (Matthews 1998, 2007).

It is possible that a more amply republican pursuit of bourgeois virtues as virtue-osities might conflict with bourgeois life as we now know it. For example, some aspects of bourgeois "publics" differ from "publics" for modern republicans (Habermas 1991; Warner 1990). How might these differences matter? How might they be reconciled? Likewise, capitalism treats private property as something close to sovereignty of individuals over objects, whereas the republican-rhetorical tradition treats all kinds of property in terms of propriety. So republican property is typically personal property, with a person's use of objects deemed appropriate (or not) by conventions for securing the community's liberty and prosperity. It is conceivable that a highly capitalist and individualist society might talk and act in terms of "private property" pretty much as Americans do now. Still there are plenty of unresolved tensions in present practices; and they might impede bourgeois virtues as a developing system, especially as a network of virtue-osities.

It is even conceivable that McCloskey's notion of bourgeois virtues strikes us as a promising insight for the same reasons that it can seem oxymoronic. Maybe there are stark incompatibilities between the two. Might cultures that love virtues in action and cultures that prize capitalism, markets, middle classes, and bourgeois life amount to clashing civilizations? To tell, we do well to assess the bourgeois virtues in action—in our "public" but also in our "private," everyday lives. For rhetoric of economics, as for the republican-rhetorical tradition, this should include recognizing bourgeois virtue-osities as styles in action.

Virtue-osities as Styles

Like rhetoric of inquiry, the discourse of virtues stems from the republican-rhetorical tradition, since it has grandfathers in the Sophists and Aristotle. And like rhetoric of inquiry, the practice of virtues involves the cultivation and criticism of our personal and disciplinary styles in both inquiry and action. In rhetoric, a style is a distinctive mode of action, communication, or construction—as well as the sensibility that informs and performs it. Modern republicans such as Machiavelli make virtues performative as virtue-osities. Therefore, the republican-rhetorical tradition encourages us to appreciate virtues as styles.

In postmodern times, constructivist epistemologies such as rhetoric of inquiry recognize that styles are seldom "mere" or strictly "formal" but generally "significant" and "substantive" (Hebdige 1979; Hariman 1995; Brummett 2008). Paradoxically, in modernist eyes, styles and symbols are among the most substantive, significant aspects of politics as community life or public action. When it comes to styles, like symbols, you can't have one without another—or, in fact, without many others. So monism is a danger only for modernists who dichotomize style and substance in the singular, pit form against content in the abstract, contrast structure with function across the board, and so on (Nelson 2013, 4–7, 88–83; Nelson 2015, 173–88).

Many of our politics are primarily styles of personal experience and conduct. Political realism has never been an ideology or formed much of a movement. Ditto political idealism. This holds also for the perfectionism promoted by Ralph Waldo Emerson, Friedrich Nietzsche, and Nike commercials. It is particularly true of the postmodern republicanism that informs much rhetoric of inquiry. It even holds for conformism, existentialism, patronism, perspectivism, and traditionalism: all prominent in the *Harry Potter* novels that now play back to current tweens and teens their daily lives in interaction with adult headlines. At the moment, though, none of these are ideologized or mobilized into movements. Instead, they appear as political styles important in our everyday lives (Rowling 1997–2007; Wolosky 2010, 1–22).

As epistemology, rhetoric of inquiry also comprehends methods of inquiry as styles of art or science, even as styles of politics. To network them into a good community of inquiry has been the modern ambition of "the republic of science." This bears comparison to the system of bourgeois virtues that McCloskey would have us recognize and refine. For some, it is already the implicit ideal of the late-modern university; for others; it maps the connecting corrections needed to rhetorize the postmodern multiversity. If we were to explicate the virtue-osities of inquiry that are propelling McCloskey from *The Rhetoric of Economics* through her books on capitalism and bourgeois culture, I suspect that they would project an updated polity of inquiry along these republican lines (Robinson 1993, 1994, 1996, 1998, 2004, 2005, 2007).

Many have promoted the republic of science as a community honor-bound to conserve knowledge and advance learning through exploration, experimentation, publication, criticism, and correction. To read in and between McCloskey's lines, her republic of rhetorized inquiry would also cultivate virtue-osities of conversation; curiosity; daring; evidence; diversity that is intellectual, cultural, and personal; humility; and more. Her republic would welcome many styles of inquiry and invention. Probably it would protect opportunities for political action outside the academic grove as well as inside it. Certainly it would encourage the specifically republican virtue of respect (not merely the thin tolerance of liberalism) for other people and ideas. And especially it would promote virtue-osity in writing (McCloskey 2000a).

Admittedly, this McCloskey sense of a republic of inquiry comes to me not only from reading but particularly from collaborating with her. In other words, I know these virtue-osities from their systematic pursuit by Deirdre, from the character who is Deirdre. The styles make the economist, the historian, the rhetorician, and the woman (McCloskey 1999). And they are McCloskey's styles in action, from inquiry to everyday life. A style of writing can be a style of acting—and politics.

McCloskey's abiding contribution to rhetorizing economics, as to rhetoric of inquiry, might turn out to be her distinctive style of writing. This is no accident. McCloskey has been working hard and well on writing style for far longer than she has been participating in rhetoric of inquiry. She is justly renowned for a bracing, biting, yet ennobling style in writing and in person, inside the discipline of economics and far beyond. In recent books, she makes the style even more full-bodied and human than before; and since rhetoricians of inquiry know how style is substance, this becomes for McCloskey another way to rhetorize even economics.

Thus McCloskey's virtue-osities feature her style in writing: in writing her rhetorized economics, in writing her memoirs, in writing her recommendations on writing economics (McCloskey 1987). For me, at least, writing style is McCloskey's strongest fulfillment of the epistemological, ethical, aesthetic, and performative projects of the republican-rhetorical tradition. In the modern republic that named itself the United States of America, the early strategies of citizen education stayed principally republican until the twentieth century. This meant lots of what people misunderstood as "rote learning," with students reciting glorious speeches and verses after their teachers. Then the students would look down to copy elegant passages from great leaders and writers past. The imitation was not meant to clone such admirable characters, nor could it. The republican aim was instead to infuse each distinctive individual with the rhythms, tropes, images, precepts, and other devices—in short, with the styles—of past masters. When they could, teachers would use pageants and other performances to have students practice the postures, gestures, even full-fledged deeds by the country's emblems of excellence. The same held for chores, sports, and other cultural rituals, including what we "privatize" these days as "volunteer work."

The virtues were in the words, deeds, and their deliveries. The virtues *were* these styles, and they could become virtue-osities for further generations through such republican education of characters by ritualized performances. All this enacts the republican-rhetorical principle—or trope—of *imitatio* (imitation). Just as the Christian "imitation of Jesus" cannot and will not make any Christian into Jesus, the republican-rhetorical imitation of Abraham Lincoln has yet to generate even the palest of replicas. But Christian recitations of words attributed to Jesus in the New Testament as well as Christian communions to reenact the Last Supper practice believers in Christian styles of thought and action. In much the same way, republican imitations of words and deeds by George Washington or Winston Churchill practice citizens in virtuoso *styles* of political performance. And just as fundamentalist Christians ask "What would Jesus do?" to maximize Bible stories for everyday conduct, so beneficiaries of republican education might ponder "What would Roosevelt do?" to maximize their political anecdotes for virtue-oso acts.

What each student brought to such learning would differ in every case, just as the class sense of each student as a public character would differ for each. The rehearsals would interact with the individuals to cultivate unique and autonomous characters, with their own distinctive virtue-osities, their personal styles in action. I have experienced this, in a way, through years of McCloskey marking my clumsy, clotted prose. (Not understanding this republican-rhetorical mode of education, I'd devoted many calendar pages of undergraduate and graduate school to copying passages from Germans writing philosophy in English and to academic translations into English from German texts of the nineteenth century: what an awful way to influence the prose of a student writing theory in English, as this overly long and complicated sentence shows!) In addition, I've analyzed and copied many paragraphs by McCloskey, hoping to grasp or even incorporate some sense of her writing style. (For me, it would be a style of inquiry and action as well.) Even at this late date, after years of intermittent but patient mentoring, you can see that I'm no McCloskey, especially in style. But you can also see a short, simple sentence in at least some of my paragraphs. In other ways, too, my recent prose manages a little more color and life—courtesy of McCloskey and other mentors but especially of McCloskey and other models.

Is it anticlimactic or belittling to exemplify virtue-osities as styles of writing—or even of action in some full-bodied sense? First, notice that the republican-rhetorical tradition features speech-in-action-in-public. Just as

McCloskey insists that we respect speech as economic action, we do well to recognize talking and writing as forms of action. Moreover, speech of some kind is intrinsic to all action in any full-fledged sense that does not collapse into mere behavior as bodily motion. Second, consider that there are no politics without speech. So attention to virtue-osities as styles—including styles of writing—is a way to emphasize the explicit and implicit politics of character, culture, goodness, and talent that any discourse on virtues seeks to engage. Some academicians in economics make public marks as advisors on corporate or government policy. Their virtue-osities are measured in politicians persuaded, events predicted, and constituents benefitted; and all these involve verbal styles, some distinctive and some not. McCloskey works more as a scholar, where her enduring virtue-osities include her disciplinary and public "voice." This is her literary voice as her characteristic style of writing. It has a persuasive politics of its own, enacting the politics of her rhetoric of economics, her brief for bourgeois virtues, and her inventive account of capitalism. It's just as provocative a contribution; and unless we want to dichotomize form and content, McCloskey's distinctive style is a virtue-osity of her work.

As a model, McCloskey's style of writing reminds me most of Judith Martin when she writes as Miss Manners for the *Washington Post*. This holds all the more now that the character of Aunt Deirdre graces McCloskey's rhetorized economics. Like Miss Manners, Aunt Deirdre sounds a tad Victorian yet pithy and down-to-earth, which is unusual for academic discourse. Both figures politely but pointedly set us readers straight on manners—that is, on appropriate styles—for conducting many matters of everyday concern. For Miss Manners, these feature society, household, and business; for Aunt Deirdre, they focus on economics, ethics, and writing.

Each is a special joy to read when showing us how to answer the scornful claims and power plays of other people with proper, seemingly simple, but devastatingly phrased words. Thus Miss Manners provides *Basic Training* in *The Right Thing to Say*, "in which Miss Manners introduces etiquette as a second language: how to talk, talk back and say 'no' without causing offense, and how to apologize when you do anyway" (Martin 1998). Likewise, McCloskey sees economics as an exercise in language: "Economics depends much more on writing (and on speaking, another neglected art) than on the statistics and mathematics usually touted as the tool of the trade. Most of the economist's skills are verbal. An economist should be embarrassed to do such a large part of the craft unprofessionally. Shame on us" (McCloskey 2000a, 6). As she adds, "Good style is above all a matter of taste. Professional economists share with college sophomores . . . the conviction that matters of taste are 'mere matters of opinion,' the notion being that 'opinion' is unarguable. A matter of taste, however, can be argued, often to a conclusion. The best argument is social practice, since that is what taste is" (McCloskey 2000a, 88). So let McCloskey also locate virtues as virtue-osities in social practices.

The best way to evidence my claim of similarity in styles is by close rhetorical analysis of many passages from each writer. But if I can pique your interest, you can enjoy the comparison and learn more by doing it yourself. Instead let us conclude the present essay by returning to its arguments on epistemics as politics, on McCloskey's inquiries as rhetorical and republican, and on the bourgeois virtues as styles in action. These, I contend, are key dynamics to acknowledge and articulate in McCloskey's rhetoric of economics. As we do, we can discern how diverse disciplines differ in the politics of their methods and discoveries. We can learn how rhetoric of inquiry becomes substantive and practical as immanent and comparative epistemology. We can consider how bourgeois virtues might cohere or clash and how they might excel or falter. We can investigate how McCloskey's writing style is intrinsic to her case for the bourgeois virtues and her rhetorizing of neoclassical economics. We can even tell how the writing of Aunt Deirdre resonates surprisingly with the prose of Miss Manners. And so, in the end, we can ask, Might it reinforce these arguments for you to learn that, in explaining proper conduct for the "private" realms of society, household, and business that often interest current economists, Miss Manners makes a telling political move? For she expressly portrays herself as walking alongside the "public" footsteps of Thomas Jefferson, since both formulate avowedly *republican* principles (Martin 1982, 1985a, b, 1989, 1999a, b, 1996, 2003).

Notes

1. This helps explain why epistemology as rhetoric-in-inquiry (and as political theory) is not on the way to becoming an institutionalized field. For one thing, it is notably adventurous and demanding work: it depends on participating in several fields of learning more or less at once and pursuing specific, substantive contributions to at least one of them. For another, its influence is as much centrifugal as centripetal. Some rhetoricians of inquiry—especially those tied to rhetoric as a tradition, communication as a field, literature as a preoccupation, or philosophy as a discipline—might focus on developing moves of rhetorical analysis and invention for detailed work in other fields. Such scholars might network into an invisible college or interdisciplinary field, and this might abet their rhetorical analysis and invention in specific studies. Still, the project must concentrate on improving substantive learning, and it must resist sidetracking into abstract epistemology for its own sake. The caution holds particularly for the sometimes thinly substantive studies that call themselves "theory." All too much literary, rhetorical, social, political, and other "theory" is little more than empty and stipulative epistemology. Most rhetorized study would proceed in specific fields, with attention to others, but with little reason to brand itself as practicing epistemology or rhetorical analysis (Kress 1979; Mitchell 1985; Gunnell 1998).

2. Nor does it help to accredit such comments as coming from anyone interested in politics, a sworn enemy of many a modernist economist (McCloskey and Nelson 1990, 155–74).

3. This fallacy of self-exception is a defect in rhetoric rather than logic. As Bertrand Russell showed long ago in regard to the paradox of the Cretan liar, who says he always tells lies, logics often can and must allow self-exception. As Russell argued, logics usually advance statements on different levels to make them assessable by different standards. The claim of always telling lies falls outside the lying statements that it describes. By contrast, rhetorics can lapse when they depend on assessing the writer or writing by different standards than the writing applies to its topic. Accusations of self-exception or double standards question the good faith of the writer or the writing rather than its logical consistency.

4. For an earlier, somewhat different formulation, see McCloskey (1994, 177–91).

5. Not all epistemic or ethical pluralists agree that humanism is good, even politically. Thus deep ecologists and other environmentalists indict modernity not only for industrialization and development but also for humanism (Enrenfeld 1978; Devill and Sessions 1985; Sessions 1995).

6. Following McIntyre following Ludwig Wittgenstein, McCloskey would take care to specify particular practices, in the plural: *The Bourgeois Virtues* (2006, 64). I concur with this (perspectivist) refinement of republican politics, especially in regard to virtues; but we can sideline it here.

7. Should it go without saying that the public figure for ancient Greeks and Romans was male?

8. McCloskey treats ethics and morality as the same. Political theorists have been loath to identify the two at least since Machiavelli consigned Christian morality to private conduct while endorsing realist ethics or politics for public performance.

9. I quote these maxims from a Smith-Barney investment commercial on TV in the last decade.

References

Arendt, Hannah. 1958. *The Human Condition*. Chicago: University of Chicago Press.

Arendt, Hannah. 1963. *On Revolution*. New York: Viking.

Arendt, Hannah. 1968a. *Between Past and Future: Eight Exercises in Political Thought*. 2nd ed. New York: Viking.

Arendt, Hannah. 1968b. "What Is Freedom?" In Arendt 1968a, 143–71.

Arendt, Hannah. 1972. *Crises of the Republic*. New York: Harcourt Brace Jovanovich.

Aristotle. 1992. *On Rhetoric: A Theory of Civil Discourse*. Translated by George A. Kennedy. New York: Oxford University Press.

Ashmore, Malcolm. 1989. *The Reflexive Thesis: Writing Sociology of Scientific Knowledge*. Chicago: University of Chicago Press.

Bacon, Francis. 2002. *The Major Works*. Edited by Brian Vickers. Oxford: Oxford University Press.

Bazerman, Charles. 1988. *Shaping Written Knowledge: The Genre and Activity of the Experimental Article in Science*. Madison: University of Wisconsin Press.

Bazerman, Charles, and Paradis, James, eds. 1991. *Textual Dynamics of the Professions: Historical and Contemporary Studies of Writing in Professional Communities*. Madison: University of Wisconsin Press.

Beardsley, Philip L. 1974. "Substantive Significance vs. Quantitative Rigor in Political Inquiry: Are the Two Compatible?" *International Interactions* 1 (1): 27–40.

Beer, Francis A., and Hariman, Robert, eds. 1996. *Post-Realism: The Rhetorical Turn in International Relations*. East Lansing: Michigan State University Press.

Bennett, William J. 1993. *The Book of Virtues*. New York: Simon and Schuster.

Bennett, William J. 1995. *The Moral Compass*. New York: Simon and Schuster.

Bentham, Jeremy. 1952. *Handbook of Political Fallacies*. Edited by Harold A. Larrabee. New York: Crowell.

Berlin, Isaiah. 1971. "The Question of Machiavelli." *New York Review of Books*, November 4, 20–32.

Booth, Wayne C. 1961. *The Rhetoric of Fiction*. Chicago: University of Chicago Press.

Booth, Wayne C. 1970. *Now Don't Try to Reason with Me: Essays and Ironies for a Credulous Age*. Chicago: University of Chicago Press.

Booth, Wayne C. 1974a. *Modern Dogma and the Rhetoric of Assent*. Chicago: University of Chicago Press.

Booth, Wayne C. 1974b. *A Rhetoric of Irony*. Chicago: University of Chicago Press.

Booth, Wayne C. 1979. *Critical Understanding: The Powers and Limits of Pluralism*. Chicago: University of Chicago Press.

Booth, Wayne C. 1988. *The Company We Keep: An Ethics of Fiction*. Berkeley: University of California Press.

Brin, David. 1985. *The Postman*. New York: Bantam Books.

Brummett, Barry. 2008. *A Rhetoric of Style*. Carbondale: Southern Illinois University.

Carlston, Donal E. 1987. "Turning Psychology on Itself: The Rhetoric of Psychology and the Psychology of Rhetoric." In Nelson, Megill, and McCloskey 1987, 145–62.

Cavell, Stanley. 1979. *The Claim of Reason: Wittgenstein, Skepticism, Morality, and Tragedy*. New York: Oxford University Press.

Cicero, Marcus Tullius. 2001. *On the Ideal Orator*. Translated by James M. May and Jakob Wisse. New York: Oxford University Press.

Cicero, Marcus Tullius. 2014. *On the Republic* and *On the Laws*. Translated by David Fott. Ithaca, NY: Cornell University Press.

Clifford, James. 1986. *Writing Culture*. Berkeley: University of California Press.

Collins, Harry M. 1982. *Frames of Meaning: The Social Construction of Extraordinary Science*. London: Routledge and Kegan Paul.

Collins, Harry M. 1985. *Changing Order: Replication and Order in Scientific Practice*. London: Sage.

Condit, Celeste Michelle. 1999. *The Meanings of the Gene*. Madison: University of Wisconsin Press.

Conway, Daniel W. 1997. *Nietzsche and the Political*. London: Routledge.

Crane, Diana. 1972. *Invisible Colleges*. Chicago: University of Chicago Press.

Crosswhite, James. 1996. *The Rhetoric of Reason: Writing and the Attractions of Argument*. Madison: University of Wisconsin Press.

Danford, John. 1978. *Wittgenstein and the Problem of Political Philosophy: A Reexamination of the Foundation of Social Science*. Chicago: University of Chicago Press.

Derrida, Jacques. 1974. *Of Grammatology*. Translated by Gayatri Chakravorty Spivak. Baltimore, MD: Johns Hopkins University Press.

Devall, Bill, and Sessions, George. 1985. *Deep Ecology: Living as If Nature Mattered*. Layton, UT: Gibbs Smither.

Dolan, Frederick M., and Dumm, Thomas L., eds. 1993. *Rhetorical Republic: Governing Representations in American Politics*. Amherst: University of Massachusetts Press.

Enrenfeld, David. 1978. *The Arrogance of Humanism*. New York: Oxford University Press.

Etzioni, Amitai. 1995. *New Communitarian Thinking*. Charlottesville: University Press of Virginia.

Etzioni, Amitai. 1999. *Civic Repentance*. Lanham, MD: Rowman & Littlefield.

Ferber, Marianne A., and Nelson, Julie A., eds. 1993. *Beyond Economic Man*. Chicago: University of Chicago Press.

Feyerabend, Paul. 1975. *Science in a Free Society*. London: NLB.

Feyerabend, Paul. 1978. *Against Method*. London: NLB.

Fleisher, Martin, ed. 1972. *Machiavelli and the Nature of Political Thought*. New York: Atheneum.

Fogel, Robert W. 1994. *Without Consent or Contract: The Rise and Fall of American Slavery*. New York: Norton.

Fogel, Robert W., and Elton, G. R. 1983. *Which Road to the Past? Two Views of History*. New Haven: Yale University Press.

Folbre, Nancy. 1993. *Women's Work in the World Economy*. New York: New York University Press.

Folbre, Nancy. 1994. *Who Pays for the Kids?* New York: Routledge.

Folbre, Nancy. 2001. *The Invisible Heart*. New York: Norton.

Foucault, Michel. 1984. *The Foucault Reader*. Edited by Paul Rabinow. New York: Pantheon.

Friedrichs, Robert W. 1970. *A Sociology of Sociology*. New York: Free Press.

Gilbert, G. Nigel, and Mulkay, Michael. 1984. *Opening Pandora's Box: A Sociological Analysis of Scientists' Discourse*. Cambridge: Cambridge University Press.

Goffman, Erving. 1959. *The Presentation of Self in Everyday Life*. Garden City, NY: Doubleday.

Goffman, Erving. 1963. *Behavior in Public Places*. New York: Free Press.

Goffman, Erving. 1971. *Relations in Public*. New York: Harper and Row.

Gould, Stephen Jay. 1977. *Ever Since Darwin: Reflections in Natural History*. New York: Norton.

Gould, Stephen Jay. 1980. *The Panda's Thumb: More Reflections in Natural History*. New York: Norton.

Gould, Stephen Jay. 1981. *The Mismeasure of Man*. New York: Norton.

Gould, Stephen Jay. 1987. *Time's Arrow, Time's Cycle: Myth and Metaphor in the Discovery of Geological Time*. Cambridge, MA: Harvard University Press.

Gould, Stephen Jay. 1989. *Wonderful Life: The Burgess Shale and the Nature of History*. New York: Norton.

Gould, S. J., and Lewontin, R. C. 1993. "Appendix: The Spandrels of San Marco and the Panglossian Paradigm: A Critique of the Adaptationist Programme." In Selzer 1993, 339–56.

Greffenius, Steven. 2002. *The Last Jeffersonian: Ronald Reagan and Radical Democracy*. Westwood, MA: TechWrite.

Gunnell, John G. 1968. *Political Philosophy and Time*. Middletown, CT: Wesleyan University Press.

Gunnell, John G. 1998. *The Orders of Discourse*. Lanham, MD: Rowman & Littlefield.

Habermas, Jürgen. 1991. *The Structural Transformation of the Public Sphere: An Inquiry into a Category of Bourgeois Society*. Translated by Thomas Burger and Frederick Lawrence. Cambridge, MA: MIT Press.

Hariman, Robert. 1995. *Political Style: The Artistry of Power*. Chicago: University of Chicago Press.

Hariman, Robert, ed. 2003. *Prudence: Classical Virtue, Postmodern Practice*. University Park: Pennsylvania State University Press.

Hauerwas, Stanley. 1974. *Vision and Virtue*. Notre Dame, IN: University of Notre Dame Press.

Hauerwas, Stanley. 1975. *Character and the Christian Life*. San Antonio: Trinity University Press.

Hauerwas, Stanley. 1981. *A Community of Character*. Notre Dame, IN: University of Notre Dame Press.

Hauerwas, Stanley. 1989. *Why Narrative?* Grand Rapids, MI: W. B. Eerdmans.

Hauerwas, Stanley. 1995. *In Good Company: The Church as Polis*. Notre Dame, IN: University of Notre Dame Press.

Hauerwas, Stanley. 1997. *Christians among the Virtues*. Notre Dame, IN: University of Notre Dame Press.

Hebdige, Dick. 1979. *Subculture: The Meaning of Style*. London: Routledge.

Hegel, G. W. F. 1977. *Phenomenology of Spirit*. Translated by A. V. Miller. Oxford: Oxford University Press.

Heidegger, Martin. 1972. *On Time and Being*. Translated by Joan Stambaugh. New York: Harper and Row.

Hempel, Carl G. 1965. *Aspects of Scientific Explanation*. New York: Free Press.

Hobbes, Thomas. 1962. *Leviathan*. Edited by Michael Oakeshott. New York: Collier.

Horwitz, Steven. 1992. *Monetary Evolution, Free Banking, and Economic Order*. Boulder, CO: Westview Press.

Horwitz, Steven. 2000. *Microfoundations and Macroeconomics*. New York: Routledge.

Hume, David. 1955. *An Inquiry Concerning Human Understanding*. Edited by Charles W. Hendel. New York: Bobbs-Merrill.

Husserl, Edmund. 1965. *Phenomenology and the Crisis of Philosophy*. Translated by Quentin Lauer. New York: Harper and Row.

Janik, Allan, and Toulmin, Stephen. 1973. *Wittgenstein's Vienna*. New York: Simon and Schuster.

Kann, Mark E. 1998. *A Republic of Men: The American Founders, Gendered Language, and Patriarchal Politics*. New York: New York University Press.

Kant, Immanuel. 1956. *Critique of Practical Reason*. Translated by Lewis Ahite Beck. Indianapolis: Bobbs-Merrill.

Klamer, Arjo, McCloskey, D. N., and Solow, Robert, eds. 1988. *The Consequences of Economic Rhetoric*. New York: Cambridge University Press.

Kress, Paul F. 1979. "Against Epistemology: Apostate Musings." *Journal of Politics* 41 (2): 526–42.

Krimerman, Leonard, ed. 1969. *The Nature and Scope of Social Science*. New York: Appleton-Century-Crofts.

Kuhn, Thomas. 1970. *The Structure of Scientific Revolutions*. 3rd ed. Chicago: University of Chicago Press.

Lakatos, Imre, and Musgrave, Alan, eds. 1970. *Criticism and the Growth of Knowledge*. Cambridge: Cambridge University Press.

Latour, Bruno, and Woolgar, Steve. 1986. *Laboratory Life*. Princeton, NJ: Princeton University Press.

Locke, John. 1996. *An Essay Concerning Human Understanding*. Edited by Kenneth P. Winkler. Indianapolis: Hackett.

Louch, A. R. 1966. *Explanation and Human Action*. Berkeley: University of California Press.

Machiavelli, Niccolò. 1970. *The Prince* and *The Discourses*. New York: Random House.

Machiavelli, Niccolò. 1992. *The Prince*. Edited and translated by Robert M. Adams. 2nd ed. New York: Norton.

MacIntyre, Alasdair C. 1984. *After Virtue*. 2nd ed. Notre Dame, IN: University of Notre Dame Press.

MacIntyre, Alasdair C. 1988. *Whose Justice? Which Rationality?* Notre Dame, IN: University of Notre Dame Press.

Martin, Judith. 1982. *Miss Manners' Guide to Excruciatingly Correct Behavior*. New York: Warner Books.

Martin, Judith. 1985a. *Common Courtesy, In Which Miss Manners Solves the Problem That Baffled Mr. Jefferson*. New York: Atheneum.

Martin, Judith. 1985b. *Miss Manners' Guide to Rearing Perfect Children*. New York: Atheneum.

Martin, Judith. 1989. *Miss Manners' Guide for the Turn-of-the-Millennium*. New York: Simon and Schuster.

Martin, Judith. 1996. *Miss Manners Rescues Civilization: From Sexual Harassment, Frivolous Lawsuits, Dissing and Other Lapses in Civility*. New York: Crown.

Martin, Judith. 1998. *Miss Manners' Basic Training: The Right Thing to Say*. New York: Crown.

Martin, Judith. 1999a. *Miss Manners on (Painfully Proper) Weddings*. New York: Crown.

Martin, Judith. 1999b. *Miss Manners' Guide to Domestic Tranquility: The Authoritative Manual for Every Civilized Household, However Harried*. New York: Three Rivers Press.

Martin, Judith. 2003. *Star-Spangled Manners, In Which Miss Manners Defends American Etiquette (for a Change)*. New York: Norton.

Marx, Karl. 1977. *Selected Writings*. Edited by David McLellan. Oxford: Oxford University Press.

Matthews, Christopher. 1988. *Hardball: How Politics Is Played—Told by One Who Knows the Game*. New York: Harper and Row.

Matthews, Christopher. 2007. *Life's a Campaign: What Politics Has Taught Me about Friendship, Rivalry, Reputation, and Success*. New York: Random House.

McCloskey, D. N. 1987. *The Writing of Economics*. New York: Macmillan.

McCloskey, D. N. 1990. *If You're So Smart: The Narrative of Economic Expertise*. Chicago: University of Chicago Press.

McCloskey, D. N. 1994a. "Bourgeois Virtue." *American Scholar* 63 (2): 177–91.

McCloskey, D. N. 1994b. *Knowledge and Persuasion in Economics*. New York: Cambridge University Press.

McCloskey, Deirdre N. 1996. *The Vices of Economists—the Virtues of the Bourgeoisie*. Amsterdam: Amsterdam University Press.

McCloskey, D. N. 1998. *The Rhetoric of Economics*. 2nd ed. Madison: University of Wisconsin Press.

McCloskey, Deirdre N. 1999. *Crossing: A Memoir*. Chicago: University of Chicago Press.

McCloskey, Deirdre N. 2000a. *Economical Writing*. Prospect Heights, IL: Waveland Press.

McCloskey, Deirdre N. 2000b. *How to Be Human, Though an Economist*. Ann Arbor: University of Michigan Press.

McCloskey, Deirdre N. 2002. *The Secret Sins of Economics*. Chicago: Prickly Paradigm Press.

McCloskey, Deirdre N. 2006. *The Bourgeois Virtues: Ethics for an Age of Commerce*. Chicago: University of Chicago Press.

McCloskey, Deirdre N. 2010. *Bourgeois Dignity: Why Economics Can't Explain the Modern World*. Chicago: University of Chicago Press.

McCloskey, Deirdre N., and Klamer, Arjo. 1995. "One Quarter of GDP Is Persuasion." *American Economic Review* 85 (2): 191–95.

McCloskey, D. N., and Nelson, John S. 1990. "The Rhetoric of Political Economy." In Nichols and Wright 1990, 155–74.

McKeon, Richard. 1987. *Rhetoric: Essays in Invention and Discovery*. Woodbridge, CT: Ox Bow Press.

McKeon, Richard. 1990. *Freedom and History and Other Essays*. Edited by Zahava K. McKeon. Chicago: University of Chicago Press.

Merleau-Ponty, Maurice. 1962. *Phenomenology of Perception*. Translated by Colin Smith. New York: Humanities Press.

Merleau-Ponty, Maurice. 1964a. *Sense and Non-Sense*. Translated by Hubert L. Dreyfus and Patricia A. Dreyfus. Evanston, IL: Northwestern University Press.

Merleau-Ponty, Maurice. 1964b. *Signs*. Translated by Richard C. McCleary. Evanston, IL: Northwestern University Press.

Mirowski, Philip. 1988. *Against Mechanism: Why Economics Needs Protection from Science*. Totowa, NJ: Rowman & Littlefield.

Mirowski, Philip. 1989. *More Heat than Light: Economics as Social Physics, Physics as Nature's Economics*. New York: Cambridge University Press.

Mirowski, Philip. 1994. *Natural Images in Economic Thought: "Markets Read in Tooth and Claw."* New York: Cambridge University Press.

Mirowski, Philip, ed. 2002. *Machine Dreams: Economics Becomes a Cyborg Science*. New York: Cambridge University Press.

Mirowski, Philip. 2004. *The Effortless Economy of Science*. Durham, NC: Duke University Press.

Mitchell, W. J. T. 1985. *Against Theory: Literary Studies and the New Pragmatism*. Chicago: University of Chicago Press.

Mulkay, Michael. 1985. *The Word and the World: Explorations in the Form of Sociological Analysis*. London: George Allen and Unwin.

Nelson, John S., ed. 1983a. *What Should Political Theory Be Now?* Albany: State University of New York Press.

Nelson, John S. 1983b. "Political Theory as Political Rhetoric." In Nelson 1983a, 169–240.

Nelson, John S. 1987a. "Stories of Science and Politics: Some Rhetorics of Political Research." In Nelson, Megill, and McCloskey 1987, 198–220.

Nelson, John S. 1987b. "Seven Rhetorics of Inquiry: A Provocation." In Nelson, Megill, and McCloskey 1987, 407–34.

Nelson, John S. 1990. "Political Foundations for Rhetoric of Inquiry." In Simons 1990, 258–89.

Nelson, John S. 1993. "Commerce among the Archipelagos: Rhetoric of Inquiry as a Practice of Coherent Education." In Stevens, Seligmann, and Long 1993, 78–100.

Nelson, John S. 1998. *Tropes of Politics: Science, Theory, Rhetoric, Action*. Madison: University of Wisconsin Press.

Nelson, John S. 2002. "A Once and Future Republic?" In Greffenius 2002: ix–xiv.

Nelson, John S. 2003. "Prudence as Republican Politics in American Popular Culture." In Hariman 2003, 229–57.

Nelson, John S. 2013. *Popular Cinema as Political Theory: Idealism and Realism in Epics, Noirs, and Satires*. New York: Palgrave Macmillan.

Nelson, John S. 2015. *Politics in Popular Movies: Rhetorical takes on Horror, War, Thriller, and SciFi Films*. Boulder, CO: Paradigm.

Nelson, John S., and Megill, Allan. 1986. "Rhetoric of Inquiry: Projects and Prospects." *Quarterly Journal of Speech* 72 (1): 20–37.

Nelson, John S., Megill, Allan, and McCloskey, D. N., eds. 1987. *The Rhetoric of the Human Sciences: Language and Argument in Scholarship and Public Affairs*. Madison: University of Wisconsin Press.

Nelson, John S., and Nelson, Anna Lorien. 1998. "Institutions in Feminist and Republican Science Fiction." *Legal Studies Forum* 22 (4): 641–53.

Nichols Jr., James H., and Wright, Colin, eds. 1990. *From Political Economy to Economics . . . and Back?* San Francisco: Institute for Contemporary Studies Press.

Nietzsche, Friedrich. 1968. *Twilight of the Idols* and *The Anti-Christ*. Translated by R. J. Hollingdale. Baltimore: Penguin.

Nietzsche, Friedrich. 1972. "On Truth and Falsity in Their Extramoral Sense." *Essays on Metaphor*. Edited by Warren Shibles. Whitewater, WI: Language Press.

Nietzsche, Friedrich. 1982. *On the Advantage and Disadvantage of History for Life*. Translated by Peter Preuss. Indianapolis: Hackett.

Pettit, Philip. 1997. *Republicanism*. Oxford: Oxford University Press.

Piketty, Thomas. 2014. *Capital in the Twenty-First Century*. Translated by Arthur Goldhammer. Cambridge, MA: Belknap Press.

Pitkin, Hanna Fenichel. 1972. *Wittgenstein and Justice*. Berkeley: University of California Press.

Pocock, J. G. A. 1975. *The Machiavellian Moment: Florentine Political Thought and the Atlantic Republican Tradition*. Princeton, NJ: Princeton University Press.

Polanyi, Karl. 1944. *The Great Transformation*. Boston: Beacon Press.

Polanyi, Michael C. 1962. "The Republic of Science." *Minerva* 1 (1): 54–73.

Popper, Karl. 1963. *Conjectures and Refutations*. New York: Harper and Row.

Popper, Karl. 1966. *The Open Society and Its Enemies*. Princeton, NJ: Princeton University Press.

Rahe, Paul A. 1994. *Republics Ancient and Modern*. 3 vols. Chapel Hill: University of North Carolina Press.

Robinson, Kim Stanley. 1993. *Red Mars*. New York: Bantam Books.

Robinson, Kim Stanley. 1994. *Green Mars*. New York: Bantam Books.

Robinson, Kim Stanley. 1996. *Blue Mars*. New York: Bantam Books.

Robinson, Kim Stanley. 1998. *Antarctica*. New York: Bantam Books.

Robinson, Kim Stanley. 2003. *The Martians*. New York: Bantam Books.

Robinson, Kim Stanley. 2004. *Forty Signs of Rain*. New York: Bantam Books.

Robinson, Kim Stanley. 2005. *Fifty Degrees Below*. New York: Bantam Books.

Robinson, Kim Stanley. 2007. *Sixty Days and Counting*. New York: Bantam Books.

Rorty, Richard. 1978. *Philosophy and the Mirror of Nature*. Princeton, NJ: Princeton University Press.

Rorty, Richard. 1982. *Pragmatism and the Consequences of Philosophy*. Minneapolis: University of Minnesota Press.

Rowling, J. K. 1997–2007. *Harry Potter*. 7 vols. New York: Scholastic Press.

Russell, Bertrand. 1962. *Freedom versus Organization, 1814–1914*. New York: Norton.

Russell, Bertrand. 1965. *On the Philosophy of Science*. Indianapolis: Bobbs-Merrill.

Sandel, Michael J. 1996. *Democracy's Discontent: American in Search of a Public Philosophy*. Cambridge, MA: Harvard University Press.

Selzer, Jack, ed. 1993. *Understanding Scientific Prose*. Madison: University of Wisconsin Press.

Sen, Amartya. 1970. *Collective Choice and Social Welfare*. San Francisco: Holden-Day.

Sen, Amartya. 1987. *On Ethics and Economics*. New York: Basil Blackwell.

Sen, Amartya. 1997. *On Economic Inequality*. 2nd ed. New York: Oxford University Press.

Sen, Amartya. 2002. *Rationality and Freedom*. Cambridge, MA: Belknap Press.

Sennett, Richard. 1974 (1992). *The Fall of Public Man*. New York: Norton.

Sessions, George, ed. 1995. *Deep Ecology for the Twenty-First Century*. Boston: Shambhala.

Simons, Herbert W., ed. 1990. *The Rhetorical Turn*. Chicago: University of Chicago Press.

Skinner, Quentin. 1998. *Liberty before Liberalism*. Cambridge: Cambridge University Press.

Stevens, L. Robert, Seligmann, G. L., and Long, Julian, eds. 1993. *The Core and the Canon*. Denton: University of North Texas Press.

Straub, Peter. 1979. *Ghost Story*. New York: Pocket Books.

Temelini, Michael. 2015. *Wittgenstein and the Study of Politics*. Toronto: University of Toronto Press.

Vico, Giambattista. 1948. *The New Science*. Translated by Thomas Goddard Bergin and Max Harold Fisch. 3rd ed. Ithaca, NY: Cornell University Press.

Walzer, Michael. 1983. *Spheres of Justice*. New York: Basic Books.

Warner, Michael. 1990. *The Letters of the Republic: Publication and the Public Sphere in Eighteenth-Century America*. Cambridge, MA: Harvard University Press.

Warner, Michael. 2002. *Publics and Counterpublics*. New York: Zone Books.

Weber, Max. 1946. "Politics as a Vocation." In *From Max Weber*, edited and translated by H. H. Gerth and C. Wright Mills. New York: Oxford University Press.

Winch, Peter. 1958. *The Idea of a Social Science and Its Relation to Philosophy*. London: Routledge and Kegan Paul.

Wittgenstein, Ludwig. 1958. *Philosophical Investigations*. Translated by G. E. M. Anscombe. 3rd ed. New York: Macmillan.

Wolin, Sheldon S. 2004. *Politics and Vision: Continuity and Innovation in Western Political Thought*. Princeton, NJ: Princeton University Press.

Wolosky, Shira. 2010. *The Riddles of Harry Potter: Secret Passages and Interpretive Quests*. New York: Palgrave Macmillan.

Ziliak, Stephen T., and McCloskey, Deirdre N. 2008. *The Cult of Statistical Significance: How the Standard Error Costs Us Jobs, Justice, and Lives*. Ann Arbor: University of Michigan Press.

10

McCloskey at Chicago

STEVEN E. LANDSBURG

In 1974, I discovered that Paradise was real. It was about ten blocks square and located on the south side of Chicago. I came to study math, and I discovered magic, a place where the air was thick with ideas and every bar or coffee shop housed a half-crazed scientist or anthropologist or student of Polish literature who would hold you with his glittering eye and share the hard-won fruits of three years' preoccupation with some bit of esoterica. In those same bars and restaurants, people ordered extra beers to use in science experiments. You could walk into a grocery store and see the world's greatest astrophysicist selecting his Cheerios.

We were dazzled, all of us—all of us who had come here hoping to escape the ordinary, to be touched by greatness, to enter into the Life of the Mind. The math students, the history students, the political science students—all of us were dazzled. But there was a special quality to the dazzlement of the economics students, who were taking a course in price theory from a certain Professor McCloskey, who kept them in a perpetual state of shock and awe.

If you went to lunch with those economics students—which I did, as often as possible—you'd get an earful of the latest. If crime prevention is expensive, then it's possible for Hyde Park to have too little crime. Perhaps the best social use for Lake Erie is as a dumping ground for chemical wastes. Rising food prices or rising oil prices can't explain inflation, at least not by the mechanisms most people imagine. A frost in Florida won't cause a shortage of oranges. When there's an increase in the price of steel, car prices will rise by less if the auto industry is monopolized than if the auto industry is competitive—though several members of the president's Council of Economic Advisors had believed otherwise. I recall that Professor McCloskey suggested running that one past your Marxist friends.

The point is not that these things were counterintuitive, though they were in fact counterintuitive—wildly, preposterously, insanely counterintuitive. The point is that McCloskey's explanations rendered them completely intuitive, completely clear, and completely incontrovertible to the point where you suddenly couldn't remember how you'd ever doubted them.

Getting this stuff second hand over the lunch table, I was blown away. That, perhaps, is not so remarkable. I was, after all, a math major who had never taken an economics course. Economic insight probably has a diminishing marginal capacity to astonish, and I was starting with a stock of zero.

But this part is remarkable: the econ students were just as astonished as I was. Think about that. These people had just spent four years studying economics, mostly at elite colleges where they'd been culled from the cream of the crop—and they were shocked to discover that if crime prevention is costly, then it's possible for Hyde Park to have too little crime. Yes, it really was possible to master Samuelson's *Foundations* and still not have the foggiest idea how to think like an economist.

Thinking like an economist—and in particular thinking like a Chicago-trained price theorist—means, first and foremost, acknowledging the pervasiveness and the logic of scarcity, pursuing that logic wherever it may lead, and accepting its consequences, no matter how unpopular or counterintuitive they may be. It means recognizing that the logic of scarcity implies the possibility—even the likelihood—of great disparities between the intended and actual effects of social policies. It means identifying a few basic implications of scarcity and learning to apply them to the widest possible range of phenomena.

As I said, students came to Chicago with no sense of how to think like an economist.

But Don McCloskey was fixing that.[1]

And then his students went out and fixed it further. They took what they'd learned from Don and, frequently armed with a remarkable new textbook called *The Applied Theory of Price*, they set out to bring price theory to the undergraduate masses.

I routinely challenge my average-quality freshmen and sophomores with the same sort of problems that stumped many of Chicago's finest in 1974. Thanks to what I learned from Don, both about economics and about how to teach, my students routinely succeed. I've taught more than ten thousand of them since I came to Rochester, and I believe I've gotten through to well over half of them. That makes five thousand people who have a better and deeper appreciation of the world—and, not incidentally, a better and deeper appreciation for the sheer joy of learning—because of what Don McCloskey made possible.

And I, of course, am only one of many. Don's disciples have carried the gospel throughout the world. And they've not forgotten their origins. I'm sure of this, because I recently contacted a few of them and asked how Don had influenced their teaching.

Rich Burkhauser has taught introductory micro to large classes at Vanderbilt and Cornell for almost forty years. He tells his students that when you first grasp the explanatory power of economic ideas, you'll feel like the movie hero who suddenly grasps The Matrix and realizes he can pull bullets out of the air. Rich remembers feeling exactly that way in Don's class, and he believes that the best of his students have had the same experience.

Many of Burkhauser's contemporaries—Aloysius Siow at Toronto, Vasan Sukhatme at Macalaster, Bart Taub at Illinois and Glasgow—have also been teaching large introductory classes for thirty years or more and attribute their successes to Don. Much like Rich, Vasan told me that for him, teaching has been a constant joy precisely because it revives the experience of taking Price Theory from Don McCloskey—by far, Vasan says, the most interesting and the most fun course that he has ever taken.

Many of these people relied heavily on *The Applied Theory of Price* or on succeeding textbooks, including my own, that, depending on your perspective, either heavily borrowed or outright stole from it. Here was a book that illuminated each new concept with a series of closely related problems that forced students to think. Like so much of the substance of what McCloskey taught, this stylistic innovation seems obvious in retrospect but was revolutionary at the time.

Don's influence was magnified by his charisma and by his legendary generosity, which many of his disciples have tried to emulate, with varying degrees of success. My own life was transformed several times by that generosity, starting with the time he agreed to meet in his office with a math grad student who had just realized that he loved economics. I expected him to tell me to stick to math. Instead, he gave me a rousing pep talk that made me love economics all the more. Later I sat in on his economic history class, and though I wasn't taking the class for credit, I chose to write a term paper. Don had no obligation to read it, but he marked it up in detail and encouraged me to publish it. It landed—partly, I suspect, due to Don's enthusiasm and influence—in the *Journal of Political Economy*.

When I decided to emulate Don by writing a price theory textbook—which I envisioned as a sort of kinder, gentler version of *The Applied Theory of Price*—I worried that he'd feel either offended or threatened. Instead, he was, from the beginning, almost fanatically supportive. That book is now in its ninth edition, but—except for the substitution of "Dee" for "Don"—the acknowledgments have not changed. Here is the first paragraph of those acknowledgments:

> I first learned economics at the University of Chicago in the 1970s, which means that I learned most of it, directly or indirectly, from Dee McCloskey. Generations of Chicago graduate students were infected by Dee's enthusiasm for economics as a tool for understanding the world, and the members of one generation communicated their exuberance to me. They, and consequently I, learned from Dee that the world is full of puzzles—not the abstract or technical puzzles of formal economic theory, but puzzles like: Could the advent of public education cause less education to be consumed? We learned to see puzzles everywhere and to delight in their solutions. Later, I had the privilege to know Dee as a friend, a colleague, and the greatest of my teachers. Without Dee, this book would not exist.

But things went even further. Don's inspiration had turned me into an evangelist, and I felt driven to share the power and beauty of economic thinking with a wider audience. So with Don's blessing and encouragement, I wrote a book called *The Armchair Economist*, and when it failed to make it past the gatekeepers at the Free Press, Don told me to call the editor in chief, Peter Dougherty, directly. I did, and as soon as I mentioned Don's name, Peter was enthusiastically on board.

Armchair has sold a lot of copies in a lot of languages, and I daresay it's done a lot of good. All of that good, from the content to the style to the Free Press imprint, flows ultimately from Don McCloskey.

Others remember Don's generosity as gratefully as I do. Wally Thurman, now at North Carolina State, scored well on a midterm and got a private note asking him to stop by so that Don could put a face with the name. To this day, Wally regrets that he never found the courage to take up that offer. Pete Linneman, now at Wharton, remembers Don's extensive advice on both theory and data collection as crucial inputs to Pete's first paper. And Don's generosity sometimes manifested itself in less conventional ways: When Bart Taub house-sat for Don in the summer of 1978, Don encouraged Bart to throw a party there.

That same generosity revealed itself in Don's relentless drive to improve other people's writing. He showered students with oral and written advice, prepared extensive handouts on writing, and even went so far as to run a sort of after-hours writers' workshop. If you submitted a paper to him, it was apt to come back looking something like this:

Craig Hakkio, now at the Kansas City Fed, remembers that Don took every opportunity to remind us that everything economists do (in academia,

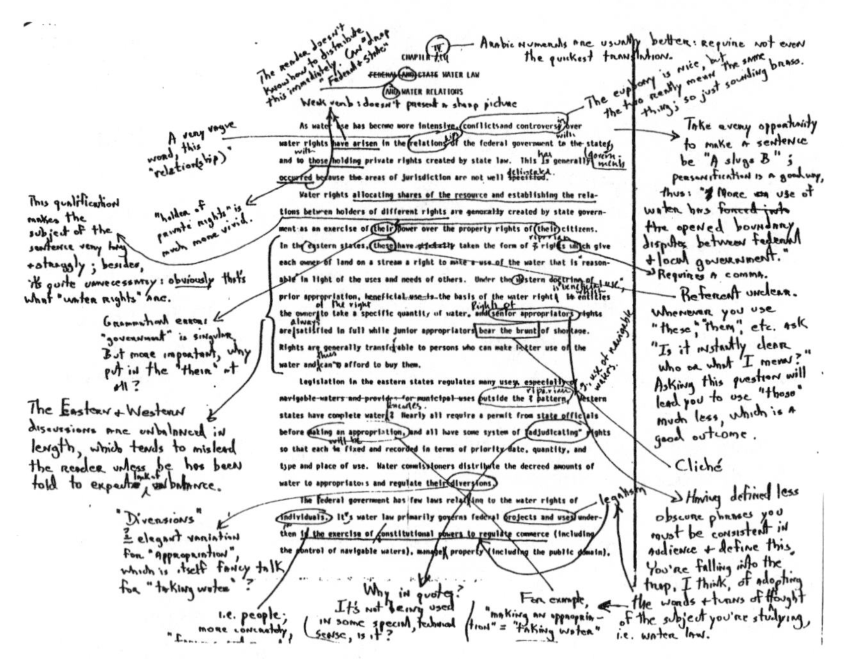
CHAPTER XIV

FEDERAL AND STATE WATER LAW

AND WATER RELATIONS

As water use has become more intensive, conflicts and controversy over water rights have arisen in the relations of the federal government to the states and to those holding private rights created by state law. This is generally occurred because the areas of jurisdiction are not well specified.

Water rights allocating shares of the resource and establishing the relations between holders of different rights are generally created by state government as an exercise of their power over the property rights of their citizens. In the eastern states, these have generally taken the form of rights which give each owner of land on a stream a right to make a use of the water that is "reasonable" in light of the uses and needs of others. Under the western doctrine of prior appropriation, beneficial use is the basis of the water right; it entitles the owner to take a specific quantity of water, and senior appropriators rights are satisfied in full while junior appropriators bear the brunt of shortage. Rights are generally transferable to persons who can make better use of the water and can afford to buy them.

Legislation in the eastern states regulates many uses, especially of navigable waters and provides for municipal uses outside the pattern. Western states have complete water codes. Nearly all require a permit from state officials before making an appropriation, and all have some system of "adjudicating" rights so that each is fixed and recorded in terms of priority date, quantity, and type and place of use. Water commissioners distribute the decreed amounts of water to appropriators and regulate their diversions.

The federal government has few laws relating to the water rights of individuals. Its water law primarily governs federal projects and uses undertaken in the exercise of constitutional powers to regulate commerce (including the control of navigable waters), manage property (including the public domain),

FIGURE 10.1 McCloskey's annotations.

at the Fed, on Wall Street, or in business) involves writing and that writing, like econometric modeling, is a skill that can't be mastered without practice. Craig, whose job involves much writing for the general public, still refers regularly to Don's book on writing. Bart Taub tells me that Don's workshop "really changed how I write . . . I try to repeat words and patterns and not to write with 'elegant variation'; I try to be concrete rather than abstract; I try to use Anglo-Saxon words rather than French and Latin."

That, at least, is how I and a few others remember things. For confirmation, I recently asked several more of Don's old students how they remembered him, and they pretty much all said exactly the same things. Here's a sampling:

From Rich Burkhauser:

> McCloskey's course profoundly shaped the way I have used economics ever since.

From Glenn Blomquist, now at the University of Kentucky:

> McCloskey's teaching epitomized how good economists think and how incredibly powerful price theory is.

From Craig Hakkio:

> He really taught me how to think like an economist.

From Todd Petzel, now a financier:

[Don's] ability to connect each lesson to a living example is what got all of us to develop an intuition for microeconomics. It wasn't good enough to know the math. One needed to feel the right answer before one solved an equation. . . . McCloskey was clearly a master. . . . McCloskey's greatest gift to students was a big leg up on how to think like an economist.

From Vasant Sukhatme:

I had done my previous economic studies in India before coming to Chicago. I had used texts by Stonier and Hague and by Henderson and Quandt. Price theory, at least as I had learned it, consisted of considerable formalism, carefully drawn diagrams, and some algebraic proofs.

It had had very little to do with how the world actually works. There had been virtually nothing concrete or personal or obvious or even intuitive in my previous economics work. McCloskey turned all this on its head.

McCloskey used to ask intriguing questions in his problem sets and course exams. I remember quite well some of the questions: What would the demand and supply curves look like for a free good? For a nonexistent good? If Congress were to pass a tax on gasoline of twenty cents per gallon, what would happen to the equilibrium quality of gasoline? To me, the answers to these questions were so intriguing and counterintuitive that I would just stare at my notebook in amazement and disbelief. But these kinds of questions slowly led me to understand that learning price theory provides deep insight into how consumers and businesses behave. I also came to appreciate for the first time in my life that understanding price theory would enable me to think about important public policy issues.

From Dan Sumner, now at the University of California at Davis:

McCloskey exposited basic economic theory using only a little mathematics, along with many examples, questions, and puzzles. Fairly soon, we realized that he was teaching us to think like economists. One of the things I learned from McCloskey was how easy it is to let the mathematics obscure rather than clarify the economics. With McCloskey we did not get any encouragement to shun mathematical modeling; rather, it was to focus on using careful formal modeling as a tool for careful economic thinking.

From Ken Clements, now at the University of Washington:

Don was a brilliant teacher . . . The content was modern and comprehensive . . . The whole package was a marvelous experience that contributed greatly to my Chicago education.

From Rick Kilcollin, now a private investment manager:

> He was one of the best, if not the best, teachers I ever had.

From Tom Macurdy, now at Stanford:

> I remember McCloskey's course fondly and have realized many times how much I benefited from this course and how unique it was.

The central lesson of all Don's teaching was that one ought to speak (and write!) mindfully, not in meaningless jargon. I think of this whenever I hear people describe, say, subsidized health care as a "compassionate" policy. Actually, if the word "compassion" means anything in this context, it means targeting expenditures where they'll do the most good for the recipients and recognizing that the same people who benefit from subsidized health care might benefit even more from a little help with the groceries or childcare or car expenses. I like to think that somewhere out there is a generation of students who, thanks to McCloskey, is too sophisticated to prefer meaningless blather over the logic of budget constraints.

And lest you fall into the trained economist's trap of thinking that such lessons are too obvious to mention, I am writing this on the day of Pope Francis's historic visit to America, where tickets to see him speak have been distributed randomly. These tickets, of course, have been scalped, leading to this lament from Cardinal Timothy Dolan: "Tickets for events with Pope Francis are distributed free [via lottery] for a reason—to enable as many New Yorkers as possible, including those of modest means, to be able to participate in the Holy Father's visit to New York. To attempt to resell the tickets and profit from his time in New York goes against everything Pope Francis stands for." This can, of course, be true only if "everything Pope Francis stands for" consists of the proposition that, for New Yorkers of modest means, nothing should take precedence over turning out to see Pope Francis—not groceries, not medicine, not car repairs, not any of the other things that people can buy with the proceeds from selling their tickets (or with the donations they could have received from the church had the tickets been sold to the highest bidders in the first place).

One hopes and expects that this is not, in fact, everything Pope Francis stands for, or even a small part of it. The fact that Cardinal Dolan would say otherwise, and be taken seriously, shows just how much the world could use a few thousand more McCloskeys.

There is nothing new under the sun. When an exhibit of artifacts related to King Tutankhamun came to Chicago in the 1970s, admission was "free" for those willing to spend a day or so waiting in a queue. Don, always the voice of reason, was eloquent in private and in public about the insanity of trying to allocate a scarce resource without using prices.

There is no end of nonsense to combat and no end to the good that economists can do by combating it. Consider the blather surrounding the recent fad for "happiness" research. An ex-president of Harvard University has been going around saying that because incomes have risen over the past several decades while reported happiness has not, policy makers should concentrate less on income growth and more on things like leisure and environmental quality—ignoring the fact that over the period in question, leisure time and environmental quality have risen about as dramatically as income (Bok 2011). Put aside all the legitimate questions about how to interpret self-reported happiness and just focus on the sheer ignorance and/or illogic behind that interpretation. It's the basis of a great McCloskey-style true/false/uncertain question, and I like to think that if a younger Derek Bok had had the experience of working through some of those questions, the older Derek Bok would have avoided such public foolishness.

Even the best economists might have done even better if only they'd spent a little time with *The Applied Theory of Price*. Two of the smartest economists of my generation are Larry Summers and Paul Krugman. But just a couple of weeks ago, Summers argued in the *Washington Post* that because gas prices have fallen and consumption is up, the case for a carbon tax is enhanced (Summers 2015). What a great true/false/uncertain question that is! I drew a few pictures and convinced myself the answer is false, or at best uncertain depending on whether externalities are increasing at the margin. Summers says it's true, but he provides no argument.

We all, of course, make mistakes, and we all, of course, sometimes embarrass ourselves in public. But what's striking to me here is not that Summers appears to be mistaken but that it seems never to have occurred to him that a conclusion requires an argument. That's exactly the core McCloskey message.

As for Krugman, there's so much more to choose from, but I'll resist temptation and limit myself to a single example. Krugman recently argued in print—and at length—that it never makes sense to cut just one government program, because, assuming expenditures are optimized to begin with, a marginal dollar is equally valuable wherever it's spent. Therefore, for small cuts it doesn't matter where you cut and for large cuts it's better to cut a little of everything instead a lot of one thing. He made this argument, of course, in the context of defending a particular program he did not want to see cut (Krugman 2015).

Of course, exactly the same argument tells you that you should never raise taxes on just one segment of the population, but that's never stopped Krugman from lobbying for higher taxes on the rich. That's because, in his saner moments, he's willing to acknowledge that existing government policies might not, in fact, always be optimal—and that if they were always optimal, we wouldn't need the advice of pundits, or even Nobel laureates.

Here the fundamental error is failing to ask whether your argument proves too much (and therefore needs to be examined with renewed skepticism). This, too, I think, is the sort of error that you're less likely to make after a healthy dose of those T/F/U questions.

Here's another great T/F/U question: If Wal-Mart can be pressured to pay higher wages, wages will tend to rise elsewhere in the economy as well. A staggering number of journalists seem to believe this, presumably because it's never occurred to them that it's possible to think before pontificating. Higher wages (and hence higher prices) at Wal-Mart make the average worker poorer, thus increasing the supply of labor and lowering the equilibrium wage in the non-Wal-Mart sector (an effect that is magnified, of course, because Wal-Mart cuts back on hiring).

Of course, the world abounds with examples of economic thoughtlessness, but I'll content myself with just one more. Journalists—even bright and thoughtful journalists like Michael Kinsley—frequently justify the taxation of capital income with an appeal to the principle that "everything ought to be taxed equally" (Kinsley 2012). If this were a T/F/U question, a good answer would touch on at least the following points:

1. There is in fact no principle that "everything ought to be taxed equally," except insofar as the most efficient tax is one that taxes everything at a marginal rate of zero. Subject to the constraint that some taxes must be positive at the margin, the most efficient tax structure depends in complicated ways on a vast number of elasticities and cross-elasticities of demand and supply.
2. A tax on capital income is equivalent to a tax on current consumption combined with a higher tax on future consumption, and so cannot in any relevant sense be said to tax everything equally.

In fact, the best case against taxing capital income relies substantially on the observation that this is one of the few cases where there is, at least in the steady state, a case for taxing everything equally (not on general principles but because of the particular structure of this particular problem), which, in light of (b), means that the tax on capital income should be zero.

Again, note the McCloskeyite themes: The notion of a general principle that "everything should be taxed equally" is pure blather, of exactly the sort that McCloskey warned us against at every turn. And if there were such a principle, it would still be incumbent on us to figure out exactly what the principle entails before jumping to any conclusions.

Incidentally, when I first worked my way through Chamley's pathbreaking paper on optimal capital taxation, I felt like I (barely) understood the math but had acquired no feel at all for what drives the result (Chamley 1986). Only after much meditation was I able to tease out the intuition. More recently, it has come to appear (in the work of Ludwig Straub and Ivan Werning) that Chamley's math might not be exactly right (Straub and Werning 2014). It's extremely important for someone to get that math right, because the process of getting it right can reveal new intuitions, or reveal limits to the old ones. But I repeat: The core intuition remains, and it's unlikely to go away.

In the end, what matters most is not the asymptotic convergence of a Lagrange multiplier but the insight that a tax on capital is equivalent to an ever-increasing tax on consumption. This highlights one last central tenet of McCloskeyism: Formal arguments matter, because they can reveal great truths. But it's the great truths we really care about.

Thank you, Deirdre.

Notes

1. One of the first lessons I learned from McCloskey was the importance of seeing the past through the eyes of those who experienced it. In any account of the 1970s, then, Dee must be Don.

References

Bok, Derek. 2011. *The Politics of Happiness: What Government Can Learn from the New Research on Well-Being*. Princeton, NJ: Princeton University Press.

Chamley, C. 1986. "Optimal Taxation of Capital Income in General Equilibrium with Infinite Lives." *Econometrica* 54 (3): 607–22.

Kinsley, Michael. 2012. "All Income Should Be Taxed Equally." *Bloomberg View*, December 26.

Krugman, Paul. 2015. "The Conscience of a Liberal." Blog post, August 30. http://krugman.blogs.nytimes.com/2011/08/30/disaster-relief-economics.

Straub, L., and Werning, I. 2014. "Positive Long Run Capital Taxation: Chamley-Judd Revisited." *NBER Working Paper*, no. 20441.

Summers, Lawrence. 2015. "Oil's Swoon Creates the Opening for a Carbon Tax." *Washington Post*, January 4.

Contributors

ROBIN L. BARTLETT is professor of economics, women's and gender studies, and queer studies at Denison University.

PETER J. BOETTKE is professor of economics and philosophy, the BB&T Professor for the Study of Capitalism, vice president for research, and director of the F. A. Hayek Program for Advanced Study in Philosophy, Politics, and Economics at the Mercatus Center at George Mason University.

STEPHEN G. ENGELMANN is associate professor of political science at the University of Illinois at Chicago.

STANLEY L. ENGERMAN is John H. Munro Professor of Economics and professor of history at the University of Rochester and is a research associate of the National Bureau of Economic Research.

RODERICK FLOUD was vice-chancellor of London Metropolitan University and provost of Gresham College, London, and is a research associate of the National Bureau of Economic Research.

JACK A. GOLDSTONE is the Elman Family Professor of Public Policy at the Hong Kong University of Science and Technology.

SANTHI HEJEEBU is associate professor of economics and business at Cornell College.

STEVEN E. LANDSBURG is professor of economics at the University of Rochester.

DAVID MITCH is professor of economics at the University of Maryland, Baltimore County.

JOHN S. NELSON is professor of political science at the University of Iowa.

ROBERT H. NELSON is professor at the School of Public Policy of the University of Maryland.

VIRGIL HENRY STORR is a research associate professor of economics in the Department of Economics and the Don C. Lavoie Senior Fellow in the F. A. Hayek Program in Philosophy, Politics, and Economics, at the Mercatus Center, George Mason University.

RICHARD SUTCH is the Edward A. Dickson Distinguished Professor Emeritus of Economics, University of California, and a research associate of the National Bureau of Economic Research.

PAUL TURPIN is associate professor of communication at the University of the Pacific in California.

Index